Experimental Philosophy of Identity and the Self

Series Editor:

James Beebe, Professor of Philosophy, University at Buffalo, USA

Editorial Board:

Joshua Alexander, Siena College, USA
James Andow, University of East Anglia, UK
Joshua Knobe, Yale University, USA
Edouard Machery, University of Pittsburgh USA
Thomas Nadelhoffer, College of Charleston, USA
Jennifer Nado, University of Hong Kong, Hong Kong
Eddy Nahmias, Georgia State University, USA
Noel Struchiner, University of Rio de Janeiro, Brazil
Jennifer Cole Wright, College of Charleston, USA

Empirical and experimental philosophy is generating tremendous excitement, producing unexpected results that are challenging traditional philosophical methods. *Advances in Experimental Philosophy* responds to this trend, bringing together some of the most exciting voices in the field to understand the approach and measure its impact in contemporary philosophy. The result is a series that captures past and present developments and anticipates future research directions.

To provide in-depth examinations, each volume links experimental philosophy to a key philosophical area. They provide historical overviews alongside case studies, reviews of current problems and discussions of new directions. For upper-level undergraduates, postgraduates and professionals actively pursuing research in experimental philosophy these are essential resources.

Titles in the series include:

Advances in Experimental Epistemology, edited by James R. Beebe

Advances in Experimental Moral Psychology,
edited by Hagop Sarkissian and Jennifer Cole Wright

Advances in Experimental Philosophy and Philosophical Methodology,
edited by Jennifer Nado

Advances in Experimental Philosophy of Aesthetics,
edited by Florian Cova and Sébastien Réhault

Advances in Experimental Philosophy of Language, edited by Jussi Haukioja

Advances in Experimental Philosophy of Logic and Mathematics,
edited by Andrew Aberdein and Matthew Inglis

Advances in Experimental Philosophy of Mind, edited by Justin Sytsma

Advances in Religion, Cognitive Science, and Experimental Philosophy,
edited by Helen De Cruz and Ryan Nichols

Experimental Metaphysics, edited by David Rose

Methodological Advances in Experimental Philosophy,
edited by Eugen Fischer and Mark Curtis

Advances in Experimental Philosophy of Free Will and Responsibility,
edited by Thomas Nadelhoffer and Andrew Monroe

Advances in Experimental Philosophy of Causation,
edited by Alex Wiegmann and Pascale Willemsen

Experimental Philosophy of Identity and the Self, edited by Kevin Tobia

Experimental Philosophy of Identity and the Self

Edited by
Kevin Tobia

BLOOMSBURY ACADEMIC
LONDON • NEW YORK • OXFORD • NEW DELHI • SYDNEY

BLOOMSBURY ACADEMIC
Bloomsbury Publishing Plc
50 Bedford Square, London, WC1B 3DP, UK
1385 Broadway, New York, NY 10018, USA
29 Earlsfort Terrace, Dublin 2, Ireland

BLOOMSBURY, BLOOMSBURY ACADEMIC and the Diana logo are trademarks of
Bloomsbury Publishing Plc

First published in Great Britain 2022
This paperback edition published 2024

Copyright © Kevin Tobia and Contributors, 2022

Kevin Tobia has asserted his right under the Copyright, Designs and Patents Act, 1988, to
be identified as Editor of this work.

For legal purposes the Acknowledgments on p. xi constitute an extension of
this copyright page.

Cover design by Catherine Wood
Cover photograph © Dieter Leistner / Gallerystock

All rights reserved. No part of this publication may be reproduced or
transmitted in any form or by any means, electronic or mechanical, including photocopying,
recording, or any information storage or retrieval system, without prior permission in
writing from the publishers.

Bloomsbury Publishing Plc does not have any control over, or responsibility for,
any third-party websites referred to or in this book. All internet addresses given in this
book were correct at the time of going to press. The author and publisher regret any
inconvenience caused if addresses have changed or sites have ceased to exist, but can
accept no responsibility for any such changes.

A catalogue record for this book is available from the British Library.

A catalog record for this book is available from the Library of Congress.

ISBN: HB: 978-1-3502-4689-8
PB: 978-1-3502-4693-5
ePDF: 978-1-3502-4690-4
eBook: 978-1-3502-4691-1

Series: Advances in Experimental Philosophy

Typeset by Deanta Global Publishing Services, Chennai, India

To find out more about our authors and books visit www.bloomsbury.com and sign up for
our newsletters.

Contents

List of Illustrations	vii
List of Contributors	ix
Acknowledgments	xi

	Introduction *Kevin Tobia*	1
1	For Whom Do Moral Changes Matter: The Influence of Change Type, Direction, and Target on Judgments of Identity Persistence *Jim A. C. Everett, Joshua A. Skorburg, Jordan L. Livingston, Vladimir Chituc, and Molly J. Crockett*	15
2	Identity Crisis *Christina Starmans*	37
3	Personal Identity and Dual Character Concepts *Joshua Knobe*	49
4	What's Left of Me?: The Role of Self-Continuity in Decision-Making and Judgments about Identity Persistence *Stephanie Chen and Oleg Urminsky*	71
5	Personal Identity and Morality *Harold Noonan*	87
6	The Whole Story: Identity and Narrative *Marya Schechtman*	99
7	What Matters in Psychological Continuity?: Using Meditative Traditions to Identify Biases in Intuitions about Personal Persistence *Preston Greene and Meghan Sullivan*	111
8	Memory as Evidence of Personal Identity: A Study on Reincarnation Beliefs *Vilius Dranseika*	127
9	The Importance of Morality for One's Self-Concept Predicts Perceptions of Personal Change after Remembering Wrongdoings *Matthew L. Stanley and Felipe De Brigard*	143
10	Uncomfortable Decisions *Paul Bloom and L. A. Paul*	157
11	Authenticity as a Pathway to Coherence, Purpose, and Significance *Rebecca J. Schlegel, Patricia N. Holte, Joe Maffly-Kipp, Devin Guthrie, and Joshua A. Hicks*	169
12	Experimental Philosophical Bioethics of Personal Identity *Brian D. Earp, Jonathan Lewis, Joshua A. Skorburg, Ivar R. Hannikainen, and Jim A. C. Everett*	183
13	Corporate Identity *Mihailis E. Diamantis*	203

14 The Essence of an Immigrant Identity: Children's Pro-social Responses to Others Based on Perceived Ability and Desire to Change *James P. Dunlea, Redeate G. Wolle, and Larisa Heiphetz* 217

15 "Human" Is an Essentially Political Category *David Livingstone Smith* 231

Index 243

Illustrations

Figures

1.1	Expected identity disruption as a function of target and type of identity change	26
1.2	Expected identity disruption as a function of target, direction of change and type of identity change	31
3.1	Jittered plot showing the results of Tobia (2015)	64
3.2	Jittered plot showing the results of the present study	65
4.1	Visual measures of psychological connectedness used in Bartels and Urminsky (2011, Study 5)	74
4.2	Illustration of task used in Chen et al. (2016) to measure the causal centrality of sixteen features of personal identity	80
8.1	Estimated marginal means for plausibility of each of the six explanations	132
8.2	Estimated marginal means for measures of (a) plausibility of an explanation in terms of reincarnation, (b) judgment of quality of evidence supporting the belief in reincarnation, ascriptions of (c) identity, and (d) remembering, grouped by afterlife beliefs	134
8.3	Estimated marginal means for how convincing different strategies were thought to be	138
8.4	Estimated marginal means for how convincing various memories differing in level of detail, availability, and type of memory are taken to be (a) and parameter estimates of the three factors (b)	139
9.1	Boxplots for moral wrongness judgments split by condition (*different self* vs. *similar self*) are depicted for Study 1	148
9.2	For actor perspective memories (A) and other perspective memories (B), boxplots are depicted for moral wrongness judgments split by self condition (*different self* vs. *similar self*) for Study 2	150
9.3	For personal change (A) and subjective distance (B) outcome variables, boxplots are depicted for ratings split by condition (actor perspective memories vs. other perspective memories) for Study 3	153
14.1	Average agreement that immigrants can (left) and want to (right) adopt American norms	222
14.2	Average attitudes toward different characters	223
14.3	Average number of resources shared with different characters	224

Tables

1.1 Items Used in Study 5 — 23
8.1 Estimated Marginal Means and Pairwise Comparisons for Measures of (a) Plausibility of Explanation in Terms of Reincarnation, (b) Judgment of Quality of Evidence Supporting the Belief in Reincarnation, Ascriptions of (c) Identity, and (d) Remembering, Grouped by Afterlife Beliefs — 133

Contributors

Paul Bloom is a professor of psychology at the University of Toronto and Brooks and Suzanne Ragen professor emeritus of psychology at Yale University.

Felipe De Brigard is the Fuchsberg-Levine family associate professor in the Departments of Philosophy and Psychology and Neuroscience, and core faculty at the Center for Cognitive Neuroscience at Duke University.

Stephanie Chen is an assistant professor of marketing at London Business School.

Vladimir Chituc is a graduate student in psychology at Yale University.

Molly J. Crockett is an associate professor at the Department of Psychology at Yale University.

Mihailis E. Diamantis is a professor of law and philosophy (by courtesy) at the University of Iowa.

Vilius Dranseika is an assistant researcher at Interdisciplinary Centre for Ethics & Institute for Philosophy, Jagiellonian University.

James P. Dunlea is a PhD student in the Department of Psychology at Columbia University. Broadly his work centers on how children and adults understand their social world.

Brian D. Earp is associate director of the Yale-Hastings Program in Ethics and Health Policy at Yale University and the Hastings Center, and a senior research fellow in moral psychology at the Uehiro Centre for Practical Ethics at the University of Oxford.

Jim A. C. Everett is a senior lecturer at the University of Kent, specializing in moral judgment, perceptions of moral character, and parochial altruism.

Preston Greene is an associate professor of philosophy at Nanyang Technological University, Singapore.

Devin Guthrie is a graduate student in the Department of Psychological and Brain Sciences at Texas A&M University.

Ivar R. Hannikainen is Juan de la Cierva research fellow in the Department of Philosophy I at the University of Granada.

Larisa Heiphetz is an assistant professor of psychology at Columbia University. Her lab studies social and moral cognition among children and adults.

Joshua A. Hicks is a professor in the Department of Psychological and Brain Sciences at Texas A&M University.

Patricia N. Holte is a graduate student in the Department of Psychological and Brain Sciences at Texas A&M University.

Joshua Knobe is a professor in the Program in Cognitive Science and the Department of Philosophy at Yale University.

Jonathan Lewis is a research fellow in Bioethics and Medical Law in the Department of Law at the University of Manchester.

Jordan L. Livingston is a postdoctoral research fellow at the University of Toronto.

Joe Maffly-Kipp is a graduate student in the Department of Psychological and Brain Sciences at Texas A&M University.

Harold Noonan is a professor of mind and cognition at the University of Nottingham.

L. A. Paul is Millstone family professor of philosophy and professor of cognitive science at Yale University.

Marya Schechtman is an LAS distinguished professor of philosophy at the University of Illinois Chicago.

Rebecca J. Schlegel is a professor in the Department of Psychological and Brain Sciences at Texas A&M University.

Joshua A. Skorburg is an assistant professor of philosophy at the University of Guelph.

David Livingstone Smith is a professor of philosophy at the University of New England in Maine.

Matthew L. Stanley is a post-doctoral research associate in the Fuqua School of Business at Duke University.

Christina Starmans is an assistant professor of psychology at the University of Toronto.

Meghan Sullivan is the Wilsey family college professor of philosophy at the University of Notre Dame.

Kevin Tobia is an associate professor of law and philosophy (by courtesy) at Georgetown University.

Oleg Urminsky is a professor of marketing at the University of Chicago Booth School of Business.

Redeate G. Wolle is a former research project manager at Columbia University.

Acknowledgments

Great thanks to Betsy Kuhn and Jennifer Lane for outstanding editorial assistance. Thanks to Josh Cape and Kayla Minton Kaufman for assistance in compiling the index.

Introduction

Kevin Tobia

I. Experimental Philosophy of the Self as Traditional Philosophy of the Self

Consider some of philosophy's most enduring questions: What makes you the same person as your childhood and future selves; which properties are essential to your identity; how should you respond to personal transformation over time; can you bind your future self, and what do you owe that person; what explains other entities' persistence through time (e.g., what makes the United States today "the same" nation as one from centuries ago); are animals, robots, or other nonhumans "persons"; and what is it to be a person?

Experimental philosophy addresses questions like these with the assistance of *empirical methods*. Although experimental philosophy is sometimes described as a new approach, empirically informed philosophy has a long history. Before any armchairs were burned, philosophers made empirical claims, offered testable hypotheses, and even employed empirical methods—all in the service of philosophical inquiry (see, for example, Naess 1938; see generally Anstey and Vanzo 2016). Experimental philosophy's novelty is not its empiricism but its use of modern empirical methods. Over the past two decades, philosophers increasingly draw on methods from contemporary experimental psychology and cognitive science to inform philosophical questions—including ones about the self, personhood, and identity.

As one example, consider a personal identity thought experiment initially raised by John Locke (1694/1975). Over two centuries later, Bernard Williams (1970) offered an empirically testable hypothesis about people's reaction to that thought experiment. And forty years later, experimentalists Shaun Nichols and Mike Bruno (2010) tested Williams's hypothesis, providing new insight into what philosophers should conclude from the traditional thought experiment.

The Lockean thought experiment involves the mixing of two people's mental and bodily properties. In the modern version, Williams (1970) invites us to imagine two persons, A and B, who will have their brains altered in a medical procedure. After the procedure, all of the psychological features now associated with A's brain (e.g., memories and character) will be associated with B's brain (and vice versa). So before the procedure, there are two people:

A, with A's psychological properties and A's body

B, with B's psychological properties and B's body

And after the procedure, there are two people:

C, with A's psychological properties and B's body

D, with B's psychological properties and A's body

Williams asks: Who is still the same person as *A*, person C or person D? If we think C, that intuition supports that psychological continuity is the criterion of personal identity; if we think D, that intuition supports that bodily continuity is the criterion of personal identity. Williams imagines that before the surgery A were told that one of the resulting persons will be tortured, and Williams proposes that if we asked A before the surgery, A would fear the torture of *person C*. Williams takes this intuition to count in favor of the conclusion that psychological continuity is the criterion of personal identity.

However, writes Williams (1970), considering a different case leads to the opposite conclusion, that personal identity is rooted in the body. Imagine that someone tells you that "you" will be tortured tomorrow, but that before the torture occurs, all of your psychological properties would be eliminated and replaced with new ones. So you stand in bodily but not psychological continuity with that future person. Yet, proposes Williams, in this case you would fear the impending torture—agreeing that the future person is really "you." That intuition supports bodily continuity as the criterion of personal identity.

Bernard Williams took these conflicting intuitions as important data for philosophers of identity. But his philosophical method also required understanding *how* we evaluate the thought experiments. Williams raised an intriguing possibility, pointing to a difference between the two cases:

> The first argument, which led to the "mentalistic" conclusion that A and B would change bodies and that each person should identify himself with the destination of his memories and character, was an argument entirely conducted in third-personal terms. The second argument, which suggested the bodily continuity identification, concerned itself with the first-personal issue of what A could expect. That this is so seems to me . . . of some significance. (1970: 179)

In experimental-philosophical terms, this proposal is an *empirically testable hypothesis*: the tension between our reactions to the two thought experiments is explained by the scenarios' differing modes of presentation. The first scenario is presented in third-personal terms, inviting reflection about *someone else* (about the person "A"), while the second scenario is presented in second-personal terms, inviting reflection about *your own situation* (about "you"). According to Williams's hypothesis, that framing difference could explain our divergent intuitions.

Modern experimental philosophy picks up the debate from here. We can make progress in assessing the truth of this hypothesis by conducting empirical studies. For example, experimenters could present some people with Williams's scenario in the second person (i.e., "Imagine that you . . .") and another group with the same scenario in the third person (e.g., "Imagine that Jerry . . ."). Comparing the responses of those groups could clarify whether the mode of presentation, in fact, makes a difference.

Nichols and Bruno (2010) conducted exactly this study. They recruited participants to assess two different versions of William's pain scenario (similar to the second scenario in the previous paragraph). Participants were randomly assigned to evaluate scenarios that varied in just one respect: one version was written in the second person (Imagine that doctors have to replace your memories in a necessary surgery . . . when the post-surgery person wakes up and feels a painful shot, do you agree or disagree that "*you* will feel the pain"?) and another was written in the third person (Imagine that doctors have to replace Jerry's memories in a necessary surgery . . . when the post-surgery person wakes up and feels a painful shot, do you agree or disagree that "*Jerry* will feel the pain").

Nichols and Bruno's findings support Williams's primary intuition about the scenario—in the second-personal case (concerning "you"), most participants (about 70%) said *yes*, the pain would be feared. But the study also found evidence counting against the hypotheses that the "yes" responses are driven by the scenario's presentation in the second person. In Nichols and Bruno's study, in the third-personal case (concerning "Jerry"), a similar percentage of participants said *yes*, the pain would be feared. There was no significant difference in responses between the second- and third-personal variations. The second versus third-person framing does not seem to affect people's judgments about this case.

This empirical study does not resolve all philosophical inquiry about personal identity. (Clearly.) But it does move the debate along. Some say there's no progress in philosophy (Dietrich 2011). But this intergenerational dialogue—from 1690 to 1970 to 2010—suggests that there can be progress. We have now learned that the divergence in these Locke-inspired personal identity case intuitions is likely not explained by second versus third-person framing. This data counts against a hypothesis contemplated by Williams, which would resolve an apparent tension between two thought experiments. So we now know it would be more useful to explore and evaluate other hypotheses about the possible divergence between case intuitions, or accept that there is intuitive support for both bodily and mental criteria of personal identity.

II. The Criteria of Identity over Time

This is just one example of contemporary experimental philosophy of identity and the self. But it illustrates that today's "experimental philosophy" approach is continuous with traditional philosophical analysis of identity. The modern approach adopts both the traditional method of thought experimentation (Locke 1694/1975; Parfit 1984) and the traditional project of interrogating the sources of our intuitive responses to those thought experiments (Williams 1970).

Much of modern experimental philosophy of identity also has a topical continuity with traditional philosophy, focusing on the most central and long-standing question in philosophy of identity: What are the criteria of personal identity over time? Consider three canonical philosophical theories of identity (quoted from Shoemaker and Tobia 2021; see also Noonan 2022; Schectman 2022):

> *The Psychological View (or neo-Lockeanism)*: X at t1 is the same person as Y at t2 just in case X is uniquely psychologically continuous with Y. (see, for example, Parfit 1984: 207)

> *The Biological View (or animalism)*: If X is a person at t1, and Y exists at any other time, then X = Y if and only if Y's biological organism is continuous with X's biological organism. (Shoemaker 2016; drawn from Olson 1997 and DeGrazia 2005)

> *The Anthropological View (or humanism)*: If X is a human being at t1, and Y is a human being at t2, then X persists as Y (paradigmatically) to the extent that enough of X's defining cluster of biological, psychological, and social features have continued in Y in order for Y to be "an identifiable locus of interaction in person-space." (Schechtman 2014: 167)

To adjudicate among these and other theories, philosophers from Locke to Parfit draw on thought experiments. Experimental philosophers continue in this tradition by conducting empirical studies to assess whether our ordinary judgments about personal identity cases reflect a psychological, biological, or anthropological criterion in assessing identity over time.

The evidence is mixed. Several empirical studies find that changes in psychological properties significantly influence people's evaluation of connectedness and identity, providing intuitive evidence for the Psychological View over the Biological View (Blok, Newman, and Rips 2005; Strohminger and Nichols 2014; Tobia 2015; Molouki and Bartels 2017; Turri and Weaver 2018). At the same time, other studies have found some support for the Biological View (e.g., Nichols and Bruno 2010).

Several especially recent studies suggest the Anthropological View's promise. For example, Newman, Bloom, and Knobe (2014) and Strohminger and Nichols (2014) find that moral and social traits (more than other psychological traits) influence people's judgment of identity and/or the self (see also Aquino and Reed 2002; Riis, Simmons, and Goodwin 2008; Strohminger and Nichols 2015; Prinz and Nichols 2016; Chen, Urminsky, and Bartels 2016; Strohminger, Knobe, and Newman 2017; Christy, Kim, and Vess 2017). This "moral self effect" has also been replicated in children (Heiphetz et al. 2018).

Everett et al. (2022) find that the relevance of moral traits to identity attributions manifests for several different targets: the self, friends, strangers, and foes. However, there is a special relationship between direction of change and the target type: friends' identities are most disrupted when they become less moral, while foes' identities are most disrupted as they become *more* moral. This finding seems particularly cohesive with anthropological views; friends and foes typically occupy different loci of interaction in person-space, and negative moral change may understandably have greater significance to a friend's cluster of features than a foe's.

These seemingly conflicting empirical results—intuitive support for the psychological, biological, and anthropological views—might be explained through a theory of "folk pluralism." Perhaps we have multiple criteria or concepts of identity (Tierney et al. 2014). If so, we should expect some empirical studies to reflect the psychological criterion, while others reflect the biological or anthropological ones. As Ted Sider puts it, conflicting intuitions about personal identity cases arise because "ordinary thought contains two concepts of persisting persons, each responsible for a separate set of intuitions, neither of which is our canonical conception to the exclusion of the other" (Sider 2001: 198). Insofar as identity is a necessary or sufficient criterion of blame, responsibility, or ownership, pluralism may be practical. Perhaps for some purposes (e.g., punishment), we identify Y with whatever X is his unique psychologically continuous predecessor, but for other purposes (e.g., ownership), we identify Y with X if and only if they are biologically continuous.

Another possible explanation of the mixed evidence begins by looking critically at what these experimental studies measure. So far, we have been discussing "personal identity," in the sense of the numerical identity relation. Experimental studies of personal identity often ask questions like, "Is the man after the surgery still the same person?" For example, in one of Strohminger and Nichols's seminal (2014) experiments, participants read about characters who experienced personal change, responding on a scale from 0% "They're the same person as before" to 100% "They're completely different now."

Consider an empirical study that asks participants to evaluate whether Jim is "still the same person" after a surgery in which he lost all of his memories. That study's question could be interpreted to mean (among other possibilities):[1]

- Is the man today *numerically identical* to the man before the surgery?
- Is the man today *qualitatively identical* to the man before the surgery?
- Is the man today *qualitatively similar* to the man before the surgery?
- Is the man today *psychologically connected* to the man before the surgery?

Philosophers have long emphasized the importance of distinguishing among numerical identity, qualitative identity, qualitative similarity, and psychological connectedness. And experimental philosophers have raised similar points about new empirical studies (e.g., Berniūnas and Dranseika 2016; Dranseika 2017; Molouki and Bartels 2017; Starmans and Bloom 2018; Schwenkler et al. 2021; Starmans 2022).

Some worry that the recent moral self findings may be reflective of qualitative similarity, not numerical identity. For example, the moral self literature finds that participants who evaluate a person who entirely loses their morals agree that the person who remains is "completely different now." But, ask Starmans and Bloom (2018), do participants really mean to endorse that the original person is now *dead*?

As another example, consider the common thought experiment about a man named Gage. As the story goes, before a railroad accident Gage was a kind and genial man, but after a tragic brain injury, the man that remains is cruel. Call this a moral *deterioration* case. But imagine the opposite story, a moral *improvement* case: Gage is a cruel man, and after a tragic injury, the man that remains is kind and genial. In an experimental study, participants were more inclined to endorse that identity breaks in the *deterioration*, compared to the improvement case (Tobia 2015). But even in the deterioration story, there is undoubtedly some sense in which the man that remains appears related to the earlier man. "[E]ven after deteriorating, postaccident Gage may still appear to be the son of pre-accident Gage's mother, to own the same house, or to owe the same taxes" (Tobia 2015).

Recent empirical work supports this hypothesis: if Gage is described as being born in Chicago and later experiencing a radical moral deterioration, participants still agree that the man after the change was "born in Chicago" (Schwenkler et al. 2021). If such intertemporal relations remain, does this not suggest that the two men are also numerically identical—and that participants who agree that the men are not the same must be expressing something else?

Other philosophers and psychologists have proposed *new* concepts related to the self, which may help clarify these debates. For example, Joshua Knobe discusses recent work on "dual character concepts," as they relate to the "true self" (Knobe 2022). Perhaps in the Gage story, participants understand the later man is still Gage but also evaluate that he is "not really the same person" in some other important sense. Bloom and Paul (2022) discuss the concept of a "transformative experience," in which one reconstructs oneself in a profoundly transformative way (while remaining numerically identical to one's past self). Chen and Urminsky (2022) reject the dichotomy between numerical identity and qualitative similarity. Instead, they propose that participants in many of these empirical studies are expressing "self-continuity judgments," judgments similar to Parfitian connectedness (Parfit 1984).

An important task for philosophers of identity is to continue clarifying what types of judgments these experiments are eliciting: Are these data about the lay notion of numerical identity, qualitative similarity, or something else entirely (e.g., the true self or self-continuity)? That inquiry could also reveal important similarities among these lay concepts. Perhaps, for example, the moral self effect arises in judgments responding to more than one of these question types.

III. Identity and Practical Concerns: Prudential, Moral, Social, Legal, and Political

Experimental philosophy of identity and the self has also looked beyond debates about *the criteria* of personal identity (e.g., psychological or biological). Recent years have seen a dazzling array of work relating identity and the self to prudential, moral, social, legal, and political issues, including authenticity to one's self, memory and responsibility, intertemporal choice, pro-social behavior, health-care decision-making, and corporate liability.

For example, recent work argues that authenticity may lead to a sense of meaning, by fostering coherence, purpose, and significance (Schlegel et al. 2022). Feeling connected to one's (true moral) self may create a sense of purpose. And, conversely, committing moral transgressions might lead us to feel out of touch with our true moral selves (e.g., Christy et al. 2016).

Insofar as your "authentic" self is a morally good one (e.g., Aquino and Reed 2002; Strohminger and Nichols 2014), how can you square this self-concept with the reality of moral transgressions? Stanley and De Brigard (2022) take up this question, finding that individuals who place morality at the center of their self-concepts tend to have a stronger sense of memory-mediated personal change, believing that they have undergone more positive change (when confronted with past wrongdoings).

Another important line of research examines the relationship between the self and decision-making. These studies suggest that concepts related to the self have concrete practical implications. Experimental studies find that lower psychological connectedness to one's future self predicts greater discounting of future rewards (Bartels and Urminsky 2011; see generally Chen and Urminsky 2022). The less connected we feel to our future selves, the more willing we are to accept smaller sooner rewards over larger later ones.

A promising and growing research area explores the intersection of experimental philosophy and bioethics. For example, imagine that a young man instructs physicians, through an advance health-care directive, of his preference for treatment to be withheld in certain future conditions. Decades later, those conditions are met—the directive would indicate that treatment should be withheld for the now old and sick man. But the older man is actually very happy with his life, and—as years have gone by—he is in some sense a completely different person from the young man who wrote the directive. Scholars in experimental bioethics study dilemmas like these with the tools of experimental philosophy (Earp et al. 2022).

Experimentalists have also examined social implications of identity and the self. For example, Dunlea, Wolle, and Heiphetz (2022) apply experimental methods to study two components of essentialist thinking about others—lack of ability to change and lack of desire to change—in the context of immigration. Their studies find that children's pro-social responses to immigrants more strongly depend on information about immigrants' *desire* to change (and less so on immigrants' *ability* to change).

Experimentalists also address the relationship between identity and legal responsibility. For example, Gomez-Lavin and Prinz (2019) find that participants are more likely to grant parole to criminal offenders whose moral values (rather than behavior) changed. Mott (2018) finds that participants' intuitions about statutes of limitations are largely explained by intuitions about intertemporal connectedness: it seems we should reduce the degree of punishment for a crime committed twenty years ago, in part, because the person today is, in some important sense, a different person.

Turning attention to the legal domain raises important practical questions about the identity conditions of many nonhuman entities. For example, what are the persistence conditions for corporations or nations? Although there are undoubtedly important differences between humans and these entities, experimental philosophy has uncovered some surprising similarities. For example, De Freitas et al. (2017) found that the same improvement/deterioration asymmetry arises for collective entities. When a five-member band substitutes out its best member for an inferior one, people are inclined to see the new (deteriorated) band as not really the same band, but when the band substitutes its worst member for a better one, people are more inclined to see the (improved) band as still the same. The same general effect arises for corporations, nations, and even science papers! These experimental findings raise new questions for philosophers of law: For example, do these lay intuitions accurately reflect corporate persistence conditions and successor liability (see Diamantis 2016, 2019a, b, 2020, 2022)?

Finally, identity and the self have important political connections. For example, David Smith addresses the long-standing question: "What is it to be human?" (Smith 2022). The answer, argues Smith, is not to be a member of a biological category (e.g., Homo sapiens). Rather, the category of "human" is ultimately a political one, demarcating "us" from "them."

IV. Conclusion: Why Ask Laypeople about Brain Swaps?

In concluding, consider one common worry about experimental philosophy of identity. Traditional philosophy of identity engages complex problems, which seem to call for *expert* analysis. However, the vast majority of empirical studies recruit *lay* participants, people without formal philosophical training. This may seem puzzling: Should philosophical analysis really care what a layperson thinks about hypothetical brain swaps?

There is a seeming tension between the expert study of identity and the empirical study of lay views of identity. In traditional personal identity debates, experts consider complex and fantastical thought experiments about brain swaps, mind/body separation, and persons fusing into one or fissioning into two. Yet, *experimental* philosophy of personal identity evaluates regular people's judgments about these questions and more ordinary ones, of prudential, moral, bioethical, and legal significance. So which is it? Is personal identity for abstract debates among experts or is it at the heart of ordinary life and experience?

This chapter's answer is both. Philosophy should not ignore either perspective. Most philosophers will already be persuaded by the relevance of the expert perspective, so this conclusion addresses the significance of the other one, *philosophy* of identity's relationship to ordinary life and experience.

In fact, traditional philosophy gives us several reasons to care deeply about laypeople's views. First, the central *method* of philosophical thought experimentation—from Locke to Parfit—involves positing an intuitive response that is presumed to be *shared* among competent language users or reasonable interlocutors (see Shoemaker and Tobia 2022; Greene and Sullivan 2022). Experimental studies of laypeople can clarify what such people intuit in personal identity test cases. This allows researchers to more robustly test thought experiments (e.g., Dranseika 2022) and debunk misleading intuitions (Earp et al. 2022).

Beyond reasons arising from traditional philosophical methods, reasons to examine lay views also come from traditional *philosophical theories*. Conventionalism about identity is the philosophical view that one's persistence conditions over time depend on one's prudential attitudes (e.g., Kovacs 2016, 2020; Braddon-Mitchell and Miller 2004, 2020). Those attitudes might include anticipation, worry, and even belief about one's identity. When philosophical theories direct us to examine people's beliefs, empirical methods can provide insight into those lay attitudes and beliefs.

A final set of reasons comes from the *aims* or goals of the philosophy of personal identity. There is a longstanding relationship between philosophy of identity and philosophical analysis of practical concerns. Philosophers have been interested in identity as it relates to prudential and moral issues. For example, in assigning blame, responsibility, and punishment for some bad act to person X, we typically seek to ensure that person X is *the same person* as person Y who committed the act. We might not explicitly refer to numerical identity when assessing these questions, but numerical identity underpins many of our most important prudential and moral concerns.

In the same way, identity is fundamental to philosophy of law. Contract law's central premise is that a present contracting self can bind their "future self" (Matsumura 2014; Toomey 2022). A promise made today binds a person in the future—namely, the same person who made that promise today. Numerical identity underpins contractual obligation, ownership of property, criminal responsibility, and many other intertemporal legal relations.

Legal scholars have also articulated how other notions, like "the self" and "personhood," play critical legal roles. For example, Radin argues that we can imbue property with a sense of self (Radin 1982). Consider someone who has lived in the same home for forty years—remembering their young children crawling across the floor; cooking holiday dinners in the kitchen; laughing, crying, and celebrating in the family room. For such a person, it seems, the home becomes central to their sense of self. Social identities, too, are of great legal significance. The law frequently categorizes and adjudicates identity, in the sense of membership in social categories (see Lane-Steele 2022). These legal determinations provide people with protection (e.g., anti-discrimination law) and assistance (e.g., asylum-granting).

In sum, philosophical study of identity (and the self) is—and has long been—closely connected to prudential, moral, social, legal, and political concerns. Insofar as the study of moral psychology and practical concerns calls for empirical data about lay beliefs and understandings (e.g., Doris 2010), the fact that philosophy of identity includes the analysis of practical concerns is another reason that questions in the field are helpfully informed by empirical study of laypeople.

In sum, the methods, theories, and aims of *traditional* philosophy all direct us to examine empirical evidence about lay understandings of identity, the self, and practical concerns. Of course, philosophers should not simply outsource debate about personal identity and the self to laypeople. The proposal is simply that it would be a mistake for modern philosophy to ignore or neglect empirical evidence of laypeople's views. Examining philosophy of identity's traditional methodology, theories, and concerns reveals its inextricability from the views of ordinary people.

Note

1 A question aiming to elicit a *numerical* identity judgment would be careful to avoid any suggestion that the person before and after the change is identical. For example, "Is Jim still the same person now?" might plausibly be read to presuppose numerical identity, insofar "Jim" refers to the post-change person. A more cautious, but wordier, question might ask whether the "pre-surgery person" is the same as the "post-surgery person" (e.g., Tobia 2015).

Bibliography

Akerlof, G. A. and R. E. Kranton (2000). "Economics and Identity." *The Quarterly Journal of Economics*, 115: 715–53.

Anstey, P. and A. Vanzo (2016). "Early Modern Experimental Philosophy." In Justine Sytsma and Wesley Buckwalter (eds.), *A Companion to Experimental Philosophy*, 87–102. West Sussex: John Wiley & Sons, Ltd.

Aquino, K. and A. Reed (2002). "The Self-importance of Moral Identity." *Journal of Personality and Social Psychology*, 83 (6): 1423–40.

Bartels, D. M. and O. Urminsky (2011). "On Intertemporal Selfishness: How the Perceived Instability of Identity Underlies Impatient Consumption." *Journal of Consumer Research*, 38: 182–98.

Berniūnas, R. and V. Dranseika (2016). "Folk Concepts of Person and Identity: A Response to Nichols and Bruno." *Philosophical Psychology*, 29: 96–122.

Blok, S., G. Newman and L. Rips (2005). "Individuals and their Concepts." In W. K. Ahn, R. L. Goldstone, B. C. Love, A. B. Markman and P. Wolff (eds.), *Categorization Inside and Outside the Laboratory*, 127–49. Washington: American Psychological Association.

Bloom, P. and L. Paul (2022). "Uncomfortable Decision-making Processes." In K. Tobia (ed.), *Experimental Philosophy of Identity and the Self*. London: Bloomsbury.

Braddon-Mitchell, D. and K. Miller (2004). "How to be a Conventional Person." *The Monist*, 87 (4): 457–74.

Braddon-Mitchell, D. and K. Miller (2020). "Conativism about Personal Identity." In A. Sauchelli (ed.), *Derek Parfit's Reasons and Persons: An Introduction and Critical Inquiry*, 129–59. London: Routledge.

Chen, S. and O. Urminsky (2022). "What's Left of Me? The Role of Self-continuity in Decision Making and Judgments about Identity Persistence." In K. Tobia (ed.), *Experimental Philosophy of Identity and the Self*. London: Bloomsbury.

Chen, S., O. Urminsky and D. M. Bartels (2016). "Beliefs about the Causal Structure of the Self-concept Determine Which Changes Disrupt Personal Identity." *Psychological Science*, 27: 1398–406.

Christy, A. G., E. Seto, R. J. Schlegel, M. Vess and J. A. Hicks (2016). "Straying from the Righteous Path and from Ourselves: The Interplay Between Perceptions of Morality and Self-Knowledge." *Personality and Social Psychology Bulletin*, 42, https://doi.org/10.1177/0146167216665095.

Christy, A. G., J. Kim and M. Vess (2017). "The Reciprocal Relationship Between Perceptions of Moral Goodness and Knowledge of Others' True Selves." *Social Psychological and Personality Science*, 8: 910–17.

De Freitas, J. and M. Cikara (2018). "Deep Down My Enemy is Good: Thinking about the True Self Reduces Intergroup Bias." *Journal of Experimental Social Psychology*, 74: 307–16.

De Freitas, J., H. Sarkissian, G. E. Newman, I. Grossmann, F. de Brigard, A. Luco and J. Knobe (2018). "Consistent Belief in a Good True Self in Misanthropes and Three Interdependent Cultures." *Cognitive Science*, 42 (Supplement 1): 134–60.

De Freitas, J., K. Tobia, G. Newman and J. Knobe (2017). "Normative Judgments and Individual Essence." *Cognitive Science*, 41 (S3): 382–402.

DeGrazia, D. (2005). *Human Identity and Bioethics*. Cambridge: Cambridge University Press.

Diamantis, M. (2016). "Corporate Criminal Minds." *Notre Dame Law Review*, 91 (5): 2049–89.

Diamantis, M. (2019a). "Corporate Essence and Identity in Criminal Law." *Journal of Business Ethics*, 154 (4): 955–66.

Diamantis, M. (2019b). "Successor Identity." *Yale Journal on Regulation*, 36 (1): 1–44.

Diamantis, M. (2020). "The Body Corporate." *Law and Contemporary Problems*, 83 (4): 133–58.

Diamantis, M. (2022). "Corporate Identity." In K. Tobia (ed.), *Experimental Philosophy of Identity and the Self*. London: Bloomsbury.

Dietrich, E. (2011). "There is No Progress in Philosophy." *Essays in Philosophy*, 12: 330–45.

Doris, J. (2010). "Introduction." In John Doris (ed.), *The Moral Psychology Handbook*, 1–2. New York: Oxford University Press.

Dranseika, V. (2017). "On the Ambiguity of 'The Same Person.'" *AJOB Neuroscience*, 8: 184–6.

Dranseika, V. (2022), "What Kind of Evidence about Personal Identity is Provided by Autobiographical Memory?." In K. Tobia (ed.), *Experimental Philosophy of Identity and the Self*. London: Bloomsbury.

Dunlea, J. P. and L. Heiphetz (2020). "Children's and Adults' Understanding of Punishment and the Criminal Justice System." *Journal of Experimental Social Psychology*, 87: 103913.

Dunlea, J. P. and L. Heiphetz (in press). "Children's and Adults' Views of Punishment as a Path to Redemption." *Child Development*, 92 (4): e398–e415. Doi: https://doi.org/10.1111/cdev.13475.

Dunlea, J., R. Wolle and L. Heiphetz (2022). "The Essence of an Immigrant Identity: Children's Pro-social Responses to Others Based on Perceived Ability and Desire to Change." In K. Tobia (ed.), *Experimental Philosophy of Identity and the Self*. London: Bloomsbury.

Earp, B. D., J. Demaree-Cotton, M. Dunn, V. Dranseika, J. A. C. Everett, A. Feltz, G. Geller, I. R. Hannikainen, L. A. Jansen, J. Knobe, J. Kolak, S. Latham, A. Lerner, J. May, M. Mercurio, E. Mihailov, D. Rodríguez-Arias, B. Rodríguez López, J. Savulescu, M. Sheehan, N. Strohminger, J. Sugarman, K. Tabb, and K. Tobia (2020). "Experimental Philosophical Bioethics." *AJOB Empirical Bioethics*, 11(1): 30–3.

Earp, B. D., I. Hannikainen, S. Dale and S. Latham (forthcoming). "Experimental Philosophical Bioethics, Advance Directives, and the True Self in Dementia." In A. De Block and K. Hens (eds.), *Experimental Philosophy of Medicine*. London: Bloomsbury.

Earp, B. D., S. Latham and K. Tobia (2020). "Personal Transformation and Advance Directives: An Experimental Bioethics Approach." *The American Journal of Bioethics*, 20 (8): 72–5.

Earp, B. D., J. Lewis, V. Dranseika and I. Hannikainen (in press). "Experimental Philosophical Bioethics and Normative Inference." *Theoretical Medicine and Bioethics*, 42: 91–111.

Earp, B. D., J. Skorburg, J. Everett and J. Savulescu. (2019). "Addiction, Identity, Morality." *AJOB: Empirical Bioethics*, 10 (2): 136–53.

Earp, B., I. Hannikainen, J. Skorburg and J. Everett (2022), "Personal Change and Experimental Bioethics." In K. Tobia (ed.), *Experimental Philosophy of Identity and the Self*. London: Bloomsbury.

Everett, J., J. Skorburg, J. Livingston, V. Chituc and M. Crockett (2022). "For Whom Do Moral Changes Matter: The Influence of Change Type, Direction, and Target on Judgments of Identity Persistence." In K. Tobia (ed.), *Experimental Philosophy of Identity and the Self*. London: Bloomsbury.

Frederick, S. (2003). "Time Preference and Personal Identity." In G. Loewenstein, D. Read and R. Baumeister (eds.), *Time and Decision*, 89–113. New York: Russell Sage Foundation.

Garfield, J. L., S. Nichols, A. K. Rai, and N. Strohminger (2015). "Ego, Egoism and the Impact of Religion on Ethical Experience: What a Paradoxical Consequence of Buddhist Culture Tells us about Moral Psychology." *The Journal of Ethics*, 19 (3–4): 293–304.

Gomez-Lavin, J. and J. Prinz (2019). "Parole and the Moral Self: Moral Change Mitigates Responsibility." *Journal of Moral Education*, 48: 65–83.

Greene, P. and M. Sullivan (2022). "What Matters in Psychological Continuity? Accommodating Profound Psychological Change in Unbiased Egoistic Concern." In K. Tobia (ed.), *Experimental Philosophy of Identity and the Self*. London: Bloomsbury.

Heiphetz, L., N. Strohminger, S. A. Gelman and L. L. Young (2018). "Who Am I? The Role of Moral Beliefs in Children's and Adults' Understanding of Identity." *Journal of Experimental Social Psychology*, 78: 210–19. doi: 10.1016/j.jesp.2018.03.007

Hussak, L. J. and A. Cimpian (2019). "It Feels Like It's in Your Body": How Children in the United States Think about Nationality." *Journal of Experimental Psychology: General*, 148: 1153–68. doi: 10.1037/xge0000567.

Knobe, J. (2022). "Personal Identity and Dual Character Concepts." In K. Tobia (ed.), *Experimental Philosophy of Identity and the Self*. London: Bloomsbury.

Knobe, J., S. Prasada and G. Newman (2013). "Dual Character Concepts and the Normative Dimension of Conceptual Representation." *Cognition*, 127: 242–57.

Kovacs, D. M. (2016). "Self-made People." *Mind*, 125: 1071–99.

Kovacs, D. M. (2020). "Diachronic Self-making." *Australasian Journal of Philosophy*, 98 (2): 349–62.

Lane-Steele, L. (2022). "Adjudicating Identity." *Texas A&M Law Review*.

Locke, J. (1694 reprint 1975). *An Essay Concerning Human Understanding*. Oxford: Oxford University.

Matsumura, K. T. (2014). "Binding Future Selves." *Louisiana Law Review*, 75: 71–125.

Mihailov, E., I. R. Hannikainen and B. D. Earp (2021). "Advancing Methods in Empirical Bioethics: Bioxphi Meets Digital Technologies." *The American Journal of Bioethics*, 21 (6): 53–6.

Molouki, S. and D. M. Bartels (2017). "Personal Change and the Continuity of the Self." *Cognitive Psychology*, 93: 1–17.

Mott, C. (2018). "Statutes of Limitations and Personal Identity." In T. Lombrozo, J. Knobe and S. Nichols (eds.), *Oxford Studies in Experimental Philosophy*, 243–69. Oxford: Oxford University Press.

Naess, A. (1938). *'Truth' as Conceived by Those Who Are Not Professional Philosophers*. Oslo: Jacob Dybwad.

Newman, G. E., P. Bloom and J. Knobe (2014). "Value Judgments and the True Self." *Personality and Social Psychology Bulletin*, 40: 203–16.
Nichols, S. and M. Bruno (2010). "Intuitions about Personal Identity: An Empirical Study." *Philosophical Psychology*, 23 (3): 293–312. doi: 10.1080/09515089.2010.490939
Noonan, H. (2022). "Personal Identity and Morality." In K. Tobia (ed.), *Experimental Philosophy of Identity and the Self*. London: Bloomsbury.
Olson, E. (1997). *The Human Animal*. New York: Oxford University Press.
Olson, E. (2003). "An Argument for Animalism." In R. Martin and J. Barresi (eds.), *Personal Identity*, 318–34. Oxford: Blackwell.
Parfit, D. (1971). "Personal Identity." *The Philosophical Review*, 80 (1): 3–27.
Parfit, D. (1984). *Reasons and Persons*. Oxford: Oxford University Press.
Paul, L. A. (2014). *Transformative Experience*. Oxford: Oxford University Press.
Phillips, B. (2021). "'They're Nott True Humans': Beliefs about Moral Character Drive Categorical Denials of Humanity." Available at https://psyarxiv.com/5bgxy/.
Prinz, J. J. and S. Nichols (2016). "Diachronic Identity and the Moral Self." In J. Kiverstein (ed.), *The Routledge Handbook of Philosophy of the Social Mind*, 449–64. Abingdon: Routledge.
Radin, M. J. (1982). "Property and Personhood." *Stanford Law Review* 34: 957–1015.
Riis, J., J. P. Simmons and G. P. Goodwin (2008). "Preferences for Psychological Enhancements: The Reluctance to Enhance Fundamental Traits." *Journal of Consumer Research* 35: 495–508.
Rose, D., K. Tobia and J. Schaffer (2020). "Folk Teleology Drives Persistence Judgments." *Synthese*, 197: 5491–509.
Russell, B. (1912). *The Problems of Philosophy*. London: Oxford University Press.
Schechtman, M. (1990). "Personhood and Personal Identity." *The Journal of Philosophy*, 87: 71–92.
Schechtman, M. (2014). *Staying Alive*. Oxford: Oxford University Press.
Schechtman, M. (2022). "The Whole Story: Identity and Narrative." In K. Tobia (ed.), *Experimental Philosophy of Identity and the Self*. London: Bloomsbury.
Schlegel, R., P. N. Holte, J. Maffly-Kipp, D. Guthrie and J. Hicks (2022). "Authenticity as a Pathway to Coherence, Purpose, and Mattering." In K. Tobia (ed.), *Experimental Philosophy of Identity and the Self*. London: Bloomsbury.
Schlegel, R. J., J. A. Hicks, J. Arndt and L. A. King (2009). "Thine Own Self: True Self-concept Accessibility and Meaning in Life." *Journal of Personality and Social Psychology*, 96 (2): 473.
Schlegel, R. J., J. A. Hicks, W. E. Davis, K. A. Hirsch and C. M. Smith (2013). "The Dynamic Interplay between Perceived True Self-knowledge and Decision Satisfaction." *Journal of Personality and Social Psychology*, 104 (3): 542–58.
Schlegel, R. J., J. A. Hicks, L. A. King and J. Arndt (2011). "Feeling Like You Know who You Are: Perceived True Self-knowledge and Meaning in Life." *Personality and Social Psychology Bulletin*, 37 (6): 745–56.
Schlegel, R. J., M. Vess and J. Arndt (2012). "To Discover or to Create: Metaphors and the True Self." *Journal of Personality*, 80 (4): 969–93.
Schwenkler, J., N. Byrd, E. Lambert and M. Taylor (2021). "One: But Not the Same." *Philosophical Studies*. https://doi.org/10.1007/s11098-021-01739-5.
Shoemaker, D. (2016). "Personal Identity and Ethics." In E. N. Zalta (ed.), *The Stanford Encyclopedia of Philosophy*. Plato.stanford.edu/entries/identity-ethics/.
Shoemaker, D. and K. Tobia (2022). "Personal Identity." In M. Vargas and J. Doris (eds.), *Oxford Handbook of Moral Psychology*. Oxford: Oxford University Press.

Sider, T. (2001). "Criteria of Personal Identity and the Limits of Conceptual Analysis." *Philosophical Perspectives*, 15: 189–209.

Smith, D. L. (2020a). *Making Monsters: The Uncanny Power of Dehumanization*. Cambridge, MA: Harvard University Press.

Smith, D. L. (2020b). *On Inhumanity: Dehumanization and How to Resist It*. New York: Oxford University Press.

Smith, D. L. (2022). "'Human' is an Essentially Political Category." In K. Tobia (eds.), *Experimental Philosophy of Identity and the Self*. London: Bloomsbury.

Stanley, M. and F. de Brigard (2022). "The Importance of Morality for One's Self Concept Predicts Perceptions of Personal Change after Remembering Wrongdoings." In K. Tobia (ed.), *Experimental Philosophy of Identity and the Self*. London: Bloomsbury.

Stanley, M. L. and F. de Brigard (2019). "Moral Memories and the Belief in the Good Self." *Current Directions in Psychological Science*, 28 (4): 387–91.

Stanley, M. L., A. Bedrov, R. Cabeza and F. de Brigard (2020). "The Centrality of Remembered Moral and Immoral Actions in Constructing Personal Identity." *Memory*, 28 (2): 278–84.

Stanley, M. L., P. Henne and F. de Brigard (2019). "Remembering Moral and Immoral Actions in Constructing the Self." *Memory and Cognition*, 47 (3): 441–54.

Stanley, M. L., P. Henne, V. Iyengar, W. Sinnott-Armstrong and F. de Brigard (2017). "I'm Not the Person I Used To Be: The Self and Autobiographical Memories of Immoral Actions." *Journal of Experimental Psychology: General*, 146 (6): 884–95.

Starmans, C. (2022). "Identity Crisis." In K. Tobia (ed.), *Experimental Philosophy of Identity and the Self*. London: Bloomsbury.

Starmans, C. and P. Bloom (2018a). "Nothing Personal: What Psychologists Get Wrong about Identity." *Trends in Cognitive Sciences*, 22 (7): 566–8.

Starmans, C. and P. Bloom. (2018b). "If You Become Evil, Do You Die?" *Trends in Cognitive Sciences*, 22 (9): 740–1.

Strohminger, N., J. Knobe and G. Newman (2017). "The True Self: A Psychological Concept Distinct from the Self." *Perspectives on Psychological Science*, 12 (4): 551–60.

Strohminger, N. and S. Nichols (2014). "The Essential Moral Self." *Cognition*, 131 (1): 159–71. doi: 10.1016/j.cognition.2013.12.005.

Strohminger, N. and S. Nichols (2015). "Neurodegeneration and Identity." *Psychological Science*, 26 (9): 1469–79. doi: 10.1177/0956797615592381.

Sullivan, M. (2018). *Time Biases: A Theory of Rational Planning and Personal Persistence*. New York; Oxford: Oxford University Press.

Tierney, H., C. Howard, V. Kumar, T. Kvaran, and S. Nichols (2014). "How Many of Us Are There?." In J. Sytsma (ed.), *Advances in Experimental Philosophy of Mind*, 181–202. London: Bloomsbury. https://www.bloomsbury.com/us/advances-in-experimental-philosophy-of-mind-9781472507334/.

Tobia, K. (2015). "Personal Identity and the Phineas Gage Effect." *Analysis*, 75 (3): 396–405.

Tobia, K. (2016). "Personal Identity, Direction of Change, and Neuroethics." *Neuroethics*, 9: 37–43. doi: 10.1007/s12152-016-9248-9.

Toomey, J. (2022). "Narrative Capacity." *North Carolina Law Review*, 100.

Turri, J. and S. Weaver (2018). "Personal Identity and Persisting as Many." In T. Lombrozo, J. Knobe and S. Nichols (eds.), *Oxford Studies in Experimental Philosophy*, Vol. 2, 213–42. Oxford: Oxford University Press.

Williams, B. (1970). "The Self and the Future." *The Philosophical Review*, 79: 161–80.

1

For Whom Do Moral Changes Matter

The Influence of Change Type, Direction, and Target on Judgments of Identity Persistence

Jim A. C. Everett, Joshua A. Skorburg, Jordan L. Livingston, Vladimir Chituc, and Molly J. Crockett

What makes you, *you*? Imagine that you were to develop severe muscular dystrophy, losing all control over your bodily movements: Would you still be you? What if you were to develop severe amnesia, losing all of your memories and having no recollection of your background or life: Would you still be you? And what if you could "catch" psychopathy, wholly losing your moral conscience and any empathy you have for those around you: Would you still be you? Such questions have long plagued philosophers. But identity change is also an enduring trope in popular fiction and entertainment, from classic children's books like Mark Twain's *The Prince and The Pauper* to cult-classic "body swap" movies like *Freaky Friday*. Moreover, identity persistence is fundamental to both folk and legal notions of blame and proportionality of punishment: whether and how much we can punish someone for a crime depends partly on whether we judge that the person we punish and the person who committed the crime are indeed the same.

The philosophical literature on personal identity is vast, but a dominant view attributed to John Locke posits that *psychological continuity* and, specifically, memories are at the heart of personal identity: if "the soul of a prince, carrying with it the consciousness of the prince's past life, enters and informs the body of a cobbler, as soon as deserted by his own soul, everyone sees he would be the same person with the prince, accountable only for the prince's actions" (*Essay*, II, 27.17). That is, if two people were to switch bodies, the "real" person would be the person with their own mind (or "soul"), not their body. This view of personal identity as dependent on psychological continuity suggests that if one were to severely disrupt parts of a person's mind (rather than their body), they might cease to be the same person after the change.

Traditionally, accounts based on psychological continuity have focused on memories as the key ingredient for identity persistence: Person X at Time 1 can be identified as Person Y at Time 2, if X and Y share an autobiographical memory (Locke 1694/1975). While philosophers have identified important flaws with psychological continuity accounts based solely on memories (Reid 1785/1975), empirical evidence suggests that such a memory-focused view does track folk intuitions (Nichols and Bruno 2010). But do laypeople really think that memories are what is *most* critical for identity persistence? Across five experiments, Strohminger and Nichols (2014) explored this, testing how other parts of the mind are perceived with respect to identity persistence. They found that *morality* was perceived as most central to identity. That is, when a person changed in terms of traits like honesty, empathy, or virtuousness, they were rated as more of a different person than when they changed in terms of their memories, preferences, or desires. This finding—henceforth "the moral self effect"—has been replicated by a number of independent groups (see Everett, Skorburg, and Livingston 2022 for a recent review), being seen in eight- to ten-year olds (Heiphetz et al. 2018) and Buddhist monks in India (Garfield et al. 2015). Moreover, it does not appear limited to hypothetical, abstract judgments, being seen in perceived identity persistence for patients with different neurodegenerative diseases (Strohminger and Nichols 2015) and people with addiction (Earp et al. 2019), and even having consequences for how we think about moral duties toward others (Everett, Skorburg, and Savulescu 2020).

Especially important for the present aims, Heiphetz, Strohminger, and Young (2017) found that changes to widely shared moral beliefs are perceived to be more disruptive to identity than changes to controversial moral beliefs. To explain this, they suggest a *community hypothesis*: perceived identity change is based on the extent to which changed attributes contribute to *communal ties*. Widely shared moral beliefs (e.g., "murder is wrong") bind one to a community, and so changes to these moral beliefs are perceived as more disruptive to identity than changes to controversial moral beliefs ("abortion is wrong") which may not bind in the same way. These results fit nicely with a related body of research showing that moral character (both one's own and the character of others) is a central element of social perception (Brambilla and Leach 2014; Goodwin, Piazza, and Rozin 2014).

In this chapter we focus on a key question about this moral self effect: *Does the importance of morality for identity persistence depend on the target of evaluation?* Existing empirical work suggests that morality is just as important when people judge their own identity persistence as when they judge others. For example, some of the earliest work on the moral self effect demonstrated that moral change was more important than memories regardless of whether it was presented in a first- or third-person perspective (Prinz and Nichols 2017). More recently, no difference was observed in a series of studies directly comparing the moral self effect for self and a hypothetical other ("Chris"), though there were stronger effects of changes in certain moral traits on the other compared to self (Heiphetz et al. 2017). And yet, there are reasons to think that perhaps the importance of morality for identity persistence *could* depend on who we're thinking about.

At least two (not mutually exclusive) lines of reasoning suggest that the importance of morality for perceived identity could vary across targets—especially as the distance becomes greater and participants move from thinking about themselves or friends to people they actively dislike or feel *negatively* about. First, people consistently overestimate their own morality compared to others (Epley and Dunning 2000), judge their friends as being better than the average person (Brown 1986), and think morality is a more important trait for the in-group than the out-group (Leach, Ellemers, and Barreto 2007). If people believe that they themselves and those close to them are more moral than average, when participants imagine themselves becoming more immoral, this should lead to a large degree of perceived identity change. This, of course, is what previous work on the moral self effect has demonstrated. However, when thinking of a stranger (assumed to be morally average) or someone that the participant does not like (assumed to be less moral than average), we might expect the moral self effect to be attenuated: in fact, disliked targets may even to some extent be defined by their *immorality*. Second, according to the community hypothesis (Heiphetz et al. 2017), morality is seen as more important for identity persistence because it binds people together, and so when evaluating someone we do *not* wish to be bound to (i.e., someone we dislike or don't get along with), morality might cease to be so important. To explore the generalizability of the moral self effect, we had participants evaluate changes to morality, warmth, competence, memories, and preferences for a number of different targets: the self (Study 1), a friend (Study 2), a stranger (Study 3), or a foe (Study 4). In answering this primary question, we take the opportunity to answer two further questions.

First, we ask, *does the direction of change matter, and does this interact with the target of evaluation?* While the vast majority of studies on the moral self effect have considered the impact of *losing* memories or *losing* morals on perceived identity persistence, it seems plausible that *gaining* memories or *gaining* morals might have different consequences. Indeed, focusing on morals (rather than memories), work on the "true self" suggests that the direction of moral change could matter. A growing number of studies have suggested that people typically regard others' true selves as being fundamentally good (Bench et al. 2015; De Freitas and Cikara 2018; Newman, Bloom, and Knobe 2014; Strohminger, Knobe, and Newman 2017), so that as people become more moral they are perceived to get closer to their true self.

In the context of identity persistence, Tobia (2015) draws on the well-worn (if potentially apocryphal) case study of Phineas Gage: a railroad worker who experienced brain damage in a horrific accident, after which he was reported to have become cruel and impulsive—so much so that "he was no longer Gage." In his work, Tobia gave participants one of two versions of this story. In a moral deterioration condition, participants saw the "standard" case of Phineas Gage, where he was kind before the accident, but cruel afterward. In another moral improvement condition, holding the magnitude of the change constant, participants saw a vignette where Gage was described as cruel before the accident, but kind afterward. In both conditions, Tobia asked participants to judge whether Phineas Gage was the same person as before the accident, and found that Gage was less likely to be judged as identical to his pre-accident self when the change was in a "bad" direction (deteriorating from kind to cruel) than when the change was in a "good" direction (improving from cruel to kind) even when the magnitude of the change was held constant. Similarly, other work has demonstrated that moral enhancement is less disruptive to perceptions of identity than moral degradation and that moral degradation is especially disruptive to perceptions of identity when people expect moral enhancement (Molouki and Bartels 2017).

On the other hand, other work has failed to replicate this effect of direction on judgments of identity. Prinz and Nichols (2017), for example, report findings suggesting that whether moral changes were in a positive or negative direction did not matter: that "moral changes are regarded as threats to identity, regardless of whether those changes are good or bad" (454). While somewhat mixed, these findings at least raise the interesting suggestion that judgments of identity change are not solely a function of the magnitude of the moral change, but could be importantly related to the *direction* of the change. When people are perceived as deteriorating (and especially when they are perceived to deteriorate morally), they might be judged to be more of a different person than when they improve or change in a positive direction.

While this work suggests that the direction of moral change could play an important role in the moral self effect (in line with what would be predicted based on the true self literature), more work is necessary on how direction and the type of change interact—and how both of these interact depending on the target of the judgment. Perhaps, for example, gaining new memories (e.g., suddenly remembering a traumatic incident that you had not known happened) is more disruptive than both losing memories *and* losing morals. Or perhaps all of this depends on whether participants are thinking about themselves, a friend, a stranger, or an enemy. In the same study mentioned earlier, Prinz and Nichols (2017) focus on judgments of the self and other, and found that the pattern for others replicated when thinking of the self: that it mattered more when the changes were moral, but it didn't matter which direction the changes were in. This, of course, goes against the suggestion in other work (e.g., Tobia 2015; Molouki and Bartels 2017)—perhaps different results would be obtained with a within-subjects "one change" paradigm used by Strohminger and Nichols (2015), and perhaps it matters on specifically who the target is.

The second additional question we ask in this work is whether *it is specifically moral attributes that are critical to identity persistence, or whether changes to warmth and competence are also more disruptive than changes to memories.* Although morality is a key dimension of person perception (Brambilla and Leach 2014; Goodwin et al. 2014), people are also perceived in terms of their *sociability* (together with morality comprising warmth) and *competence* (or agency) (e.g., Abele and Wojciszke 2014; Fiske, Cuddy, and Glick 2007; Rosenberg, Nelson, and Vivekananthan 1968). These three dimensions account for 80% to 90% of variance in social perception (Wojciszke 2005), and reflect our fundamental need to know whether another social entity has good or bad intentions (morality); whether they are able to enact these intentions (competence); and whether they are able to recruit others to help them in enacting these intentions (warmth) (Goodwin 2015). Most intriguingly, according to the dual perspective model of Abele and Wojiske, agency (competence) and communion (warmth) have different relevance depending on who we're thinking of: when thinking of ourselves, competence is more relevant, but when thinking of others, warmth—that is morality and sociability—is more relevant (Abele and Wojciszke 2014). Surprisingly, then, previous work on the moral self effect has not systematically considered these two fundamental dimensions of social perception, instead focusing on general "personality" changes. In this work, we sought to begin bridging this gap between work from experimental philosophy and moral psychology on the effect of moral changes on identity persistence (e.g., Strohminger and Nichols 2014), with work from traditional social cognition research on person perception and impression formation (e.g., Abele and Wojciszke 2014; Brambilla and Leach 2014; Fiske et al. 2007). To do this, we chose to compare changes to memories and preferences with not just changes to morals (e.g., "X no longer tells the truth") but also changes in warmth (e.g., "X no longer enjoys spending time with other people") and competence (e.g., "X no longer achieves their goals"). In doing so, we tried to make sure that the items we used in each category were unambiguous exemplars and broadly equivalent in specificity (see also discussion in the sub-section "Materials" in Study 1).

I. Open Science

In all studies our design, hypotheses, and analysis plan were all pre-registered at the Open Science Framework. We report all measures, manipulations, and exclusions. In the interest of space for this chapter in an edited book, we have moved some details on participants, power analyses, and analysis plans (including minor deviations) to a supplementary open science appendix. This, along with all data, analysis code, and experiment materials, is available for download at: https://osf.io/65f92/.

A. Study 1

1. Method

Participants: We recruited 150 participants online via Amazon MTurk, and participants were paid $2.40 for their time, in accordance with a minimum wage of $7.25 and the survey taking approximately 20 minutes. In accordance with the pre-registration, we excluded participants if they completed the study more than once ($N = 2$), or failed one or both of two simple attention checks embedded in the survey requiring them to enter a specific scale point to confirm they were paying attention ($N = 16$). This left us with a final sample of 132 participants (116 female; $M_{age} = 34.96$, $SD = 10.26$).

Design: This study had a fully within-subjects design with five conditions where participants thought about themselves and imagined that they were treated for a virus, but that a side-effect of treatment included a change to one of the following: morals (e.g., "*After the treatment, you are the same in every way as before, except now you do not tell the truth*"), warmth/sociability (e.g., "*... except now you do not tend to be in a good mood*"), competence (e.g., "*... except now you are not able to achieve your goals*"), memories (e.g., "*... except now you do not remember cherished time spent with family*"), or preferences (e.g., "*... except now you do not like your favorite food*"). The full list of items can be seen in the Supplementary Table 1 at the Open Science Foundation (OSF) (https://osf.io/65f92/).

Procedure: At the start of the survey, participants were told to imagine:

> It is some time in the near future, and a deadly virus has been spreading around the world. While the virus can be treated and the patient's life can be saved,

the treatment can have unexpected side-effects. Patients may recover and be physically exactly the same as before, but the side-effects can include memory loss, personality trait changes, and changes in what the patient likes and dislikes. In the questions that follow, we want you to imagine that you contracted the virus. Fortunately, you were able to receive treatment quickly and your life was saved. As a side-effect of this treatment, however, you changed in a specific way.

We informed participants that over the course of the study we would give them "25 different ways to imagine that they had changed, and for each we want you indicate how much you think that you would still be the same or a different person after the change."

After reading these instructions, participants began the main part of the study. In twenty-five separate blocks presented in a randomized order, participants were given a specific change ("Y") from across the five categories (morality, warmth, competence, memories, and preferences) and told that "you are the same in every way as before, except now you are no longer Y." Participants completed the five dependent measures for each change in the same fixed order on a single page. After completing these questions for each change, participants were told, "Thank you for answering these questions. On the next page you'll answer some questions about a different trait. You are Y again, but now you will have changed in a different way."

Materials: For our studies, we created a set of twenty-five items that expressed deterioration in morality, warmth, competence, memories, and preferences (see Supplementary Table 1: https://osf.io/65f92/). These differ in several ways from the original items in Strohminger and Nichols (2014). First, we made the items less extreme. For example, while Strohminger and Nichols's (2014) moral items included changes such as someone becoming a pedophile or a psychopath, we used less extreme changes (e.g., someone no longer tells the truth) that would be more comparable to attributes on other dimensions of interest (warmth and competence). Second, we did our best to better match the specificity of the items across dimensions. For example, while many of Strohminger and Nichols's (2014) moral items are fairly abstract personality descriptors (e.g., "virtuousness," "cowardice," "criminality"), the memory items were more specific (e.g., "knowing how to ride a bike"). To reduce this potential confound of differential specificity across dimensions, we used more specific examples across all five dimensions (though given the difference between specific memories and broad personality traits, differences in specificity are of course difficult to eliminate entirely). Third, we ensured that the items across dimensions captured general attributes that many people in the population would possess. For example, for memory changes, Strohminger and Nichols's used items like forgetting how to play the piano, and for the preferences items like craving cigarettes or enjoying rock music. Of course, many people do not play the piano, smoke cigarettes, or like rock music. To ensure that our items could be applicable in general to participants' themselves and people they knew, we chose items that we judged would be applicable to most people (e.g., instead of enjoyment of rock music, we simply mention favorite type of music). While we do not claim, of course, that we have obtained a perfect set of stimuli, we believe that it does represent an improvement upon those used in previous work.

Measures: Our first dependent measure, for which we pre-registered our hypotheses, looked at identity persistence or change: To what extent is someone a different person after experiencing the change? This was measured with two dependent measures, and since they were both intended to measure the same thing and results were the same for both, in the interest of space we have created an average composite score that we report in this chapter for all four studies. Across each category of change these composite scores were very reliable: $\alpha^{morality} = 0.88$; $\alpha^{warmth} = 0.85$; $\alpha^{competence} = 0.84$; $\alpha^{memories} = 0.86$; $\alpha^{preferences} = 0.90$ (though see the Supplementary Results on the OSF for full results across all four studies, looking at the measures separately).

DV 1a measured psychological identity persistence by looking at the extent to which participants thought they would be identified as the same person after the change: "Now that you are no longer Y, to what extent are you the same or a different person to how you were before?" (*1 = completely identical/the same person; 7 = completely different person*).[1] DV 1b also measured psychological identity persistence, but this time focused on participants judgments of whether their *essence* or *true self* would be the same. Participants were asked to rate "Now that you are no longer Y, how much has your 'essence', or your deepest, truest self—the thing that makes you, you—changed?" (*1 = not changed at all; 7 = completely changed*). Again, higher scores indicate greater identity disruption.

In addition to our key, pre-registered DV, we also had two additional, more exploratory measures which—on the advice of reviewers—are not included in the main text but reported in full at the OSF. The first of these additional measures had participants rate "Now that you are no longer Y, to what extent will you now behave differently?" (*1 = not at all; 7 = very much*), and the second had participants rate "Now that you are no longer Y, to what extent do you think other people will see you differently?" (*1 = not at all; 7 = very much*). Results for these dependent measures, in Study 1 and the subsequent studies, were highly consistent with the main identity persistence measure.

2. Results

A repeated measures ANOVA showed a significant effect of change type on perceptions of identity change, or how much participants thought they would be a "different person" after the changes, $F(4, 524) = 195.48$, $p < 0.001$, $\eta_p^2 = 0.6$. Pairwise comparisons using Bonferroni correction revealed significant differences between all pairs (most $ps < .005$; morality vs. competence significant at $p < 0.001$), with the exception of memories and preferences, which were not significantly different. Participants thought that changes to morality would be the most disruptive to their identity, judging that they would be more of a different person after changes to morality than when they changed in terms of warmth, competence, memories, and preferences (all $ps < .005$). And while morality was more important than warmth and competence, changes in these non-moral dimensions of person perception still led to significantly greater identity disruption than changes to memories and preferences. Interestingly in light of the results in the later studies (where warmth is either more important than competence, or there is no difference between them), we actually find here that participants judged changes to their own competence as more important for identity change than changes to their own warmth.

Overall, moral attributes were perceived to be the most central to identity, followed by competence, warmth, memories, and finally preferences. When imagining themselves to have changed morally, more so than the other types of changes, participants felt they would be more of a different person, and that their "essence, or their deepest, truest self" would have changed most.

3. Discussion

Our first study explored how a variety of changes would impact judgments of identity persistence in the self. In line with previous research, we found that morality is perceived to be highly identity-conferring such that changes to one's morals led participants to report that they would be more of a different person *and* their truest self would change most. It is noteworthy that these results were found even after attempting to deal with potential criticisms of the items used in the original paradigm (namely, that they differed substantially in valence and extremity).

Moreover, while previous work has mainly focused on the comparison between moral attributes and memories, we took a more systematic approach to non-moral personality traits by introducing changes on the two fundamental dimensions of person perception: warmth and competence. We found that while morality was perceived as most central to the self, changes to warmth and competence were more disruptive than memories and preferences. Interestingly, we found that while participants judged moral changes as most disruptive, they judged changes to their own competence as more disruptive than changes to their own warmth. This is broadly consistent with Abele and Wojciszke's (2014) Dual Perspective Model of Agency and Communion, which follows Peeters's (1983) distinction between primarily self-profitable traits (competence) and other-profitable traits (warmth) in positing that while warmth is more relevant when judging other people, competence is more relevant when judging the self.

B. Study 2

In Study 2, we turned away from looking at judgments of the self to see how different types of changes would influence perceptions of identity persistence for a friend.

1. Method

Participants: We recruited 270 participants online via Amazon MTurk, and participants were paid $2.40 for their time. In accordance with the pre-registration, we excluded participants if they completed the study more than once ($N=7$), or failed one or both of two simple attention checks embedded in the survey requiring them to enter a specific scale point to confirm they were paying attention ($N=16$). This left us with a final sample of 247 participants (116 female; $M_{age}=34.94$, $SD=10.26$).

Design: As in Study 1, we used a fully within-subjects design with the same five conditions (morality, warmth/sociability, competence, memories, preferences).

However, in this study, participants thought about their closest friend of the same gender: a third person, but one which is usually highly overlapping with the self. The vignette text was identical, except that we substituted the friend's name for the self and asked the participants to imagine that their friend was treated for the virus. The full list of items, along with means and standard deviations, can be seen in Table 1.1.

Procedure: The procedure was identical to Study 1 with the following exceptions. At the start of the survey, participants entered the name of their "closest friend of the same gender" and then throughout the study, piped text was used to insert this into the instructions and text for the dependent measures. It was made clear to participants that we were not going to ask any identifying information about this friend, but that we just needed to make sure they were thinking of the same specific friend throughout the study. After confirming their decision, participants were asked to rate how long they have known their friend ("X"), how close they feel to them, and how similar they are to them. Participants were then showed the same vignette as Study 1 (but with their friend's name substituted for the self).

Measures: The key dependent measure of identity persistence was identical to Study 1. This was supplemented with additional exploratory measures of expected behavior change and expected change in the eyes of others (as in Study 1), as well as two questions concerning how the changes would influence participants' desire to continue interacting with their friend, and how much would it influence how close

Table 1.1 Items Used in Study 5

Category	Decrease	Increase
	After the treatment X is the same in every way as before, except now they . . .	*After the treatment X is the same in every way as before, except now they . . .*
Morality		
	Do not tell the truth	Always tell the truth
	Do not respect people's differences	Care much more about respecting people's differences
	Do not care about helping others	Care much more about helping others
Warmth		
	Do not enjoy spending time with other people	Much more enjoy spending time with other people
	Do not tend to be in a good mood	Are more likely to be in a good mood
	Are not easygoing and relaxed	Are much more easygoing and relaxed
Competence		
	Do not achieve their goals	Are much better at achieving their goals
	Are not competent at taking on new tasks	Are much more competent at taking on new tasks
	Do not easily learn new skills	Find learning new skills much easier
Memories		
	Do not remember cherished time spent with family	More vividly remember cherished time spent with family
	Do not remember the worst thing that has ever happened to them	More clearly remember the worst thing that has ever happened to them
	Do not remember the house they grew up in	Better remember the house they grew up in

participants felt toward them. Again, results for these additional measures were highly consistent and are reported in the supplementary results.

2. Results

A repeated measures ANOVA on perceptions of identity change showed a significant effect of change type condition, $F(4, 984) = 367.95$, $p < 0.001$, $\eta_p^2 = 0.6$, with pairwise comparisons using Bonferroni correction revealing significant differences between all pairs except warmth and competence. Changes to morality were most disruptive to their friend's identity, with participants judging that their friend was more of a different person than when they changed in terms of warmth, competence, memories, and preferences (all p s < .001). And while morality was more important than warmth and competence, changes in warmth and competence still led to significantly greater identity disruption than changes to memories and preferences.

3. Discussion

In Study 1, we considered the moral self effect in the context of judgments about the self. Here in Study 2, we extended this investigation to explore the moral self effect in the context of judgments about a close friend. We replicated and extended our previous findings with a new target, demonstrating that changes to morality were most disruptive to a friend's identity. As before, changes to warmth and competence were also perceived to be more identity-conferring than memories or preferences.

C. Study 3

In Study 3, we sought to further explore the generalizability of the moral self effect by looking at judgments of both a friend and a stranger.

1. Method

Participants: We recruited 300 participants online via Amazon MTurk, and participants were paid $2.40 for their time. In accordance with the pre-registration, we excluded participants if they completed the study more than once ($N=6$), or failed one or both of two simple attention checks embedded in the survey requiring them to enter a specific scale point to confirm they were paying attention ($N=14$). This left us with a final sample of 281 participants (138 female; $M_{age} = 37.79$, $SD = 10.04$).

Our sample size was determined through a power analysis using G*Power (Faul et al. 2009) which revealed that for each between-subjects variant (friend and stranger) separately, assuming a conservative small-effect size of $f=0.10$, and an α of .05 and power of .80, we would need a sample size of 121 participants for both friend and stranger conditions. To account for participant exclusions—we recruited a total of 300 participants. A post hoc sensitivity analysis revealed that for each variant separately (with α of .05 and power of .80), we had sufficient power to detect a small effect of $f=0.09$.

Design: This study had a mixed design with the same five change conditions used in Studies 1 and 2 as a within-subjects factor (morality, warmth, competence, memories, preferences), and a between-subjects factor of whether participants were thinking about their closest friend of the same gender ("friend condition") or a matched-gender stranger named Jordan ("stranger condition").

The procedure for participants in the friend condition was identical to Study 2. Participants in the stranger condition were presented with a description of "Jordan," who had male pronouns for male participants ($n = 142$), female pronouns for female participants ($n = 137$), and randomly either male or female for non-binary gendered participants ($n = 3$). We gave participants a short description of this stranger to ensure all participants were thinking broadly of the same person, and devised the text to be a neutral portrait that was reasonably ambiguous with regards to race, social class, and political ideology. "Jordan" was described as being in their mid-thirties, living just outside Cleveland, Ohio, with their partner and two children, having a middle-management position in a large department store, and in their free time enjoying spending time with their children, going to the movies, and spending time in nature. Piped text was used to either input the name of the participants' friend (for the friend condition), or the name Jordan (for the stranger condition) into the text and DVs. All the change items and dependent measures were identical to those used in Study 2.

2. Results

An ANOVA revealed a main effect of change type on how much participants thought the target (i.e., their friend or stranger) would be a "different person" after the changes, $F(4, 1,116) = 470.01$, $p < 0.001$, $\eta_p^2 = 0.63$, but no significant interaction of change type and target condition, $F(4, 1,116) = 2.04$, $p = 0.086$, $\eta_p^2 = 0.01$. Bonferroni-corrected pairwise comparisons revealed significant differences between every pair except warmth and competence, and memories and preference (all other $ps < .005$). In other words, *how* a person changed mattered, but the target of the change did not. Social changes, and specifically moral changes, were again the most disruptive to a person's identity, with changes to memories and preferences having significantly less effect on identity change than changes to morality, warmth, and competence (see Figure 1.1).

3. Discussion

In Study 1, we explored judgments of identity change for the self, and in Study 2, within the context of close friendships. In Study 3, we replicated and extended these findings by adding a "stranger" condition. We found that *how* targets change matters a great deal, but *who* changes seems comparatively less important. For friends and strangers alike, changes to morality were perceived to be the most disruptive to identity. Consistent with the findings in Studies 1 and 2, changes to warmth and competence were perceived to be more disruptive to identity than memories or preferences. But might these findings be specific to thinking about either neutral or positively tinged others? What about those who we might think *negatively* about, those whom we might already think of in ways that downgrade their morality and warmth? How important, in other words, is morality when we're thinking not of a friend or a stranger, but a foe?

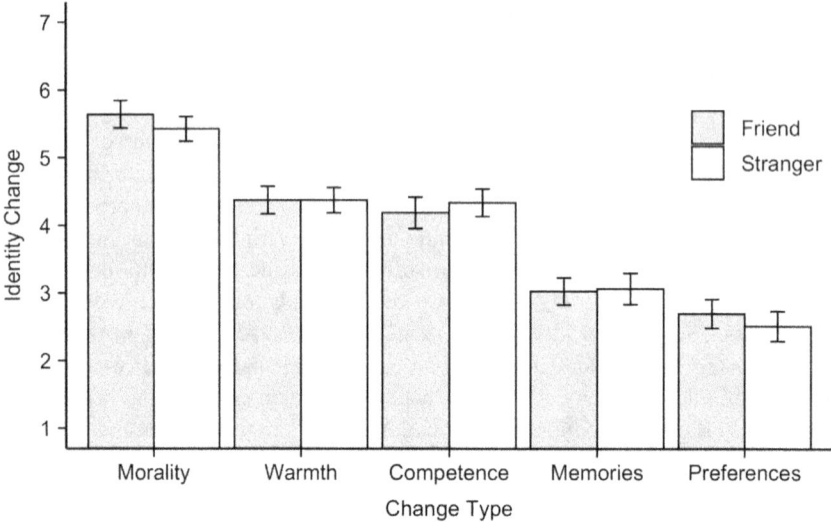

Figure 1.1 Expected identity disruption as a function of target and type of identity change. For both a friend and stranger, social changes—and especially moral ones—were perceived as more disruptive to psychological identity persistence than changes to memories or preferences. Higher numbers represent greater perceived identity change, and error bars represent 95% confidence intervals.

D. Study 4

In Study 4 we extend our investigation of whether the importance of morality for identity persistence depend on the target of evaluation by considering how people think about both friends *and* foes.

1. Method

Participants: We recruited 300 participants online via Amazon MTurk, and participants were paid $2.40 for their time. Our sample size was determined through the same power analysis used in Study 2. Out of the 300 participants, 299 completed the survey in full. Again, we excluded participants if they completed the study more than once ($N = 7$) or failed one or both of two simple attention checks ($N = 24$). This left us with a final sample of 268 participants (115 female; $M_{age} = 36.22$, $SD = 10.56$).

Design: This study had the same mixed design as used in Study 3, with the five change conditions as a within-subjects factor (morality, warmth, competence, memories, preferences), and a between-subjects factor of whether participants were thinking about a person they like and feel positively about ("friend" condition) or someone they do dislike and feel negatively about ("foe" condition). While the dependent measures and categories of change were identical to those used in Studies 1–3, in this study we only used a subset of the full set of change items, using four changes from each category instead of five (see supplementary file for exact items).

The main difference between this study and the previous two was the focus of the change. In Study 2, participants thought about their "closest friend of the same gender," and in Study 3 participants thought about either their closest friend of the same gender, or a matched-gender stranger. In this study, we moved away from having participants think about their closest friend to instead just think of someone with whom they have a positive relationship, and we compared this to participants thinking about someone with whom they have a negative relationship.

Participants were asked to think about:

> someone that you like [dislike] and get along [have difficulty] with. This person should not be part of your immediate family and should not be someone you have a current romantic relationship with. Maybe this person has helped [wronged] you in the past, or maybe they just [don't] wish you well. You probably have positive [negative] thoughts and emotions about this person.

Importantly, these instructions were chosen to be fairly moderate for both the friend and foe conditions. Instead of thinking of a closest friend, participants simply think of someone they have a positive relationship with. Moreover, while we refer to participants' "foe," even this terminology is likely too strong, for participants were merely instructed to think of someone they don't like, not their mortal enemy.

To get information about the person that participants were thinking of, we asked participants some questions about the person they had chosen before they were introduced to the thought experiment component of the study. Participants were asked to indicate the person's gender, how they knew the person, how close they felt to them, how much in general they wanted to interact with them, how much the person has helped/harmed them in the past, and overall how positive/negative they felt about them (see supplementary results file for full details).

Analysis Plan: Our primary pre-registered analysis was for the first two key DVs measuring identity persistence, in which we conducted a repeated measures ANOVA in which we entered as a within-subjects factor the five categories of change (morality, warmth, competence, memories, and preferences), and as a between-subjects factor the target that changed (friend vs. stranger). There are, however, only reported at the OSF (https://osf.io/65f92/) because—unsurprisingly—participants rated a friend as higher in morality, warmth, and competence than they did for an enemy. Given this, any interaction effect suggesting that changes to social dimensions were more important for a friend than an enemy (as we found in the ANOVA) could be explained just through a friend having higher baseline ratings and thus more room for change when they were describing as losing these traits. In an attempt to address this, our main analyses we report are from a within-subjects ANCOVA where, as well the within-subjects factor of the five categories of change and the between-subjects factor of the target, we also entered as three separate covariates participants' average baseline rating of how much the friend or foe exhibited the morality, warmth, and competence attributes used later in the study right now, prior to the thought experiment. Then, across target conditions and for the friend and foe separately, we then compared between specific change conditions using Bonferroni-corrected pairwise comparisons.

Person Ratings: Before beginning our key analyses, we looked at how participants described the person they were thinking of. For participants instructed to think of a friend, on a 1–7 scale, participants reported feeling close to their friend ($M = 5.11$, $SD = 1.09$), and on scales where +3 indicates maximum positivity and −3 indicates maximum negativity, participants felt that their friend had helped, not harmed, them ($M = 1.94$, $SD = .99$); wanted to interact with, not avoid, the person ($M = 2.02$, $SD = 0.95$); and overall felt positive, not negative, about the person ($M = 2.41$, $SD = 0.77$). Finally, participants reported high baseline levels of morality ($M = 6.09$, $SD = 0.88$), warmth ($M = 5.58$, $SD = 0.94$), and competence ($M = 5.95$, $SD = 0.93$) for their friend.

For participants instructed to think of a foe, on the 1–7 scale, participants reported feeling not close to the person ($M = 1.88$, $SD = 1.15$), and on the −3 to 3 scales, participants felt that their foe had harmed, not helped, them in the past ($M = -1.49$, $SD = 1.37$); wanted to avoid, not interact with, the person ($M = -2.02$, $SD = 1.28$); and overall felt negatively, not positively, about the person ($M = -2.02$, $SD = 1.06$). Finally, participants reported low-to-medium baseline levels of morality ($M = 3.31$, $SD = 1.29$), warmth ($M = 3.65$, $SD = 1.17$), and competence ($M = 4.00$, $SD = 1.42$) for the foe.

2. Results

An ANCOVA revealed a significant main effect of change type on perceptions of identity change, $F(4, 1{,}052) = 8.36$, $p < .001$, $\eta_p^2 = 0.03$, but no interaction of change type and person condition, $F(4, 1{,}052) = 1.42$, $p = .23$, $\eta_p^2 = 0.01$. Collapsing across both targets, we found significant differences between every pair (all $ps < .005$) except warmth and competence. While the interaction was not significant, for consistency with the previous study we looked at friend and foe separately. For a friend, there were significant differences between every pair (all $ps < .005$), but for a foe there were no significant differences between changes to morality and changes to memories, warmth, or competence; changes to preferences led to the least change, and only this was significantly different from all other categories.

3. Discussion

As in Studies 2 and 3, we found again that for a friend, moral ones were perceived as more disruptive to identity than changes to warmth and competence, changes to which were in turn more disruptive to identity than changes to memories or preferences. For a foe, results were more ambiguous. When ignoring baseline levels of a friend or foe's morality, warmth, and competence, analyses suggested that changes to morality were more detrimental to identity for a friend and a foe. We judged that these analyses were inadequate, however, because foes were naturally perceived as having lower baseline levels of morality, warmth, and competence. It is plausible that because foes are already seen as deficient in morality and warmth, being asked to imagine that such a foe has lost their morality or warmth will not have as strong an effect as when imagining someone who is previously seen as high in morality and warmth. Indeed, when controlling for these baseline levels using three separate covariates, across the DVs we found no interaction of person condition and change type, only the main effect of change type with the same pattern as in the other studies (i.e., morality > warmth > competence > memories > preferences). At the same time, however, on our main DV of identity persistence, post hoc comparisons for a friend and foe separately revealed the expected pattern was only for a friend, while for a foe only preferences were significantly different from the others (i.e., morality = warmth = competence = memories > preferences). Given these mixed findings, it is difficult to draw firm conclusions about the moral self effect when it comes to foes from Study 4 alone.

E. Study 5

In Study 5 we sought to address the potential concern from Study 4 that we looked at how a decrease in morals (compared to memories) would influence perceptions of identity persistence for both a friend and foe, but because foes were already seen as less moral than friends, it is unsurprising that further deterioration in their morality would be less impactful than deterioration in the morality of a good person. To address this, in Study 5 we also manipulated the direction of change, looking at whether just as a friend who becomes less moral is seen as more of a different person, so too might a foe who becomes *more* moral.

1. Method

Participants: We recruited 741 participants online via Amazon MTurk, and participants were paid $1.80 for their time. Of our 741 participants who completed the survey, as in the previous studies we excluded participants if they completed the study more than once ($N = 52$) or failed one or both of two simple attention checks ($N = 50$). This left us with a final sample of 639 participants (293 female, 3 other; $M_{age} = 37.32$, $SD = 10.83$).

Design: This study had a mixed design, with four change conditions as a within-subjects factor (morality, warmth, competence, memories), and two between-subjects factors. First, participants were assigned to a between-subjects condition in which we varied participants who were thinking about a person they like and feel positively about ("friend" condition) or someone they do dislike and feel negatively about ("foe" condition). Second, participants were assigned to an additional between-subjects condition in which we varied the direction of change: whether each trait decreased (e.g., became less moral, as in the previous studies) or increased (e.g., became more moral). The "decreasing" conditions were identical to Study 4; the key change was the addition of the "increasing" conditions. The wording of the increase conditions was designed to parallel the original direction (see Table 1.1 for items).

Note that to reduce the length of the survey, we only used four types of change (instead of five), and used only three instantiations of each category (instead of the four used in the previous study). Given that the category of preference changes were functioning mainly as a comparison control condition and not of specific theoretical interest, we removed the items related to preferences to only have the four key change types: morality, memories, warmth, and competence, each with three examples. The dependent measures used were the same as in Study 4, but again we only report in the main text the results for our key, pre-registered dependent measure of identity persistence.

Person Ratings: Before beginning our key analyses, we looked at how participants described the person they were thinking of. For participants thinking of a friend, on a 1–7 scale, participants reported feeling close to their friend ($M = 5.22$, $SD = 1.17$), and on scales where +3 indicates maximum positivity and −3 indicates maximum negativity, participants felt that their friend had helped, not harmed, them ($M = 1.20$, $SD = .84$); wanted to interact with, not avoid, the person ($M = 1.30$, $SD = 0.69$); and overall felt positive, not negative, about the person ($M = 1.27$, $SD = 0.59$). Finally, participants reported high baseline levels of morality ($M = 5.96$, $SD = 0.92$), warmth ($M = 5.82$, $SD = 0.88$), and competence ($M = 5.75$, $SD = 0.93$) for their friend.

For participants instructed to think of a foe, on the 1–7 scale, participants reported feeling not close to the person ($M = 2.11$, $SD = 1.58$), and on the −3 to 3 scales, participants felt that their foe had harmed, not helped, them in the past ($M = -1.55$, $SD = 1.42$); wanted to avoid, not interact with, the person ($M = -1.96$, $SD = 1.46$); and overall felt negatively, not positively, about the person ($M = -1.90$, $SD = 1.35$). Finally, participants reported low-to-medium baseline levels of morality ($M = 2.94$, $SD = 1.46$), warmth ($M = 3.65$, $SD = 1.47$), and competence ($M = 3.76$, $SD = 1.51$) for the foe.

2. Results

First, we looked at perceptions of identity change. An ANOVA revealed a significant interaction of change type, person condition, and direction condition: $F(3, 1,905) = 123.00$, $p < .001$, $\eta_p^2 = 0.16$; along with significant main effects of change type: $F(3, 1,905) = 82.78$, $p < .001$, $\eta_p^2 = 0.12$; direction condition: $F(1, 635) = 68.97$, $p < .001$, $\eta_p^2 = 0.10$; and person condition: $F(1, 635) = 4.33$, $p = .038$, $\eta_p^2 = 0.16$.

Breaking this interaction down, we first looked at participants in the friend condition. For a friend and across all categories, decreasing a trait was seen as more disruptive for identity than increasing the same trait: it was more disruptive for perceived identity when a friend became less moral than when they became more moral: $t(317.35) = 18.36$, $p < .001$; more warm rather than less warm: $t(301.54) = 14.84$, $p < .001$; and more competent rather than less competent: $t(295.33) = 7.83$, $p < .001$. Similarly, it was more disruptive for perceived identity when a friend lost their memories than when their memories became more vivid: $t(290.02) = 8.86$, $p < .001$. Looking at the relative disruptiveness of the various kinds of change, we found that for the decrease conditions, replicating the previous studies, changes to morality were seen as more disruptive than warmth, competence, and memories (all $ps < .001$). For the increase conditions, we found that morality was equally disruptive as changes to warmth and competence ($ps = 1.00$), and weakly but significantly more disruptive than memories ($p = .002$, mean$^{morality} = 2.79$, mean$^{memories} = 2.52$).

Next, we looked at participants in the foe conditions. Consistent with the findings for a friend, when a foe lost their memories this was perceived as more disruptive for identity than when their memories increased, $t(316.19) = 5.55$, $p < .001$. For morality, however, we found the opposite pattern: the foe was perceived to be more of a different person when they become more moral than when they became less moral,

$t(311.02) = 9.71$, $p < .001$. While not statistically significant, the same pattern was observed for warmth, $t(315.47) = 1.83$, $p = .068$; and there was no effect of direction of change in competence, $t(316.90) = 0.02$, $p = .99$. Looking at the relative disruptiveness of the various kinds of change, we found that for the decrease conditions, changes to morality were seen as *less* disruptive to a foe's identity than changes to warmth ($p < .001$), competence ($p = .03$), and memories ($p < .001$). For the increase condition, we found results paralleling those found in previous studies for a friend and stranger: changes to morality were perceived as more disruptive than changes to warmth, competence, and memories ($p < .001$).

Overall, then, results from our main dependent measure of identity persistence revealed that that changes to morality were most disruptive to perceived identity, but that the direction of change mattered: a friend became more of a different person when they became less moral, but a foe became more of a different person when they became more moral (see Figure 1.2).

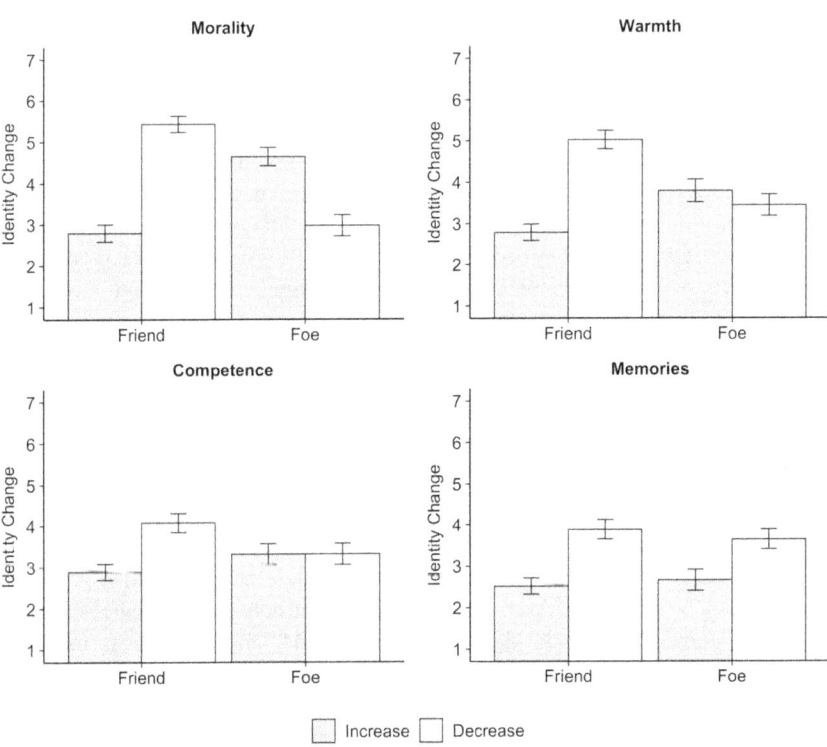

Figure 1.2 Expected identity disruption as a function of target, direction of change, and type of identity change. Changes to morality were more disruptive to perceived identity than memories, but the direction of change mattered: a friend became more of a different person when they became less moral, but a foe became more of a different person when they became more moral Higher numbers represent greater perceived identity change, and error bars represent 95% confidence intervals.

II. General Discussion

What makes someone the same person over time? Philosophers have typically argued that what is essential for identity persistence is continuity of memories. In more recent years, however, work at the intersection of psychology and experimental philosophy has suggested a *moral self effect* (Heiphetz et al. 2017; Strohminger and Nichols 2014, 2015), whereby laypeople judge morality as the core of personal identity. While illuminating, there remain several questions about the precise nature of this moral self effect (Heiphetz et al. 2017; Strohminger and Nichols 2014, 2015). In this chapter we focus on how sensitive the moral self effect is to who we're thinking of, investigating the moral self effect in the context of judgments of the self, a stranger, a close friend, a generic friend, and a foe. In answering this primary question, we also take the opportunity to shed light on two other questions: first, whether the direction of change matters; and second, whether it is specifically moral attributes that are critical to identity persistence, or whether changes to warmth and competence are also more disruptive than changes to memories.

We found consistent support for the moral self effect, showing that changes to morality were seen as more disruptive than changes to warmth, competence, memories, and preferences, for the self (Study 1), a close gender-matched friend (Study 2), a stranger (Study 3), a positive friend (Study 4), and a "foe" (Studies 4–5). Most interestingly, we found that while changes to morality were most disruptive to perceived identity, but that the direction of change mattered based on whether participants thought of a positively or negatively viewed target: a friend became more of a different person when they became less moral, but a foe became more of a different person when they became *more* moral. These results highlight that even if morality is seen as generally more important than memories, we must also consider the direction of change.

Our results support the moral self effect in showing that judgments of identity persistence are more impacted by changes to morals than memories across a variety of targets, but what they cannot speak to is precisely *what* participants are thinking about when they respond to statements like "Now that X is no longer Y, to what extent are they the same or a different person to how they were before?" The traditional interpretation in work on the moral self effect is that participants are treating such responses at face value, reporting perceptions of identity disruption. Some scholars have, however, disputed this interpretation by arguing that participants are more plausibly thinking about similarity rather than numerical, personal identity (Berniūnas and Dranseika 2016; Starmans and Bloom 2018). Starmans and Bloom (2018), for example, argue that work on the moral self effect has "fail[ed] to properly distinguish similarity from personal identity, and therefore certain conclusions regarding common-sense intuitions about identity are not supported." They claim that while Strohminger and colleagues have sought to make claims about quantitative identity ("After changing morally, can I identify X as the same person?"), they are actually obtaining participants' intuitions about qualitative identity ("After changing morally, is X dissimilar to how they were before?"). It is beyond the scope of this chapter to deal fully with this interesting theoretical debate, though see Everett et al. (2020) and Everett et al. (2022) where we push back against this view on both empirical and theoretical grounds, respectively. For now, suffice it to say that even if our work, like that which we build on, is better understood as about similarity than numerical identity (which we would partly resist), the numerous theoretical and methodological extensions we make here still advance our knowledge about identity, just in the qualitative sense of similarity, not the numerical sense of identification. Our work still clarifies and extends the existing work: it highlights the importance of non-moral social attributes, still establishes boundary conditions depending on the person one thinks of, and still establishes the consequences of perceived identity change for interpersonal relationships. Ordinary conceptions of personal identity are deeply social and wedded to their role in the community.

Acknowledgments

This work was supported by a sub-award given to Jim A. C. Everett, Joshua Skorburg, Jordan Livingston, and Michael Ferguson through the 2016 Summer Seminars in Neuroscience and Philosophy (SSNAP) program, funded by the John Templeton Foundation. We gratefully acknowledge Walter Sinnott-Armstrong and Felipe De Brigard for all their efforts in organizing this summer seminar series that allowed us to develop this work. JACE was further supported by the European Union's Horizon 2020 research and innovation program under the Marie Skłodowska-Curie grant (707404).

Note

1   One potential philosophical problem with this wording is that because we say as the prelude "Now that X is longer Y . . .," this strictly speaking assumes numerical identity because it implies that the person at Time-2 is the same person as Time-1. This is mainly a problem for philosophical interpretation, however, not for the interpretation of our empirical results, and that we yield the same results as other studies using different wording suggests that this is not a major concern regardless.

Bibliography

Abele, A. E. and B. Wojciszke (2014). "Communal and Agentic Content in Social Cognition: A Dual Perspective Model." In J. M. Olson and M. P. Zanna (eds.), *Advances in Experimental Social Psychology*, Vol. 50, 195–255. Academic Press. doi: 10.1016/B978-0-12-800284-1.00004-7.

Bench, S. W., R. J. Schlegel, W. E. Davis and M. Vess (2015). "Thinking about Change in the Self and Others: The Role of Self-Discovery Metaphors and the True Self." *Social Cognition*, 33 (3): 169–85. doi: 10.1521/soco.2015.33.3.2.

Berniūnas, R. and V. Dranseika (2016). "Folk Concepts of Person and Identity: A Response to Nichols and Bruno." *Philosophical Psychology*, 29 (1): 96–122. doi: 10.1080/09515089.2014.986325.

Brambilla, M. and C. W. Leach (2014). "On the Importance of Being Moral: The Distinctive Role of Morality in Social Judgment." *Social Cognition*, 32 (4): 397–408. doi: 10.1521/soco.2014.32.4.397.

Brown, J. D. (1986). "Evaluations of Self and Others: Self-Enhancement Biases in Social Judgments." *Social Cognition*, 4 (4): 353–76. doi: 10.1521/soco.1986.4.4.353.

De Freitas, J. and M. Cikara (2018). "Deep Down my Enemy is Good: Thinking about the True Self Reduces Intergroup Bias." *Journal of Experimental Social Psychology*, 74: 307–16.

Earp, B. D., J. A. Skorburg, J. A. C. Everett and J. Savulescu (2019). "Addiction, Identity, Morality." *AJOB Empirical Bioethics*, 10 (2): 136–53. doi: 10.1080/23294515.2019.1590480.

Epley, N. and D. Dunning (2000). "Feeling 'Holier than Thou': Are Self-Serving Assessments Produced by Errors in Self- or Social Prediction?" *Journal of Personality and Social Psychology*, 79 (6): 861–75.

Everett, J. A. C., J. A. Skorburg and J. Livingston (2022). "Me, My (Moral) Self, and I." In Felipe de Brigard and Walter Sinnott-Armstrong (eds.), *Neuroscience and Philosophy*. MIT Press.

Everett, J. A. C., J. A. Skorburg and J. Savulescu (2020). "The Moral Self and Moral Duties." *Philosophical Psychology*, 0 (0): 1–22. doi: 10.1080/09515089.2020.1789577.

Faul, F., E. Erdfelder, A. Buchner and A.-G. Lang (2009). "Statistical Power Analyses using G*Power 3.1: Tests for Correlation and Regression Analyses." *Behavior Research Methods*, 41 (4): 1149–60. doi: 10.3758/BRM.41.4.1149.

Fiske, S. T., A. J. C. Cuddy and P. Glick (2007). "Universal Dimensions of Social Cognition: Warmth and Competence." *Trends in Cognitive Sciences*, 11 (2): 77–83. doi: 10.1016/j.tics.2006.11.005.

Garfield, J. L., S. Nichols, A. K. Rai, and N. Strohminger (2015). "Ego, Egoism and the Impact of Religion on Ethical Experience: What a Paradoxical Consequence of Buddhist Culture Tells us about Moral Psychology." *The Journal of Ethics*, 19, no. 3–4: 293–304.

Goodwin, G. P. (2015). "Moral Character in Person Perception." *Current Directions in Psychological Science*, 24 (1): 38–44. doi: 10.1177/0963721414550709.

Goodwin, G. P., J. Piazza and P. Rozin (2014). "Moral Character Predominates in Person Perception and Evaluation." *Journal of Personality and Social Psychology*, 106 (1): 148–68. doi: 10.1037/a0034726.

Heiphetz, L., N. Strohminger, S. A. Gelman and L. L. Young (2018). "Who am I? The Role of Moral Beliefs in Children's and Adults' Understanding of Identity." *Journal of Experimental Social Psychology*. doi: 10.1016/j.jesp.2018.03.007.

Heiphetz, L., N. Strohminger and L. L. Young (2017). "The Role of Moral Beliefs, Memories, and Preferences in Representations of Identity." *Cognitive Science*, 41 (3): 744–67. doi: 10.1111/cogs.12354.

Leach, C. W., N. Ellemers and M. Barreto (2007). "Group virtue: The Importance of Morality (vs. Competence and Sociability) in the Positive Evaluation of In-Groups." *Journal of Personality and Social Psychology*, 93 (2): 234–49. doi: 10.1037/0022-3514.93.2.234.

Locke, J. (1694 reprint 1975). "Of Identity and Diversity." In *Essay Concerning Human Understanding*, reprinted in Perry John (ed.), *Personal Identity*, 33–52. Berkeley: University of California Press.

Molouki, S. and D. M. Bartels (2017). "Personal Change and the Continuity of the Self." *Cognitive Psychology*, 93: 1–17. doi: 10.1016/j.cogpsych.2016.11.006.

Newman, G. E., P. Bloom and J. Knobe (2014). "Value Judgments and the True Self." *Personality and Social Psychology Bulletin*, 40 (2): 203–16. doi: 10.1177/0146167213508791.

Nichols, S. and M. Bruno (2010). "Intuitions about Personal Identity: An Empirical Study." *Philosophical Psychology*, 23 (3): 293–312. doi: 10.1080/09515089.2010.490939.

Peeters, G. (1983). "Relational and Informational Patterns in Social Cognition." In W. Doise and S. Moscovici (eds.), *Current issues in European Social Psychology*, Vol. 1, 201–37. Cambridge: Cambridge University Press.

Prinz, J. J. and S. Nichols (2017). "Diachronic Identity and the Moral Self." In J. Kiverstein (ed.), *The Routledge Handbook of Philosophy of the Social Mind*, 449–64. London and New York: Routledge.

Reid, T. (1785 reprint 1975). "Of Mr. Locke's Account of Our Personal Identity." In J. Perry (ed.), *Personal Identity*, 113–18. Berkeley: University of California Press.

Rosenberg, S., C. Nelson and P. S. Vivekananthan (1968). "A Multidimensional Approach to the Structure of Personality Impressions." *Journal of Personality and Social Psychology*, 9 (4): 283.

Starmans, C. and P. Bloom (2018). "Nothing Personal: What Psychologists Get Wrong about Identity." *Trends in Cognitive Sciences*, 22 (7): 566–8. doi: 10.1016/j.tics.2018.04.002.

Strohminger, N., J. Knobe and G. Newman (2017). "The True Self: A Psychological Concept Distinct from the Self." *Perspectives on Psychological Science*, 12 (4): 551–60. doi: 10.1177/1745691616689495.

Strohminger, N. and S. Nichols (2014). "The Essential Moral Self." *Cognition*, 131 (1): 159–71. doi: 10.1016/j.cognition.2013.12.005.

Strohminger, N. and S. Nichols (2015). "Neurodegeneration and Identity." *Psychological Science*, 26 (9): 1469–79. doi: 10.1177/0956797615592381.

Tobia, K. P. (2015). "Personal Identity and the Phineas Gage Effect." *Analysis*, 75 (3): 396–405. doi: 10.1093/analys/anv041.

Wojciszke, B. (2005). "Morality and Competence in Person- and Self-Perception." *European Review of Social Psychology*, 16 (1): 155–88. doi: 10.1080/10463280500229619.

2

Identity Crisis

Christina Starmans

When I was seven years old, my sister and I attended a local fair—the kind with carnival barkers and games with giant stuffed animals. Among the sea of plushies, my sister and I spotted real prizes—and for such a simple game. All we had to do was toss a ping pong ball into a sea of glass jars, and hope it landed inside one. Swimming in each jar was the prize we had our eyes on. Much to our delight, we both won, and were each handed a small plastic bag containing a cup or so of water and a bright orange goldfish.

We brought our new pets home, ignored the looks exchanged between our parents, and deposited them together into a fishbowl. Each day, I'd make sure to feed the fish, always hoping to direct the food a little more toward my own goldfish, who I'd named Sharky. Which of the two goldfish was actually Sharky was impossible to say, since they were identical. But I was sure that I owned a particular one of these goldfish and was determined to take good care of him.

Alas, after a few days had passed, I went downstairs one morning, and discovered a goldfish floating on the surface of the bowl. Even at seven, I knew what this meant, and I ran back up to my parents and sister, and broke the news: "Amy's goldfish died!"

* * *

We'll never know whose goldfish really died. But the story illustrates the relationship between, and the different consequences of, being identical in a *qualitative* sense versus being identical in a *numerical* sense.

Qualitative identity is a form of similarity. To say that two apples are identical is to say that they share the same properties (except for location); you cannot tell them apart. This is the sense in which identical twins are identical, and the sense in which the Starmans sisters had identical goldfish.

Numerical identity is persistence over time. This is the sense in which the fish from the fair were the very same fish that were later in my house. It is the sense that one of the fish and not the other was Sharky, even though perhaps only God himself could tell the difference.

Importantly, numerical identity does not require qualitative identity. The clearest examples of this are with people. Throughout your lifetime, you will survive a great many such changes. You will morph from a seven-pound infant, less than two feet long, to a more-than-hundred-pound adult three times that size. Your hair will grow, change color, and may even disappear altogether. You'll develop wrinkles, freckles, and scars. The cells in your body will die and be replaced. You may donate one of your kidneys to help a relative in need. In some tragic cases, you may even lose a limb, and perhaps gain a prosthesis to replace it. Your favorite foods, sports teams, and companions may completely change. Life may alter your character, so a once sweet young girl becomes a sour old woman, or a painfully shy little boy becomes a confident and gregarious young man. Your deepest desires, most strongly held convictions, and highest goals—those things you consider most fundamental to who you are—may change. You will forget many of the events of your past, and you may even forget most of the people you have ever known and cared about. If the seven-year-old goldfish owner who threw her sister under the bus is taken to be the same individual who is currently typing this manuscript, then clearly qualitative identity is not at the heart of personal identity.

* * *

Qualitative identity—which I'll just call *similarity* in what follows—matters in countless ways. Our intuitions about similarity form the basis of concepts; to recognize that something is an apple is to infer that it is similar along relevant dimensions to other instances of the category of apples (Murphy 2004). Without similarity, we couldn't have concepts, and without concepts, most of mental life is impossible.

But identity is also important. Consider moral responsibility. Our legal system reflects our intuitive moral judgments in recognizing that you are only morally responsible for an action if *you* committed the action. Pinker (1997) discusses the real-world arrest of identical twins who both participated in an attempted burglary that resulted in a scuffle with a police officer. During the scuffle, one of the brothers bit off the officer's ear. Although the officer saw the twin that bit him, his inability to distinguish them in court resulted in neither brother being sentenced to prison. Our justice system cares about *which individual* committed a crime, not simply the characteristics of that individual.

Much of what we do in our daily lives depends on personal identity. Each day upon waking, you get out of your bed, gather a selection of your clothes, and perhaps make breakfast for your spouse or your children. You might promise to pick up milk on your way home from work, or pay a colleague back for lunch. None of these actions would be reasonable if it did not seem that you were the same person who had acquired the bed and the clothes, married your spouse, had your children, and borrowed money from your co-worker. Your promise to pick up milk would not carry much weight if you did not believe that the person returning home from your office later in the day would in fact be you. Your feeling of obligation toward your colleague cannot be felt on behalf of someone else, no matter how similar they may be to you. Moral responsibility, reward, punishment, ownership, promises, debts, self-conscious emotions, and relationships all depend upon a continuity of personal identity.

* * *

Intuitions about similarity and intuitions about identity interact in important ways. We are sensitive to the similarity of an individual across different periods of their life. Friendships can end if people change too much, particularly if they stop sharing the same values (Kalmijn and Vermunt 2007; Silka 1984, 2012). And sufficient change in personal properties has long been considered legal grounds for divorce (Freed 1974).

Intrapersonal similarity also matters. Imagine that you have the choice between a reward now and a reward five years from now. We discount the future (if the rewards are equal, we're likely to choose the immediate one), but if the future reward is large enough, we will choose to wait. But this willingness to defer immediate gratification is influenced by how we think of ourselves in the future. If people believe, or are led to believe, that they will become greatly dissimilar to their present self (because of converting to a new religion, say), they are less willing to give up present resources for future ones (Bartels and Rips 2010; Bartels and Urminsky 2011). It's not just that we feel more fondly toward similar others, then, we also feel more fondly toward similar versions of our future selves. This finding is consistent with the view that we see our future selves in some sense as distinct individuals, an interesting proposal that falls outside the scope of this chapter (Bartels and Rips 2010; Ersner-Hershfield, Winner, and Knutson 2009; Mitchell et al. 2011; Pronin 2008; Parfit 1984; Starmans 2017).

Furthermore, the most obvious cue to identity, and the one we use more than any other, is perceptual similarity. If a woman walks into your apartment, and she looks just like your roommate, you will likely assume she is your roommate. Someone might be convicted of a crime based on eyewitness accounts or video footage. If a person looks enough like Mary, it is a reasonable inference that she is Mary. Again, though, the fact that we don't hold one twin responsible for the sins of the other shows that while our identity intuitions may relate to similarity, they do not reduce to it.

So what *does* give rise to our intuitions about identity? In what follows, I will explore three hypotheses about the psychology of personal identity; about what we think makes someone the same person over time. I will suggest that all of them are interesting and capture some important phenomena—and all are ultimately mistaken. And I'll conclude with a tentative suggestion about a future direction of inquiry.

Before getting to these, it's worth emphasizing that this is not a metaphysical enterprise. I am not asking what personal identity really is. That is a philosopher's question, though I'll add that people who are not philosophers are very interested in the answer. Just as one example, many are intrigued by the possibility that we will soon be able to unload all the information contained within our brains into the cloud, or, even better, into sleek robotic bodies, and once this is done, destroy our original bodies, brains, and all. You can wonder what this would feel like. Would you blink and open your eyes to find yourself in a robotic body? What if your original body still existed—would your consciousness now seem to exist in two places at once? Would this process make you immortal, or would it just kill you (see Dennett 1978 for a related question)?

The first hypothesis is that we track personal identity as we track the identity of more mundane physical objects, through making inferences about their continuity over space and time.

How do we determine whether the Frisbee I throw and the Frisbee you catch are one and the same Frisbee? It's obvious: we consider the spatiotemporal history of the object (see Scholl 2007 for review). If you watch the disc closely as it leaves my hand, you can follow its path through a continuous series of points in space and time. If you are watching closely but fail to see this continuous path, you may conclude that there must have been two Frisbees. (Many magic tricks work by convincing us that there is no spatiotemporal continuity between two objects, when in fact there is.)

Perhaps we treat people just like objects; we judge an individual at time A and an individual at time B to be the same individual if and only if there is an unbroken spatiotemporal path between their bodies. After all, if a person runs from one of us to the other as we are playing in the park, we track the person through the same sort of inference that we use for the Frisbee.

Indeed, even young children make this sort of inference. Sorrentino (2001) found that three-year-old children would extend a proper name to an individual with a unique spatiotemporal path even if its appearance changes. Gutheil and colleagues (2008) showed preschoolers pairs of individuals who looked identical but differed in their spatiotemporal history (e.g., two physically distinct but identical Winnie-the-Pooh dolls), and asked the children whether both members in the pair would have access to knowledge that had been supplied to only one of the members. Most children responded that only the individual who had been present when the knowledge was supplied would have access to the knowledge, suggesting that they were using spatiotemporal history, rather than perceptual similarity, to guide their assessments of identity.

This theory needs sharpening, though. In the soapy 1986 movie *Who Is Julia?*, a beautiful and wealthy young model has a horrible accident that destroys most of her body, but leaves her brain undamaged. At the same time, a poor and plain-looking housewife suffers brain death. Doctors are able to save one of the women by transplanting the healthy brain into the healthy body. But which woman have they saved? Our strong intuition is that they have saved the model, whose brain survived the accident, despite the resulting person being largely comprised of the housewife's body. Presumably, then, if a person is tracked as an object, it's not the whole person, it's the person's brain.

Empirical investigations of analogous scenarios suggest that the intuitions of both adults and children are compatible with this view. Blok and colleagues (2001) gave undergraduate students a story about Jim, who had his brain transplanted into a robot. The majority indicated that Jim still existed, though he now had the body of a robot. Even children, by the age of seven, follow the brain rather than the body when considering personal identity. Johnson (1990) told children a story in which their own brain was transplanted into the body of a pig. The children reported that the pig would now be a person, respond to and identify himself with the child's name, and have the memories, preferences, and relationships of the child, rather than the pig. In other words, children thought that after this brain transplant, the pig would be them.

But there is reason to doubt this simple account. Returning to fictional examples, consider the plot of the movie *Freaky Friday*, in which a teenaged daughter and her middle-aged mother wake up after an odd event in a Chinese restaurant to find themselves occupying each other's bodies. In stories like this—repeated in many forms, from science fiction movies, to Sunday morning cartoons, to books for children such as *Help! I'm Trapped in My Gym Teacher's Body!*—the original brain does not move anywhere, and may even be discarded or destroyed. That this trope shows up in so many forms suggests that we naturally understand what it would mean for one person's psychology to enter another person's body, with no transfer of physical matter. And again, when these scenarios have been tested experimentally, adults and children have not hesitated to locate a person wherever his or her psychology is located, regardless of whether there is any spatiotemporal connection to the body it now occupies (e.g., Corriveau, Pasquini, and Harris 2005). This presents a serious challenge to the spatiotemporal theory of personal identity—nothing physical has been transferred and yet our intuition is that a transfer of identity has nonetheless occurred.

Perhaps our intuitions about personal identity don't reduce to physical intuitions because, intuitively, we don't think of people as objects. Descartes famously argued that human beings consist of two fundamentally distinct types of entities: a physical body and an immaterial soul, and children and adults, whether religious or not, intuitively understand human beings from this dualist perspective (e.g., Bloom 2004; Chudek et al. 2013; Forstmann and Burgmer 2015; Nichols and Bruno 2010; Tierney et al. 2014; see Starmans and Bloom 2011 for review; but see Barlev and Shtulman, 2021, for a recent critique).

* * *

A focus on psychological properties rather than physical ones brings us to the second hypothesis, famously put forth by John Locke (1632–1704/1959). (This was intended as a metaphysical claim, but I am treating it here as a proposal about our intuitions.)

Locke proposed that what really matters for identity is memory. According to Locke's theory, you are numerically identical to that past person whose memories you share, and that future person who will share your memories, regardless of whether these people are spatiotemporally continuous with you. Returning to the "body swap" stories we considered earlier, Locke's theory does an excellent job of explaining our intuition that the teenaged body with the middle-aged mind in *Freaky Friday* is the mother, despite looking like and being spatiotemporally continuous with the daughter.

Philosophers have raised several counterexamples to this view, however. One such problem concerns the instability of memory. There are many events in what I take to be my past that I can't remember at all. I can't now recall anything that happened to me while I was asleep last night, or while I was an infant. Yet the very thing we want to explain is how it can be that I am the same person now as when I was an infant. And presumably, I am not extinguished and reborn as a new person every time I fall asleep and later wake up.

Further, identity is transitive, but memory is not. That is, if Person A is identical to Person B, and Person B is identical to Person C, then Person A *must* be identical to Person C. Memory, on the other hand, has no such property. Reid (1785/1975) illustrates this by imagining a young boy who is flogged at school for stealing from an orchard. Later this boy becomes a brave officer who defeats his enemy in battle, and later still the officer becomes a general. The young officer remembers the flogging at school, while the general, advanced in age, remembers his previous bravery in battle, but no longer recalls being beaten as a boy. If memory is necessary for identity, it would seem that the boy is identical to the officer, and the officer is identical to the general, but the general is not identical to the young boy. (Locke's response is to propose that as long as a person has even one memory of a past action that he can experience "with the same consciousness as he had of it at first," this will be sufficient for identity; Locke 1632–1704/1959, xxvii, 12.)

Another challenge to Locke's theory was raised by Williams (1973). Suppose a scientist discovers a procedure for copying memories from any brain and transferring them to another brain. In his first successful procedure, the scientist erases all the memories of his lab assistant Charles, and replaces them with the memories of Guy Fawkes, a man hung in 1606 for trying to blow up the English Parliament. According to Locke, Charles now *really is* Guy Fawkes. This is somewhat of a challenging assumption—Are we to conclude that after having been dead for over 400 years, Fawkes has now come back to life? But assuming we can accept this conclusion, there is a further problem for Locke. For now, spurred on by the success of his first experiment, the scientist can cause the very same memories to be held by another person, Robert. On Locke's theory, both Charles and Robert are psychologically continuous with Fawkes, and therefore both men *are* Fawkes. To conclude this, however, is to conclude that Charles and Robert are numerically identical to each other. But this is impossible—Charles and Robert are two different individuals, who could very well meet and discuss their unusual similarities.

Very little empirical work has explored people's intuitions about memory duplication as a method of probing our theory of personal identity. However, several experimental findings peripherally touch on this issue, and are worth considering briefly. As mentioned earlier, adults judge that if a person's brain is transplanted into a robotic body, the robot will retain the identity of the person (Blok et al. 2001). This is consistent with both the spatiotemporal continuity theory (i.e., continuity of the brain), and Locke's theory. However, the researchers then conducted a second study in which participants read a similar scenario, but instead of a brain transplant, the original person's memories were copied onto a sophisticated computer, which was then implanted into the robot and used to control its actions. In this scenario, participants were much less likely to accept that the robot retained the identity of the person. This suggests that people do not generally share Locke's assumption that memory is sufficient for personal identity.

* * *

The third hypothesis also presupposes that we track individuals differently than we track objects, drawing on intuitions about continuity about psychological traits. But here the relevant trait is not memory, it is morality.

This conclusion arises from studies in which individuals are described as going through certain transformations (due to a pill, brain injury, or the simple passage of time). These transformations are described as influencing various psychological traits, including morality, memory, and personality, and participants are asked whether the individuals are still the same person after the transformations (Strohminger and Nichols 2014, 2015). The findings suggest that people believe that if the moral traits change sufficiently, an individual ceases to be the same person. Other work suggests that we are more likely to see moral decline as extinguishing identity than moral improvement (Tobia 2015; Molouki and Bartels 2017).

This is a significant line of research, but the conclusion that a radical change in morality extinguishes personal identity seems implausible. There are all sorts of cases, after all, in both fiction and real life, where people become morally worse over time. It might well be that this change in morality makes them very dissimilar to their previous selves, and true as well that someone whose morality has worsened is seen as more dissimilar than someone who has morally improved. But does it really fit our intuitions that someone who becomes evil ceases to exist, that moral degradation leads to *death*?

Consider an example from Starmans and Bloom (2018a), in which Bob, aged twenty, the sweetest of people—generous, warm, and loving—undergoes some sort of change so that, by age thirty, he has become a scoundrel—mean, selfish, and psychopathic. Presumably, people who knew Bob would not assume that he ceased to exist, and that a new person came into existence. Nobody would give away his property; his debts would not be forgiven. Rather they would simply assume that he changed in a very unfortunate way (see also Starmans and Bloom 2018b).

But if we don't think moral decline leads to death, how do we explain the results of the forgoing studies? One concern is that it's unclear what sort of intuition the questions are tapping. For example, several of these studies ask participants whether someone who has undergone a change is (for example) "Still Jim." This can be taken as a question about personal identity: Does Jim still exist? But it can also be taken as a question about similarity. After all, if Jim changes radically, one can sensibly say "Jim just isn't Jim anymore," and in at least some such cases, we mean that Jim is very dissimilar to how he was before, not that he died (Dranseika 2017; Starmans and Bloom 2018a,b). The same concern arises when participants are asked to rate whether the person is "The same person as before" or "Completely different now" (Earp et al. 2019; Heiphetz, Strohminger, and Young 2017; Strohminger and Nichols 2015). These can be taken as remarks about changes in identity (as in "Mary got divorced and she is now married to a completely different person") but they can also be taken as referring to dissimilarity (as in "After Mary's husband went to therapy, it's like she is now married to a completely different person").

Researchers have been aware of this problem and have tried to address it, trying to make clear to participants that what is being asked about is numerical identity and not similarity. For instance, Nichols and Bruno (2010) asked whether, after a procedure that wipes out your personality and memories, it would still be "*you*" (in italics) who felt a subsequent painful shot. While it does seem that this question picks out identity more so than similarity, the intuition here is subtle, and it's difficult to rely solely on a font choice to convey subtle philosophical distinctions to participants.

In what is probably the most careful attempt to date to address this issue, Tobia (2015) presented subjects with two characters, Art and Bart, and use them to clarify the distinction between identity and similarity for participants. But when he did so, it turned out that the findings of previous studies (e.g., Earp et al. 2019; Heiphetz et al. 2017, 2018; Strohminger and Nichols 2014, 2015) did not replicate—people didn't tend to judge that moral change influenced identity. It might be that people had problems understanding the philosophical views that these characters were expressing. But another possibility is that when the concepts of identity and similarity are carefully distinguished, people don't believe that moral changes disrupt identity—a possibility that Melissa Finlay and I explored in a set of recent studies (Finlay and Starmans 2022).

In these studies, we developed a novel training method that allowed participants to distinguish between sameness in the sense of similarity, and sameness in the sense of identity. We also included a condition in which participants were asked whether the person after the brain transplant was "Still Jim" (Blok, Newman, and Rips 2005; Nichols and Bruno 2010; Strohminger and Nichols 2014). And then we tested participants across five types of changes that had been previous explored in the literature, including changes in morality.

We replicated the "Still Jim" findings from previous work; subjects in this condition believed that significant moral changes suggested that the individual was no longer Jim. The pattern of judgments participants made in this condition was much like the pattern observed when participants were asked about similarity, but markedly different from the pattern observed when participants were asked about identity. When asked about identity, participants who understood the distinction between similarity and identity largely disagreed that any of these changes resulted in a new identity. In other experiments, we showed that under the right circumstances, such as a full brain transplant or "soul swap," people *do* judge that identity has changed, showing that these methods are sensitive enough to detect intuitions about identity changes when they are seen as warranted.

Our findings support the claim that people view morality as central to the self (Strohminger and Nichols 2014; Goodwin, Piazza, and Rozin 2014; Wojciszke, Bazinska, and Jaworski 1998). However, the fact that participants made this judgment when considering similarity, but not when considering identity, helps to clarify that these previous findings should be interpreted as judgments about similarity, rather than numerical identity. Most of all, our own findings suggest that morality is not central to personal identity.

* * *

I've discussed three hypotheses about our intuitions about personal identity—object tracking, continuity of memory, and continuity of morality—and suggested that they are all lacking. I'll end with a hypothesis of my own.

Consider a modified version of the first proposal. Perhaps we do see spatiotemporal continuity as the necessary and sufficient criterion for identity, but it is spatiotemporal continuity of the soul, rather than of the body. This is a hybrid account, suggesting that we consider the essence of personal identity to consist in the psychological, but we treat this psychological essence as if it were a physical object—albeit a physical object with some unusual properties.

In a classic passage, Descartes writes, "I realized that I was a substance whose essence, or nature, is nothing but thought, and which, in order to exist, needs no place to exist nor any other material thing." I proposed earlier that people are, in a sense, natural-born Cartesian dualists, but there is one part of Descartes's passage that does not ring true—that the soul "needs no place to exist."

Indeed, when asked directly, adults are quite willing to pinpoint a precise location within their bodies as the location of their soul. Bertossa et al. (2008) guided participants through a semi-structured interview designed to generate a verbal report of their phenomenological experience of the location of the self. The majority indicated a precise point inside the head, midway behind the eyes, as the location for what the researchers called the "I-that-perceives." Limanowski and Hecht (2011) obtained a similar finding when they asked participants to mark a "self" on a rectangle with its brain, heart, eyes, and ears in varying locations.

One might object here that these findings don't capture common-sense intuitions, rather they were parroting back the contemporary view that the brain is the seat of consciousness. Indeed, even subjects blind from birth tended to locate the self in the head (Bertossa et al. 2008). This is despite their different everyday phenomenal experiences, and thus consistent with a cultural account.

To address this issue, Starmans and Bloom (2012) explored whether adults and children share an intuitive sense that the self is located in a particular place within the body. To access participants' intuitions, rather than their explicit theories about the self, the study used an indirect method that asked when an object is closest to a person. Participants saw pictures of a cartoon character who had an object (either a snowflake or a fly) positioned in one of five locations on her body. If participants consider the self to be equally distributed across the body, or if they think the self has no spatial location, then they should judge that objects are equally close to the character regardless of where on her body they are positioned. However, both children and adults judged that objects near a person's eyes were closer to her than objects near other parts of her body. These findings suggest that children and adults intuitively think of the self as occupying a precise location within the body, at or near the eyes.

Is the soul thought to possess other physical characteristics? There is indirect evidence that at least some people have a strong intuition that the soul has weight. A now discredited study carried out in 1907 by a Haverhill, Massachusetts, doctor by the name of Duncan MacDougall claimed to have discovered that the soul weighs 21 grams (MacDougall 1907). MacDougall put six dying people on a bed equipped with sensitive springs and claimed to have observed a sudden loss of weight—about 21 grams—at the exact moment of their death. Having reasoned that such loss could not be explained by bowel movements or evaporation, he concluded he must have measured the weight of the soul. This claim was immortalized in the 2003 movie titled *21 Grams*, and a quick search on Google turns up thousands of discussions about whether the soul has weight, and if so, how much.

A further question about the extent to which our concept of the soul is physical relates to whether the soul is subject to the laws of physics. Little research has directly examined people's natural intuitions about this question. But here again, the popular representation of the soul in fiction and science fiction can give us a clue to the kind of thing we tend to think the soul is. Souls (and angels, demons, ghosts, gods, and other bodiless entities) are often depicted as being transparent—often entirely invisible—and non-solid—able to pass through solid objects like walls (and bodies!). However, the popular conception of souls also depicts them as being bounded, having a shape, occupying a particular time and place, and having to follow a continuous path of motion to travel from one place to another. These properties are consistent with a conception of the soul as a physical object, and inconsistent with the Cartesian, or "theologically correct," idea of an immaterial soul.

In sum, our intuitive theory of personal identity may be a hybrid of the physical and psychological accounts previously discussed. On this view, we conceive of a person as consisting of two separable components—body and soul—and we consider the psychological component essential to the continuation of personal identity. However, our conception of the soul includes certain physical characteristics, such as a location in space, and possibly weight, shape, and size. As such the laws of physics that seem to apply to bodies may be extended to the soul itself, even when separated from the body. This "physical soul" hypothesis explains the seeming conflict in our intuitions about the relevant factors for personal identity: we are concerned with spatiotemporal continuity as well as with psychological continuity because we conceive of the psychological essence of a person as a special kind of physical object.

Many questions remain, as there is little research examining exactly what kind of entity we think the soul is. Do we conceive of it more like a solid object, a liquid or gel, or a cloud of gas? What physical limitations does it have? How well do the depictions of souls in various religious traditions, as well as in fictional and science fictional stories, capture our natural intuitions about their composition and behavior?

Once we better understand our intuitive ideas about the nature of the soul, a further step will be to directly investigate whether spatiotemporal continuity of the soul predicts our judgments of personal identity. Can the physical soul theory accurately capture our intuitions about body swaps, brain transplants, and the afterlife? Can it resolve the paradox of duplication, and explain why a duplicate seems to be the same person in some circumstances, but not in others? This is an exciting line for future research.

Bibliography

Barlev, M. and A. Shtulman (2021). "Minds, Bodies, Spirits, and Gods: Does Widespread Belief in Disembodied Beings Imply that We are Inherent Dualists?" *Psychological Review*, 128 (6): 1007.

Bartels, D. M. and L. J. Rips (2010). "Psychological Connectedness and Intertemporal Choice." *Journal of Experimental Psychology: General*, 139 (1): 49.

Bartels, D. M. and O. Urminsky (2011). "On Intertemporal Selfishness: How the Perceived Instability of Identity Underlies Impatient Consumption." *Journal of Consumer Research*, 38 (1): 182–98.

Bertossa, F., M. Besa, R. Ferrari and F. Ferri (2008). "Point Zero: A Phenomenological Inquiry into the Subjective Physical Location of Consciousness." *Perceptual and Motor Skills*, 107: 323–35.

Blok, S., G. Newman, J. Behr and L. J. Rips (2001). "Inferences about Personal Identity." In *Proceedings of the 23rd Annual Conference of the Cognitive Science Society*, 80–5. Mahwah: Erlbaum.

Blok, S. V., G. Newman and L. J. Rips (2005). "Individuals and Their Concepts." In W.-k. Ahn, R. L. Goldstone, B. C. Love, A. B. Markman, and P. Wolff (eds.), *Categorization Inside and Outside the Laboratory: Essays in Honor of Douglas L. Medin*, 127–49. American Psychological Association.

Bloom, P. (2004). *Descartes' Baby*. New York: Basic Books.

Chudek, M., McNamara, R. A., Birch, S., Bloom, P., and Henrich, J. (2018). Do minds switch bodies? Dualist interpretations across ages and societies. *Religion, Brain & Behavior*, 8 (4): 354–68.

Corriveau, K., E. Pasquini and P. Harris (2005). "'If it's in Your Mind, it's in Your Knowledge': Children's Developing Anatomy of Identity." *Cognitive Development*, 20: 321–40.

Dennett, D. (1978). *Brainstorms: Philosophical Essays on Mind and Psychology*. Cambridge, MA: MIT Press.

Dranseika, V. (2017). "On the Ambiguity of 'the Same Person.'" *AJOB Neuroscience*, 8 (3): 184–6.

Earp, B. D., J. A. Skorburg, J. A. Everett and J. Savulescu (2019). "Addiction, Identity, Morality." *AJOB Empirical Bioethics*, 10 (2): 136–53.

Ersner-Hershfield, H., G. E. Wimmer and B. Knutson (2009). "Saving for the Future Self: Neural Measures of Future Self-Continuity Predict Temporal Discounting." *Social Cognitive and Affective Neuroscience*, 4 (1): 85–92.

Finlay, M. and C. Starmans (2022). "Not the Same Same: Distinguishing Between Similarity and Identity in Judgments of Change." *Cognition*, 218: 104953.

Forstmann, M. and P. Burgmer (2015). "Adults are Intuitive Mind-Body Dualists." *Journal of Experimental Psychology: General*, 144 (1): 222.

Freed, D. J. (1974). "Grounds for Divorce in the American Jurisdictions (as of June 1, 1974)." *Family Law Quarterly*, 8: 401–23.

Goodwin, G. P., J. Piazza and P. Rozin (2014). "Moral Character Predominates in Person Perception and Evaluation." *Journal of Personality and Social Psychology*, 106 (1): 148.

Gutheil, G., S. A. Gelman, E. Klein, K. Michos and K. Kelaita (2008). "Preschoolers' use of Spatiotemporal History, Appearance, and Proper Name in Determining Individual Identity." *Cognition*, 107 (1): 366–80.

Heiphetz, L., N. Strohminger, S. A. Gelman and L. L. Young (2018). "Who am I? The Role of Moral Beliefs in Children's and Adults' Understanding of Identity." *Journal of Experimental Social Psychology*, 78: 210–19.

Heiphetz, L., N. Strohminger and L. L. Young (2017). "The Role of Moral Beliefs, Memories, and Preferences in Representations of Identity." *Cognitive Science*, 41 (3): 744–67.

Johnson, C. N. (1990). "If You Had My Brain Where Would I Be? Children's Understanding of the Brain and Identity." *Child Development*, 61: 962–72.

Kalmijn, M. and J. K. Vermunt (2007). "Homogeneity of Social Networks by Age and Marital Status: A Multilevel Analysis of Ego-Centered Networks." *Social Networks*, 29 (1): 25–43.

Limanowski, J. and H. Hecht (2011). "Where Do We Stand on Locating the Self?" *Psychology*, 2: 312–17.

Locke, J. (1632–1704 reprint 1959). *An Essay Concerning Human Understanding*. New York: Dover Publications.

MacDougall, D. (1907). "Hypothesis Concerning Soul Substance Together with Experimental Evidence of the Existence of Such Substance." *Journal of the American Society for Psychical Research*, 1: 237–44.

Mitchell, J. P., J. Schirmer, D. L. Ames and D. T. Gilbert (2011). "Medial Prefrontal Cortex Predicts Intertemporal Choice." *Journal of Cognitive Neuroscience*, 23: 857–66.
Molouki, S. and D. M. Bartels (2017). "Personal Change and the Continuity of the Self." *Cognitive Psychology*, 93: 1–17.
Murphy, G. (2004). *The Big Book of Concepts*. Cambridge, MA: MIT Press.
Nichols, S. and M. Bruno (2010). "Intuitions about Personal Identity: An Empirical Study." *Philosophical Psychology*, 23 (3): 293–312.
Parfit, D. (1984). *Reasons and Persons*. Oxford: Oxford University Press.
Pinker, S. (1997). *How the Mind Works*. New York: Norton.
Pronin, E. (2008). "How We See Ourselves and How We See Others." *Science*, 320: 1177–80.
Reid, T. (1785/1975). "Of Mr. Locke's Account of Personal Identity." In R. Perry (ed.), *Personal Identity*, 113–18. London: University of California Press.
Scholl, B. J. (2007). "Object Persistence in Philosophy and Psychology." *Mind & Language*, 22 (5): 563–91.
Silka, L. (1984). "Intuitive Perceptions of Change: An Overlooked Phenomenon in Person Perception?" *Personality and Social Psychology Bulletin*, 10 (2): 180–90.
Silka, L. (2012). *Intuitive Judgments of Change*. New York: Springer.
Sorrentino, C. M. (2001). "Children and Adults Represent Proper Names as Referring to Unique Individuals." *Developmental Science*, 4: 399–407.
Starmans, C. (2017). "Children's Theories of the Self." *Child Development*, 88 (6): 1774–85.
Starmans, C. and P. Bloom (2011). "What Do You Think You Are?" *Annals of the New York Academy of Sciences*, 1234 (1): 44–7.
Starmans, C. and P. Bloom (2012). "Windows to the Soul: Children and Adults see the Eyes as the Location of the Self." *Cognition*, 123 (2): 313–18.
Starmans, C. and P. Bloom (2018a). "Nothing Personal: What Psychologists Get Wrong about Identity." *Trends in Cognitive Sciences*, 22 (7): 566–8.
Starmans, C. and P. Bloom (2018b). "If You Become Evil, Do You Die?" *Trends in Cognitive Sciences*, 22 (9): 740–1.
Strohminger, N. and S. Nichols (2014). "The Essential Moral Self." *Cognition*, 131: 159–71
Strohminger, N. and S. Nichols (2015). "Neurodegeneration and Identity." *Psychological Science*, 26 (9): 1469–79.
Tierney, H., C. Howard, V. Kumar, T. Kvaran, and S. Nichols (2014). "How Many of Us Are There?" In J. Sytsma (ed.), *Advances in Experimental Philosophy of Mind*, 181–202.
Tobia, K. P. (2015). "Personal Identity and the Phineas Gage Effect." *Analysis*, 75 (3): 396–405.
Williams, B. (1973). *Problems of the Self*. Cambridge: Cambridge University Press.
Wojciszke, B., R. Bazinska and M. Jaworski (1998). "On the Dominance of Moral Categories in Impression Formation." *Personality and Social Psychology Bulletin*, 24 (12): 1251–63.

3

Personal Identity and Dual Character Concepts[1]

Joshua Knobe

In an important recent study, Tobia (2015) gave participants a vignette about a person who gets into an accident:

> Phineas is extremely kind; he really enjoys helping people. He is also employed as a railroad worker. One day at work, a railroad explosion causes a large iron spike to fly out and into his head, and he is immediately taken for emergency surgery. The doctors manage to remove the iron spike and their patient is fortunate to survive. However, in some ways this man after the accident is remarkably different from Phineas before the accident. Phineas before the accident was extremely kind and enjoyed helping people, but the man after the accident is now extremely cruel; he even enjoys harming people.

Participants then received a simple question. Consider the man after the accident. Is that man Phineas, or would it be more accurate to say that he is not Phineas at all?

Participants answered this question on a scale that went from completely agreeing that the man is Phineas to completely agreeing that he is not Phineas. Strikingly, the mean response was about the midpoint of the scale. In other words, people regarded this as a difficult case. They were drawn in some way toward the view that the man after the accident is Phineas, but they were also drawn in some way toward the view that he is not Phineas. Since this is an intuition about a case of radical moral change, let's refer to it as the *moral change intuition*.

In what follows, we will be looking in detail at recent empirical findings regarding the moral change intuition, but before we discuss any of those findings, it is important to see that the intuition is deeply surprising just in itself. After all, there seems to be some straightforward sense in which people think the man after the accident is *obviously* Phineas, and it's hard to see what people could possibly mean by saying that he is not.

To illustrate, suppose the man went to a bank and tried to withdraw money. People would presumably not find it remotely plausible to say: "You can't withdraw money from Phineas's account—you aren't Phineas." Similar points would no doubt hold for many of the other ordinary practices that depend on intuitions about personal identity (see Starmans and Bloom 2018). In short, it seems that we face a puzzle about the moral change intuition. Given that there is a sense in which the man after the accident is obviously Phineas, what exactly do people mean when they say that he is not Phineas?

I will argue that if we want to understand people's intuitions in cases like this one, it will prove helpful to look to frameworks from a literature that might at first seem quite remote from the study of personal identity. Specifically, I suggest that it might be helpful to look to the literature on what are called *dual character concepts* (Del Pinal and Reuter 2017; Flanagan and Hannikainen in press; Guo, Dweck, and Markman 2021; Knobe, Prasada, and Newman 2013; Leslie 2015; Liao, Meskin, and Knobe 2020; Reuter 2019; Tobia, Newman, and Knobe 2020).

What is a dual character concept? For a simple example, consider the criteria people ordinarily employ to determine whether or not someone counts as a scientist. Now imagine a physics professor. She spends her days running experiments and writing up papers, but she doesn't really care about getting at the truth regarding scientific questions and is dogmatically clinging to some theory in a way that ignores all of the evidence. Is this person a scientist?

In cases like this one, people tend to agree with both of the following two statements:

(1) There is a sense in which this person is a scientist.
(2) Ultimately when you think about what it really means to be a scientist, you would have to say that this person is not truly a scientist.

The fact that people agree with both of these statements provides some evidence that people actually have two different criteria for the application of this concept, hence the claim that the concept shows "dual character."

My claim will be that the frameworks developed within the study of dual character concepts give us the tools we need to understand the moral change intuition. On this view, people actually have the following pair of intuitions:

(1) There is a sense in which the man after the accident is Phineas.
(2) Ultimately, when you think about what it really means to be Phineas, you would have to say that the man after the accident is not truly Phineas.

The complicated intuition people have about the man after the accident—that he is obviously Phineas in one sense but is somehow not really Phineas in another—can then be understood as just one example of a far broader phenomenon, and it can be explained using the frameworks that have been developed to understand that phenomenon more generally.

I. A Framework for Understanding Dual Character Concepts

In this section, I introduce a general framework for understanding dual character concepts. Then, in the remaining sections, we will be looking at specific empirical results regarding the moral change intuition and using this framework to explain those results.

Within existing research, the study of dual character concepts has focused on people's use of concepts that might seem a bit distant from the moral change intuition, and I recognize that much of the material in this first section might at first appear to be irrelevant to the specific phenomenon we are trying to explain. But I promise, although many elements of this framework were originally developed to understand other concepts, every one of them will be used very directly in subsequent sections to explain the results of experiments on the moral change intuition.

A. Characteristic Values

To begin with, let's consider the concept of *hip-hop*. Suppose we are listening to a new hip-hop song, and we start wondering about the degree to which it is continuous with the existing tradition of hip-hop music. It will be helpful here to distinguish two different ways in which we might do this.

First, we might ask whether the new song is *similar* to previous hip-hop songs. Some hip-hop songs are similar to previous songs, whereas others take things in radically new directions. This distinction might be important for various purposes.

But, importantly, we could also ask a very different question. We could ask whether the new song *embodies what hip-hop is really all about*. In this latter inquiry, we also seem to be looking at some kind of continuity with the past, but the continuity in question is of a very different type. We aren't just asking whether the new song is similar to the previous songs. Instead, we are doing something more complex. We look at the existing hip-hop songs, extract from them some deeper property ("what hip-hop is really all about"), and then ask whether the new song has that deeper property.

Importantly, this approach might yield very different judgments from the ones we would arrive at if we were just judging based on similarity. People might think that a particular song is not very similar at all to previous hip-hop songs and yet nonetheless believe that this song fully embodies what hip-hop is really all about. Or, conversely, people might think that a particular song is in most respects pretty similar to previous hip-hop songs and yet nonetheless believe that this song fails to embody what hip-hop is really all about.

One can then use this same approach when applying numerous other concepts. One can ask whether a new religious practice embodies what Christianity is all about, whether a new law embodies what the United States is all about, whether a particular scientist embodies what being a scientist is all about, and so forth. In each case, this approach enables us to think about a certain kind of continuity with the past, but in each case, that continuity is clearly not just a matter of similarity to past exemplars.

Let's now introduce some terminology that allows us to talk about these sorts of judgments. Instead of saying "what X is really all about," I will sometimes speak of the *characteristic values* of X. So I will be speaking in what follows about the characteristic values of hip-hop, the characteristic values of Christianity, and so forth.

Ultimately, our goal will be to use the notion of characteristic values to understand the moral change intuition, but first we will need to get clear in a more general way on the role of these judgments in people's cognition.

B. Characteristic Values Are Not a Matter of the Features an Object Actually Has

Judgments about the degree to which an object embodies the characteristic values of a concept should not be seen as just some minor variation on the idea of checking for similarity; it is a fundamentally different thing.

Suppose we want to determine whether something is similar to a given object X. We would do this by trying to figure out whether that thing has the features that X has. For present purposes, it will be important to emphasize one specific aspect of this process:

> The degree to which something is similar to object X is a matter of the degree to which it has certain features. But object X itself always has all of those features.

An obvious corollary is that nothing can ever be more similar to X than X is to itself. This is a pretty fundamental fact about the nature of similarity.

Although this might all seem pretty obvious and straightforward, it will perhaps be helpful to take a moment just to hammer home the key point. Suppose we are thinking about contemporary science (i.e., the practice of science as it exists right now). We might imagine various possible ways in which science could change, and we could ask how similar each of those possibilities would be to contemporary science. In doing so, we would be asking whether those other possibilities have certain features. However, contemporary science itself would have all of the features we were asking about. Thus, these other possibilities might be more or less similar to contemporary science, but none of them could ever be more similar to contemporary science than contemporary science is to itself.

The notion of embodying characteristic values does not work like that. To determine whether something embodies the characteristic values of X, we arrive at a judgment of the characteristic values of X, and then ask whether something embodies those values. But now notice an important fact:

> The degree to which something embodies the characteristic values of object X is a matter of the degree to which it embodies certain values. But object X might not itself perfectly embody all of those values.

A corollary is that something else might embody the characteristic values of X more perfectly than X does itself.

To illustrate, consider again the example of contemporary science. If we want to know whether something embodies the characteristic values of contemporary science, we will need to have some understanding of what the characteristic values of contemporary science are. But will we conclude that contemporary science itself perfectly embodies these values? Surely not. Thus, we might well think that some other practice—one that is a lot like contemporary science but that differs in a few specific respects—would actually more fully embody the characteristic values of contemporary science than contemporary science does itself.

If we are going to successfully make sense of this sort of judgment, we will need a conception of characteristic values according to which things can fail to perfectly embody their own characteristic values. Existing research has led to the development of a number of different theories that aim to do this. One family of theories says that people's ability to attribute characteristic values is closely tied to *teleology* (e.g., Rose, Schaffer, and Tobia 2020), while another says that it is closely tied to *psychological essentialism* (e.g., Bailey, Knobe, and Newman 2021; Newman and Knobe 2019; Ritchie and Knobe 2020). Some recent work has sought to unify these two approaches in a theory of "teleological essentialism" (Rose and Nichols 2019). Nothing in what follows will depend on the resolution of this controversy, and we can therefore remain neutral as between the different possible theories.

Instead, the key point in what follows will be a relatively straightforward one that should be compatible with any plausible theory. That point is that what an object is "really all about" is not just a matter of features that the object actually has and that, as a result, an object can sometimes fail to perfectly embody the very thing that it is really all about.

C. When and Why Do People Care about Characteristic Values?

A question now arises as to why people care about characteristic values and what role they play in people's lives. As far as I know, no existing research has tackled this question directly. I will therefore introduce a tentative hypothesis, which could be put to the test in future empirical work.

Consider a case in which people think that an object falls under a given concept. Now suppose that people conclude that the object fails to embody the characteristic values of that concept. In such cases, people will tend to think that something has gone wrong.

As an example, suppose we arrive at a conception of the characteristic values of punk rock. We might then conclude that almost all music does not embody those values. (For example, Bach's partitas don't embody the characteristic values of punk rock.) But in most cases, we would not regard this as a problem. There is no particular reason why most music ought to embody the characteristic values of punk rock, and there is therefore nothing wrong with cases in which it does not. However, something different happens when we conclude that a given piece of music actually *is* punk rock but nonetheless fails to embody the characteristic values of punk rock. In those cases, there is a mismatch, and we might feel that something has gone wrong.

This phenomenon also seems to arise for numerous other concepts. Consider the characteristic values of philosophy. Presumably, people would think that most objects do not embody these characteristic values. (Math papers, action movies, and punk rock songs typically do not embody the characteristic values of philosophy.) Yet none of this is itself a problem. However, it does seem that there is a problem when a philosophy paper fails to embody the characteristic values of philosophy. In that case, there is a mismatch, and people may feel that something has gone wrong.

In introducing this idea, I mean to be making a very weak claim. The point is not that people will necessarily think that it would be better all-things-considered for every object to embody the characteristic values of the concepts it falls under. In some cases, they might think that there are also strong countervailing reasons that outweigh this one. Similarly, the point is not that people specifically think that the best way to address these mismatches is by changing the object so that it embodies the right characteristic values. In some cases, people might think it would be better to make the opposite change. For example, if a philosophy paper fails to embody the characteristic values of philosophy but does embody the characteristic values of math, people might think that the best way to address the mismatch is to turn the paper into a straight-up math paper.

With any luck, future empirical research will more directly put this claim to the test. For the moment, I adopt it as a provisional hypothesis. If it forms a part of a package that, taken together, provides an explanation for the moral change intuition, this explanation will itself provide at least some small measure of empirical support for the hypothesis itself.

D. Dual Character Statements

Consider now cases in which people represent an object as falling under a concept but think that the object fails to embody the values associated with that concept. A series of studies have explored the statements people are inclined to use in cases like this (Knobe et al. 2013).

For example, consider the hypothetical scientist we discussed in the introduction. As we noted there, participants who receive this example tend to agree with both of the following statements:

(1) There is a sense in which this person is a scientist.
(2) Ultimately when you think about what it really means to be a scientist, you would have to say that this person is not truly a scientist.

This result seems to suggest that people actually have two different sets of criteria for determining whether someone counts as a scientist. One set of criteria involves more superficial features, while the other involves characteristic values. For this reason, concepts like the concept of being a scientist are known as *dual character concepts*.

Interestingly, in existing studies on dual character concepts, it is not as though one sample of participants receives a sentence like (1) and another, completely separate sample of participants receives a sentence like (2). Rather, each individual participant receives both sentences. So participants are agreeing with both of these sentences even when they see them back to back. Indeed, participants agree even when they are conjoined to form a single sentence.

> There's a sense in which she is clearly a scientist, but ultimately, if you think about what it really means to be a scientist, you'd have to say that there is a sense in which she is not a scientist at all.

Sentences of this form have played a large role in the study of dual character concepts, and they have sometimes been referred to as "dual character statements." Studies show that people generally think that dual character statements make sense when used with dual character concepts but do not make sense when used with other concepts (Knobe et al. 2013). For example, participants think that the following sentences make sense:

> There's a sense in which she is clearly a **friend**, but ultimately, if you think about what it really means to be a **friend**, you'd have to say that there is a sense in which she is not a **friend** at all.

> There's a sense in which this is clearly a **poem**, but ultimately, if you think about what it really means to be a **poem**, you'd have to say that there is a sense in which this is not a **poem** at all.

But they think that the following sentences do not make sense:

> There's a sense in which she is clearly a **second cousin**, but ultimately, if you think about what it really means to be a **second cousin**, you'd have to say that there is a sense in which she is not a **second cousin** at all.

> There's a sense in which this is clearly a **table of contents**, but ultimately, if you think about what it really means to be a **table of contents**, you'd have to say that there is a sense in which this is not a **table of contents** at all.

Drawing on this finding, previous studies have used agreement with dual character statements as a measure of the degree to which concepts show dual character (Liao et al. 2020).

People's use of dual character statements raises a host of deep and very difficult issues. Those issues have been discussed in a number of existing papers (Del Pinal and Reuter 2017; Guo et al. 2021; Knobe et al. 2013; Leslie 2015; Liao et al. 2020; Reuter 2019), but I think it's fair to say that they have not yet been satisfactorily resolved. Further research on this topic is clearly needed.

In what follows, we will not be attempting to make progress on the broader questions that arise here. Instead, we will be focusing just on one very specific issue. Consider the second conjunct within a dual character statement. These are sentences like "Ultimately, she is not a scientist at all" or "Ultimately, this is not a poem at all." We can refer to these as *ultimately-not statements*. When a person uses an ultimately-not statement, what exactly does she thereby accomplish?

E. Downstream Effects

In thinking about this question, it will be helpful to explore some specific examples. As we will see, even a brief look at some examples suggests that things are not exactly the way we might have expected them to be if we had just considered the matter in the abstract.

Imagine that you are thinking about what is so deeply valuable in the work of Biggie, Tupac, Nas—when you are interrupted by the sound of some new song on your local hip-hop radio station. Now suppose you use an ultimately-not statement: "Ultimately, this isn't even hip-hop at all." What exactly are you doing when you use a sentence like this?

The first thing to note is that you seem to be *disparaging* the object you are discussing. Any account of these sentences that left out the disparagement would be missing something very fundamental. But the disparagement here is a complex one, and it might at first be difficult to see precisely how sentences like these can serve to disparage the objects they discuss.

To begin with, notice that it would not normally be considered disparaging to say that a song is not hip-hop. Lots of songs are not hip-hop, and there is nothing wrong with that. Of course, one might add that the sentence seems to be suggesting that the song doesn't embody the characteristic values of hip-hop, but that addition doesn't immediately address what is puzzling here. After all, lots of songs don't embody the characteristic values of hip-hop, and there is nothing wrong with that either. The disparagement in this case seems to arise from something very specific about the application of the claim to a case involving the use of a dual character concept. Let us therefore refer to it as a *dual character diss*.

Very roughly, the force of a dual character diss comes from the combination of two elements. On the one hand, a certain object does fall under a concept, but on the other hand, the object does not embody those characteristic values. Thus, there is a mismatch. In some important sense the object is failing to be the very thing it actually is.

The phenomenon of dual character disses is a pervasive one, which arises in numerous different domains. Suppose you read through this chapter and say: "Ultimately, this isn't even really philosophy." You would thereby be disparaging the chapter, but only because there is a clear sense in which this chapter *is* philosophy. Or suppose that a racist is talking about a member of some other racial group and says: "Ultimately, she isn't even really human." This is a way of disparaging that person— perhaps the worst thing that can be said about a person—but even here, one can only see that the sentence is disparaging if one understands that she actually *is* human (Phillips 2021; cf. Smith, this volume).

In short, ultimately-not statements seem to have quite distinctive downstream effects. Consider again our ultimately-not statement:

Ultimately, this isn't even hip-hop at all.

One might at first think that the downstream effects of a statement like this one would be at least roughly similar to the downstream effects of a more straightforward statement saying that something does not fall under a concept. For example, one might think that they would be at least roughly similar to the downstream effects that would arise if someone were simply wondering whether a song was hip-hop and you answered:

No, that one isn't hip-hop.

I have been trying to suggest that this is actually not the case. The downstream effects of an ultimately-not statement aren't even roughly similar to the effects of these more straightforward statements. Rather, the downstream effects of an ultimately-not statement are closely tied to the idea of a *mismatch*. Fundamentally, what an ultimately-not statement is doing is saying that there is a mismatch between what an object is and which values it embodies.

F. Summary

Thus far, we have been developing a framework for understanding dual character concepts. This framework includes claims about the criteria people use in applying such concepts (characteristic values), about the linguistic expressions associated with them (dual character statements), and about the role of such linguistic expressions in people's lives (dual character disses).

The dual character framework was originally developed to understand a class of concepts that might seem quite distant from questions about personal identity, and we have been exploring that framework through a discussion of those other concepts. The key question in what follows will be whether this very same framework can also give us insight into the moral change intuition.

II. Normative Standards and Similarity

Admittedly, however, this is not the obvious place to go in looking for an explanation. A more natural approach would be to look to the frameworks developed within existing research on the way people think about personal identity over time. Recent studies show that these frameworks have been extraordinarily successful in explaining numerous different phenomena that seem closely related to personal identity, and one might therefore be tempted to assume that they can also be used to explain the moral change intuition.

A core goal of much of this recent research has been to understand the way people think about the various normative standards associated with being a particular person. If we determine that a particular person is me, it immediately seems to follow that this person ought to treat others in certain ways and ought to be treated in certain ways by others. If a person is me, that person has to keep my promises, teach my courses, and raise my children. And, similarly, if a person is me, that person should be cared for by my friends, should be punished for my misdeeds, and so forth.

So then, how do people actually make judgments about whether a person has these normative statuses? Experimental work on this question has been deeply influenced by frameworks coming out of philosophy. Some philosophical theories suggest that personal identity is not a matter of continuity of the body but rather a matter of continuity of the mind (Locke 1690). But, as philosophers have noted, continuity of the mind seems to be a matter of degree (Parfit 1984). If you undergo a radical change of personality, you might be said to have a lower degree of continuity in this respect than if your personality remains pretty much constant. Experimental work has drawn on this idea in exploring the ways in which people ordinarily attribute normative standards. For example, consider a person who undergoes various changes, in the normal way, over the course of a number of years. Depending on various factors, such a person's psychology might change relatively little, or it might change quite a lot. Systematic studies show that this difference has an important effect on how people regard the agent after the change. People are less concerned with the welfare of their own future self if they believe that they will undergo very substantial psychological changes in the future (Bartels and Urminsky 2011; Bartels, Kvaran, and Nichols 2013), and they are less inclined to punish a person for her former misdeeds if she underwent substantial psychological changes in the time since those misdeeds (Mott 2018).

This line of research seems to be pointing to something truly profound about the way people ordinarily understand identity over time, and it raises some fundamental, and philosophically rich, questions about the relationship between personal identity and normative status (e.g., Hershfield and Bartels 2018; Tierney et al. 2014; Tierney 2020). In this chapter, however, I will not be grappling with those questions. Instead, I just want to focus on one very specific issue. Should we be using the framework coming out of this recent research to understand the moral change intuition?

In addressing this issue, it might be helpful to start by making two simple points. First, at a very straightforward level, the thing being measured in this line of research is different from the thing being measured in studies on the moral change intuition. Studies in this line of research are concerned with the degree to which participants are inclined to help a person, or to blame a person, or to punish a person. By contrast, studies on the moral change intuition are concerned with the degree to which people agree with statements like "The man after the accident is not really Phineas." Of course, one might well think that the very same psychological processes that explain the former will also explain the latter. This is a plausible view—and I agree that it is an obvious first place to start—but all the same, it is clearly an empirical hypothesis. It might well turn out to be correct, but it is also possible that it will turn out to be wrong.

Second, in the previous section, I introduced a somewhat complex framework for thinking about certain kinds of continuity, but no one has suggested that this complex framework would be necessary for understanding the phenomena being studied in this other line of research, and my sense is that such a suggestion wouldn't even be plausible. Those other phenomena really are just a matter of *similarity*.

For example, Mott (2018) looked at judgments about punishment. The results showed that if you perform a morally bad act and then change a lot, people are disinclined to punish you for the act you performed before the change. This is a fascinating finding, but it doesn't seem at all helpful to think of it using the framework I introduced in the previous section. It is not that people are disinclined to punish you because they think that you are failing to embody what the person who performed the original act was really all about. Rather, the effect here seems to be driven by a straightforward judgment regarding similarity. People are disinclined to punish you because you are now so different from the way you were at the time you performed the act.

In sum, existing research on intuitions about personal identity has uncovered some very surprising effects on people's judgments about normative standards, and those judgments appear to be driven by perceived similarity. What we want to know now is whether the frameworks that have proven so helpful in explaining these effects will help us in understanding the moral change intuition.

III. The Moral Change Intuition

To address this question, let's now turn to existing empirical work on the moral change intuition. We will be focusing on four major findings.

A. Moral versus Non-moral

Strohminger and Nichols (2014) reported a series of studies that looked at which specific changes led to the intuition that personal identity was disrupted. For example, in one study, all participants were asked to imagine a person named Jim who suffers a brain injury in a car accident. They were then randomly assigned to be told that one specific aspect of Jim's previous mental states was lost as a result: his memories, his desires, his perceptual abilities, or his moral conscience. Participants were then asked about the degree to which they agreed with the sentence: "The transplant recipient is still Jim."

In a striking result, Strohminger and Nichols found that a loss of moral conscience led to a different pattern of responses than any of the other sorts of psychological changes. In all other conditions, participants tended on the whole to agree with this sentence, but in the condition where Jim loses his moral conscience, they tended on the whole to disagree.

This same finding also emerged in numerous further studies, including everything from studies in which participants are asked to imagine that one person's soul enters another person's body to studies on people whose spouses actually are undergoing psychological changes due to dementia (Heiphetz, Strohminger, and Young 2017; Prinz and Nichols 2016; Strohminger and Nichols 2014, 2015). There seems to be a pervasive tendency whereby people's use of these sentences is much more affected by changes in moral traits than by other sorts of changes.

This is not the pattern we would have expected to find if we thought that these intuitions were driven by straightforward judgments of similarity. After all, similarity does not seem to be just a matter of having the same moral traits; it seems to be a matter of having the same features more generally (same memories, same preferences, etc.). We might be able to accommodate this result on a theory that emphasizes similarity, but to do so we would have to introduce some additional complexities into our account of the similarity judgment that plays a role here. For example, we could say that it isn't a matter of similarity across the board but rather a matter of similarity in one specific respect (e.g., similarity with regard to moral traits).

B. Good versus Bad

Thus far, we have seen that intuitions about personal identity depend especially on changes in moral traits, but does it matter whether those changes involve morally good traits or morally bad traits?

To address this question, Tobia (2015) conducted an elegant experiment. Participants were randomly assigned to receive either a vignette in which Phineas loses morally good traits or morally bad traits. In the condition in which the morality good traits are lost, participants received the vignette quoted at the beginning of this chapter. In the condition in which morally bad traits are lost, participants received a modified version (changes in boldface type):

> Phineas is extremely **cruel**; he really enjoys **harming** people. He is also employed as a railroad worker. One day at work, a railroad explosion causes a large iron spike to fly out and into his head, and he is immediately taken for emergency surgery. The doctors manage to remove the iron spike and their patient is fortunate to survive. However, in some ways this man after the accident is remarkably different from Phineas before the accident. Phineas before the accident was extremely **cruel** and enjoyed **harming** people, but the man after the accident is now extremely **kind**; he even enjoys **helping** people.

In both conditions, participants were asked whether they thought that the man after the accident was not Phineas.

The results showed a surprising asymmetry. In the condition where the morally good traits are lost, participants' ratings were at about the midpoint of the scale (indicating that they were uncertain whether to say that the man after the accident was Phineas). By contrast, in the condition where the morally bad traits were lost, participants were specifically inclined to say that personal identity was not disrupted and that the man after the accident was still Phineas.

Subsequent studies found similar effects with other materials (Earp et al. 2019), across a wide variety of cultures and languages (Dranseika et al., unpublished data), and even in studies with children (Lefebvre and Krettenauer 2020). For example, in a study that we will be discussing further in a later section (Tobia 2015; based on a case from Parfit 1984), participants were given a vignette about a Russian nobleman. In one condition, participants were told that he started out with egalitarian ideals and then lost those ideals (morally good traits lost). In the other condition, participants were told that he started out with anti-egalitarian ideals and then lost those ideals (morally bad traits lost). Participants were more inclined to say that the person after the loss of ideals was not the same as the original nobleman in the condition where morally good traits were lost.

This pattern in the results looks even farther from the pattern one would expect if these intuitions were driven by similarity judgments. To hold onto the idea that these intuitions are driven by similarity judgments, we would therefore have to introduce even more complexity into our account of the similarity judgments themselves. Not only would we need to say that they are a matter of similarity in one specific respect, we would have to say that the notion of similarity at work here is asymmetric. Notice the structure of the studies we are discussing. In both conditions, the person is described as undergoing a change between the very same two states (being morally good, being morally bad), and the only difference is the direction in which the person is moving (good to bad vs. bad to good). Thus, to explain this result in terms of similarity, we would have to say that being morally good is seen as more similar to being morally bad than being morally bad is seen as similar to being morally good.

At this point, it is beginning to seem that the concept of similarity is not actually playing any helpful role in explaining the results. What the studies show is that people are especially inclined to use a certain sort of sentence in cases where a person fails to show a morally good trait that he or she showed previously. We might be able to rig up a very complex account of similarity that allowed us to accommodate this result, but is the concept of similarity actually helping us in any way to make sense of it?

C. Beyond Human Beings

So far, we have been looking at intuitions about human beings and their psychological states. A question arises, however, as to whether these same effects would emerge if one looked at other types of objects.

In a series of studies, De Freitas and colleagues therefore took the effect that Tobia found for intuitions about Phineas and asked whether that same effect would emerge for intuitions about nonhuman objects (De Freitas et al. 2017). For example, in one study, participants were asked to imagine a physics paper called "Atom Dynamics." They were told that the authors revised the paper, deleting some of the existing sections and adding some new sections. In one condition, participants were told that these changes involved eliminating all of the good parts of the paper, while in the other condition, participants were told that these changes involve eliminating all of the bad sections of the paper. All participants were then asked whether the paper after the changes genuinely was "Atom Dynamics." The results showed the same effect observed for people's intuitions about persons. Participants were more inclined to say that the paper was no longer really "Atom Dynamics" when it lost its *good* properties. This effect also arose for nonhuman objects of many other types: a university, a nation, a conference, and a rock band.

In short, when we look specifically at intuitions about human beings, we find a difference between losing good traits and losing bad traits. But this effect does not appear to be due to something unique about human beings. Rather, it seems to be just one instance of a far more general effect involving a difference between losing good properties and losing bad properties.

D. Downstream Effects

We have seen that people are more inclined to have a certain sort of intuition when a person loses morally good traits then when that person loses morally bad traits. A question now arises about the downstream effects of this intuition. If people are more inclined to think that the man after the accident is not really Phineas when he loses morally good traits, what impact will this have on the way they actually think about or interact with him?

Work on the role of similarity has emphasized one specific type of downstream effect. Specifically, this work points to an impact of similarity judgments on intuitions about normative standards. Does the moral change intuition work in that very same way? If people are more inclined to think that the man after the accident is not truly Phineas when he loses morally good traits, will they be less inclined to think that the normative standards that applied to the original Phineas still apply after he loses morally good traits?

Although existing studies have not explored this question using the Phineas case in particular, Earp and colleagues explored this question by looking at intuitions about advance directives (Earp, Latham, and Tobia 2020). Suppose Robin signs an official document saying that if she ever ends up in a certain kind of medical condition, she does not want to be resuscitated. Subsequently, she undergoes a radical psychological change as a result of dementia, and she either loses her morally good traits or her morally bad traits. Then the person who exists after the psychological change gets pneumonia and ends up in precisely the medical condition described by the advance directive. Should the doctors' treatment of the person after the onset of dementia be governed by the advance directive that the original Robin signed?

The question being asked here has very much the same structure as the questions asked in the many existing studies on personal identity and normative standards. There is a normative standard that applies to a person before a change (the advance directive), followed by a change in that person's psychological state (the onset of dementia). Participants are then asked a question design to see whether they continue to apply the normative standard even after this change. The key question is whether participants will be less inclined to apply the normative standard when the change involves the loss of morally good traits than when the change involves the loss of morally bad traits. Strikingly, the results showed that people were *not* less inclined to apply the normative standard when the change involved a loss of morally good traits. That is, there was no effect at all such that participants were less inclined to think that the doctors should obey the advance directive in the condition where morally good traits were lost than in the condition where morally bad traits were lost.

Because this study came out only very recently, I worry that the field might not yet have absorbed its full significance. Previous studies consistently find that people are more inclined to have a certain sort of intuition when morally good traits are lost than when the morally bad traits are lost, and a question now arises about the downstream effects of that intuition. The obvious first hypothesis would be that it has exactly the same sorts of downstream effects that have been demonstrated in numerous existing studies on the effects of similarity judgments. But we are now getting some evidence that it does *not* have those same sorts of downstream effects. This provides at least some reason to suspect that it is not the same thing but is something else entirely.

E. Summary

Our aim here has been to understand the intuition people express when they use sentences like: "The man after the accident isn't even really Phineas." One initial question we face is whether this intuition can be straightforwardly explained using the sorts of frameworks that come out of the existing philosophical literature on personal identity or whether we will need a new sort of framework to understand it.

To make progress on this question, we reviewed four findings from the existing empirical literature: (1) people's use of these sentences is especially affected by changes in moral traits and (2) even more so by the loss of morally good traits. (3) This same basic pattern arises for the way people describe things other than human beings. (4) Although the loss of morally good traits has an especially large impact on use of these sentences, it does not have an especially large impact on people's intuition about the normative standards that apply to the person after the loss. None of these findings seems to follow in any obvious way from the frameworks that have been so successful in helping us understand the relationship between normative standards and psychological similarity.

So then, how are the findings to be explained? One possible approach would be to try fiddling with the frameworks developed within this prior work. We might then end up with something that resembled those frameworks but that also differed from them in various details. For example, we might say that people have some very complex notion of similarity that is actually asymmetric. Or we might say that, for some complex reason, intuitions about personal identity don't have the impact one might think they would on judgments about advance directives.

Although there is a chance that this strategy will ultimately prove successful, I will be pursuing a very different approach. On the view I will be developing, these findings do not provide any reason to revise existing frameworks. Those frameworks are fine just as they are; the issue is simply that the moral change intuition is completely unrelated to the phenomena they were originally designed to explain. Thus, if we want to explain the moral change intuition, we will have to switch over to an entirely different approach.

IV. The Moral Change Intuition and Dual Character Concepts

Let's therefore shift gears and ask instead whether we can make sense of these results within the framework introduced to understand dual character concepts. On the hypothesis I will be proposing, it is not just that there is some loose analogy between the moral change intuition and dual character concepts. Rather, the moral change intuition simply *is* an example of the use of a dual character concept.

On this view, then, what people are doing when they say "The man after the accident isn't really Phineas" is deeply similar to what people are doing when they say things like "Ultimately, this song isn't really hip-hop." The best way of understanding the sentence about Phineas is through an application of the framework that was first developed to understand those other cases.

Now, of course, these two cases look very different from a metaphysical perspective. In the former case, we have a concept that applies to various different *objects*. We are now thinking about a particular object, and we are wondering whether this concept applies to it. By contrast, in the latter case, we have a concept that applies to various different time slices of a person, that is, to what metaphysicians sometimes call *person-stages*. We are now thinking about a particular person-stage, and we are wondering whether the concept applies to it. Clearly, there is an important difference between thinking about objects and thinking about person-stages.

Given this obvious difference, it would certainly be reasonable to suspect that it won't be possible to find a single overarching framework that helps make sense of both sorts of cases. Nonetheless, I will be arguing that the dual character framework actually does capture a more abstract structure that applies across both. To see how this might work, we need to engage in a more detailed examination of the moral change intuition itself.

A. Dual Character Statements

As we noted earlier, one way to test whether a concept has dual character is to see whether people are willing to use it in sentences of a specific form that we have called "dual character statements." To see whether people are inclined to express the moral change intuition using sentences of this form, I conducted a simple experiment.

In all, 205 participants were recruited using Amazon MTurk. All participants received one of Tobia's (2015) vignettes about Phineas. Participants in one condition

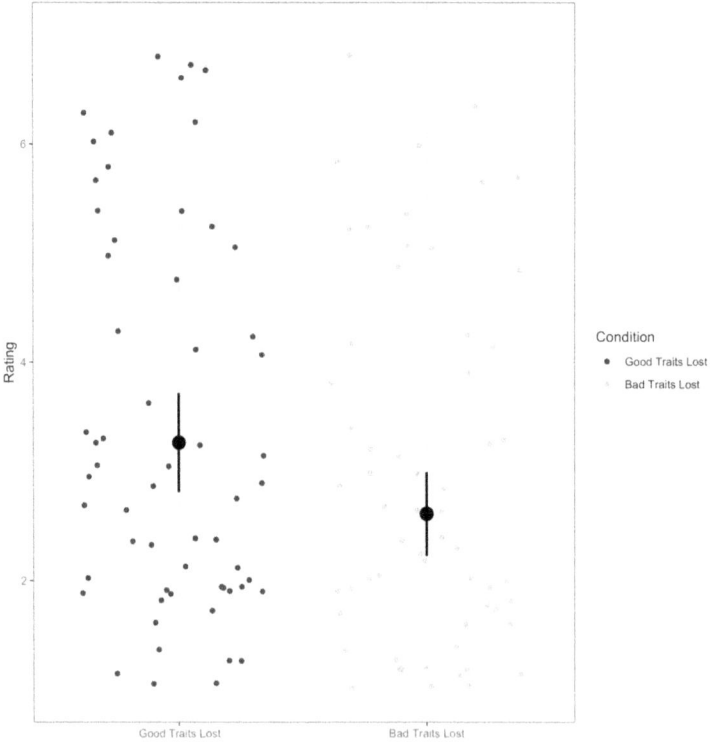

Figure 3.1 Jittered plot showing the results of Tobia (2015). Each small circle represents the rating given by one individual participant. Large black circles show the means for each condition. Error bars show 95% CI.

received the version in which Phineas loses morally good traits; participants in the other condition received the version in which Phineas loses morally bad traits. All participants then received the dual character statement:

> There's a sense in which the man after the accident is clearly still Phineas, but ultimately, if you think about what it really means to be Phineas, you'd have to say that he is not truly Phineas at all.

Participants rated this statement on a scale from 1 ("completely disagree") to 7 ("completely agree").

Ratings in the condition where the morally good traits were lost ($M = 5.5$, $SD = 1.4$) were significantly higher than were ratings in the condition where the morally bad traits were lost ($M = 4.6$, $SD = 1.7$), $t(204)=3.7$, $p < .001$. (All data and R code for this study are available at https://osf.io/w842x/.)

To get a better understanding of these results, it might be helpful to compare them to the results of the original Tobia study. Figure 3.1 shows the original Tobia results; Figure 3.2 shows the present results.

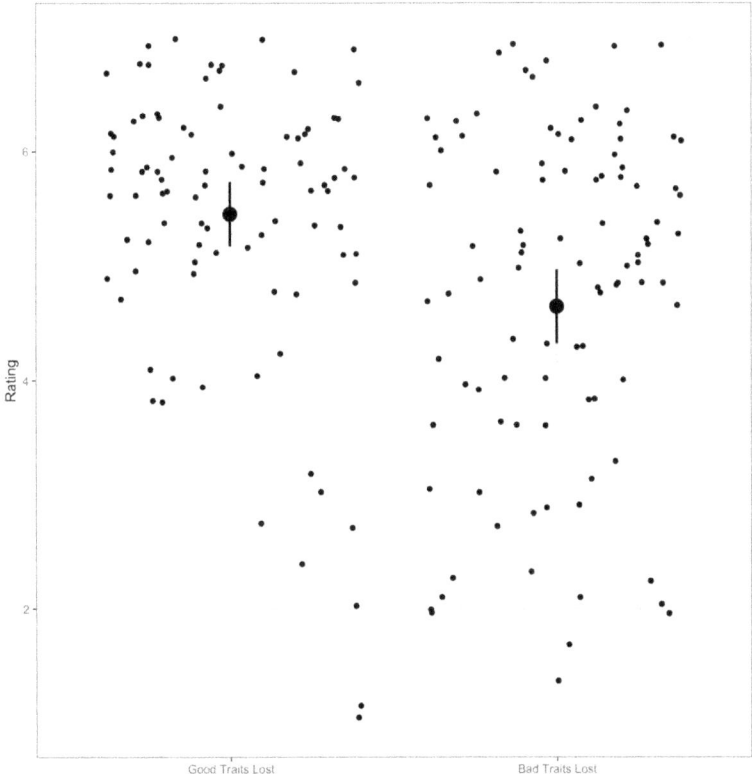

Figure 3.2 Jittered plot showing the results of the present study. Each small circle represents the rating given by one individual participant. Large black circles show the means for each condition. Error bars show 95% CI.

This simple study yields two findings that we will be trying to explain.

First, in the condition where morally good traits were lost, participants tended on the whole to agree with the dual character statement. This result contrasts with the result from the original Tobia study. In that original study, participants showed at least some willingness to say that the man after the accident was not truly Phineas, but it was not the case that they actually tended on the whole to agree with that statement. What we find here is that when participants are given the more complex dual character statement, the majority actually *agree*. The obvious conclusion would be that this more complex statement more accurately captures their opinions about this case.

Second, the results from the condition in which morally bad traits were lost were very different from the results in the conditions in which morally good traits were lost. In the condition in which morally bad traits were lost, participants' judgments were all over the place. Some agreed with the dual character statement, others disagreed. Thus, an adequate account of people's judgments in these cases needs to explain why this second condition is different from the first and why it leads to so much disagreement in people's intuitions.

In sum, this study provides at least some evidence for the hypothesis that the moral change intuition is best understood in terms of dual character concepts. The key question now is whether we can use the dual character framework to explain the exact pattern of intuitions that people show in these cases.

B. Criteria

Consider the original Phineas, as he existed before the accident. In the actual text of the vignettes participants received, there is a certain amount of information about what the original Phineas was actually like, and this information makes it clear that he was morally good in one condition, morally bad in the other. But to apply the dual character framework, we need to look at something that goes beyond just what Phineas was actually like. We need to look at *what he was really all about*. Importantly, these two things might sometimes differ substantially; what Phineas was actually like might involve a failure to embody the characteristic values that constituted what he was really all about.

What will participants conclude in each of these conditions about what Phineas was really all about? This sort of question has been explored in a number of recent studies, and we now have at least some amount of evidence regarding the answer. When an agent is described as having morally good features, people tend to think that the agent is fundamentally morally good. By contrast, however, when an agent is described as having morally bad features, people don't just conclude that the agent is fundamentally morally bad. Instead, people seem to regard this as a difficult or confusing case. Some people say that the agent is morally bad, while others say that there is some sense in which, deep down, the agent is morally good (Newman, De Freitas, and Knobe 2015).

Of course, further questions immediately arise as to why people think about morally bad agents in this way. These questions have been a major preoccupation of recent work in this area. The tendency people show in these cases seems to be related to a more general tendency to believe that, deep down, all agents are morally good (Newman, Bloom, and Knobe 2014; Strohminger, Knobe, and Newman 2017), which in turn seems to be related to an even more general tendency to think that all objects, including nonhuman objects, have good essences (e.g., De Freitas et al. 2017). The question as to how to explain this more general tendency is a difficult one, and I don't have anything new to contribute to it here. The key point for present purposes is just that if people's judgments do show this pattern, we can use those judgments to explain the moral change intuition.

First, consider the condition in which Phineas loses his morally good traits. In that condition, people tend to think that the man after the accident is failing to embody the characteristic values of the original Phineas. For this reason, they say that, ultimately, the man after the accident is not truly Phineas.

Now consider the condition where Phineas loses his morally bad traits. In that condition, the man after the accident is certainly very dissimilar from the original Phineas, so if these intuitions were driven by similarity judgments, people should again say that the man after the accident is not Phineas. However, on the view we have been developing, these intuitions are *not* driven by similarity judgments. Instead, they are driven by judgments about characteristic values.

This gives us a very different way of explaining the results in that condition. Given the way in which people attribute characteristic values, it seems likely that people will be all over the place when it comes to judgments about what the original Phineas was really all about. Some people will think that the cruelty he shows on the surface is what he is really all about, while others will think that despite the features he shows on the surface, what he was really all about was something more morally good. These different people should have different intuitions about whether the man after the accident embodies the characteristic values of the original Phineas. Those people who think that what the original Phineas was all about was something morally bad should conclude that the man after the accident does not embody the characteristic values of the original Phineas, but those participants who think that what the original Phineas was all about was something morally good should reach the opposite conclusion. They should conclude that the man after the accident embodies the characteristic values of the original Phineas even *more* than the original Phineas himself did.

C. Downstream Effects

When one first encounters the moral change intuition, it is only natural to seek to understand it in terms of a familiar web of concerns involving normative standards. After all, if we learn that a particular person is Phineas, we immediately begin to attribute to that person certain normative standards. He has to fulfill Phineas's promises, he has the right to use Phineas's possessions, he should be punished for Phineas's misdeeds, and so forth. If someone says that the man after the accident is not truly Phineas, an obvious first thought is that this person is saying that some of these normative standards do not fully apply to the man after the accident.

I have been arguing that the moral change intuition should not be understood in this way. It doesn't have anything to do with any of the concerns that are familiar from the existing literature on personal identity. Rather, it should be understood as closely connected to the use of ultimately-not sentences with dual character concepts.

As soon as one begins thinking in this way, a completely different set of concerns immediately suggest themselves. Suppose we think about Phineas and thereby extract a view about what he is all about. We could then pick out any person and ask whether that person embodies Phineas's characteristic values. For example, we could ask whether Barack Obama embodies Phineas's characteristic values, or whether Alexander the Great embodies those values. Yet, though we could ask this question about any arbitrary person, we usually would not care very much about the answer. However, there is one specific person who has a special relationship to Phineas's characteristic values. That person is *Phineas*. To the extent that Phineas fails to embody what Phineas is all about, it seems that something is going wrong. He is failing to *be himself*.

This point comes out even more clearly when we consider more ordinary cases. Take the case of the Russian nobleman (Parfit 1984). Suppose you knew the Russian nobleman back when he passionately believed in the cause of liberating the serfs. Then you see him again, years later, and he seems interested only in preserving his own power and privilege. You say: "It isn't even really *him* anymore." What exactly would you be conveying with a sentence like that?

On the hypothesis we are exploring here, you would be pointing to a certain sort of mismatch. The person you are seeing is clearly still the person you once knew, but at the same time, he is tragically failing to embody the values of the person you once knew. Therein lies the force of the claim you are making about him—that he is failing to be the very thing that he is.

V. Conclusion

Our inquiry has been concerned with the relationship between two things. On the one hand, there are very general theories about dual character concepts. On the other hand, there are a series of specific empirical findings concerning the moral change intuition. We have been exploring the hypothesis that the former can explain the latter.

To evaluate this hypothesis, we have been looking at some theories regarding dual character concepts in general and at some findings regarding the moral change intuition in particular. If we consider just the findings that are already available, it does seem that the theories provide good explanations for the findings. This gives us at least some reason to suspect that our hypothesis might be on the right track.

But of course, the hypothesis makes predictions that go far beyond anything that can be verified just by looking at existing findings. In the years to come, we will presumably uncover further facts both about dual character concepts in general and about the moral change intuition in particular. The hypothesis we have been exploring makes a prediction about those further facts. It predicts that even after we know much more about the dual character concepts and about moral change intuition, we will continue to find an explanatory relationship between the two.

Note

1   I am grateful for comments from Paul Bloom, Brian Earp, James Kirkpatrick, Shaun Nichols, John Schwenkler, Marya Schechtman, and Kevin Tobia.

Bibliography

Bailey, A., J. Knobe and G. E. Newman (2021). "Value-based Essentialism: How Beliefs about Shared Values Promote Essentialist Beliefs." *Journal of Experimental Psychology: General*, 150 (10): 1994–2014.
Bartels, D. and O. Urminsky (2011). "On Intertemporal Selfishness: The Perceived Instability of Identity Underlies Impatient Consumption." *Journal of Consumer Research*, 39: 182–98.
Bartels, D. M., T. Kvaran and S. Nichols (2013). "Selfless Giving." *Cognition*, 129: 392–403.
De Freitas, J., K. P. Tobia, G. E. Newman and J. Knobe (2017). "Normative Judgments and Individual Essence." *Cognitive Science*, 41 (Supplement 3): 382–402.
Del Pinal, G. and K. Reuter (2017). "Dual Character Concepts in Social Cognition: Commitments and the Normative Dimension of Conceptual Representation." *Cognitive Science*, 41 (Supplement 3): 477–501.
Dranseika, V., E. Lauraitytė and Experimental Jurisprudence Cross-Cultural Study Swap Consortium (unpublished data). "Cross-cultural Replication of Tobia (2016)."
Earp, B. D., S. R. Latham and K. P. Tobia (2020). "Personal Transformation and Advance Directives: An Experimental Bioethics Approach." *American Journal of Bioethics*, 20 (8): 72–5.
Earp, B. D., J. A. Skorburg, J. A. C. Everett and J. Savulescu (2019). "Addiction, Identity, Morality." *AJOB: Empirical Bioethics*, 10: 136–53.
Flanagan, B. and I. Hannikainen (in press). "The Folk Concept of Law: Law is Intrinsically Moral." *Australasian Journal of Philosophy*.
Guo, C., C. S. Dweck and E. M. Markman (2021). "Gender Categories as Dual-Character concepts?" *Cognitive Science*, 45 (5): e12954.
Heiphetz, L, N. Strohminger and L. Young (2017). "The Role of Moral Beliefs, Memories, and Preferences in Representations of Identity." *Cognitive Science*, 41: 744–67.
Hershfield, H. E. and D. M. Bartels (2018). "The Future Self." In G. Oettingen, A. T. Sevincer, and P. M. Gollwitzer (eds.), *The Psychology of Thinking about the Future*, 89–109. New York: The Guilford Press.
Knobe, J., S. Prasada and G. Newman (2013). "Dual Character Concepts and the Normative Dimension of Conceptual Representation." *Cognition*, 127: 242–57.
Lefebvre, J. P. and T. Krettenauer (2020). "Is the True Self Truly Moral? Identity Intuitions across Domains of Sociomoral Reasoning and Age." *Journal of Experimental Child Psychology*, 192: 104769.
Leslie, S.-J. (2015). "'Hillary Clinton is the Only Man in the Obama Administration': Dual Character Concepts, Generics, and Gender." *Analytic Philosophy*, 56 (2): 111–41.
Liao, S. Y., A. Meskin and J. Knobe (2020). "Dual Character Art Concepts." *Pacific Philosophical Quarterly*, 101(1): 102–28.

Mott, C. (2018). "Statutes of Limitations and Personal Identity." In T. Lombrozo, J. Knobe and S. Nichols (eds.), *Oxford Studies in Experimental Philosophy*, Vol. 2, 243–69. Oxford: Oxford University Press.

Newman, G. E., P. Bloom and J. Knobe (2014). "Value Judgments and the True Self." *Personality and Social Psychology Bulletin*, 40: 203–16.

Newman, G. E., J. De Freitas and J. Knobe (2015). "Beliefs about the True Self Explain Asymmetries Based on Moral Judgment." *Cognitive Science*, 39: 96–125.

Newman, G. E. and J. Knobe (2019). "The Essence of Essentialism." *Mind & Language*, 34: 585–605.

Parfit, D. (1984). *Reasons and Persons*. Oxford: Clarendon Press.

Phillips, B. (2021). "'They're Not True Humans': Beliefs About Moral Character Drive Categorical Denials of Humanity." Unpublished manuscript. Available online: https://psyarxiv.com/5bgxy

Prinz, J. and S. Nichols (2016). "Diachronic Identity and the Moral Self." In Julian Kiverstein (ed.), *The Routledge Handbook of Philosophy of the Social Mind*, 449–64. Abingdon: Routledge.

Reuter, K. (2019). "Dual Character Concepts." *Philosophy Compass*, 14 (1): e12557.

Ritchie, K. and J. Knobe (2020). "Kindhood and Essentialism: Evidence from Language." *Advances in Child Development and Behavior*, 59" 133–64.

Rose, D. and S. Nichols (2019). "Teleological Essentialism." *Cognitive Science*, 43: 12725.

Rose, D., J. Schaffer and K. Tobia (2020). "Folk Teleology Drives Persistence Judgments." *Synthese*, 197 (12): 5491–509.

Smith, D. L. (this volume). "'Human' Is an Essentially Political Category." In K. Tobia (ed.), *Experimental Philosophy of Identity and the Self*. London: Bloomsbury.

Starmans, C. and P. Bloom (2018). "Nothing Personal: What Psychologists Get Wrong about Identity." *Trends in Cognitive Sciences*, 22 (7): 566–8.

Strohminger, N. and S. Nichols (2014). "The Essential Moral Self." *Cognition*, 131 (1): 159–71.

Strohminger, N. and S. Nichols (2015). "Neurodegeneration and Identity." *Psychological Science*, 26 (9): 1469–79.

Strohminger, N., J. Knobe and G. Newman (2017). "The True Self: A Psychological Concept Distinct from the Self." *Perspectives on Psychological Science*, 12 (4): 551–60.

Tierney, H. (2020). "The Subscript View: A Distinct View of Distinct Selves." *Oxford Studies in Experimental Philosophy*, 3 (3): 126.

Tierney, H., C. Howard, V. Kumar, T. Kvaran and S. Nichols (2014). "How Many of Us are There?" *Advances in Experimental Philosophy of Mind*, 181–202.

Tobia, K. (2015). "Personal Identity and the Phineas Gage Effect." *Analysis*, 75 (3): 396–405.

Tobia, K. P., G. E. Newman and J. Knobe (2020). "Water is and is Not H_2O." *Mind & Language*, 35 (2): 183–208.

4

What's Left of Me?

The Role of Self-Continuity in Decision-Making and Judgments about Identity Persistence

Stephanie Chen and Oleg Urminsky

I. Introduction

Personal identity is an important driver of choice and behavior. While a large literature in philosophy and psychology has explored questions of how people represent the self-concept and what changes people think will disrupt their identity, a growing literature has focused on understanding how these beliefs underlie decision-making. By connecting beliefs about personal identity with common decisions like financial and consumption choices, we explore how people are likely to think about the self in their everyday lives.

In this chapter, we first situate our work on personal identity and the self-concept in the broader literature about personal identity. A central distinction in the philosophical study of personal identity is the distinction between numerical and qualitative identity. Recent accounts have debated whether these two types of identity have been confused in recent research on personal identity (Dranseika 2017; Starmans and Bloom 2018a). We suggest that the types of beliefs about the self that underlie decision-making are those that are likely to reflect how people think about the self in everyday life. We further suggest that the type of beliefs about identity that track these decisions, self-continuity beliefs, do not fit neatly into the numerical-qualitative identity dichotomy and challenge current ideas about what identity researchers are and should be studying.

We then review emerging research that we believe leverages a more psychologically realistic conceptualization of how people think about identity to explain decisions that are driven by beliefs about personal identity. First, we review research on how intertemporal choice is influenced by psychological connectedness to the future self—the extent to which a person believes that she shares key psychological characteristics with her future self. Second, we examine choices that are driven by the norms of the various social categories that people belong to. We review work that suggests that how likely a person is to make choices consistent with the norms of a social category is a function of her beliefs about how that social category is causally related to the other aspects of her self-concept.

A. What Is Identity?

While the meaning of "identity" may seem intuitively obvious, different scholars in philosophy and psychology have brought different understandings and assumptions to their work on identity, resulting in different operational definitions. For example, social psychologists often treat a person's identity (or identities) in terms of social categories (Markus and Wurf 1987; Tajfel 1978), while work in philosophy and cognitive science has thought of identity in terms of the features that would need to be preserved to maintain identity (Blok, Newman, and Rips 2005; Strohminger and Nichols 2014).

A recent debate has attempted to clarify the meaning of identity and to question whether researchers' operationalizations in studying identity have actually explored the construct that they conceptually intended to study (Starmans and Bloom 2018a, b; De Freitas et al. 2018). Starmans and Bloom (2018a) highlight the important distinction between *numerical* and *qualitative* identity in people's intuitions about the identity of the self and others undergoing change. Numerical identity concerns whether the person literally ceases to exist after a change, such that the person who occupied the body is no longer there, akin to death of the individual, even if the body is still alive. By contrast, qualitative identity relates to the similarity between the person at different points in time (e.g., before vs. after a change), defined as the degree to which the post-change person's features overlap with the original person's features.

Starmans and Bloom (2018a) suggest that researchers aiming to study changes in numerical identity (i.e., whether a person literally ceases to exist after a change) have instead studied changes to qualitative identity (i.e., changes to similarity). Consider a moral person who suffers a cognitive impairment and begins behaving immorally, as in the classic case of railway worker Phineas Gage (Damasio et al. 1994). When family members say that the person no longer seems like the same person underneath or that the person seems like a stranger (e.g., as was found for changes in morality, in Strohminger and Nichols 2015), what does that mean? Do they mean that the person is no longer there, has ceased to exist, and there is another person in the physical body? Or do they mean that the same person is still there, but is now so dissimilar from the person they used to be that loss-of-identity metaphors are appropriate for characterizing the large degree of dissimilarity?

While clarity on these concepts is important, the distinctions being drawn in this debate may perpetuate a false dichotomy, between literal cessation of existence at one extreme and "mere" dissimilarity of any kind (e.g., reduction in feature overlap between the past and present self, Starmans and Bloom 2018a). In our view, much recent research on the role of identity in people's lives instead explores a third type of identity, distinct from both numerical and qualitative identity. This type of identity can be referred to as *self-continuity*[1] (e.g., Urminsky and Bartels 2019; Molouki and Bartels 2017), building on characterizations of change in the self over time and partially overlapping selves in Parfit (1984). We believe that the notion of self-continuity best aligns with how people make subjective judgments about their own and others' identities in everyday situations, particularly ones that underlie common decisions.

B. Assessing Self-continuity and Persistence of Subjective Identity

Self-continuity judgments are not all-or-nothing numerical identity judgments about whether a change causes the prior self to literally cease to exist. Instead, they are continuous judgments about how much of the self, in terms of people's subjective perceptions of what defines a person as oneself, persists over time (Bartels and Rips 2010; Bartels and Urminsky 2011; Chen, Urminsky, and Bartels 2016; Mott 2018). Going from being a shy child to an outgoing teenager is unlikely to make a person feel that they have ceased to exist, but it may make her feel like she's changed into a somewhat different person than she had been, perhaps losing an important part of herself or gaining a new aspect of the self in the process.

Importantly, self-continuity judgments are not simply defined by feature overlap (e.g., qualitative identity), because changes to some features are more important to the definition of the self than others. In fact, we have found that changing the same number of features (i.e., equivalent changes in feature overlap/qualitative identity) can result in different judgments about self-continuity (Chen et al. 2016), depending on which features change. While becoming an outgoing teenager may make a previously shy child feel a sense of being a somewhat different person, going from always having long hair as a child to having short hair as a teenager likely doesn't make one feel like a significantly different person. That said, which features disrupt subjective self-continuity is idiosyncratic—giving Rapunzel or Samson a haircut might make them feel more like a different person than would giving the average person a haircut. In our view, much recent research should be understood as aiming to examine which features are weighted most heavily in such subjective judgments of self-continuity (e.g., Blok et al. 2005; Haslam, Bastian, and Bissett 2004; Strohminger and Nichols 2014) and, importantly, why.

Consistent with this conceptualization, many explorations of personal identity use continuous measures of self-continuity judgments, asking participants to rate to what extent a change will make them into a different person (see Figure 4.1 for an example). This is similar to the notion in cognitive psychology that categorization judgments are, ironically, continuous, not categorical. Items vary on how likely they are to be categorized in a given category and how typical they are of the category. Typical items are those that not only share a lot of properties with other category members but also do *not* share properties with the members of other categories. Atypical members of a category are the converse: they share fewer properties with category members and tend to resemble members of other categories (Rosch and Mervis 1975).

For example, a platypus is a terrible member of the mammal category, in part, because it has properties that make it resemble the bird category (e.g., lays eggs, has a beak). Nonetheless, it is still (generally) categorized as a mammal. In the same way, some changes to personal identity may be significant enough that an individual starts to resemble a "new" individual and become a less good example of the previous version

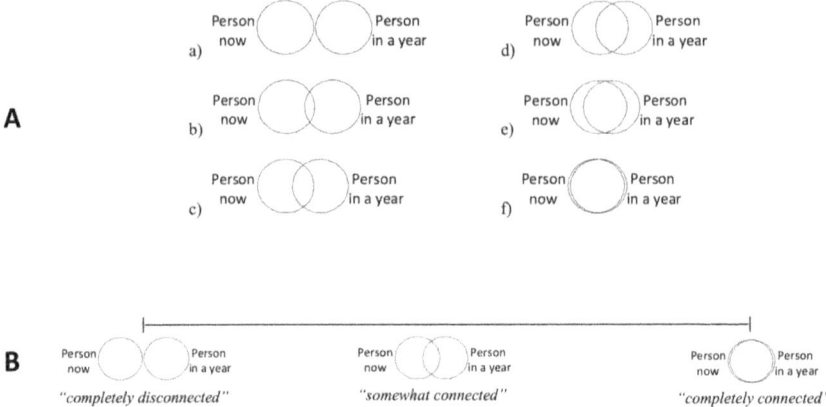

Figure 4.1 Visual measures of psychological connectedness used in Bartels and Urminsky (2011, Study 5). Participants chose the set of circles (panel A) or marked the position on the line (panel B) that best represented their belief about how much their current self's defining psychological traits overlap with their future self's psychological traits. Figures from "Daniel M. Bartels and Oleg Urminsky, On Intertemporal Selfishness: How the Perceived Instability of Identity Underlies Impatient Consumptions," © 2011 Oxford University Press. Reproduced with permission of Oxford University Press through CCC RightsLink.

of the self, despite remaining the same individual in numerical terms. Thus, we argue that characterizations of change in terms of loss of identity (e.g., no longer the same person, a stranger) often do not constitute metaphorical exaggeration, but instead may be accurate representations of the decline in perceived self-continuity over time: some of what made you the person you were then is no longer part of who you are now.

If self-continuity is not mere similarity, but is instead determined by change specifically in those features of the self that are perceived as defining of the person, what determines the degree to which a given feature is identity-defining? Building on the idea that people fundamentally reason in causal terms, including in reasoning about numerical identity in objects (Rips, Blok, and Newman 2006), a growing body of research suggests that causal beliefs shape self-continuity judgments (Chen et al. 2016). Unlike most people (who likely see their hair as causally linked to few features of the self), Rapunzel likely believes that her hair is causally linked to many aspects of the self—for example, her relationship with the prince, her role as a prisoner, and her magical powers. For Rapunzel, changing that feature would therefore likely be more disruptive to her self-continuity than it would be to most others' self-continuity.

Furthermore, deviations from a person's expected causal trajectory of the self are seen as more disruptive of self-continuity than expected changes (Molouki and Bartels 2017). For a person who expected to remain a shy wallflower forever, becoming outgoing will disrupt self-continuity more than if that person expected to eventually become popular and outgoing. Thus, the exact same change (and the same difference in mere similarity between an individual before and after the change) will influence self-continuity to the degree that it is expected. This can help explain research suggesting that the direction of change matters to persistence of identity judgments—

improvements in moral qualities are seen as more consistent with the self than declines in these traits (Newman, De Freitas, and Knobe 2015). If one expects to improve over time (as most do, including in their moral qualities), then improvements will match expectations and preserve self-continuity. However, in those cases where people expect to worsen, anticipating improvements disrupts self-continuity (Molouki and Bartels 2017).

If the goal is to understand how people commonly think about their own identity and to explore the role of identity change in decision-making, we believe that self-continuity is the most relevant and useful construct to study. Both researchers and laypeople often tend not to think in terms of numerical identity, despite its philosophical significance, because literally ceasing to exist rarely occurs. For example, Starmans and Bloom (2018b) suggest that even the case of Phineas Gage's dramatic transformation is not a change in numerical identity. It follows that most changes that people experience and think about are not about numerical identity. However, we believe that people have a richer and more nuanced understanding than is captured by qualitative identity that is better captured by self-continuity. Framing identity in terms of self-continuity enables us to study the role of identity beliefs in decision-making and explore why changes to some features impact self-continuity more than others.

II. Psychological Connectedness and Future-Oriented Decisions

Many of the decisions that people face can be characterized as trade-offs between immediate and future benefits. The decision to save money for the future means forgoing the enjoyment that you would get from spending that money in the present. Working hard today to ensure that you have better opportunities in the future means giving up all the fun that you could have now if you weren't working. A large literature on such intertemporal choices documents that people are generally impatient; they prefer immediate rewards and discount future rewards in ways that cannot be explained by rational (economic) considerations (see Frederick, Loewenstein, and O'Donoghue 2002; Urminsky and Zauberman 2016 for reviews).

While people's intertemporal choices are influenced by a number of factors, recent research has identified an aspect of self-continuity, *psychological connectedness*, as a key driver of these choices. Psychological connectedness was first defined by philosopher Derek Parfit (1984) as the degree of overlap in psychological traits (e.g., one's values, memories, ambitions, disposition) that people believe exists between their current and future selves. Parfit (1984) makes a normative argument that people ought to discount future outcomes more when they are less psychologically connected to their future selves. This is because people who are more connected to the future self will be the ones reaping future benefits for which they have sacrificed immediate benefits, more so than people who are less connected to the future self. While such normative claims are controversial, Parfit's ideas provide a useful framework to examine the descriptive psychological drivers of intertemporal choice. The research reviewed in this section leaves aside the question of whether people *ought to* discount future rewards to the extent that they are psychologically connected to the future self and instead asks the question of whether people *do* act in this way.

Recent research has found that people do, in fact, discount future rewards more when they are less connected to their future selves (see Urminsky 2017 for a review). For example, Bartels and Urminsky (2011) manipulated psychological connectedness among a set of graduating college seniors by having them read passages about the stability of personal identity. Those in the low-connectedness condition read that graduation was likely to change many of their important psychological traits (e.g., "The characteristics that make you the person you are"). Those in the high-connectedness condition read that personal identity was relatively stable and graduation was unlikely to change their core psychological traits. Participants then made a series of trade-offs about a real lottery, between receiving a $120 gift certificate in one week and a larger reward later in one year. Consistent with the hypothesis that people who are more connected to the future self will be more willing to forgo more immediate rewards for future ones, participants in the high-connectedness condition were significantly more willing to wait for the larger reward (requiring $16 less to wait, on average) than those in the low-connectedness condition.

A number of researchers have also found that lower measured psychological connectedness to the future self predicts greater discounting of both real and hypothetical future rewards (Bartels and Rips 2010; Bartels and Urminsky 2011; Ersner-Hershfield et al. 2009; but not in Frederick 2003). For instance, Bartels and Urminsky (2011) measured psychological connectedness with continuous measures. First, participants rated how much they felt that the future self would be the same person as they are today on a scale of 0 (completely different to the current self) to 100 (exactly the same as the current self). Second, participants completed two visual measures in which they saw pairs of circles that overlapped to different extents, representing their perceived overlap with their future self (see Figure 4.1). Participants either selected the set of circles (Figure 4.1A) or marked the position on the line (Figure 4.1B) that they felt best represented how much overlap they saw between their current and future self. Bartels and Urminsky (2011) found that a composite of these measures of psychological connectedness predicted participants' willingness to forgo a payment in the present for a larger payment in the future. Further, using similar measures of psychological connectedness, Ersner-Hershfield et al. (2009) found that the degree of connectedness to the future self predicted differences in accumulated financial assets (controlling for age and education).

Recent research has examined the conditions under which psychological connectedness is more likely to predict differences in intertemporal choice. More specifically, Bartels and Urminsky (2015) examined the relationship between psychological connectedness and consideration of opportunity costs. As people often neglect opportunity costs when making purchasing decisions (i.e., do not think about alternative uses for unspent money; Frederick et al. 2009, but see Spiller 2011 for exceptions), the authors hypothesized that consideration of opportunity costs may be necessary for psychological connectedness to influence decisions. That is, neglecting opportunity costs means not being aware that spending in the present often means forgoing future resources or consumption. Thus, when neglecting opportunity costs, people may not be motivated to forgo immediate benefits, no matter how connected they are to the future self, since they are not thinking in terms of depriving the future self of a benefit.

Bartels and Urminsky (2015) found that people did, in fact, need to consider opportunity costs for psychological connectedness to influence intertemporal choice. In one study, psychological connectedness and opportunity cost salience were independently manipulated and the dependent measure was participants' choices between more expensive and cheaper products in a number of product categories. When opportunity costs were made salient (by having participants rank the importance of the product categories), those in the high-connectedness condition were more likely to choose cheap products than those in the low-connectedness condition. However, when opportunity costs were not made salient, there was no difference in choices between the high- and low-connectedness conditions. Thus, consideration of opportunity costs may be necessary for psychological connectedness to influence choices with non-explicit intertemporal consequences. As these findings illustrate, anticipated self-continuity can be an important input into decision-making, but its role depends on how the decision is conceptualized.

III. Causal Centrality Approach to the Self-Concept

A. What Features Define the Self?

Thus far, we have suggested that people see some features as more defining of the self, and therefore as more relevant to assessments of self-continuity. However, this begs the question of which features are more defining and why. Notably, the empirical research on psychological connectedness discussed earlier essentially punts on this question, relying on people's idiosyncratic definitions and interpretations of what constitutes their "core" or "important" psychological traits.

A large literature has explored which feature of the self people think defines their self-concept, such that a change in that feature would reduce self-continuity. Theories of identity-based consumption and choice have focused on social categories as central to the self-concept. In contrast, other disciplines have debated which individual-level aspects of the self are most defining of the self-concept. Autobiographical memories have long been suggested by philosophers to be defining of personal identity as they are unique to each individual. Consistent with this proposal, psychological studies have found that disrupting a person's memories leads to perceptions that the person has become a different person (Blok et al. 2005; Nichols and Bruno 2013). Other accounts have instead suggested that personality traits are particularly important in defining the self-concept (Haslam et al. 2004; Gelman, Heyman, and Legare 2007), while more recent research has emphasized moral qualities (Strohminger and Nichols 2014, 2015). While these approaches select a different feature to place at the center of the self-concept, they all conceptualize the self-concept as defined by a set of core features in general.

Our *causal centrality* approach to the self-concept instead suggests that the representation of the self-concept is not simply a set of features but also critically includes beliefs about the causal relationships between these features. Our approach was inspired by research on conceptual representation in cognitive psychology which has found that features are defining of a concept to the extent that the features are seen as causally central (Rehder and Hastie 2001; Sloman, Love, and Ahn 1998)— causally connected to many other features of the concept. Following Rehder and Hastie (2001), we define causal centrality of a feature as the total number of other features of the self-concept a given feature is seen as causally linked to, as either a cause or an effect. This definition has most consistently explained participants' judgments across our explorations of self-concept representation and identity-based choice (and in particular better than a common alternative definition that suggests that only causing other features counts in the calculation of causal centrality,[2] Ahn et al. 2000; Sloman et al. 1998). However, the issue of the role of causes versus effects in defining causal centrality is still debated (Chen and Urminsky 2019; Rehder and Kim 2010).

While ideas about causal centrality have been influential in the study of people's concepts of categories, there are at least two important ways that the self-concept differs from the concepts in which causal centrality has previously been explored. First, the self-concept is a concept of a single individual (the self) and is not a concept of a category (a set of items). Second, the self-concept, unlike many of the artificial, biological, and artifact categories commonly studied, is one which people have a wealth of knowledge about and may have very idiosyncratic beliefs about. Thus, unlike the commonly studied concepts of categories, the self-concept is both a concept of an individual and a highly individualized concept.

The key prediction of our approach is that features of the self-concept would be seen as defining of the self-concept to the extent that they were seen as causally central. That is, changes to causally central features will disrupt self-continuity more than changes to causally peripheral features. To illustrate, imagine two academics, Stephanie and Oleg, who went to Princeton. Stephanie believes that her experiences at Princeton shaped her choice of profession and many of her academic interests. Oleg instead believes that it was his academic interests that led him to become both an academic and a Princetonian. As a result, even though the features of Stephanie and Oleg's self-concepts are identical, the differences in their causal beliefs lead to differences in what they believe define their self-concept. Because she believes that it is connected to more features of her self-concept (her interests *and* her profession), Stephanie will see being a Princetonian as more defining her self-concept than Oleg does (since he sees being a Princetonian as connected to his academic interests *only*). In contrast, Oleg's interests will be more defining of his self-concept because he sees them as relatively more causally central (connected to both being a Princetonian and to his profession). And, to foreshadow the next section on identity-consistent behavior, the causal centrality approach to the self-concept also predicts that Stephanie will be more likely to follow the norms of being a Princetonian (e.g., donating to the school) than Oleg will be.

As the previous example demonstrates, causal beliefs about the features of the self-concept are subjective—people have different beliefs about how their features fit together. So, the causal centrality approach to the self-concept can explain why a given feature may be more important for some people than to others (i.e., because of differences in the subjective casual beliefs as in the previous example). It can also explain why some features or feature types can, on average, be perceived as more defining of the self (i.e., because they are seen as more causally central by more people).

Chen, Urminsky, and Bartels (2016) tested the hypothesis that changes to features that are more causally connected are perceived as more disruptive to self-continuity than changes to features that are seen as less causally connected (i.e., more causally peripheral). They had participants report which cause-effect relationships they believed existed between sixteen aspects of the self-concept that had been identified as important to the self-concept in previous research (memories, moral qualities, personality traits, preferences/desires; Strohminger and Nichols 2014, see Figure 4.2). As discussed earlier, the causal centrality of a feature was calculated by summing the number of other features a given feature was causally linked to as either a cause or an effect (Rehder and Hastie 2001). Participants also reported how defining each feature was to their self-concept by stating to what extent changing each feature would impact their self-continuity—that is, to what extent they felt that they would still be the same person versus a different person after the change. The results supported our hypothesis: participants reported that changes to causally central features were more disruptive to self-continuity (transformed them into a different individual to a greater extent) than changes to causally peripheral features. Further, people also saw causally central features as more defining of the self-continuity of *other* people, suggesting that causal relationships are an important part of not only the self-concept but also of concepts of other people.

While the results of the experiments described earlier support the hypothesis that features that are seen as causally central are perceived as more defining of the self-concept, a perhaps more interesting question is whether the exact same feature can be made more or less defining by simply changing the feature's causal connections with other features—that is, by changing people's beliefs about how causally central the feature is. This is an important question because many of the accounts of the self-concept discussed earlier emphasize feature type (moral quality, memory, social categories, etc.) as the main determinant of how defining the feature is. However, if changing the perceived causal connections of a feature with other features makes the exact same feature more or less defining, there has to be more that determines how defining a feature is than just feature type—that is, its causal relationships.

To isolate the effect that causal centrality has on how defining a feature is, Chen et al. (2016) manipulated the causal centrality of a feature in descriptions of people's self-concepts. For example, half of the participants read that a person named Jack believes that his memories of being a lonely child caused him to develop a shy personality *and* a preference for solitary activities. Here, Jack's memories were relatively causally central because they were connected to two other features (his shy personality and his preferences for solitary activities). The other half of the participants read that Jack's memories were relatively causally peripheral; they read that Jack had the same three features but believed that his memories were causally connected to only one other feature (his shy personality). Participants were then introduced to a person who had all of Jack's features except for one (e.g., his memories) and judged whether the

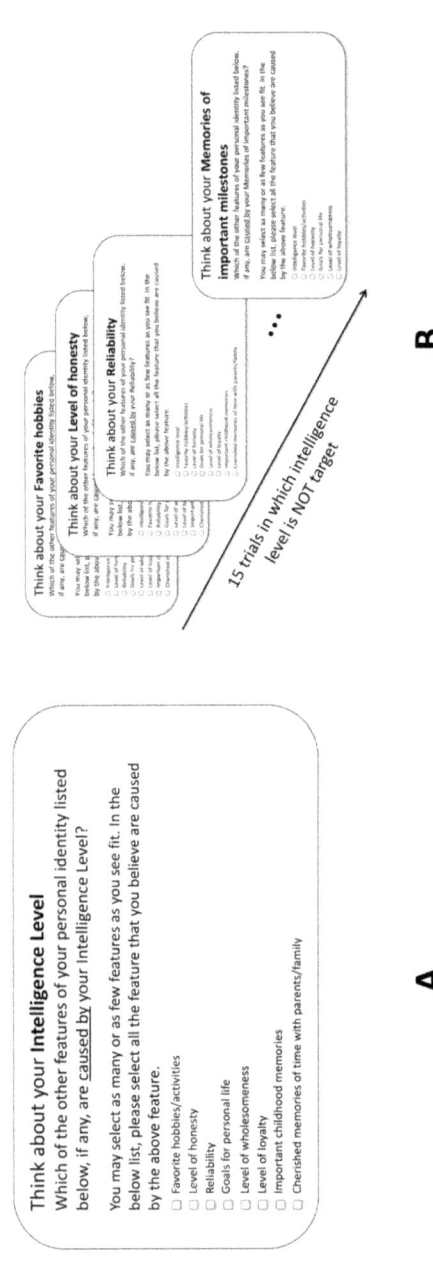

Figure 4.2 Illustration of task used in Chen et al. (2016) to measure the causal centrality of sixteen features of personal identity. Each of the sixteen features was the target feature for one trial, so participants completed sixteen total trials. What follows is an explanation of how causal centrality was calculated for all sixteen features using intelligence level as the example feature. Panel A. Trial in which intelligence level was the target feature. Participants selected all the other features that intelligence level caused from the checklist which included the other fifteen features (truncated in the illustration). From this trial the number of features that intelligence level *caused* is calculated by summing the number of features selected as being caused by intelligence level in this trial. Panel B. In fifteen trials, intelligence level was not the target and was listed in the checklist of possible effects of the target feature. The number of times intelligence level was selected as an effect of other features across these fifteen trials was the number of things that intelligence was *caused by*. The sum of the number of features that intelligence level caused and the number of features that caused intelligence level was the causal centrality of intelligence level.

person was "still Jack." Supporting the theory, people were less likely to say a version of Jack without his memories was "still Jack" when those memories were manipulated to be causally central (as in the first scenario) than when they were manipulated to be causally peripheral. Across a number of features types, manipulating the changed feature to be causally central disrupted the (hypothetical person's) self-continuity more than manipulating the exact same feature to be causally peripheral.

B. Implications for Identity-Consistent Behavior

The notion that more causally central aspects are seen as more defining of the self and more necessary for self-continuity provides a new perspective on the role of social category memberships (i.e., "*social identities*") in people's decisions. A large literature across social psychology, economics, and marketing suggests that behaviors and choices are influenced by the social categories that people belong to (e.g., Akerlof and Kranton 2000, 2010; Markus and Wurf 1987). This research suggests that people who belong to a social category are more likely to act in ways consistent with the norms of that category—display identity-consistent behaviors—than those who do not belong to the social category.

While social identity provides a good explanation for differences in behavior at a *category* level (e.g., people who are vs. are not in the category), it does not provide much insight into variance in identity-consistent behaviors at an *individual* level, among people who belong to the same social category. To explain such variance in identity-consistent behaviors, prior research has largely relied on differences in situational factors, particularly identity salience. In this view, members of a social category are likely to display identity-consistent behaviors to the extent that those social identities are made salient in the environment (LeBoeuf, Shafir, and Bayuk 2010; Reed II 2004). However, two people who belong to the same social category and are in similar situations may still behave differently. We propose that such differences in behavior can be explained, at least in part, by differences in people's internal representations of their self-concept.

The causal centrality approach provides a new way of thinking about differences across people in identity-consistent behaviors. As causally central features are seen as more defining of the self-concept, among people who hold a social identity, those who perceive the social identity as more causally central are predicted to be more likely to act in ways consistent with the norms of the group than those who see the same identity as more causally peripheral. The causal centrality account extends prior theoretical accounts which suggest that aspects of the self influence behavior to the extent that they are seen as important to or central to the self-concept (e.g., Markus and Wurf 1987) by providing a psychological explanation (based on a large literature on conceptual representation) of what makes a particular aspect important to the self-concept.

During the 2016 US presidential election, Chen and Urminsky (2019) investigated whether the causal centrality of political identities (Democrat and Republican) predicted identity-consistent behavior (voting for the party's candidate) among holders of each identity. The day before the election, participants reported the causal relationships that existed between the features of their self-concept, including political party. The day after the election, participants reported who they voted for and their satisfaction with their party's candidate. Running the study at a time when political identity would have been highly salient to everyone allowed us to focus on differences in internal representations, as differences in choice were unlikely to be due to differences in political identity salience.

Consistent with the hypothesis that the causal centrality of a social identity predicts how likely people are to act in identity-consistent ways, participants who saw their political party as more causally central were more likely to vote for their party's candidate,[3] even when controlling for satisfaction with the candidate. These findings suggest that causal centrality of political identity is associated with greater norm-compliance, not just greater preference for the party's candidate (Chen and Urminsky 2019). Thus, among people who personally do not approve of their party's candidate, if their political identity is causally central enough, they may still behave in line with the norms of the group. Chen and Urminsky (2019) also found that among people who identified as British or English, the more causally central they believed that those identities were, the more likely they were to vote for Brexit, consistent with the perceived norms for those nationalities (as reported by the participants).

More recent research using both measured and manipulated causal centrality has extended these findings to a wide range of consumer behaviors. For example, Chen, Urminsky, and Yu (2020) found that the causal centrality of the environmentalist identity among self-identified environmentalists predicted reported willingness to purchase more expensive environmentally friendly products (e.g., rechargeable batteries) over their cheaper traditional counterparts. Further, the causal centrality of the environmentalist identity predicted willingness to purchase environmentally friendly products even when the judgments of identity and the purchase task were separated in time. For example, in one study, the causal centrality of the environmentalist identity predicted willingness to purchase measured one year later. These results suggest that the causal centrality of a social identity predicts a wide range of choices and that an identity's causal centrality may generally be a relatively stable belief that predicts choices over time.

III. Conclusion

As the introduction to this chapter noted, there are many ways to think about personal identity and many judgments that can be made about the persistence of the self over time. While some researchers have aimed to study numerical identity and investigate what changes make a person literally cease to exist, we have aimed to study how people think about personal identity in their everyday lives. A key criterion that we used to identify the types of beliefs about the self that are involved in everyday thought is that they should underlie common forms of decision-making. That is, to understand how people commonly think about the self, we have put beliefs about the self into the context of decision-making and asked: What beliefs drive people's future-oriented decisions and decisions to follow group norms? In both cases, we have found that beliefs about self-continuity, a continuous judgment about how much of the self remains over time, underlie a wide range of choices.

Self-continuity represents a new characterization of beliefs about whether identity persists over time—distinct from numerical and qualitative identity—that has not only allowed for a better understanding of decision-making but also provided insight into judgments of the persistence of the self over time and the representation of the self-concept. Unlike qualitative identity, not all features of the self are equal in shaping judgments about self-continuity. Thus, a key question is why some features impact self-continuity more than others. An emerging line of research reviewed in this chapter has identified causal reasoning as a key determinant of how influential features are on self-continuity judgments and as a critical component of self-concept representation. Continuing to answer questions about why changes to some features impact self-continuity judgments more than others and about how causal beliefs guide these judgments will be key issues for future research, particularly because judgments of self-continuity have important consequences for decision-making.

Notes

1 The notion of self-continuity we introduce here is distinct from notions of psychological continuity that are characterized by lack of variability in psychological connections over time (Parfit 1984).
2 For the self-concept specifically, there is also a theoretical reason to believe that a given feature's causal centrality should not solely be determined by the number of other features of which it is the cause. According to such models, causes are always more central than their effects. Since causes always occur before their effects, these models imply that people would always be more defined by things that happened and/or the features that developed earlier in life than those that happened/developed later. By also including the number of features that a given feature is an effect of in our calculation of causal centrality, what is most defining of the self can change over time—that is, features that develop later in life can become more defining of the self-concepts than their causes.
3 To ensure that the relationship between an identity's causal centrality and choice was not driven by the fact that some participants reported more causal relationships between the features of their self-concept, in general, in the analyses for all studies we controlled for the number of total causal relationships reported.

Bibliography

Ahn, W., N. S. Kim, M. E. Lassaline and M. J. Dennis (2000). "Causal Status as a Determinant of Feature Centrality." *Cognitive Psychology*, 41: 361–416.
Akerlof, G. A. and R. E. Kranton (2000). "Economics and Identity." *The Quarterly Journal of Economics*, 115: 715–53.
Akerlof, G. A. and R. E. Kranton (2010). *Identity Economics: How Our Identities Shape Our Work, Wages, and Well-Being*. Princeton: Princeton University Press.

Bartels, D. M. and L. J. Rips (2010). "Psychological Connectedness and Intertemporal Choice." *Journal of Experimental Psychology: General*, 139 (1): 49.

Bartels, D. M. and O. Urminsky (2011). "On Intertemporal Selfishness: How the Perceived Instability of Identity Underlies Impatient Consumption." *Journal of Consumer Research*, 38: 182–98.

Bartels, D. M. and O. Urminsky (2015). "To Know and to Care: How Awareness and Valuation of the Future Jointly Shape Consumer Savings and Spending." *Journal of Consumer Research*, 41: 1469–85.

Blok, S., G. Newman and L. J. Rips (2005). "Individuals and Their Concepts." In W. Ahn, R. L. Goldstone, B. C. Love, A. B. Markman and P. Wolff (eds.), *Categorization Inside and Outside the Lab*, 127–49. Washington: American Psychological Association.

Chen, S. Y. and O. Urminsky (2019). "The Role of Causal Beliefs in Political Identity and Voting." *Cognition*, 188: 27–38.

Chen, S.Y., O. Urminsky and D. M. Bartels (2016). "Beliefs About the Causal Structure of the Self-Concept Determine which Changes Disrupt Personal Identity." *Psychological Science*, 27: 1398–406.

Chen, S.Y., O. Urminsky and J. Yu (2020). "We Do What We Are: Representations of the Self-Concept and Identity-Based Consumption." http://home.uchicago.edu/ourminsky/WeDoWhatWeAre_Chen_Urminsky_Yu.pdf

Damasio, H., T. Grabowski, R. Frank, A. M. Galaburda and A. R. Damasio (1994). "The Return of Phineas Gage: Clues About the Brain from the Skull of a Famous Patient." *Science*, 264 (5162): 1102–5.

De Freitas, J., M. Cikara, I. Grossmann and R. Schlegel (2018). "Moral Goodness is the Essence of Personal Identity." *Trends in Cognitive Sciences*, 22 (9): 739–40.

Dranseika, V. (2017). "On the Ambiguity of 'the Same Person.'" *AJOB Neuroscience*, 8: 184–6.

Ersner-Hershfield, H., M. T. Garton, K. Ballard, G. R. Samanez-Larkin, and B. Knutson (2009). "Don't Stop Thinking about Tomorrow: Individual Differences in Future Self-Continuity Account for Saving." *Judgment and Decision Making*, 4 (4): 280.

Frederick, S. (2003). "Time Preference and Personal Identity." In G. Loewenstein, D. Read and R. Baumeister (eds.), *Time and Decision*. New York: Russell Sage Foundation, 89–113.

Frederick, S., G. Loewenstein and T. O'Donoghue (2002). "Time Discounting and Time Preference: A Critical Review." *Journal of Economic Literature*, 40 (2): 351–401.

Frederick, S., N. Novemsky, J. Wang, R. Dhar and S. Nowlis (2009). "Opportunity Cost Neglect." *Journal of Consumer Research*, 36: 553–61.

Gelman, S., G. Heyman and C. Legare (2007). "Developmental Changes in the Coherence of Essentialist Beliefs About Psychological Characteristics." *Child Development*, 78 (3): 757–74.

Haslam, N., B. Bastian and M. Bissett (2004). "Essentialist Beliefs About Personality and Their Implications." *Personality and Social Psychology Bulletin*, 30 (12): 1661–73.

LeBoeuf, R. A., E. Shafir and J. B. Bayuk (2010). "The Conflicting Choices of Alternating Selves." *Organizational Behavior and Human Decision Processes*, 111 (1): 48–61.

Markus, H. and E. Wurf (1987). "The Dynamic Self-Concept: A Social Psychological Perspective." *Annual Review of Psychology*, 38 (1): 299–337.

Molouki, S. and D. M. Bartels (2017). "Personal Change and The Continuity of the Self." *Cognitive Psychology*, 93: 1–17.

Mott, C. (2018). "Statutes of Limitations and Personal Identity." In T. Lombrozo, J. Knobe and S. Nichols (eds.), *Oxford Studies in Experimental Philosophy*, Vol. 2, 243–69. Oxford: Oxford University Press.

Newman, G. E., J. De Freitas, and J. Knobe (2015). "Beliefs about the True Self Explain Asymmetries based on Moral Judgment." *Cognitive Science*, 39 (1): 96–125.

Nichols, S. and M. Bruno (2013). "Intuitions about Personal Identity: An Empirical Study." In Joachim Horvath and Thomas Grundmann (eds.), *Experimental Philosophy and Its Critics*, 23–42. New York, NY: Routledge.

Parfit, D. (1984). *Reasons and Persons*. Oxford: Oxford University Press.

Reed II, A. (2004). "Activating the Self-Importance of Consumer Selves: Exploring Identity Salience Effects on Judgments." *Journal of Consumer Research*, 31 (2): 286–95.

Rehder, B. and R. Hastie (2001). "Causal Knowledge and Categories: The Effects of Causal Beliefs on Categorization, Induction, and Similarity." *Journal of Experimental Psychology: General*, 130 (3): 323–60.

Rehder, B. and S. Kim (2010). "Causal Status and Coherence in Causal-Based Categorization." *Journal of Experimental Psychology: Learning, Memory, and Cognition*, 36 (5): 1171–206.

Rips, L. J., S. Blok, and G. Newman (2006). "Tracing the Identity of Objects." *Psychological Review*, 113 (1): 1.

Rosch, E. and C. B. Mervis (1975). "Family Resemblances: Studies in The Internal Structure of Categories." *Cognitive Psychology*, 7: 573–605.

Sloman, S., B. C. Love and W. Ahn (1998). "Feature Centrality and Conceptual Coherence." *Cognitive Science*, 22 (2): 189–228.

Spiller, S. A. (2011). "Opportunity Cost Consideration." *Journal of Consumer Research*, 38: 595–610.

Starmans, C. and P. Bloom (2018a). "Nothing Personal: What Psychologists Get Wrong About Identity." *Trends in Cognitive Sciences*, 22 (7): 566–8.

Starmans, C. and P. Bloom (2018b). "If You Become Evil Do You Die?" *Trends in Cognitive Sciences*, 22 (9): 740–1.

Strohminger, N. and S. Nichols (2014). "The Essential Moral Self." *Cognition*, 131: 159–71.

Strohminger, N. and S. Nichols (2015). "Neurodegeneration and Identity." *Psychological Science*, 26 (9): 1469–79.

Tajfel, H. (1978). *Differentiation between Social Groups: Studies in the Social Psychology of Intergroup Relations*. London: Academic Press.

Urminsky, O. (2017). "The Role of "Psychological Connectedness to the Future Self" in Decisions Over Time." *Current Directions in Psychological Science*, 26 (1): 34–9.

Urminsky, O. and D. M. Bartels (2019). "Identity, Personal Continuity and Psychological Connectedness Across Time and Over Transformation." In A. Reed II and M. Forehand (eds.), *Handbook of Research on Identity Theory in Marketing*, 225–39. Northampton: Edward Elgar.

Urminsky, O. and G. Zauberman (2016). "The Psychology of Intertemporal Preferences." In G. Keren and G. Wu (eds.), *The Wiley Blackwell Handbook of Judgment and Decision Making*, 141–81. Chichester: John Wiley and Sons.

5

Personal Identity and Morality

Harold Noonan

I

Does the true account of personal identity undermine everyday moral thinking? Do every day moral practices presuppose a false account of our nature and persistence conditions? For example, it seems a fundamental platitude of our moral thought that only the doer of a deed merits punishment or reward for it (call this "the principle of the moral necessity of agency"). But this principle is challenged in the debate about personal identity from the mid-twentieth century. Can it be retained? Another principle challenged, also seemingly fundamental to our moral thought, is what I shall call "the principle of the intrinsicality of moral status": no relation any sentient being has to another can deprive it, qua patient, of moral status. I shall consider the three main accounts of personal identity in the contemporary literature: the neo-Lockean psychological continuity account presented paradigmatically by Shoemaker (1963, see also Shoemaker and Swinburne 1984), animalism (as defended by Olson (1997, 2003) and David Lewis's perdurance account (1983, 1986). In each case it will be concluded that the account is inconsistent with what we take to be fundamental elements of our moral thought being so.

II

I begin with the contemporary neo-Lockean psychological continuity account of personal identity, the paradigm of which is Sydney Shoemaker's. This, of course, developed from Locke's account, which is intended to be in accordance with the status of "person" as a "forensic term appropriating actions and their merits, [which] belongs only to intelligent agents, capable of a law, and happiness and misery" (Essay II, xxvii.26), whence, according to Locke, "in this personal identity is founded all the right justice of reward and punishment; happiness being that for which everyone is concerned for himself, and not mattering what becomes of any substance not join to or affected by that consciousness" (Essay II, xxvii.18). Nevertheless, as Parfit's famous argument (1971, 1984) reveals, it follows from the neo-Lockean story, at least its paradigmatic form, that personal identity lacks the foundational moral status Locke affirms, but is of merely derivative importance. It is not fundamentally "what matters."

The basis for the contemporary neo-Lockean account is the argument based on the "transplant case," which makes it all but undeniable that suitably caused psychological continuity can in some circumstances be sufficient for personal identity.

Shoemaker (1963) tells the story. In the late twenty-first century surgeons can transplant brains and brain parts, specifically cerebra. Suppose that the cerebrum of a Mr. Brown is transplanted into the skull of a Mr. Robinson, with consequent transference of psychological traits. The resultant person, Brownson, is a completely healthy person, with Robinson's body, but in character, memories, and personality traits quite indistinguishable from Brown, not as a consequence of a freak accident but because of his possession of Brown's cerebrum. Now who will this person be?

Most modern philosophers, reflecting on this case, have found that they could not honestly deny that Brownson is Brown, and so they have been led to accept, as Parfit puts it (1984: 263), that "receiving a new skull and a new body is just the limiting case of receiving a new heart, new lungs and so on."

The position to which this "transplant intuition" seems to point is that personal identity is constituted by psychological facts. The essence of this is that, given the importance for our attitudes toward persons of their memories, character, and personality traits, continuity in respect of these should be taken to constitute personal identity—whether or not caused by the persistence of some bodily organ, such as the brain; and absence of continuity in these respects entails absence of personal identity.

This position is called "neo-Lockean," of course, because the simplest version of it is suggested by Locke's discussions. Reading Locke to mean memory by "consciousness" we arrive at the memory criterion of personal identity.

Contemporary neo-Lockeans revise this in two ways. First, they say that other psychological facts as well as memory must be mentioned in defining personal identity. In general, any causal links between past psychological facts and present psychological facts can be subsumed under the notion of "psychological connectedness." Secondly, they introduce the notion of psychological continuity, to mean the obtaining of overlapping chains of psychological connections, to ensure conformity with the transitivity of identity.

At this point the problem of fission raises its head. Consider the variant of the Brown/Brownson case in which only half of Brown's brain is transplanted with consequent transfer of psychological traits, the other half being destroyed. The neo-Lockean must say this preserves personal identity. But now consider the case—the fission case—in which both hemispheres are transplanted, but into different heads. Both later people cannot be the same as the one original. But there is nothing to choose between them. So we must say that neither is. But then psychological continuity is not a sufficient condition of personal identity.

Most psychological continuity theorists, including Shoemaker (in Shoemaker and Swinburne 1984), respond to this problem by revising the psychological continuity account to make psychological continuity sufficient for personal identity only absent an equally good rival candidate. This is to reject the principle, the only x and y principle (Noonan 2019), implicit in a seminal argument given by Bernard Williams (1956–7, see also his 2014: Chapter 39), that, to put it roughly, whether an individual x is identical with an earlier individual y can depend only on facts about them and the relations between them; no facts about any individuals other than x or y can be relevant (for less rough formulations, see Noonan 2019).

To see the intuitive objection to the revised continuity account, consider the fission case again. Suppose I am told that my brain is to be divided into two and then the two halves transplanted into different heads. Then, according to the revised psychological continuity account, I know that I will cease to exist, and two new people will come into being. However, I know that if someone destroys the right brain hemisphere before it is transplanted, thereby eliminating the plurality of candidates, I will continue to exist and be the recipient of the left-brain hemisphere. Thus, according to the revised psychological continuity criterion, in this case my continued existence is logically dependent upon the non-existence of someone, the person resulting from the right brain hemisphere transplant, who would not be me even if he were to exist. But how can my continued existence thus be logically dependent on the non-existence of someone else?

Reflecting on the fission case with these considerations in mind leads Parfit to his remarkable thesis that identity is not what matters in survival. Thinking about this will lead us on to the question whether the neo-Lockean psychological continuity account accords with our everyday moral thinking.

To get clear before turning to the argument for it we must first see what Parfit's thesis means.

What it means is that, contrary to what we are all inclined to think, we do not have a non-derivative concern for our own future existence. What is of fundamental importance to us is that there be in the future people related by psychological continuity to ourselves as we are now—call these our Parfitian survivors. My having a Parfitian survivor tomorrow guarantees, as things are, that I will exist tomorrow, but it does not entail it, and in conceivable circumstances, like fission, the two come apart. Parfit's thesis is that given our fundamental desires we would have no reason, in such a conceivable circumstance, to prefer a situation in which we continued to exist to one in which we had merely a multiplicity of (equally comfortably off) Parfitian survivors.

Intuitively this is very implausible. We can imagine a society in which *Star Trek* variety teletransportation is in general use as a means of transportation of inanimate objects and food animals—even though it is acknowledged that it is not transportation at all but, in reality, the destruction of one object and the creation elsewhere of a mere replica. But if we try to imagine that the people in this society, *while continuing to acknowledge that this is what the process really involves*, nonetheless allow themselves and their loved ones to be teletransported and regard teletransportation as a convenient alternative to travel, we run into immediate difficulties; at first sight it seems as if we have succeeded only imagining a society of madmen.

But according to Parfit we have not. These people are acting as it would be rational for us to act, *given our actual non-derivative desires*, if we lived in their society and shared their beliefs in the destructive nature of the teletransportation process. For our fundamental desires do *not* include a desire for our own continued existence but merely one for the future existence of a Parfitian survivor.

Parfit's argument for this thesis arises from reflection on the fission case. And to understand it we need to make a distinction between two types of opinion that reflection on such puzzle cases about personal identity generates. First, there are opinions about how the language of personal identity is to be applied to the case, what the true statements about personal identity to be made about it are. These opinions reflect our mastery of our language and particularly those parts that are expressive of the concept of personal identity. In short, they reflect our semantic intuitions. They are akin to our opinions about identity in puzzle cases about non-persons, such as, for example, the case of the Ship of Theseus (Noonan 2019). But thinking about puzzle cases about personal identity generates opinions of a second sort. These are opinions about how it is rational for the people whose identity is at issue in the case to behave, given the beliefs they are described as holding. These opinions reflect our fundamental desires. For we arrive at them by imagining *ourselves* to be involved in the case and asking how *we* should then rationally behave.

Parfit's argument for his thesis can be explained as follows. First, he describes a fission case. Next, he argues that (a) the correct description of the case, the one which accords with our semantic intuitions, is that the original person ceases to exist but would not have done so if only one of the fission products had existed, and that the fission products are new existents (in accordance with the revised psychological continuity criterion of personal identity), but that (b) the correct opinion about what it is rational to do in such a case, the one in accord with our fundamental desires, is that it would be quite irrational, if you were the original in the case, to be concerned about your impending fission as you would be about an impending heart attack, or to think that you could gain anything by preventing the fission by ensuring that only one hemisphere was transplanted (if you were given the choice), even though it is correct there were you to do so you *would* ensure your own future existence. (See also Shoemaker's exposition in Shoemaker and Swinburne [1984: 119] where this choice situation is emphasized.) The conclusion is then that this *combination* of opinions can be explained only by accepting that the fundamental desires we have are not the ones we think we have and do not include a desire for our own future existence; that desire, which we do have, is a merely derivative one, and what it is derivative from is a desire for a future Parfitian survivor, which as a matter of fact, as things are, we can ensure only by ensuring our own continued existence.

The argument can be resisted by denying that the description of the fission case given in (a), the description implied by the revised psychological continuity criterion, is correct. An alternative is to say that no one ceases to exist when the fission takes place. Rather, two people who have been spatially coincident now become spatially distinct. But if no one ceases to exist when the fission takes place of course it must be absurd to view it as death. This multiple occupancy view is the straightforward consequence of accepting Bernard Williams's only x and y principle. Given the intuitiveness of this principle it cannot be regarded as an absurd view, but it is a minority one.

Another way of resisting the argument is to deny that we do have the type (b) opinion about fission. Few have taken this line; one who does is Jerome Schaffer who writes:

> Psychological continuity is important where there is identity, but not otherwise. Returning to our case of the man who splits, we would say that since identity is not preserved even though psychological continuity is preserved, the man should feel quite differently about it from the way he should feel about single transplantation. (1977: 157)

However, the difficulty with this is just that it is just so plausible that we have the (b)-type opinion.

But it is obvious that if we accept Parfit's conclusion we must abandon the principle of the moral necessity of agency, that only the doer of a deed merits punishment or reward for it, as a fundamental element of our everyday moral thinking.

Of course, as things are, fission does not happen. But imagine a society in which it does—and where it is frequently occurring and can be voluntarily chosen. And suppose that in the society people still have only the fundamental desires which according to Parfit we actually have, that is, they do not have a non-derivative desire for their continued existence. Then a legal system and societal norms in accordance with the principle of the moral necessity of agency would be wholly inappropriate.

Locke writes, in support of his claim that "person" is a forensic term: "in this personal identity is founded all the right justice of reward and punishment; happiness and misery being that for which everyone is concerned for himself" (Essay II, xxvii.18). Here what follows the semicolon is intended to give a reason for what precedes. But if Parfit is right, what follows the semicolon is false. Hence in the society imagined, in which, perhaps merely because of the advanced state of medical technology, fission is frequent, reward and punishment founded on personal identity would be purposeless. For people would not be much motivated to act well by the prospect of reward given only to the doers of good since fission would too often supervene before any reward was possible; nor would they be motivated to refrain from wrong-doing by the prospect of future punishment meted out only to evildoers since they could easily avoid it by choosing fission. Thus, if Parfit is right, the principle of the moral necessity of agency is not a fundamental part of our moral thinking but merely a rule of thumb the utility of which depends very largely on the present limited state of medical technology.

III

The same conclusion can be derived if animalism is accepted. The reasoning is parallel.

Animalism is the claim that we, you and I, and any other readers of this book at least, are animals of a certain kind, human beings. So we have the persistence conditions of human beings; and these involve *no* sort of psychological continuity whatsoever. Psychological continuity is irrelevant to personal identity because it is irrelevant to the persistence of animal identity generally. Hence for each of us there was a time when he was a fetus, but not a person, possessed of no psychology whatsoever, and again for some of us there will be times in the future, after brain damage or decay when we will still exist, but merely as human beings, not persons, wholly devoid of any psychological life. In addition, in the cerebrum transplant case, the person does not go with the cerebrum since no animal does; he remains, devoid of a cerebrum and entirely without psychology. However, if the entire brain, including the brain stem, the biological control center of the human animal, is transplanted, the person (i.e., the animal), who is the original owner of the brain, goes with it.

This animalist position is, of course, wholly opposed to the neo-Lockean account, and the strongest argument against it is the main argument for the latter, the transplant argument. Animalists must therefore respond to it.

Eric Olson does so by an appeal to Parfit's thesis that identity does not matter. The recipient of the cerebrum transplant, he says, does have what matters in the survival of the donor. Therefore, the donor has the same reason to care about the welfare of the recipient as you have to care about your own welfare. It is the recipient who should be held responsible for the donor's actions, and, rather than the surviving donor (if provided with cerebrum replacement), who should be regarded for practical reasons as the same person. These facts cause us to believe, mistakenly, that the recipient is the donor. We recognize that he is the Parfitian survivor, and so we mistakenly believe he has what matters for identity. Olson suggests that we use "the same person" in ordinary speech in a "practical" sense in which it expresses not numerical identity but just the holding of those relations of psychological continuity and connectedness which according to Parfit matters in survival. His "bold conjecture" is that (in a cerebral transplant version of Locke's cobbler-prince example): "The fact that Brainy is the same person after the operation as Prince was before it in this practical sense of 'same person' is the main source of the transplant intuition" (1997: 69).

Of course, this explanation depends on Parfit's thesis being correct. But as we have seen it is controversial; additionally, it is not clear that an animalist can endorse it.

Parfit's argument rests on the claim that our opinions about the fission are in accord with a "best candidate" account, so that whether I continue to exist depends on whether there is anyone who is *uniquely* best qualified to count as me at the later time (as will be the case if the fission is botched but not if it is successful). This conflicts with Williams's only x and y principle.

But it is not at all obvious that an animalist should endorse the uniqueness requirement on a sufficient condition of personal identity. Olson himself writes, "no one accepts the Uniqueness Requirement because it sounds right. The transplant intuition has led us into a quandary and the Uniqueness Requirement is seen as the best way out; it is a theoretical necessity" (Olson 1997: 49). However, if the animalist is to endorse Parfit's argument for his thesis, so that he can call on it to explain the seeming evidence of the transplant intuition, he must accept the uniqueness requirement. Thus, the transplant intuition seems to remain a very strong argument against animalism.

But there are also strong arguments for animalism, in particular, the thinking animal argument, also called the "too many thinkers" argument, which points out that since it is undeniable that human and other animals are thinkers it appears to follow that, according to the neo-Lockean position, there are two thinkers where I am, the person and the thinking animal, and that there are at least twice as many highly sophisticated thinking beings on this planet as there are persons.

So let us assume the correctness of animalism and ask what it implies about everyday moral thinking. The first thing to note is that the animalist can argue for Parfit's thesis in his own way without needing to appeal to the problematic uniqueness requirement on the condition of personal identity that Parfit's own argument requires.

Imagine that:

> Your brain stem is replaced by an inorganic substitute . . . bit by bit. The rest of you is left intact . . . there is never a period when your life-sustaining functions are left without an organ to coordinate them, or when your cerebrum is not aroused and coordinated in a normal way by a brainstem. As a result, there need be no interruption of consciousness throughout the operation (suppose the surgeon uses only a local anaesthetic). The result would be a conscious rational being with your mind. . . . [Animalism] entails that you would not survive this. The resultant being would not be you . . . it would not be a human being at all. For something with an inorganic brainstem would not be an animal at all. . . . If you are an animal you will not survive without an [organic] brain stem. (Olson 1997: 141–2)

Now suppose that you are faced with a choice between this operation (inorganic replacement) and an operation in which your brain stem is repaired and patched up, retaining its biological identity (maybe your brain stem is riddled with cancer so either replacement or repair is necessary). In each case the outcome is a person psychologically continues with you. The difference between brain stem repair and patch up and inorganic replacement makes no difference to that. According to animalism, our opinion about this case, if we reflect on it carefully, should be (a) that we do not persist through inorganic replacement of brainstem but do persist through repair. But reflection on this case also generates, Olson would insist, and very plausibly, the opinion (b) that it would be quite irrational if you were facing this choice to prefer repair to inorganic replacement (as irrational as preferring to have your heart repaired rather than replaced if both procedures were equally safe and effective) or to think that you could gain anything by choosing repair, even though it is correct to say that by doing so you would ensure your own future existence. The conclusion is then Parfit's: to reconcile these opinions we must say that we in fact have no non-derivative desire for our continued existence.

Imagine now a society with advanced medical treatment technology in which brain stem replacement by inorganic substitutes is a frequent occurrence and easily obtainable. Also suppose the people still have only the fundamental desires which, according to Parfit we actually have, that is, they do not have a non-derivative desire for their own continued existence. Then a legal system and societal norms according with the principle of the moral necessity of agency would be wholly inappropriate. In this society, given the advanced state of medical technology, reward or punishment founded on personal, that is, animal, identity would be purposeless. For people would not be much motivated to act well by the prospect of rewards given to the doer of good deeds since brainstem replacement would too often intervene; nor would they be motivated to refrain from acting wrongly by the prospect of future punishment meted out only to evildoers, since they could easily avoid it by electing for brain stem replacement. Thus, if animalism is correct, the principle of the moral necessity of agency is again revealed as a mere rule of thumb, the utility of which depends very largely on the present limited state of medical technology.

IV

I now turn to the Lewis's perdurance account of personal identity. Perdurantism is, in fact, neutral concerning the dispute over the role of psychological continuity in the explanation of personal identity. A perdurantist can think this as crucial or totally irrelevant. According to the perdurantist, persons persist by having temporal parts at different times. For our present purposes the crucial thing is that for him their temporal parts are the *subjects* of mental states, as persons are. Lewis explains this very clearly:

> A person stage is a physical object, just as a person is . . . . It does many of the . . . things that a person does: it walks and talks and thinks, it has beliefs and desires. (Lewis 1983: 76)

The apparent conflict between the perdurance view and our everyday thinking is immediate. We think it unproblematic that in some circumstances at least, when there are no extenuating circumstances or excuses, and no other person (or animal) will suffer as a consequence, an evildoer should be punished for his deeds. But according to the perdurantist view, whenever punishment is meted out, some subject of psychological states, who only fails to be a person because he is part of a temporally longer one and is entirely innocent of the crime since he did not even exist when it was committed, is punished or at least made to suffer along with the morally responsible agent.

The apparent conflict is more general, as Olson (2010) and Johnston (2016, 2017) bring out. Olson calls the psychologically endowed temporal parts of persons the perdurantist posits "subpersons" and Johnston calls them "personites." They note that, for example, if there is a subperson/personite now coinciding with me, which will no longer exist tomorrow, this renders morally problematic my planned visit to the dentist today since the subperson/personite, unlike me, will suffer the pain today but not live long enough to experience gain. The same reasoning renders morally problematic spending time learning a difficult language for a trip abroad. And irritatingly, in accordance with this reasoning, the child who claims that making him do his homework isn't fair is arguably right. Moreover, since not only subpersons/personites as well as persons exist if perdurantism is the case, but also, for example, what we might call "subdogs" or "caninites," and these also need to be counted in the moral calculus, at least if dogs do, it follows that just as it is morally problematic to force a lazy child to do homework, it is morally problematic to put an obese dog on a diet. Underpinning the reasoning here is the principle of the intrinsicality of moral status, the thought that no relation one sentient being can have to another can deprive it of the right to be counted in the moral calculus (qua patient). *Being the wife of* cannot, *being a child of* cannot, *being the creation of* cannot. Nor can *being a temporal part of*. Thus, it seems that the perdurantist's ontology does not accord with our fundamental moral thinking.

It renders morally problematic activities which according to our ordinary thinking are utterly unproblematic.

As Olson and Johnston note the conflict is not merely between perdurantism and ordinary moral thought. Any "generous" ontology which includes short-lived person-like entities or short-lived dog-like entities, and so on, coincident with longer-lived persons or dogs, generates the same conflict; it does not matter whether they are correctly thought of as parts of longer ones; it matters only that they can suffer.

In fact, seen in this way the challenge to the generous ontologist from our everyday moral thinking is anticipated by Locke. Locke has a tripartite ontology. He distinguishes not only between persons and human beings (men, as he puts it) but also between these and thinking substances, which may be material or immaterial:

> It is not . . . unity of substance that comprehends all sorts of identity . . . but we must consider what idea it is applied to stand for; it being one thing to be the same substance, another the same man and a third the same person, if *person*, *man*, and *substance* are three names standing for three different ideas. (Essay II, xxvii.7)[1]

Hence it may be that:

> Different substances by the same consciousness [are] united into one person . . . For it being the same consciousness that makes a man be himself to himself personal identity depends on that only, whether it be annexed to one individual substance, or can be continued in the succession of many. (Essay II, xxvii.9)[2]

So Locke notes, the question whether "if the same [immaterial] thinking substance be changed it could be the same person?" cannot be resolved "but by those who know what kind of substance they are they do think and whether the consciousness of past action can be transferred from one thinking substance to another" (Essay II, xxvii.13). He goes on:

> But why one intellectual substance may not have represented to it, as done by itself, what it never did, and perhaps was done by some other agent, will be difficult to conclude from the nature of things. And that it never is so will by us, till we have clear views of the nature of thinking substances, be best resolved into the goodness of God, who as far is the happiness or misery of any of his sensible creatures is concerned in it will not, by a fatal error of theirs, transfer from one to another that consciousness that draws reward or punishment with it.[3]

Locke's thought is that if, as his tripartite ontology allows, one thinking substance may be conscious of the actions of another, the two will make but one person. But then in punishing that person for his sins God will make suffer the thinking substance then coincident with it, even if it was never present at any past crime. So it will be punished for what it never did but was done by some other agent.

This is too much for Locke, so he appeals to God's goodness to rule out such a "fatal error." But his concern is clearly the same as Olson's and Johnston's about the generous ontology, and contemporary generous ontologists cannot answer the challenge by appeal to such a deus ex machina.

V

It appears from the forgoing that to ensure absence of conflict with our everyday moral thinking and to allow the fundamental place in our moral thought of the principles we have discussed (the principle of the moral necessity of agency and the intrinsicality of moral status) an account of personal identity (a) must not involve a generous ontology, (b) cannot deny the relevance of psychology to personal identity, and (c) must be consistent with the only x and y principle. These constraints rule out the familiar accounts of Lewis, Olson, and Shoemaker. What is left?

Notes

1 Excerpt from "John Locke, An Essay Concerning Human Understanding" © 1975 Oxford Publishing Limited (Academic). Reproduced with permission of The Licensor through PLS clear.
2 Excerpt from "John Locke, An Essay Concerning Human Understanding" © 1975 Oxford Publishing Limited (Academic). Reproduced with permission of The Licensor through PLS clear.
3 Excerpt from "John Locke, An Essay Concerning Human Understanding" © 1975 Oxford Publishing Limited (Academic). Reproduced with permission of The Licensor through PLS clear.

Bibliography

Johnston, M. (2016). "Personites, Maximality and Ontological Trash." *Philosophical Perspectives*, 30: 198–228.
Johnston, M. (2017). "The Personite Problem: Should Practical Reason be Tabled?" *Noûs*, 51: 617–44.
Lewis, D. (1983). *Philosophical Papers*, Vol. I. Oxford: Oxford University Press.
Lewis, D. (1986). *On the Plurality of Worlds*. Oxford: Blackwell.
Locke, J. (1694 reprint 1975). *An Essay Concerning Human Understanding*. Oxford: Oxford University Press.
Noonan, H. (2019). *Personal Identity*, 3rd ed. London: Routledge.
Olson, E. (1997). *The Human Animal*. New York: Oxford University Press.
Olson, E. (2003). "An Argument for Animalism." In R. Martin and J. Barresi (eds.), *Personal Identity*, 318–34. Oxford: Blackwell.
Olson, E. (2010). "Ethics and the Generous Ontology." *Theoretical Medicine and Bioethics*, 31: 259–70.
Parfit, D. (1971). "Personal Identity." *The Philosophical Review*, 80 (1): 3–27.
Parfit, D. (1984). *Reasons and Persons*. Oxford: Oxford University Press.

Shaffer, J. (1977). "Personal Identity." *Journal of Medicine and Philosophy*, 2:147–61.
Shoemaker, S. (1963). *Self-Knowledge and Self-Identity*. Ithaca: Cornell University Press.
Shoemaker, S. and R.G. Swinburne (1984). *Personal Identity*. Oxford: Blackwell.
Williams, B. A. O. (1956-7). "Personal Identity and Individuation." *Proceedings to the Aristotelian Society*, 57: 229–52.
Williams, B. A. O. (2014). *Essays and Reviews: 1959-2002*. Princeton: Princeton University Press.

6

The Whole Story

Identity and Narrative

Marya Schechtman

The burgeoning use of experimental methods to consider questions of human nature and personal identity has been a fruitful and exciting development. Rigorously designed studies investigating how we think about these concepts have yielded robust and sometimes surprising results, especially concerning our moral evaluation of the true self. As welcome and important as this new methodology has proved, this chapter argues for the value of focusing also on another long-used means of gaining insight into how we think about identity and human nature, namely reflection on the treatment of these themes in narrative fiction. The case for fiction is not based on a suggestion that experimental methods are defective, only incomplete. The brevity and clarity of experimental vignettes, which is a great strength of the experimental approach, also imposes limitations. The format of fiction allows for exploration of forms of messiness and ambiguity inherent in the human condition that are harder to investigate in an experimental context. Questions of identity and morality are complex and multidimensional, and different aspects of these questions call for different approaches. Bringing these two approaches into dialogue thus promises to yield broader and richer insights than are obtained by relying on either alone.

I begin with a brief review of some experimental results that have been interpreted as implying that we tend to believe people are fundamentally morally good (Section 1), after which I look at an alternate interpretation of these results that has been offered within experimental philosophy (Section 2). I turn next to an example from fiction which touches on the debate introduced in Sections 1 and 2, reflecting on the way in which viewers are led to judge Tony Soprano in the television series *The Sopranos* to be intrinsically bad (Section 3). Next, I contrast how viewers make moral judgments about Tony Soprano with how participants make moral judgments in responding to an experimental vignette involving a professional assassin. This juxtaposition shows how the more expansive nature of fiction can explain the divergent reactions found in these two contexts, underscoring the importance of remaining clear on the distinction between generic and individual questions about moral nature (Section 4).

I. The True and the Good

A striking series of recent studies suggests that we tend to believe that people are fundamentally good "deep down." This conclusion is gleaned from a variety of experiments which reveal asymmetrical responses to a range of different vignettes depending upon their moral valence. For instance, when an agent acts on desires that conflict with her beliefs participants are more inclined to say that she "values" what she is doing if they view her desires as morally good than if they view them as morally objectionable (Knobe and Roedder 2009). Someone who acts on overwhelming and irresistible emotion is judged by participants to deserve less blame for a bad action than someone who acts coolly on considered motives, even though someone who is driven by overwhelming emotion to perform a morally good action is not typically seen as less praiseworthy than someone who undertakes such an action as the result of coolheaded deliberation but, if anything, as more praiseworthy (Pizarro, Uhlmann, and Salovey 2003).

One explanation that has been given for these and related asymmetries in judgment is that they stem from the implicit assumption that the true self is morally good. Faraci and Shoemaker (2019: 606) call this the "good true self" (GTS) theory. Further investigation, aimed at testing directly whether assumptions about the nature of the true self mediate these responses, supports this interpretation. Newman, De Freitas, and Knobe (2015), for instance, undertake a series of five experiments. Four reproduce existing experiments that generate asymmetrical judgments based on moral valence with the addition of a separate question about whether the relevant actions or attitudes represent the agent's true self. The fifth directly manipulates beliefs about the true self and measures effects on the application of the concepts involved in the asymmetries.

For what follows it will be useful to have an example in hand, and here I choose one that will serve as a useful foil to the fictional case I will consider later. One of the studies Newman et al. undertook replicated an earlier study by Sousa and Mauro (2015) involving asymmetries in judgments concerning weakness of will. Sousa and Mauro gave one group of participants the following vignette:

> John is a professional assassin. He has started to think about quitting this profession because he feels that it is wrong to kill another person. However, he is strongly inclined to continue with it because of the financial benefits.
>
> John is in conflict, but after considering all aspects of the matter, he concludes that the best thing for him to do is to quit his profession. Accordingly, he decides that the next day he will look for a job that does not involve violence.
>
> The next day, while still completely sure that the best thing for him to do is to look for a job that does not involve violence, John is swayed by the financial benefits. Against what he had decided, he kills another person for money.

Another group received a modified version of this vignette:

John is in conflict, but after considering all aspects of the matter, he concludes that the best thing for him to do is to continue with his profession. Accordingly, he decides that the next day he will kill another person for money.

The next day, while still completely sure that the best thing for him to do is to kill another person for money, John is swayed by the feeling that it is wrong to kill. Against what he had decided, he looks for a job that does not involve violence. (Reproduced in Newman et al. 2015: 14–16)

Although each condition involves John acting against what he has decided to do, and so, on most philosophical accounts, as exhibiting weakness of will, participants tended to judge him to be weak of will only in the first condition, where he acts immorally against his good impulses, and not in the second, where he acts morally against immoral impulses.

Newman et al. not only replicated these results but also asked participants to respond to a question about whether the agent went against his true self in the action. The results indicated that beliefs about the true self did in fact mediate the judgments about weakness of will. The other studies produced similar results. These findings are taken to provide strong evidence for the view that the asymmetries based on moral valence are, as the authors suggest, "symptoms of a single unified phenomenon: the tendency to assume that, deep down, others are morally good" (Newman et al. 2015: 28). Other studies (e.g., Tobia 2015) have produced similar results. There is, however, always room for another point of view. The next section considers an alternate interpretation of these data proposed by Faraci and Shoemaker.

II. An Alternative Explanation

Faraci and Shoemaker approach these issues through work on attributability theory, the view, roughly, that "for an agent to be the proper target of praise or blame *for* the action of a particular moment, that action must be expressive *of* that agent" (2019: 607), it must, in other words, represent the deep or true self. In this context, Faraci and Shoemaker (2014) had conducted studies that had revealed asymmetries in attributions of praise and blame consistent with those found by others. These studies employed four scenarios involving a white male named Tom. Tom_A was raised in New Orleans and taught to respect all people equally but as an adult decides to embrace the identity of a proud racist. When he is twenty-five, he encounters a Black man who has tripped and fallen outside his home and, in keeping with his beliefs, spits on the man as he walks by. Tom_B was raised on an isolated island in the bayous of Louisiana and was taught, growing up, that all non-white people are inferior. As an adult he embraces what he has been taught. When he is twenty-five, he encounters a Black man who has tripped and fallen outside his home and, in keeping with his beliefs, spits on the man as he walks by. Participants overall found Tom_A to be more blameworthy for his action than Tom_B. The presumption was that Tom_B's morally impoverished background led subjects to attribute his action to him less fully, and hence to find him less culpable than Tom_A.

At the same time, however, they included a second set of cases about which they surveyed additional participants. Tom_C, like Tom_A, was taught to respect all people equally but decided, as an adult, to embrace racism. Like the previous Toms, at age twenty-five he encounters a Black man who has fallen in front of his home, but unlike them, Tom_C goes against his considered moral beliefs and helps the man up. Tom_D, like Tom_B, was raised on an isolated island and taught to believe that all non-white people are inferior, a view he embraces as an adult. Like the others, at age twenty-five he encounters a fallen Black man in front of his house and, like Tom_C helps him up despite his beliefs that he should spit on him. In these cases, subjects were asked about praiseworthiness, and were inclined to say that Tom_D was *more* praiseworthy than Tom_C. This asymmetry raises questions about the simple hypothesis that a morally deprived upbringing decreases attributability and so mitigates both blame and praise.

Faraci and Shoemaker's original thought was that this difference could be accounted for by the "Difficulty Hypothesis," that moral ignorance of the sort depicted in the cases of Toms B and D affects assessments of blameworthiness or praiseworthiness insofar as it affects the level of difficulty involved in doing the right thing. The idea is that it is more difficult for Tom_B than for Tom_A to help the Black man, given how he was raised, so he is less blameworthy. Likewise, it was more difficult for Tom_D than for Tom_C to recognize the rightness of helping the Black man up, so he deserves extra praise. While this is an intuitive explanation for the asymmetries, the work of Newman et al. inspired them to undertake a new study to see if the response was mediated by beliefs about the true self. Their results replicated those of Newman et al., suggesting that despite their parallel childhood deprivation and moral ignorance, participants judged Tom_A and Tom_B as both being less themselves when spitting on the Black man, and Tom_C and Tom_D as both being more themselves when they helped him up.

While these findings do support the GTS theory, Faraci and Shoemaker point out that these are not the only relevant data. Within these and other experiments are also examples of cases where we judge bad actions to be more representative of the true self than good ones. In their own studies, they note, subjects tended to judge Tom_A to be more blameworthy for spitting on the Black man than Tom_C is seen to be praiseworthy for helping him up. If the true self were straightforwardly figured as the good self, one would expect the opposite to be true. Earlier work by Knobe, moreover, showed that when presented with a case where a CEO doesn't care about how a decision about company policy will predictably affect the environment, participants tend to judge those environmental effects as intentional when they are detrimental, but unintentional when they are positive (Knobe 2006) quoted in (Faraci and Shoemaker 2019: 616).

Faraci and Shoemaker (2019: 619) acknowledge that these data do not show the GTS theory to be false, but they do speak against the claim that it is the obvious interpretation of experimental results. They thus suggest an alternative hypothesis. This alternative interprets our patterns of attribution as showing that we judge bad behavior as representative of the true self in the absence of another available explanation. It is widely recognized, they point out, that imperfect conditions can cause someone who is not intrinsically bad to act badly. When someone behaves badly, it *might* be because she is a bad person deep down, but it also might be because she is under intense stress or overcome with emotion she cannot control. As an alternative to the GTS theory, which sees the data as showing that participants assume that people are good deep down, and so that bad actions almost never represent the true self, Faraci and Shoemaker propose instead what I will call the "benefit-of-the-doubt" (BD) theory. BD theory holds that that when an excusing explanation of bad behavior is available we will, to a point at least, give the agent the benefit of the doubt, assuming that it is some interfering condition rather than intrinsic badness that is responsible for the bad action (2019: 617–20).

Faraci and Shoemaker acknowledge that this is only one possible interpretation of the data, and that the GTS theory can also explain them. They thus suggest the need for further investigation of the precise nature of our moral assessments in these cases and their relation to judgments about the true self. Presumably, they are thinking most immediately of further work in experimental philosophy, and undoubtedly there is a great deal of progress to be made in this way. There is, however, another venue in which questions about our patterns of attribution and assessment are explored, and that is narrative fiction. There is reason to hope that such explorations also have something to add to our overall attempts to understand these difficult matters. In the next section I describe a narrative that bears directly on the questions Faraci and Shoemaker raise.

III. The Good, the Bad, and the Complicated

The past few decades have been hailed by many as a golden era of television because of the rise of "prestige dramas" like *Breaking Bad* and *The Sopranos*, which are recognized as serious aesthetic accomplishments. In each of these dramas we are presented with a complex, charismatic, and fascinating character who engages in horrific, immoral behavior. It is generally agreed that viewers who watch these series are ultimately forced to acknowledge that these characters are truly bad deep down.

The protagonists of these series are what A. W. Eaton calls, taking a phrase from Hume, "rough heroes" (2012: 281). The defining features of rough heroes can be seen by contrasting them with antiheroes. The latter, though flawed, have redeeming features which ultimately outweigh their deficits. The rough hero, by contrast, has flaws that are "grievous" and "an integral part of his personality rather than peripheral failings or foibles." He "fully intends to do bad and is remorseless about his crimes." The narratives in which these heroes are portrayed do not offer "reasons to dismiss his misdeeds as the result [of] misfortune, weakness, folly, or ignorance," and his "vices are not outweighed by some more redeeming virtues" (Eaton 2012: 284). Examples of rough heroes outside of prestige dramas include Humbert Humbert in *Lolita*, Satan in *Paradise Lost,* and Alex in *A Clockwork Orange*. It is a critical feature of rough heroes, Eaton argues, and the unique aesthetic accomplishment of the works that contain them, that we simultaneously recognize them as deeply and intrinsically bad and feel a sympathetic attraction to them. To get the viewer to see them as they truly are, it is necessary to get them to overcome whatever tendencies we have to see people as fundamentally good or benefit of the doubt we are inclined to give in judging them. By offering an extended and detailed picture of a case in which we do overcome initial impulses to judge a character positively, these dramas thus potentially have something to say about when and how we come to judge someone to be fundamentally bad, including the role excusing explanations might play.

To explore what might be learned by reflection on a fictional narrative, I take Tony Soprano as my example, since his case will present a useful contrast with the vignette about John the assassin presented earlier. There is general critical agreement that Tony Soprano is an extraordinarily complex and intriguing character. He is a mob boss, who lives an extremely violent life and regularly commits monstrous, immoral acts. He is also, however, a husband and father who loves his family and friends and does a great deal to enhance their well-being. He is charming, affable, and intelligent. We learn that Tony had an upbringing of deep moral deprivation: that his mother was an abusive and uncaring parent and that growing up he received none of the love or attention humans need to thrive. As an adult, he is vulnerable and sensitive. At the beginning of the series, he suffers a panic attack which leads him to therapy. His therapist links his symptoms to the departure of a family of ducks that had been nesting in his pool. His investment in the ducks, she suggests, represents his deep investment in his family and fear of abandonment. Throughout the series we see him attend therapy sessions and undertake various other efforts aimed at self-improvement, all of this alongside intensely vicious actions and general moral depravity.

We have, of course, seen complicated and conflicted mob bosses before in fiction. The Mafioso with a heart of gold, who commits despicable acts but is fiercely loving and loyal to family and friends, has a rigid code of honor that he follows scrupulously, and is pushed to his life of crime through external forces, is a paradigmatic antihero. What makes Tony Soprano different is that although the series frequently invites the viewer to understand him in just this way, it also repeatedly undercuts attempts to do so. He *is* genuinely good to his family and friends, often supporting and mentoring them, but he also regularly betrays and hurts them, sometimes turns on them violently, and is willing to murder those close to him if they become inconvenient, seemly with no real remorse. He *is* vulnerable and sensitive at times, but he is also often remarkably callous and unconcerned about the pain he causes to others, even those he loves. He gestures toward a code of honor, but violates it readily, and although he does try to improve, he is not interested in doing any difficult work in this regard and easily becomes bored with the project. Tony is without question an immensely complicated person. Unlike the antihero Mafioso, however, in the end, he does not seem terribly conflicted.

Crucial for our purposes is the way in which the different sides of Tony's personality emerge over time. The viewer starts out clear that Tony is a violent man who acts immorally but is also immediately exposed to his positive traits and vulnerabilities. Moving the viewer from an assessment of Tony as a tragic antihero to the recognition that he is a truly disturbing and violent rough hero takes a carefully orchestrated set of incidents through which viewers are repeatedly invited to accept an excusing explanation of Tony's behavior of the sort Faraci and Shoemaker suggest, only to see him then behave in a way so violent or insensitive or malicious that it is not only difficult to find any explanation other than malevolence for the current behavior but also increasingly difficult to believe that bad behavior explained away earlier is not, after all, representative of who Tony truly is deep down. After many iterations of this cycle, the viewer is forced to conclude that Tony is, as Eaton puts it, "a liar, a thief, an extortionist, and a womanizer; he is pathologically callous, selfish, bigoted, racist, homophobic, and self-centered" (2012: 281).

I have suggested that reflection on fictional treatments of these issues can provide useful insights to complement experimental work. In the next section I provide an example of the way in which thinking about *The Sopranos* might contribute to discussion of these topics.

IV. Implications

One way to see the kind of contribution fiction is especially well placed to make is to contrast the story of Tony Soprano with the vignette of John the assassin, mentioned earlier. A television series that follows a character over multiple seasons will obviously contain a great deal more detail about his behavior and the possible causes for it than a vignette designed for experimental purposes. In the case of Tony and John, this is a difference that potentially makes a difference in the way we assess their behavior and its relation to their true nature. There are isolated incidents within the trajectory of Tony Soprano in which he decides not to carry out some particular act of violence but ends up doing so anyway. Presented with only this sequence of events, the viewer is likely to judge that Tony has displayed weakness of will as participants in the experimental studies judge John to do. This would be the initial step in the dynamic described in the last section. Seen within the context of the entire series, however, viewers are likely in the end to revise that initial judgment and conclude that in fact Tony did exactly what he wanted to do. That is the final step of an extended dynamic that is possible to portray in fiction, but not in an experimental vignette.

What, then, do we learn from considering the more extended and detailed depiction of Tony's reversal rather than the more abbreviated one that we find in the case of John? One might take the differing judgments in the cases of John and Tony to support BD theory over the GTS theory. It seems that in viewing *The Sopranos* viewers do offer Tony the benefit of the doubt up to a point, but when excusing explanations are no longer viable, they withdraw it and conclude that he is bad. While I find this an intriguing possibility, it is a conclusion that we cannot draw without more work. There are two reasons. First, the GTS theory does allow that we can, in rare and extreme circumstances, judge someone to be fundamentally bad. The data, after all, do not show that all participants always judge everyone to be entirely good. Second, the case of Tony does not quite show excusing explanations to be discarded. While ultimately viewers tend to judge that he cannot be excused for what he does, it is not as if what had been taken as excusing explanations are shown to be false; they just play a somewhat different role in his life than we originally thought. Further reflection on the nature of excusing explanations thus seems indicated. While I think that there is real potential for further reflection on Tony's case to shed light on the dispute between the GTS theory and BD theory, more work is required to determine just what the implications are.

Another possible conclusion is that the judgments that come from reflection on fictional accounts are somehow more reliable than those found in experimental philosophy, since they are based on more complete information. There is clearly a great deal that speaks against this conclusion, however, at least as a general claim. The detail found in fictional narrative is bought at the cost of the control, quantifiability, reproducibility, and generalizability experimental philosophy offers. *The Sopranos* generates judgments about and reactions to one (fictional) man, one that leads a very unusual life. There is no straightforward route from our judgments about Tony Soprano to our judgments about people in general. I have talked about how viewers react to Tony's exploits, but data about how "we" react to Tony, while I believe it to be generally accurate, is collected in a highly unsystematic way. There is nothing, in the case of fiction, like the concrete responses to survey questions found in experimental philosophy, and so no firm data about what percentage of viewers felt exactly what way about Tony's actions or true self. In multiple senses, then, the judgments that come from the data in experimental philosophy are more reliable than those that come out of discussing fiction.

The contributions of reflection on fictional narratives that I would argue for thus lie not in providing additional or different data of the sort that experimental philosophy collects. Fiction will always be worse at that. Juxtaposing these different ways of thinking about moral assessment of the true self can, however, help to distinguish different kinds of questions about the moral assessment of the true self, and to see that different methods may be indicated depending on which we are asking. Looking at the cases of Tony and John side-by-side uncovers a certain ambiguity about what question is being answered by participants in the experimental studies. On the one hand, there is a question about human nature—whether humans as a kind are fundamentally good. On the other hand, there is a question about a particular person, whether Phineas, or John, or Tony is fundamentally good.

The experimental vignettes, in some sense, ask about particular people. There are protagonists, and they have names. Since the information given about each is so limited, however, it is not clear that they are really being interpreted as about particular individuals by the participants as opposed to being seen as generic representatives of humankind. In everyday life, it is a truism that if you want to know whether someone is truly good (or bad) deep down, you need to know more than a few sentences about his history and the circumstances of one particular action he took. Nonetheless, participants in the experimental setting subjects *do* make such judgments, based on just such information, and the judgments they make are remarkably consistent. Since there is little particular information about the people in these vignettes, and since it is, after all, general information we are looking for, it is reasonable to assume that in making them participants are consulting their generic views about what humans are like (as the GTS theory implies) or what protocols we should use for judging humans in general (as BD theory suggests). Either way, however, these results yield conclusion about how we morally assess *people* in general, and not about how we assess a particular person.

The difference between these questions can be made sharper by looking at how experimental philosophers have characterized what it means to say that we take the true self to be fundamentally good. Shoemaker and Tobia (in press) mention two possibilities for thinking about the picture of the true self that explains the asymmetries in moral assessment found in the experimental data. One refers to essences, suggesting that human nature is seen as essentially good and so that any deviation from goodness is a corruption of one's true essence (e.g., Strohminger, Knobe, and Newman 2017).

Another emphasizes teleological persistence, suggesting that moral improvement represents a person's true purpose (e.g., Rose, Tobia, and Schaffer 2020). What these and related accounts have in common is that claims about the good true self are normative rather than descriptive, either insofar as fundamental goodness is seen as criterial for humanness or as the proper purpose of humans. Neither version implies that all, or even most, individual humans are actually good, only that insofar as they are not good, they deviate from the way humans are "meant" to be.

The question of individual nature, however, while it is a moral judgment and so normative in that sense, is descriptive insofar as it captures the particularities that make an individual the unique character that he is, including the various ways in which he deviates from generic human nature. To say that Tony is fundamentally bad is to say that his badness is an intrinsic part of who he is as an individual. Determining this, I have suggested, requires more information than can be supplied in an experimental vignette. If we are interested in determining whether *this* person is fundamentally good or evil, rather than whether *people* are, it is necessary to look at the confluence of choices and influences and opportunities in his life. Presenting these details is something that fiction is well suited to do. Following an individual through a narrative and coming to an ultimate judgment about his nature will not provide a set of general conditions under which we judge an individual to be good or bad but, as I hope the case of Tony Soprano shows, it can provide general insights about what goes into making such determinations.

Recent work by Knobe (in press) challenges the distinction I have just drawn between questions about the fundamental nature of generic humans and that of individuals. Knobe proposes using the framework of dual character concepts to explain asymmetric judgments in cases of moral change. This framework applies in situations where we recognize that an individual formally falls under a particular category but also feel that it fails to instantiate the truest norms of that category. The person who engages in scientific research but has no intellectual curiosity is in some sense a scientist but is "when you think about it" not really a scientist at all. Similar claims may be made of the artist who writes and performs punk rock but is motivated by banal commercialism, or the churchgoer who is merely going through the motions. Knobe suggests that something similar may be at work in our assessments of identity through moral change.

On the surface, this framework seems to favor the distinction between generic and individual questions of one's nature that I have been urging. We have on the one hand the question of what it means to *really* be a scientist, or Christian, or punk rocker, and on the other hand a question about *this* individual who in some crude, formal sense falls under one of these categories but fails to instantiate the true nature of the kind. Knobe argues, however, that preliminary research suggests that we make similar kinds of judgments about individuals.

When subjects are presented with a scenario like that in Tobia (2015) where someone named Phineas changes from a morally good person to a morally bad one, they tend to agree with the statement: "There's a sense in which the man after the accident is clearly still Phineas, but ultimately, if you think about what it really means to be Phineas, you'd have to say that he is not truly Phineas at all" (Knobe in press).

This can be interpreted to show that the nature of the individual is just an instance of the nature of the kind. Since Phineas is a human, what it means to "really be" Phineas is what it "really means" to be human, and when Phineas loses the good essence of humankind, he ceases to be himself.

If this is right, the question I suggested was better addressed by fiction just *is* an example of the general question experimental philosophy is especially well placed to answer. This is not, however, the only way to interpret Knobe's results. Given the very limited information provided about Phineas in these vignettes, participants may well be taking him to stand in for generic humanity in the way I described in the previous paragraphs. Phineas Gage is a specific individual, but this Phineas is really just "a person named Phineas." Some support for this suggestion is found in the results obtained in the condition where Phineas is described as changing from a morally bad person to a morally good one. When participants in this condition are presented with the question about whether he is truly Phineas at all after the change, their "judgments were all over the place. Some agreed with the dual character statement, others disagreed" (Knobe in press). A possible explanation for this result is that in the moral improvement case, Phineas's initial moral badness presents him immediately as an individual who does *not* instantiate paradigmatic humanness, and this may signal some participants to interpret this as a case in which they are asked about the individual nature of a specific person rather than about generic humanity. The variable answers may thus result from the difficulty of making such judgments with limited information.

Obviously, more investigation is needed to draw any conclusions here, and additional work in experimental philosophy is going to be an essential part of this investigation. If the distinction between generic and individual questions can be maintained, however, there is also work in which reflection on fictional treatments of these matters is especially well suited to do. In any event, bringing these considerations into the mix can only help us to recognize that these questions can be asked either about particular individuals or about humans as a kind, and to think more clearly about how these two types of questions are related to one another.

Experimental work is without question a valuable addition to philosophical discussions of personal identity. It provides controlled, qualified, and reproducible data about how key concepts are understood, and has produced a great many valuable and provocative results. The very strengths of these experiments in investigating the questions for which they were designed can, however, represent drawbacks in other contexts. There are many dimensions to our thinking about human nature, and correspondingly different questions about the moral nature of the true self. To map out, let alone civilize, this messy and exciting terrain will require multiple tools in our methodological toolbox. Luckily, we have a great many, and there is a great deal to be hoped for as we learn how to use them together.[1]

Note

1 I am grateful to Kevin Tobia, Joshua Knobe, and David Shoemaker for immensely helpful comments on an earlier draft of this chapter.

Bibliography

Eaton, A. (2012). "Robust Immoralism." *The Journal of Aesthetics and Art Criticism*, 70 (3): 281–92.

Faraci, D. and D. Shoemaker (2014). "Huck vs. JoJo: Moral Ignorance and the (A)symmetry of Praise and Blame." In T. Lombrozo, J. Knobe and S. Nichols (eds.), *Oxford Studies in Experimental Philosophy*, 7–27. Oxford: Oxford University Press.

Faraci, D. and D. Shoemaker (2019). "Good Selves, True Selves: Moral Ignorance, Responsibility, and the Presumption of Goodness." *Philosophy and Phenomenological Research*, 98 (3): 606–22.

Knobe, J. (2006). "The Concept of Intentional Action: A Case Study in the Uses of Folk Psychology." *Philosophical Studies*, 130: 203–31.

Knobe, J. (in press). "Personal Identity and Dual Character Concepts." In K. Tobia (ed.), *Experimental Philosophy of Identity and the Self*. London: Bloomsbury.

Knobe, J. and E. Roedder (2009). "The Ordinary Concept of Valuing." *Philosophical Issues*, 19: 131–47.

Newman, G. E., J. De Freitas and J. Knobe (2015). "Beliefs About the True Self Explain Asymmetries Based on Moral Judgement." *Cognitive Science*, 39: 96–125.

Pizarro, D. A., E. Uhlmann and P. Salovey (2003). "Asymmetry in Judgments of Moral Blame and Praise: The Role of Perceived Metadesires." *Psychological Science*, 14: 267–72.

Rose, D., K. Tobia and J. Schaffer (2020). "Folk Teleology Drives Persistence Judgments." *Synthese*, 197: 5491–509.

Shoemaker, D. and K. Tobia (in press). "Personal Identity." In M. Varga and J. Doris (eds.), *Oxford Handbook of Moral Psychology*. Oxford: Oxford University Press.

Sousa, P. and C. Mauro (2015). "The Evaluative Nature of the Folk Concepts of Weakness and Strength of Will." *Philosophical Psychology*, 28 (4): 487–509.

Strohminger, N., J. Knobe and G. Newman (2017). "The True Self: A Psychological Concept Distinct from the Self." *Perspectives on Psychological Science*, 12: 551–60.

Tobia, K. P. (2015). "Personal Identity and the Phineas Gage Effect." *Analysis*, 75: 396–405.

7

What Matters in Psychological Continuity?

Using Meditative Traditions to Identify Biases in Intuitions about Personal Persistence

Preston Greene and Meghan Sullivan

I. Egoistic Concern and the Method of Thought Experiments

Thought experiments have played a central role in philosophy since at least the time of the Greeks, and they have long served as evidence for and against theories, as means of exploring the entailments of commitments and as probes for exposing concepts and values latent in our thinking. In recent decades, academic philosophy has become more interested in studying not only the intuitions elicited by thought experiments but also the potential biases that act on these intuitions. The question is no longer simply, "What is the intuitive answer?" but "What could explain why this answer feels intuitive?" In some cases, the explanation for why a particular response to a thought experiment feels intuitive appeals to processes that we have discovered to be unreliable, noisy, or systematically influenced by arbitrary considerations. This, in turn, has made academic philosophers more sophisticated in their use of thought experiments. These improvements are thanks in large part to the contributions of experimental philosophers and greater interdisciplinarity between philosophy, psychology, and other social sciences.

Our focus in this chapter is on how this methodological expansion can be further developed within the study of one subfield of philosophy: psychological continuity theories of personal identity and egoistic concern.

This is a topic where, from Descartes and Locke onward, the method of thought experiments has been central to philosophical argument. Take as a case study Jeff McMahan's agenda-setting 2002 book *The Ethics of Killing*. McMahan opens with an extended defense of a psychological connectedness theory of egoistic concern. He conducts a close conceptual analysis of what we take to matter when it comes to being the same person over time and change. His goal is to distill principles which we can then use to make arguments about what we ought to care about in margins of life and radical change cases—abortion and miscarriage, mental and physical change, and death. McMahan's opening chapter on egoistic concern and personal identity has fifteen extended thought experiments, with topics like "Whole Body Transplantation" and "Teletransportation." In each thought experiment, you are asked to imagine a situation where some aspect of your mind or physical organism is changed and then register the extent to which the change would cause you to be less concerned for the resulting person's interests. With this method, he follows Derek Parfit (1984), who deploys similar thought experiments in defending his view that psychological connectedness is the rational and ethical basis for self-concern. Similar examples can be found throughout the recent literature on personal identity. They often serve the claim that concern for the self over time ought to diminish as the self undergoes psychological changes.

McMahan assumes (in line with many philosophers) that there is a reliable route from imaginatively engaging with a thought experiment to realizing a conceptual truth about how change affects normative judgments about the self. Consider McMahan's (2002: 77) reasoning about a case he calls *The Cure*:

> Imagine that you are twenty years old and are diagnosed with a disease that, if untreated, invariably causes death (though not pain or disability) within five years. There is a treatment that reliably cures the disease but also, as a side effect, causes total retrograde amnesia and radical personality change. Long-term studies of others who have had the treatment show that they almost always go on to have long and happy lives, though these lives are informed by desires and values that differ profoundly from those that the person had prior to treatment. You can therefore reasonably expect that, if you take the treatment, you will live for roughly sixty more years, though the life you will have will be utterly discontinuous with your life as it has been. You will remember nothing of your past and your character and values will be radically altered. Suppose, however, that this can be reliably predicted: that the future you would have between the ages of twenty and eighty if you were to take the treatment would, by itself, be better, as a whole, than your entire life would be if you do not take the treatment.[1]
>
> Would it be egoistically rational for you to take the treatment? Most of us would at least be skeptical of taking the treatment and many would be deeply opposed to it.

The thought experiment is meant to reveal that we care about the connectedness of memory and personality more than we care about (disconnected) improvements to well-being.

This method of thought experiments aims to be both psychologically descriptive and rationally probative. And for both of these projects, the method partially answers to standards of evidence from psychology. Do people have the patterns of egoistic concern that philosophers hypothesize? And upon reflection, do we think the patterns of egoistic concern revealed by these thought experiments are justified? Recent work in social psychology has raised challenges for thought experiments on both counts, indicating that our intuitions on these examples are vulnerable to a bias—we tend to dissociate from negatively valenced moral or social changes and to associate with positively valenced moral or social changes. This is one of the primary upshots of recent work on "good true self" attributions in social psychology (Tobia 2015; Shoemaker and Tobia forthcoming; Strohminger, Knobe, and Newman 2017). Though we discover many desires, intentions, and personality features through introspection, we tend to distinguish an enduring "true self" around a cluster of psychological traits that house and develop our morally and socially valued characteristics.

This effect becomes a bias when we realize that thought experiments like McMahan's *Cure* are meant to reveal metaphysical data but are likely to be influenced by features of the case that are irrelevant to the facts of personal persistence (Strohminger et al. 2017).[2] Why think our self histories are ones of uninterrupted moral and social improvement? As Strohminger et al. (2017: 7) put it: "The true self is posited rather than observed. It is a hopeful phantasm." Consider a thought experiment that is structurally similar to *The Cure* but does not involve illness or disability. We might call this thought experiment *The School*:

> Imagine you are eighteen years old, from a working-class background, and offered a full scholarship to attend an elite university far from your family. This experience is known to significantly, rapidly, and permanently shape your personality, desires, and values over the next five years.

Would you be indifferent between dying and attending the school? More importantly, what intuitions differ between *The Cure* and *The School*? Perhaps the psychological disconnection in the positive valence school case feels far less threatening to self-interest than the negative valence disease case. And if we reflect on these intuitions, we realize that the brute metaphysical facts about being a persisting self shouldn't depend on arbitrary factors like whether the relevant change is caused by education or disability. This bias becomes still more urgent once we realize how many of the philosophical thought experiments (like *The Cure*) involve imagined disability or otherwise negatively valenced changes.[3]

If this reasoning is on the right track, then our ability to think clearly about personal identity and egoistic concern has improved thanks to our newfound awareness of a bias in our intuitive judgments, and this bias has been revealed with the help of social-scientific methods. Research into cognitive biases is useful to philosophy not because it establishes philosophical conclusions directly, but instead because it sometimes calls into question the intuitions that are behind such conclusions. In some cases, the relevant biases are general and far-reaching: for example, ethical theory has benefited from awareness of the fact that our intuitions tend to be affected by whether an event is framed as a loss or a gain, and epistemology has benefited from awareness of how our intuitions are distorted as events change from "near certain" to merely "probable."[4] In other cases, research on biases is more targeted to specific philosophical intuitions, like the "good true self" effect discussed earlier.

One potential methodological principle to draw from this is that philosophers should pay more attention to empirical psychological research. This is true. Nevertheless, we submit that the more general, and better, lesson to be drawn is that *philosophical theorizing can be improved by greater awareness of potential biases in intuitive judgments*. Notice that if we are committed to the latter principle, we should be interested in the identification of biases *however it occurs*. In other words, we should cultivate as many resources as we can for identifying biases in intuitions that are relevant to philosophical theorizing.[5]

What resources for identifying biases are currently available but underutilized? Plausibly, the answer depends on the domain of philosophical inquiry. For theories of personal identity, especially those that focus on psychological continuity, we contend that a rich and underutilized potential source of data are traditions of *sustained inquiry into the direct observation of the mind*—a practice which is often called "meditation."

"Meditation research" in academia tends to refer to empirical research on the biological and psychological effects of meditation. In contrast, there is currently little precedent for treating meditation as a tool for *conducting* research, though some philosophers have in recent times advocated for the use of meditation in this role.[6] A primary contention of this chapter is that a third option is available, and it reveals a role that meditative traditions can and should play in philosophical discourse. In this role, meditation is not used to directly establish metaphysical, epistemological, or ethical claims, but to reveal potential illusions or biases in the intuitions of philosophers engaged in the standard analytic methodology.

Of course, claiming that data from meditative traditions *can* play this role is not yet to show how that is best accomplished. In the context of philosophical theories of personal identity, we believe the main barrier to the incorporation of meditative insights is the misperception that if taken seriously, this data would only push toward grand conclusions about the erroneous nature of Western philosophical reasoning— conclusions such as "there is no self."[7] Instead, in this chapter we try to show how meditation traditions can play the more reasonable role of revealing potential biases (which, in the context of Buddhist meditative traditions, are usually called "illusions" or "delusions") that are relevant to philosophical thinking about personal identity.

The claim that we will focus on in this chapter is that there is a ubiquitous tendency to misidentify ourselves with our thoughts, emotions, memories, aspects of our personality, or combinations of these. This is a consistent report from many meditative traditions, and we will have much more to say about it in the next section. The claim is intriguing because if true, it seems to cut at the heart of much philosophical theorizing about personal identity over time, and especially that which focuses on the method of thought experiments. In philosophical discussions of psychological connectedness views, it is taken for granted that we identify a persisting self with our thoughts, memories, intentions, and the like, and the changing personality is viewed as inextricably linked with the changing self. (Recall, for instance, the role that changes to memory and personality are assumed to play in McMahan's *The Cure*.) We might call this the *dualistic assumption* in personal identity. According to several traditions of inquiry into our nature—most immediately Buddhist meditation practice—this dualistic perspective is a *delusion*. You are *not* your memories, desires, emotions, thoughts, or any combination of these. And if this really is a delusion, then it is one that could affect the layperson in the same way that it affects philosophers as venerable as Descartes.

Our primary task in this chapter will be to interpret reports on the identification delusion in a way compatible with developing the psychological connectedness theory of rational egoistic concern within analytic philosophy. So, our study is one *within* the study of psychological connectedness theory, which nevertheless draws on uncommon or underexplored resources in the existing literature. As our task is such, we will not present an in-depth analysis of Buddhist theory, but instead introduce applied material as appropriate to reveal a potential bias in intuitions about thought experiments concerning psychological connectedness. We hope that the view we formulate is plausible as a model for study by psychologists and philosophers, without any necessary appeal to scripture or mystical writing offered to defend this as a religious tradition.

Our thesis is that people who have undergone the sustained inquiry into the observation of their psychologies, in many cases over a lifetime, have insights worth paying attention to when interpreting the results of the method of thought experiments as applied to psychological connectedness theories of personal identity over time. Thus, we claim that psychological connectedness views can be improved by incorporating data from meditative traditions, and that the improvement can be seen most clearly in thinking about potential biases in intuitions about cases of psychological change. According to the positive proposal we will sketch, the basis for psychological connectedness and egoistic concern is less susceptible to change than intuitions gleaned from the method of thought experiments would suggest—there is a foundational form of experience, or what we call "ur-experience," that may be the subject of what matters and the basis for self-persistence. We present evidence for this proposal from new and underappreciated sources in Western analytic philosophy, namely a tradition of Tibetan Buddhist meditative practices.

II. Meditation and Methodology

We should at the outset say more about our conception of Buddhist meditation and what forms of it we take to be most relevant to this project. This is important because we will be focusing on a different type of practice from those often associated with the current "mindfulness" movement in the West—with which we expect our readers to be most familiar. We will argue that these types of meditation are not the most useful practices for the purposes of analytic philosophy. So, it will be helpful for us to say more about the kind of practice from which we aim to draw insights.

"Meditation" can mean many different things depending on the context. Empirical research on meditation practices categorizes them into three types: (1) focused attention, (2) open monitoring, and (3) nondual awareness.[8] As Albahari (2019a: 19) explains:

> Meditation is . . . the systematic training of attention to go against that current of mind which keeps it unwittingly lost in the content of various objects to enable, eventually, a keen percipience of the objects' status as unfolding, present-moment events. The attention can for instance be trained to (1) focus on one object (such as the breath, mantra, or an idea of God), perhaps eliciting states of absorption [focused attention], or (2) become aware of different objects as they arise and

pass away [open monitoring], or (3) go beyond objects to the field of conscious awareness in which they arise and pass away [nondual awareness meditation].

In the West, books on "mindfulness," as well as meditation centers and teachers, almost exclusively engage with Theravada or Zen traditions of Buddhism (e.g., *vipassana*) that emphasize (1) and (2)—focused attention and open monitoring. These styles of meditation are sometimes described as "dualistic" because they "contain an essentially dualistic orientation of 'subject-observing-object'" (Josipovic 2010: 1120). For example, meditators might be instructed to sit and pay attention to their breath and encouraged to gently return to the breath when they become lost in thought or their attention wanders to something external (focused attention). Meditators with some experience may be invited to simply sit and notice thoughts and emotions come and go, without attempting to direct the flow of their experience (open monitoring). These are the kinds of practice that most Westerners associate with the mindfulness movement.

All Buddhist meditation practices aim for the practitioner to achieve some degree of enlightenment or awakening to insights about the nature of reality. However, a common feature of focused attention and open-monitoring practices is that they are *indirect* and *gradual*. They are indirect because they aim to shift the mental makeup of the practitioner to a place where they arrive at nondual insights independently. And they are gradual in that they view the process of achieving the insights as proceeding slowly over a very long period of time with great effort. Aspiring meditators are often encouraged to meditate for an hour or more a day in their normal circumstances, and to go on sustained meditation retreats that can last for months or even years.

Nondual awareness meditation, in contrast, reverses this process (at least in some traditions—more on this in the following paragraphs). Nondual awareness meditation often begins by *directly pointing out* an aspect of conscious experience that goes unnoticed in the everyday mind. By receiving this pointing-out instruction, the person glimpses a nondual way of perceiving the world. They are then encouraged to remind themselves of what has been pointed out during "short moments" as they go about their lives (Mingyur Rinpoche and Tworkov 2019: 52). This practice helps shift the mind into a place where recognition of the insights is sustained and natural. Thus, the process of awakening is reversed in the sense that recognition of insights drives a shift in one's mental makeup, as opposed to a shift in mental makeup driving the recognition of insights. In the Tibetan Buddhist nondual awareness tradition *Dzogchen*, this is described as "taking the goal of meditation as the path" (Josipovic 2010: 1120).

There are psychological benefits touted from all three forms of meditation.[9] And all have practices that are taken as legitimate routes to awakening within the traditions. Nevertheless, traditions that emphasize nondual awareness meditation are particularly suited to the task of gleaning insights from practitioners for the purposes of philosophical inquiry. After all, the methodology of the practice proceeds by *the direct pointing out of the insights*, as a method to foster further practice. Of course, it is not the case that one can fully appreciate the nature of an insight without sustained engagement with the practice. Even so, if one has an open mind, there is at least a chance to glean something of value, even at the very beginning. In contrast, few people are inclined to spend the better part of a lifetime training their mind with dualistic practice, including philosophers.

Consider another prominent nondual awareness tradition, *Sutra Mahamudra* (sometimes called "Mahamudra"),[10] a tradition in Tibetan Buddhism that its practitioners claim offers a "direct path" to awakening that is "especially swift" (Dorje 2003: xiii). This practice, according to the Dalai Lama, goes "straight to the point" (Dalai 2003: xi). Mahamudra was initially developed not by people living in monasteries but instead by lay practitioners in India looking for a way to awaken within the context of everyday life. As Dzogchen Ponlop Rinpoche explains: "[Mahamudra] is seen as a very profound method because it does not require any of the sophisticated and complex tantric rituals, deity yoga visualization practices or [vows] . . . Sutra Mahamudra has a tradition of skillful means that contains profound methods of directly pointing out the selfless and luminous nature of mind."

So, what insights about the nature of the self does Mahamudra reveal, and how do these bear on what matters in psychological continuity? We can distinguish between two projects. One is the negative project of pointing out what we are *not*—the common illusions that occur when people try to understand themselves, which are claimed to afflict the vast majority before meditation training. The other is the more positive project of describing what we are—the features of our *nature of mind* (*rigpa* in Tibetan Buddhism). In what follows, we focus on the negative project for two reasons. First, because the negative project alone is (nearly) sufficient for the aims of the chapter. Second, because understanding the proposed illusions and mistakes is easier for the uninitiated than understanding the positive proposals. (The positive proposals are often interpreted as gibberish or as false metaphysical theses by those unenthusiastic about contemplating spiritual-sounding claims.) Nevertheless, we do include some discussion of the positive project later.

While throughout this chapter we cite the reports of both Buddhist monks and Western practitioners, in discussing the negative project we draw heavily from the work of Loch Kelly. Kelly initially studied in Nepal under the prominent Mahamudra teachers Dzogchen Ponlop Rinpoche and Tulku Urgyen Rinpoche,[11] and then continued with the two sons of Urgyen Rinpoche, Tsoknyi Rinpoche and Yongey Mingyur Rinpoche. In 2004, he was asked by Mingyur Rinpoche to work on synthesizing Mahamudra with contemporary science and to teach it to Westerners. Kelly's phrasings make Mahamudra teachings more accessible to contemporary Western ears than reading directly from the esoteric language of ancient manuals, and his comparisons to contemporary science and the history of Western philosophy create easy-to-spot points of contact between nondual awareness insights and analytic philosophy.

Another feature of Kelly's work that makes it unique to our purposes is his focus on perfecting the pointing-out instructions. In the Mahamudra tradition, pointing-out instructions are called "an introduction to awareness," which are "hints on how and where to look" to see through our "mistaken identity" (Kelly 2017: 37). These instructions are intended to describe a kind of insight that occurs at the end of awakening or enlightenment, which can nevertheless be partially glimpsed at the beginning if delivered with skill. It is these kinds of instructions, we believe, that offer the most immediate and fruitful data for the philosophical study of identity and personal persistence.

One of the primary aims of Buddhist meditation is to help you "awaken" from the illusion of being what is sometimes called a *small self* or "mini-me" located inside your head behind your eyes. This illusory small self is created through the process of *identification with thought*: the feeling that you are choosing the thoughts that arise and that they are you talking.

To understand this proposal, it may help at the outset to consider the common phenomenon of having a piece of a song stuck in one's head. For example, consider an unfortunate case where you've gotten stuck with the chorus of "Who Let the Dogs Out?" by the Baha Men. This is a rare instance where you are *not* identifying with mental chatter; it doesn't feel like it is "you" (i.e., the small self) who is singing the song. Nevertheless, if you try, you might find that you can identify, on command, with the repeating chatter, by choosing to mentally "sing" the next line as it replays (not singing it out loud, but instead silently "singing" it in your mind). For example, you might try to create the following identification pattern, where **bold** text represents the inner hearing you identify with, and standard text represents the inner hearing that you do not identify with.

> "Who let the dogs out? Who, who, who, who? **Who let the dogs out? Who, who, who, who?** Who let the dogs out? Who, who, who, who?"

You can identify, and thus create the feeling of "this is me, I am doing this" selectively as the lyric replays. But in this case, it is clear that the replaying of the lyric is not under your control—after all, it's been replaying for the last several minutes, and will continue to replay whether you like it or not.

The Buddhist proposal is that *all* inner talk arises like the song lyric. "You" (i.e., the small self) do not select a thought to occur next; there are just thoughts popping up. What makes this hard to see is that in typical cases—cases in which the Baja Men have not invaded your mind—identification with mental hearing happens automatically and immediately. In other words, what you just did with the song lyric deliberately is what you do with your other mental hearing automatically. We thus find ourselves with the feeling that we are what we hear. As Kelly (2017: 130) explains:

> You are not the voices in your head. . . . The . . . thoughts that you hear are not you talking. You are not even the second voice that comments on the first thoughts. You start by listening to the thoughts, then you believe the thoughts, and then you believe the thoughts are you. It is important that you directly experience that you are primarily the awareness that hears all voices and thoughts.[12]

How does one glimpse that one is the awareness that hears thoughts? A lot of discursive mental talk concerns *problem-solving* in a general sense. Problem-solving can range from deciding what one is going to do next, to crafting what one will say to persuade another person, to hypothesizing about why one is feeling unhappy, and so on. As such, a pointer that has helped many people glimpse what is beyond identification with thought is the inquiry:

> What is here now if there is no problem to solve? (Kelly 2017: 29; 2019: 25)

This is an inquiry you might try sitting with for a minute or two. What is here if "there is nowhere to go and nothing to do? Nothing to know or create or become? What is here, just now, when you are not the problem solver" (Kelly 2017: 29)? Remember that instances of thinking like "how long am I going to sit here?" or "what is the point of this?" are themselves directed at solving problems. What aspects of your conscious experience are here, right now, if there are no problems?

A related pointer begins with a focused-attention instruction and then expands into a nondual insight:

1. Sit and focus your attention on the breath in your chest or stomach as it rises and relaxes.
2. Take a minute to notice the sensations of breath in this one specific area.
3. Next, become aware of the area you are focusing *from*. This is usually in the head, behind your eyes.
4. Ask: What is the awareness that is aware of both what you are focusing on and where you are focusing from? Does it have a location?
5. Open to the awareness that is aware of both what you are focusing on and where you are focusing from.[13]

The aim of these pointers is to glimpse an alternative to understanding one's identity within the constructed illusion of the small self and its thought-based identity. The small self is a "self-referencing loop" (Kelly 2019: 81) that is created when a thought orients to a previous thought, and then that thought refers to the next thought, which itself then orients back again to the initial thought (Kelly 2017: 129). This loop "creates a limited thought-based sense of self" (Kelly 2019: 81) that Tibetan Buddhism calls "afflictive consciousness." Our minds then project this looping, or "selfing," onto our spatial representation of the location behind and around our eyes.

We've learned from an early age that our brains are responsible for our thinking, and so it is perhaps no surprise that many of us project our thoughts onto the area we know our brains to be located. The projection is often on a spatial representation of our brain area, but since we typically do not feel much sensation in this area, some people project their thoughts onto the closest place to their brain in which dynamic sensation occurs—the little muscles around the eyes. But nondual awareness meditators have found that this habit of projection can be broken. We don't *need* to imagine that our "inner" mental contents are all somehow crammed into a small area of our spatial representation. Thought experiments popular in the study of personal identity already strongly suggest that there is no necessary connection between where one's brain is located and where one takes oneself to be.[14] The feeling that your mental life is happening where you represent your brain to be located is not a result of your biology—it is a result of your beliefs about your biology.

The proposal, then, is that experienced meditators in the nondual awareness tradition have managed to break the illusion of being a small thought-based "mini-me" located behind or around the eyes, and they have done this by repeatedly glimpsing pointers like those suggested here. The pointers are designed to draw one out of identification with mental talk and the looping thought patterns that create the feeling of being a small self. Thus, the project of "awakening," in Buddhism, is primarily the process of transitioning out of the delusion of the small self. As Kelly (2017: 27) explains, "When you awaken, you awaken from a looping thought pattern that has been called 'me' and feels located behind your eyes, in the middle of your head." To do this, as Mingyur et al. (2019: 45) puts it, one must "become bigger than the thought."

The afflictive consciousness insists on the delusion:

Thoughts occur within your spatial representation of your brain and eyes, they are chosen, and they are you.

When one awakens, one realizes:

True nature of mind is not represented as spatially located, it is aware of thoughts occurring unchosen, and it is not thought-based.[15]

In this discussion, we have been focusing on thoughts, and especially their occurrence as inner chatter or mental hearing. Thoughts have been our initial target because of the exalted status that philosophers have placed on discursive thought in establishing identity. This can, of course, be seen clearly in the work of Descartes. In interpretations of Descartes's meditations, thought is often interpreted as a tool not only for reasoning but also for establishing one's identity as a "thinking thing." Compare this perspective with that presented by Kelly (2017: 125):

The most crucial mistake we make is turning to thought to know who we are. Unfortunately, philosopher René Descartes's famous statement "I think, therefore I am" is often misunderstood to mean "I am my thinking," or "I am a thinker." When we identify ourselves as our thoughts, we become anxious, isolated, and obsessively caught in our own self-images and stories. To grow beyond afflictive consciousness, we need to experience [nature of mind], the feeling of "am" that is not thought based.[16]

Identification with inner chatter thus seems to play an important role in our conception of ourselves, but such identification also occurs with other forms of experience. One can identify with imagined images, emotions, and, of course, *memories*. Just as one can have the feeling that "this is me, I am doing this" as thoughts come and go, as one remembers something, one can feel "I am choosing to remember this, this is me."

The proposal is that as thoughts, emotions, memories, and the like come and go, the process of illusory identification occurs automatically and immediately. Our true identity—our nature of mind, or *rigpa*[17]—is not to be found in these kinds of contents of consciousness but instead in the broader context in which they occur.

III. Ur-Experience as Replacement for the Small Self in Theories of Psychological Connectedness

Buddhist theory of mind does not view thinking as having a special status in relation to the five senses. Thinking, appearing as "inner hearing" or "inner seeing," has no more or less claim to being one's identity than the hearing and seeing of external objects. (This is why Buddhism views thinking as the "sixth sense.") We usually don't think of thoughts and memories as experiences like visual and auditory sensing because of the illusion of a small self that is *choosing* thoughts and memories; a small self that is, in some sense, *composed* of thoughts and memories. But this is an illusion that is consistently seen for what it is with the help of meditation.

Thus, if these claims are correct, there is more to our experience than thinking and the five senses. There is a form of experience that is prior to the arising of these. We do not wish to take a stand on the more specific attributes of this form of experience, but we think it is helpful to have at least a catch-all term for it. We thus propose to call this form of experience, whatever its specific nature, *ur-experience*. Meditation is the project of ceasing the habit of identifying with thoughts, emotions, and memories, and building awareness of ur-experience. Ur-experience remains even if there are no problems to solve, and it explains why one can at the same time experience the location one is focusing on and from. Ur-experience is not dependent on one's experience of oneself as a thinker or as having a personality. Ur-experience is the experience of being immediately aware of these phenomena as experiences.[18]

This view proposes that what matters in psychological continuity is the connectedness of ur-experience. This contrasts with existing theories that focus on the connectedness of memory, thought, personality, and other mental phenomena commonly involved in identification delusions.

The proposal has stark implications for cases of radical psychological change. Many of these implications are acknowledged in the Buddhist tradition. As Dzogchen Ponlop Rinpoche (2003: 14–5) admits, "from a conventional point of view," the view is "a little bit insane." For example, ur-experience remains constant through the transitions from waking to sleeping, and thus those who recognize ur-experience as the foundation of their identity "see little difference between being awake and being asleep."

What this implies, for our purposes, is that ur-experience is a candidate to endorse and explain perceived psychological continuity through radical change. The crucial claim is that psychological continuity is in no way threatened by any changes, radical or otherwise, to one's personality, memories, emotions, or patterns of thought. It is the connectedness of ur-experience, which notices the arising of these contents, and not these contents themselves, that matters to personal persistence. For many people, the realization that ur-experience is the foundation of their identity makes sense of the deep-set intuition that their identity has remained constant even as their personality and thought patterns have undergone drastic changes as they grow older. A common sentiment is: "This is the feeling of who I've been at all ages in my life, which hasn't changed" (Kelly 2017: 27).

IV. Conclusion

Research into cognitive biases is useful to philosophy not because it establishes philosophical conclusions directly, but instead because it sometimes calls into question the intuitions that are behind such conclusions. In this chapter, we have developed an account of how some Tibetan Buddhist meditation traditions can play the same role: revealing potential biases relevant to philosophical thinking about personal identity and egoistic concern.

Specifically, we have claimed that there is a tendency to identify ourselves with a "small self" composed of thoughts, emotions, memories, aspects of our personality, or combinations of these. Just as psychologists suggest that the "good true self" is a persistent illusion, one that we must be careful of when we distill philosophical insights about personal identity and egoistic concern from thought experiments, meditative practices suggest that the "small self" is a similar illusion. This has important implications for philosophical theories (most notably psychological connectedness theories) that identify the self with thoughts and memories. Given that this illusion is pervasive and requires sustained observation to overcome, it would not be surprising if this bias went undetected even by philosophers like Descartes, Parfit, and McMahan who engage in sustained but non-meditative reflection on philosophical prompts. Centuries of cultivated meditative practices suggest that the route from intuitions about thought experiments to data about the nature of psychological continuity is suspect.

We can endorse this regulatory role for Buddhism while still remaining open to theories about the nature of a persisting self. And if, of course, these claims about supposed biases, such as the identification delusions of the small self, can themselves be challenged or explained away by empirical psychological research, then that would also be an intriguing and welcome development.

Notes

1 Excerpt from "Jeff McMahan, The Ethics of Killing: Problems at the Margins of Life" © 2002 Oxford Publishing Limited (Academic). Reproduced with permission of The Licensor through PLS clear.
2 Indeed, while the origin of the effect is still being studied, the leading hypotheses are that the effect shows a form of motivated cognition on the part of subjects and reflects evolved heuristics that aid in social coordination. See Strohminger et al. (2017).
3 See Chapters 4 and 8 of Sullivan (2018). A similar tendency to focus only on negative cases is seen in philosophical arguments in favor of the rationality of future bias. Greene et al. (2021a,b) found that people are more future biased about negative hedonic events than they are positive hedonic events, and they suggest that it is therefore no surprise that philosophers who defend the rationality of future bias focus almost exclusively on thought experiments involving negative hedonic events.
4 These are well-established features of prospect theory, developed in the work of Daniel Kahneman and Amos Tversky.

5 It is important to note that in some instances philosophers have used thought experiments as a method for calling intuitions into question. The best example of this, in the study of personal identity, may be Dennett's (1978) essay "Where Am I?" Indeed, the thought experiments Dennett presents can help show us that there is *something* off about our common conception of ourselves as spatially located behind our eyes, and thus pave the way for taking seriously meditative practices that aim to reveal this intuition as an illusion. See Section II and Footnote 12. (Another prominent example of thought experiments used in the latter way, this time in epistemology, is Gendler and Hawthorne (2005)). So, when we refer to the "method of thought experiments" in this chapter, we have in mind the method of using thought experiments to elicit intuitions as data for theories, and not the method of using thought experiments to call intuitions into question.
6 See the work of Miri Albahari: for example, her 2019a and b. See also Sparby (2015: 216), who notes the ambiguity in the term "meditation research." There has been a recent resurgence in Western philosophers arguing for greater engagement between Buddhist and analytic philosophical traditions. See, for example, Garfield (2015) and Bommarito (2020).
7 Intriguingly, recent work in experimental philosophy shows that among Monastic Tibetan Buddhists who deny the existence of any continuity of self (an extreme view with which we do not engage in this chapter), there are still significant indicators of forms of future-directed egoistic concern, like fear of death (Nichols et al. 2018; Garfield et al. 2016). This data cries out for further explanation.
8 See, for example, the survey article of Millière et al. (2018).
9 There now exists a large empirical literature suggesting benefits from meditation to physical and emotional well-being, as well as to attributes like attention, memory, and mental quickness. Most of this research is on the benefits of focused-attention and open-monitoring meditation, and it is only recently that studies have started to regularly include nondual-awareness meditation. An early study by Josipovic et al. (2011) found that focused-attention meditation suppresses the internally focused default-mode network, while open-monitoring meditation suppresses the externally focused task-positive network. In contrast, nondual-awareness meditation tended to balance the activity of each network. A subsequent study by Schoenberg et al. (2018) found that nondual-awareness meditation created high gamma frequencies, which occur when separate areas of the brain fire in harmony. There is also recent work about potential harmful effects of sustained meditation practice (e.g., Lindahl et al. 2019), including conjecture about whether there is a "U" shaped trajectory to meditation training where initially positive effects turn negative (Britton 2019). (Though see the recent review of Farias et al. (2020), which concludes that the rate of observed adverse effects due to meditation is similar to that of psychotherapy in general). Josipovic (2013: 12) suggests that the network-suppression effects of focused attention and open monitoring are the most likely cause of long-developing adverse effects, because it is questionable whether the ongoing suppression of networks, leading to an attenuation of their activity, is a viable long-term strategy.
10 Mahamudra and Dzogchen share many methodological similarities and are often thought to be complementary practices.
11 "Rinpoche" is not a surname but an honorific term used in Tibetan Buddhism. It can be translated as "precious one."

12 Excerpt from "Shift into Freedom: The Science and Practice of Open-Hearted Awareness" © 2017 Loch Kelly used with permission from the publisher, Sounds True Inc.
13 Adapted from Kelly (2019: 58–9). Excerpt from "The Way of Effortless Mindfulness: A Revolutionary Guide for Living an Awakened Life" © 2019 Loch Kelly used with permission from the publisher, Sounds True Inc.
14 For example, Dennett (1978). See footnote 4 of this chapter.
15 It is important to note that these claims concern what is true at the level of experience. They are not claims about metaphysics; for example, they are not claims concerning whether consciousness is spatially located.
16 Excerpt from "Shift into Freedom: The Science and Practice of Open-Hearted Awareness" © 2017 Loch Kelly used with permission from the publisher, Sounds True Inc.
17 Kelly translates *rigpa* as "awake awareness." Other translations include "no-self self," "true nature," "unity consciousness," "ground of being," "source of mind," "optimal mind," "natural awareness," "heart-mind," "unchanging essence," "open-hearted awareness," and "Self 2."
18 To avoid a regress, we would predict that awareness *of* ur-experience *as* experience would not be possible in the same way that ur-experience makes possible awareness of the experience of thinking, having a personality, or remembering. This prediction is consistent with the fact that the attributes of ur-experience are usually presented as either indescribable or only describable in "mystical" language, which itself seems to offer little in the way of concrete description. Given the proposed nature of ur-experience, we would expect to only be capable of describing its functions and not its attributes. If one views mystical language as *not* successfully describing the attributes of ur-experience, then this expectation is satisfied. See Albahari (2019a) for more on "mystical" passages describing the nature of *rigpa* and an interesting discussion on the evidential status of mystical reports for the study of analytic metaphysics.

Bibliography

Albahari, M. (2019a). "The Mystic and the Metaphysician: Clarifying the Role of Meditation in the Search for Ultimate Reality." *Journal of Consciousness Studies: Controversies in Science and the Humanities*, 26 (7–8): 12–36.

Albahari, M. (2019b). "Perennial Idealism: A Mystical Solution to the Mind-Body Problem." *Philosophers' Imprint*, 19 (44): 1–37.

Bommarito, N. (2020). *Seeing Clearly: A Buddhist Guide to Life*. Oxford: Oxford University Press.

Britton, W. (2019). "Can Mindfulness Be Too Much of a Good Thing? The Value of a Middle Way." *Current Opinions in Psychology*, 28: 159–65.

Dalai, L. (2003). *Forward, in Ponlop Rinpoche, D., Wild Awakening: The Heart of Mahamudra and Dzogchen*. Boston: Shambhala.

Dennett, D. C. (1978). "Where Am I?" In *Brainstorms*, 55–68. Cambridge, MA: MIT Press.

Dorje, O. T. (2003). *Forward, in Ponlop Rinpoche, D., Wild Awakening: The Heart of Mahamudra and Dzogchen*. Boston: Shambhala.

Farias, M., E. Maraldi, K. C. Wallenkampf and G. Lucchetti (2020). "Adverse Events in Meditation Practices and Meditation-Based Therapies: A Systematic Review." *Acta Psychiatrica Scandinavica*, 142: 374–93.

Garfield, J., S. Nichols, A. Rai and N. Strohminger (2016). "Ego, Egoism and the Impact of Religion on Ethical Experience: What a Paradoxical Consequence of Buddhist Culture Tells Us About Moral Psychology." *Journal of Ethics: An International Philosophical Review*, 19: 2.

Garfield, J. L. (2015). *Engaging Buddhism: Why it Matters to Philosophy*. New York: Oxford University Press.

Gendler, T. S. and J. Hawthorne (2005). "The Real Guide to Fake Barns: A Catalogue of Gifts for Your Epistemic Enemies." *Philosophical Studies*, 124 (3): 331–52.

Greene, P., A. J. Latham, K. Miller and J. Norton (2021a). "Hedonic and Non-Hedonic Bias toward the Future." *Australasian Journal of Philosophy*, 99 (1): 148–63.

Greene, P., A. J. Latham, K. Miller and J. Norton (2021b). "On Preferring that Overall, Things are Worse: Future-Bias and Unequal Payoffs." *Philosophy and Phenomenological Research*. doi: 10.1111/phpr.12819.

Josipovic, Z. (2010). "Duality and Nonduality in Meditation Research." *Consciousness and Cognition*, 19: 1119–21.

Josipovic, Z. (2013). "Neural Correlates of Nondual Awareness in Meditation." *Annals of the New York Academy of Sciences*, 1307: 9–18.

Josipovic, Z., I. Dinstein, J. Weber and D. J. Heeger (2011). "Influence of Meditation on Anti-Correlated Networks in the Brain." *Frontiers in Human Neuroscience*, 5: 183.

Kelly, L. (2017). *Shift into Freedom: The Science and Practice of Open-Hearted Awareness*. Boulder: Sounds True.

Kelly, L. (2019). *The Way of Effortless Mindfulness: A Revolutionary Guide for Living an Awakened Life*. Boulder: Sounds True.

Lindahl, J. R., W. B. Britton, D. J. Cooper and L. J. Kirmayer (2019). "Challenging and Adverse Meditation Experiences: Toward a Person-Centered Approach." In M. Farias, D. Brazier and M. Lalljee (eds.), *The Oxford Handbook of Meditation*. doi:10.1093/oxfordhb/9780198808640.001.0001

McMahan, J. (2002). *The Ethics of Killing: Problems at the Margins of Life*. Oxford: Oxford University Press.

Millière, R., R. L. Carhart-Harris, L. Roseman, F. Trautwein and A. Berkovich-Ohana (2018). "Psychedelics, Meditation, and Self-Consciousness." *Frontiers in Psychology*, 9: 1475.

Mingyur Rinpoche, Y. and H. Tworkov (2019). *In Love with the World: A Monk's Journey Through the Bardos of Living and Dying*. New York: Random House.

Nichols, S., N. Strohminger, A. Rai and J. Garfield (2018). "Death and the Self." *Cognitive Science: A Multidisciplinary Journal*, 42 (S1): 314–32.

Parfit, D. (1984). *Reasons and Persons*. Oxford: Oxford University Press.

Ponlop Rinpoche, D. (2003). *Wild Awakening: The Heart of Mahamudra and Dzogchen*. Boston: Shambhala.

Schoenberg, L. A. P., A. Ruf, J. Churchill, D. P. Brown and J. A. Brewer (2018). "Mapping Complex Mind States: EEG Neural Substrates of Meditative Unified Compassionate Awareness." *Consciousness and Cognition*, 57: 41–53.

Shoemaker, D. and K. P. Tobia (forthcoming). "Personal Identity." In J. Doris and M. Vargas (eds.), *Oxford Handbook of Moral Psychology*. Oxford: Oxford University Press.

Sparby, T. (2015). "Investigating the Depths of Consciousness through Meditation." *Mind & Matter*, 13 (2): 213–40.
Strohminger, N., J. Knobe and G. Newman (2017). "The True Self: A Psychological Concept Distinct from the Self." *Perspectives on Psychological Science*, 12 (4): 551–60.
Sullivan, M. (2018). *Time biases: A Theory of Rational Planning and Personal Persistence*. New York: Oxford University Press.
Tobia, K. P. (2015). "Personal Identity and the Phineas Gage Effect." *Analysis*, 75 (3): 396–405.

8

Memory as Evidence of Personal Identity

A Study on Reincarnation Beliefs

Vilius Dranseika

Derek Parfit in his book *Reasons and Persons* writes:

> There might [. . .] have been evidence supporting the belief in reincarnation. One such piece of evidence might be this. A Japanese woman might claim to remember living a life as a Celtic hunter and warrior in the Bronze Age. On the basis of her apparent memories she might make many predictions which could be checked by archaeologists. Thus she might claim to remember having a bronze bracelet shaped like two fighting dragons. And she might claim that she remembers burying this bracelet beside some particular megalith, just before the battle in which she was killed. Archaeologists might now find just such a bracelet buried in this spot, and their instruments might show that the earth had not here been disturbed for at least 2,000 years. This Japanese woman might make many other such predictions, all of which are verified. (1984: 227)[1]

In this chapter, I will not discuss whether such a case—should we really encounter it—would constitute evidence supporting the belief in reincarnation. In contrast to Parfit, my aim here is purely descriptive. I want to understand how people think about the role of memory claims in establishing facts about personal identity.

In empirical literature, there is work on various questions dealing with folk reasoning about memory and personal identity. Is continuity of memory taken to be necessary for the continuity of personal identity (Blok, Newman, and Rips 2005; Nichols and Bruno 2010)? How important are facts about possession of memories in reidentification of a person in reincarnation (White 2015, 2016a) or fission (Woike, Collard, and Hood 2020)? What is the role of memory in convincing people that they have lived past lives (White, Kelly, and Nichols (2016))? Existing work, however, does not look into the role of memory *claims* in establishing facts about personal identity.

Let us thus distinguish between three descriptive questions that can be asked about Parfit's imaginary case and others like it (e.g., Ayer 1956: 220), assuming, for the sake of argument, that such alternative explanations as a deliberate hoax are taken to be definitively ruled out. First, would these cases be taken to provide evidence supporting the belief in reincarnation? Second, if yes, would they be taken to provide evidence of personal identity retained through cycles of reincarnation? Third, what exactly in these cases would be taken to constitute such evidence?

Let us briefly discuss these three questions. The answer to the first one plausibly depends on what alternative explanations are considered. In discussing Parfit's case, Steven Hales claims that "there are indefinitely many [...] hypotheses" that are superior explanations than reincarnation in a sense that they are consistent with our best current theories about the mind and physics in general, as well as being in principle empirically testable (2001: 342). He provides the following alternative hypothesis as an example:

> There are intelligent, technologically advanced extra-terrestrials who regard humans with great amusement, and secretly monitor and occasionally interfere with our lives. One thing they enjoy is performing super-advanced psychosurgery on select humans that provides these humans with quasi-memories of having lived past lives, verifiably true beliefs about where ancient bracelets are hidden, and previously non-existent linguistic or musical talents. (2001)

Alternatively, one may be willing to consider alternative supernatural explanations (Ducasse 1961: 300–4), like mediumistic communication (the Japanese woman communicates with [the spirit of] the Celtic warrior), possession (the spirit of Celtic warrior possesses the Japanese woman), or extrasensory perception (ESP) (the Japanese woman has access to either the mind of the Celtic warrior or current facts about locations of buried artifacts). Thus, we can expect that the answer to the first question would depend both on what prior plausibility was assigned to the reincarnation hypothesis and also on what alternative hypotheses are salient in the context (and how much initial plausibility is assigned to them).

Moving to the second question, the answer would depend on the precise understanding of reincarnation or rebirth. While the most familiar conception of reincarnation in Western culture seems to assume personal identity through cycles of reincarnation, this is arguably not the case in the Buddhist understanding of rebirth (Perrett 1987; Siderits 2015). Memories of past lives do not presuppose continuous personal identity, at least on the level of the religious and philosophical doctrine, if not always on the level of folk conceptualizations.[2]

Finally, and most centrally for this chapter, let's look into the nature of evidence involved in such cases as Parfit's. The only available systematic analysis of ethnographic evidence suggests that in cultures that have procedures of identification of reincarnates, these procedures tend to primarily focus on "physical marks that correspond to those on the deceased when they were alive [...]; behavioral similarities that indicate similar personal traits [...]; and the recognition of places or people the deceased knew" (White 2016b: 3–4). Furthermore, in a series of studies with participants from cultures that do not practice identification of reincarnates (Americans and Indian Jains), White gave the participants a story about a village in which the true reincarnation needs to be chosen from a number of candidates, each of whom has one feature in common with the deceased. She found that possession of memories and bodily marks were preferred cues in identifying reincarnated people (2015, 2016a).

Now, memory comes in different kinds and flavors. Which aspect of it is taken to provide evidence of reincarnation? For ethnographic accounts, White claims that the recognition of places or people the deceased knew "assumes the continuity of episodic autobiographical memory" (2016b: 4). The same was true about empirical studies (White 2015, 2016a), where presence of an episodic autobiographic memory ("He remembered seeing a shoe for the first time.") was taken to constitute better evidence of reincarnation than the presence of a semantic ("He remembered the names of shoe parts.") or a procedural ("He remembered how to mend shoes.") memory. Autobiographic memory of past events, however, can also be semantic. Thus we can ask whether the reason why verifiable memory claims are considered to provide evidence for the belief in reincarnation is (otherwise unexplainable) possession of information about past events—a feature shared by both episodic and semantic memories—or rather some feature of memory claims that signals the presence of specifically episodic memories.

I present two studies in which I look into these three questions.

I. Study 1: Celtic Warrior

In the first study, I test whether (a) judgments of quality of evidence supporting the belief in reincarnation provided by Parfit's Celtic warrior case depend on study participants' initial beliefs about the possibility of reincarnation and also whether (b) evidence can be weakened by making alternative explanations salient.

Participants: Three hundred study participants were recruited on Prolific: 63% female, 37% male, 1 person identified as non-binary, M_{age} = 37.0, age SD = 13.4, age range 18–75. In both studies reported in this chapter, participants were nationals of the United States or the United Kingdom who indicated English as their first language.

Materials: Study participants were asked to read a short story based on Parfit's scenario:

> A Japanese woman claims to remember living a life as a Celtic hunter and warrior in the Bronze Age. On the basis of her apparent memories, she makes many predictions which can be checked by archaeologists. For example, she claims to remember having a bronze bracelet, shaped like two fighting dragons. And she claims that she remembers burying this bracelet beside some particular megalith, just before the battle in which she was killed.
>
> Archaeologists now find just such a bracelet buried in this spot, and their instruments show that the earth has not here been disturbed for at least 2,000 years. This Japanese woman makes many other such predictions, all of which are verified.
>
> Suppose you learn that there indeed is a woman who (a) claims to remember living a life as a Celtic hunter and warrior in the Bronze Age and (b) many of the

things she claims to have experienced are verified by archaeologists. What would be your best explanation of what could be happening here?

Study participants were asked to write a one- or two-sentence-long explanation and then they proceeded to the next two tasks which were presented in a counterbalanced order over the two subsequent pages.

One of these tasks asked to suppose that it is shown that the woman is sincere in her claims, that she sincerely believes remembering the Bronze Age events, and then respond to the following two questions (in randomized order) on a scale from 1 (Completely unlikely) to 7 (Very likely):

[Identity][3] After learning of such a case, would you think that this woman in fact is the same person as the Celtic warrior?

[Memory] After learning of such a case, would you think that this woman in fact personally remembers (and not only thinks that she remembers) the Bronze Age events?

In the other task, participants were provided with a list of attempts to explain what could be happening in this situation (in randomized order) and asked to indicate how plausible each attempted explanation is, on a scale from 1 (Totally implausible) to 7 (Very plausible):

[Reincarnation] The Celtic warrior reincarnated as the Japanese woman.

[Possession] The spirit of the Celtic warrior possessed the Japanese woman.

[Telepathy] The Japanese woman had telepathic access to the mind of the Celtic woman.

[Clairvoyance] The Japanese woman used clairvoyance to learn where various Bronze Age artifacts are.

[Insertion] Technologically advanced extra-terrestrials planted memories of or true beliefs about past events they witnessed into the Japanese woman (for amusement or as an experiment).

[Immortality] The Japanese woman was the same immortal being as the Celtic warrior.

Half of the participants responded to identity and memory questions before considering alternative explanations, and the other half in the opposite order.

On the next page, participants were asked to suppose again that there indeed is such a woman and then asked whether they would consider this to provide evidence in favor of a belief in reincarnation (on a scale from 1 ["No evidence"] to 7 ["Very strong evidence"]).

Finally, on the next page, they were asked which of the following descriptions best captures what they think happens after we die (first three options provided in a randomized manner, "unsure" always last):

[Annihilation] The person ceases permanently after the body dies.

[Immortal soul] The person continues to exist as a soul after the body dies.

[Reincarnation] After the body dies, the person continues to exist in a new body.

[Unsure] I don't know what happens to the person after the body dies.

A. Results

Free text explanations: Seventy percent of the participants provided one explanation; 24%, two explanations each; and a further 2%, three each. The remaining 4% did not provide any explanations either by saying that they have none or simply claiming that the story is false.

Explanation in terms of reincarnation was mentioned most frequently, by 51% of the participants. The second most common explanation was in terms of educated guess— 26% of the participants speculated that the reason why archaeologists were able to verify the claims is that the claims were based on familiarity with Celtic culture and history, for example, general knowledge about types of Celtic jewelry or funerary rituals. Twelve percent referred to precise knowledge. Most of these were in terms of testimony through family line (twenty-one participants), followed by access to an authentic written source, for example, the Celtic warrior's diary (fourteen). Ten indicated that the relevant knowledge was acquired via archaeological means, for example, in a non-invasive way, like sonar or x-ray, which is compatible with ground not being disturbed. There were also six participants who referred to knowing or having information without specifying any details. Thirteen percent entertained a possibility of sheer coincidence, some referring to the fact that if there are many people making claims, some are likely to be true, other referring to the claims being vague enough. Finally, 13% referred to various other supernatural explanations, such as ESP (eight participants), communication with spirits (five), messages in dreams (four), time traveling (three), genetic memory (three), collective consciousness (two), possession (two), being a multidimensional being (two), and a number of other explanations each mentioned by only one participant.

Order effects: Ascriptions of identity were higher before ($M = 3.54$, $SD = 1.97$) than after evaluating alternative explanations ($M = 3.00$, $SD = 1.92$), $t(298) = 2.40$, $p = .017$, $d = 0.28$. The same was true for memory, $M_{before} = 4.08$, $SD = 1.85$, $M_{after} = 3.64$, $SD = 1.92$), $t(298) = 2.04$, $p = .043$, $d = 0.24$. Ascriptions of identity and ascriptions of memory were strongly correlated, $r = .782$, $p < .001$.

Explanations: A mixed-effects model was fit with participants as a random factor, explanations and order of presentation as fixed factors, and plausibility as an outcome. There were differences in evaluations of plausibility between different explanations, $F(1, 1490) = 34.7$, $p < .001$. Order of presentation did not affect evaluations ($p = .545$) nor was there an interaction between the two factors ($p = .399$).

Post hoc pairwise comparisons suggest that reincarnation was taken to be a more plausible explanation than all the other five explanations (all $p_{holm} < .001$), while extraterrestrial memory insertion was taken to be the least plausible of all (all $p_{holm} < .001$). See Figure 8.1.

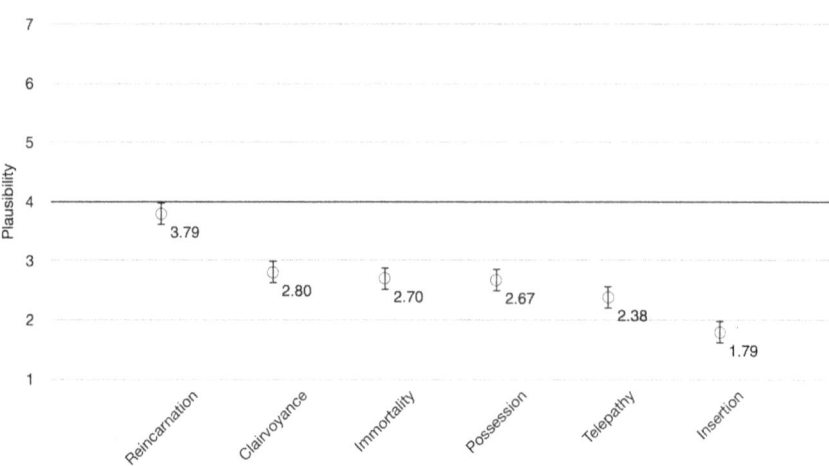

Figure 8.1 Estimated marginal means for plausibility of each of the six explanations. Error bars indicate 95% CI.

Principal component analysis using varimax rotation on the six explanations returned a two-factor solution that cumulatively explains 68% of variance. Factor 1 includes three explanations that presuppose the presence of the Celtic warrior in the Japanese woman: reincarnation (factor loading .874), immortality (.850), and possession (.717), explaining 38% of variance. Factor 2 includes three explanations that presuppose mental access to the relevant facts: insertion (.769), clairvoyance (.736), and telepathy (.681), explaining 30% of variance. When measures of memory and identity are also added, they strongly load in Factor 1: identity, .914; memory, .853.

Quality of evidence: Evidence for reincarnation was on average judged to be inconclusive, no different from the middle of the scale, $M = 3.99$, $SD = 1.95$, $t(299) = 0.09$, $p = .929$.

Afterlife beliefs: Nine percent of participants indicated that they believe that after the body dies, the person continues to exist in a new body (reincarnation). Thirty-one percent said that the person continues to exist as a soul after the body dies (immortal soul). Twenty-nine percent said that the person ceases permanently after the body dies (annihilation), while the remaining 31% were unsure.

Effect of afterlife beliefs: A series of one-way ANOVAs showed that afterlife beliefs were associated with responses to questions about how plausible an explanation in terms of reincarnation is, $F(3, 296) = 27.9$, $p < .001$, and how good the evidence in favor of belief in reincarnation was taken to be, $F(3, 296) = 22.5$, $p < .001$, as well as with ascriptions of identity, $F(3, 296) = 15.0$, $p < .001$, and remembering, $F(3, 296) = 15.3$, $p < .001$. Estimated marginal means and pairwise comparisons are presented in Table 8.1 and Figure 8.2. The same pattern can be observed in all four cases. Scores are the highest in those who believe in reincarnation, closely followed by those who believe in the immortal disembodied soul, while scores are low in those who believe in annihilation.

Table 8.1 Estimated Marginal Means and Pairwise Comparisons for Measures of (a) Plausibility of Explanation in Terms of Reincarnation, (b) Judgment of Quality of Evidence Supporting the Belief in Reincarnation, Ascriptions of (c) Identity, and (d) Remembering, Grouped by Afterlife Beliefs

Measure	Group	EMM	95% CI	Immortality		Annihilation		Unsure	
				t(296)	p_{holm}	t(296)	p_{holm}	t(296)	p_{holm}
(a) Plausible explanation	Reincarnation	5.81	[5.10, 6.52]	2.97	.007**	7.62	<.001***	5.70	<.001***
	Immortality	4.60	[4.22, 4.97]	—	—	6.99	<.001***	4.12	<.001***
	Annihilation	2.68	[2.30, 3.07]			—	—	2.96	.007**
	Unsure	3.49	[3.12, 3.86]					—	—
(b) Evidence	Reincarnation	5.38	[4.70, 6.07]	1.48	.141 n.s.	6.18	<.001***	4.07	<.001***
	Immortality	4.80	[4.44, 5.17]	—	—	7.05	<.001***	3.92	<.001***
	Annihilation	2.94	[2.55, 3.31]			—	—	3.22	.003**
	Unsure	3.79	[3.43, 4.15]					—	—
(c) Identity	Reincarnation	4.77	[4.06, 5.48]	2.20	.053 n.s.	5.62	<.001***	4.16	<.001***
	Immortality	3.87	[3.49, 4.25]	—	—	5.12	<.001***	2.95	.010*
	Annihilation	2.47	[2.08, 2.85]			—	—	2.23	.053 n.s.
	Unsure	3.07	[2.70, 3.45]					—	—
(d) Memory	Reincarnation	5.12	[4.43, 5.80]	1.59	.112 n.s.	5.35	<.001***	3.50	.002**
	Immortality	4.49	[4.13, 4.85]	—	—	5.64	<.001***	2.87	.013*
	Annihilation	3.00	[2.63, 3.37]			—	—	2.83	.013*
	Unsure	3.74	[3.39, 4.10]					—	—

Significance levels: n.s. $p > .05$; * $p \leq .05$; ** $p \leq .01$; *** $p \leq .001$.

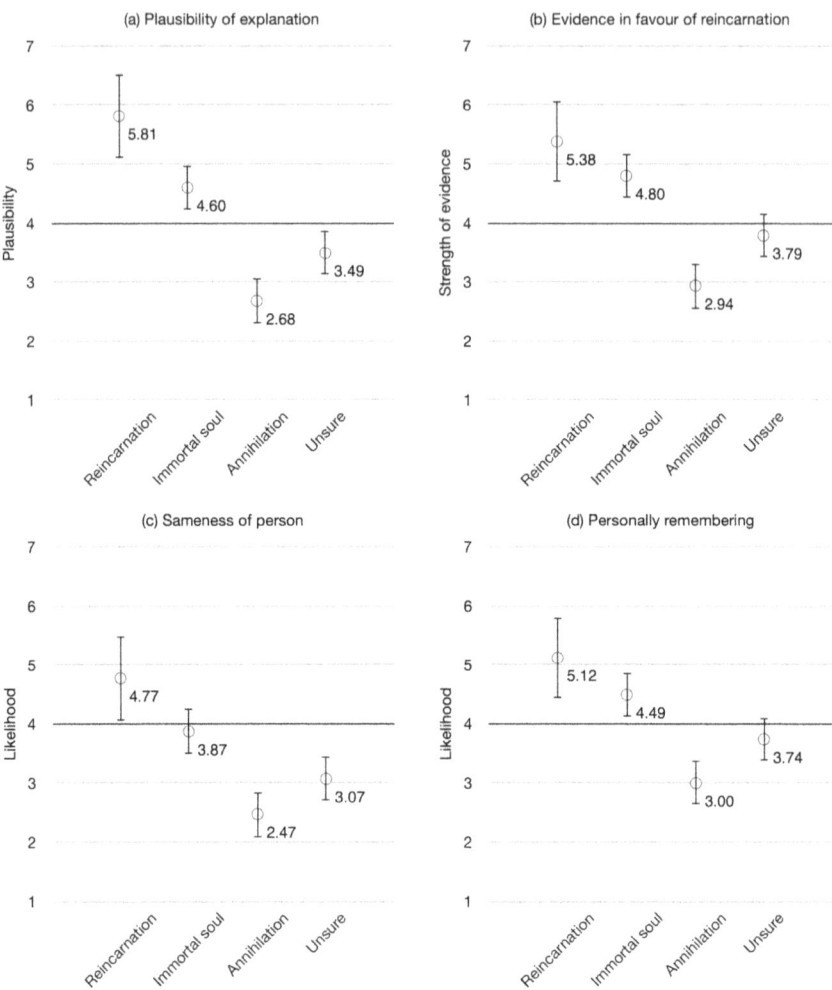

Figure 8.2 Estimated marginal means for measures of (a) plausibility of an explanation in terms of reincarnation, (b) judgment of quality of evidence supporting the belief in reincarnation, ascriptions of (c) identity, and (d) remembering, grouped by afterlife beliefs. Error bars indicate 95% CI.

The same pattern of responses is also observed in looking at how frequently participants mention reincarnation as an explanation in free text responses. Reincarnation was mentioned by 85% of those who believe in reincarnation, 64% of those who believe an in immortal soul, and only 33% of those who believe in annihilation. Among those who were unsure, 45% mentioned reincarnation. Binomial logistic regression suggests that probability of mentioning reincarnation depended on the type of afterlife beliefs, $\chi^2(3) = 32.6, p < .001$.

Discussion: While on average Parfit's Celtic warrior case was not judged to constitute strong evidence in support of belief in reincarnation, judgments of quality of evidence depended on study participants' initial beliefs about the afterlife. For instance, those who believe in reincarnation (and those who believe in an immortal soul) thought that such a case would constitute strong evidence supporting the belief in reincarnation, while this was denied by those who believe that the person ceases permanently after death. A similar pattern was observed on a number of other measurements: how plausible an explanation in terms of reincarnation was taken to be, how likely participants thought it is that they would ascribe personal identity and remembering in such a case, and how often participants suggested an explanation in terms or reincarnation in a free text response. Furthermore, evidence can be weakened by making alternative explanations salient. Study participants who had a chance to consider alternative explanations before ascribing identity and remembering ascribed lower scores.

II. Study 2: The Strategy

In Study 2, I build upon a study design used by White (2015, 2016a). There are some differences, however. First, the task does not require the study participant to suppose that reincarnation can in fact occur. Second, participants are asked to create the most convincing strategy in favor of a particular candidate rather than simply to choose from a predefined set of candidates. Third, the strategies can rely only on what is observable (thus, for instance, memory *claims* rather than presence of memories themselves). Furthermore, I check how different aspects of memory claims (level of detail, availability of information, type of remembering) contribute to how convincing the memory claim is taken to be.

Participants: One hundred study participants were recruited on Prolific. Fifty-one percent female, 44% male, remaining 5% chose "non-binary/other," M_{age} = 32.0, age SD = 11.6, age range 18–76.

Materials: Study participants were given the following task:

> Imagine that it is the middle of the nineteenth century and you are a secret operative sent to a far-away country on a secret mission. Your mission is to make sure that a tribe that lives in one of the valleys does not interfere with the business people from your home country building railroads and mines in the territory adjacent to the tribe's territory. You were given this mission because thirty years ago you spent several years with this tribe, learned its language and traditions. You knew the chief of the tribe well; you know a lot about his life, appearance, character. You also know that the chief died from an arrow shot into his heart.
>
> You realize that if your mission fails and you do not manage to convince the tribe to cooperate, your country will use its army against the tribe and the whole tribe is likely to perish.
>
> After thorough analysis, you come to the conclusion that the only way to secure the support of the tribe is to convince them that your close associate (who was born

in this tribe, but kidnapped and raised by a neighboring tribe) is the reincarnated tribal chief. In this tribe, everyone believes that people reincarnate after they die and also that the tribe should be governed by the reincarnate of the previous chief. If the tribe can be convinced that your associate is the true reincarnation of the deceased chief, your associate will become the new chief and you will secure the tribe's cooperation.

Now you need to come up with the best way for your associate to convince the tribe that he is the true reincarnation of the deceased chief.

Participants then were asked to answer the following two questions (one or two sentences each):

What advice would you give to your associate on how to convince the tribe that he's the true reincarnation of the deceased chief?

Why, in your opinion, will the tribe find your suggested strategy convincing?

On the next page, they were provided with a list of possible strategies (presented in randomized order) and asked to indicate whether they think it would be found by the tribe to be convincing (on a scale from 1 [Completely unconvincing] to 7 [Completely convincing]):

[Tattoo] Your associate tattoos a birthmark on the chest exactly where the chief was shot with an arrow.

[Memory] Your associate claims to remember various events from chief's life and is able to describe those events.

[Limp] Your associate walks in a limping manner, exactly like the chief did.

[Jewelry] Your associate is able to recognize jewelry that was owned by the chief.

[Name] Your associate claims that his name is the same as the chief's.

[Claim] Your associate claims that he is the reborn chief.

[Style] Your associate has hair and clothes in the same style as the chief.

[Character] Your associate exhibits character traits that are exactly similar to the chief's.

Finally, on the last page participants received the following task:

Let's look further into the strategy "Your associate claims to remember various events from the chief's life."

Which features of memory would be found to be the most convincing? Consider the following three pairs of features.

[Availability] Event known only to very few / Event known to many.

[Level of detail] Event is described with a lot of detail / Event is described very abstractly.

[Memory type] Associate claims "I personally remember this event" / Associate claims "I just know that this happened to me."

After reading these instructions, participants were asked to indicate for each of the eight possible combinations[4] (presented in random order) whether they think it would be found by the tribe to be convincing. Responses were collected on a scale from 1 (Completely unconvincing) to 7 (Completely convincing).

A. Results

Free text responses: Looking at bare word frequencies in responses, "knowledge" and "to know" in various forms (seventy-seven instances) is mentioned three times more frequently than "memory" and "to remember" (in various forms, twenty-five instances). These results hint that it is unlikely possession of information rather than presentation of this information in a form of a memory claim that is taken to be key element in assessing evidence.

To look into the suggested strategies in more detail, the following coding-scheme was applied (some participants mentioned more than one strategy):

1. Strategies based on possession of information;
2. Strategies based on possession of traits;
3. Strategies based on possession of bodily signs.

Sixty-five percent of participants mentioned possession of information, 33% possession of traits, 7% possession of bodily signs. There were also several additional isolated strategies, like staging a miracle, but they were not mentioned by more than one or two participants each.

In the first category, it was often not possible to discern what form should communication of information take. Where it was presented explicitly enough, twenty-nine participants talked about demonstrating knowledge about the chief and the tribe while only eleven participants mentioned that the associate should claim to have memories of events from the chief's life. The fact that memories were relatively rarely mentioned may suggest that it was the unlikely possession of information that was thought to play the crucial role.

For traits, no comparable classification difficulties emerged. Twenty-four participants mentioned that the strategy should involve mimicking behavioral patterns, such as mannerisms, and a further fifteen mentioned mimicking character and personality traits.

Only seven participants mentioned bodily signs, in all cases associated with the manner in which the chief died, such as presenting a scar or a birthmark on the spot where the arrow hit the chief or pains in the heart.

Comparison of strategies: Mixed-effects linear regression with random intercepts by participant and strategy as a fixed factor showed that there were differences in how convincing various strategies were taken to be, $F(7, 693) = 54.9$, $p < .001$. Estimated marginal means for each strategy are plotted in Figure 8.3. Post hoc pairwise

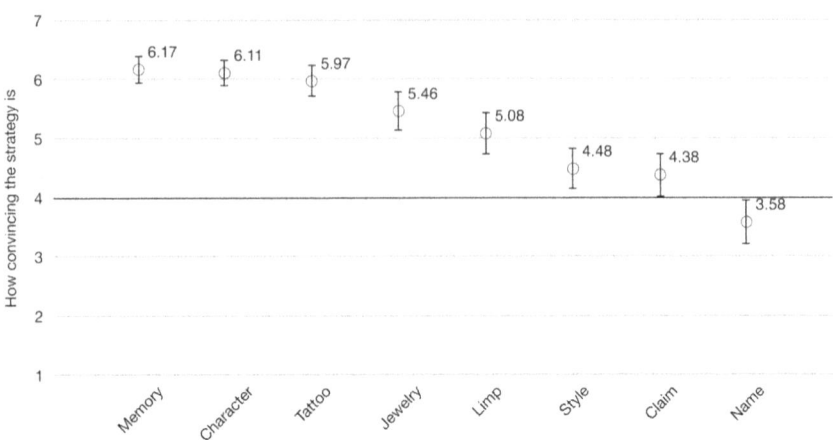

Figure 8.3 Estimated marginal means for how convincing different strategies were thought to be. Error bars indicate 95% CI.

comparisons suggest that there were no differences in how convincing the top three strategies (Memory, Character, Tattoo) were taken to be, all p_{holm} = 1.00. Second-tier strategies (Jewelry, Limp, no difference, p_{holm} = .176) were seen to be less convincing than those in the first-tier (all p_{holm} < .030) but more convincing (all p_{holm} < .010) than those in the third group (Style, Claim, no difference, p_{holm} = 1.00). The least convincing strategy (all p_{holm} < .001) was Name.

A mixed-effects model was fit with participants as a random factor, three fixed within-subject factors: level of detail (detailed vs. abstract), availability (known to few vs. known to many), and memory type (personally remembers vs. knows) and convincingness as an outcome. All three factors were statistically significant predictors of how convincing the memory is going to be taken to be (Level of detail, $F(1, 693) = 79.6$, $\beta = 0.97$, 95% CI [0.76, 1.18], $t(697) = 8.93$, $p < .001$; Availability, $F(1, 693) = 52.7$, $\beta = 0.79$, 95% CI [0.58, 1.00], $t(697) = 7.27$, $p < .001$; Memory type, $F(1, 693) = 14.1$, $\beta = 0.41$, 95% CI [0.20, 0.62], $t(697) = 3.76$, $p < .001$). There were no two- or three-way interactions between the factors (all $ps > .250$). See Figure 8.4.

Memory type, however, was the weakest predictor of the three, weaker than Level of detail ($z = 3.66$, $p < .001$) and Availability ($z = 2.48$, $p = .013$). No difference was observed between Availability and Level of detail ($z = 1.18$, $p = .24$).

Discussion: While the study confirms that accurate memory claims are taken to constitute evidence of reincarnation—strategy based on memory was perceived to be highly convincing, on a par with strategies based on mimicking the character of the deceased chief and also bodily marks—both free text responses and direct comparisons between the level of detail, availability of information about the event, and memory type suggest that it is otherwise hard-to-explain knowledge of facts that plays the key evidential role. While memory claims in which the agent is explicitly claiming to personally remember an event from the chief's life were taken to be more convincing than those claims in which the agent claims to simply know that the event happened to

Memory as Evidence of Personal Identity 139

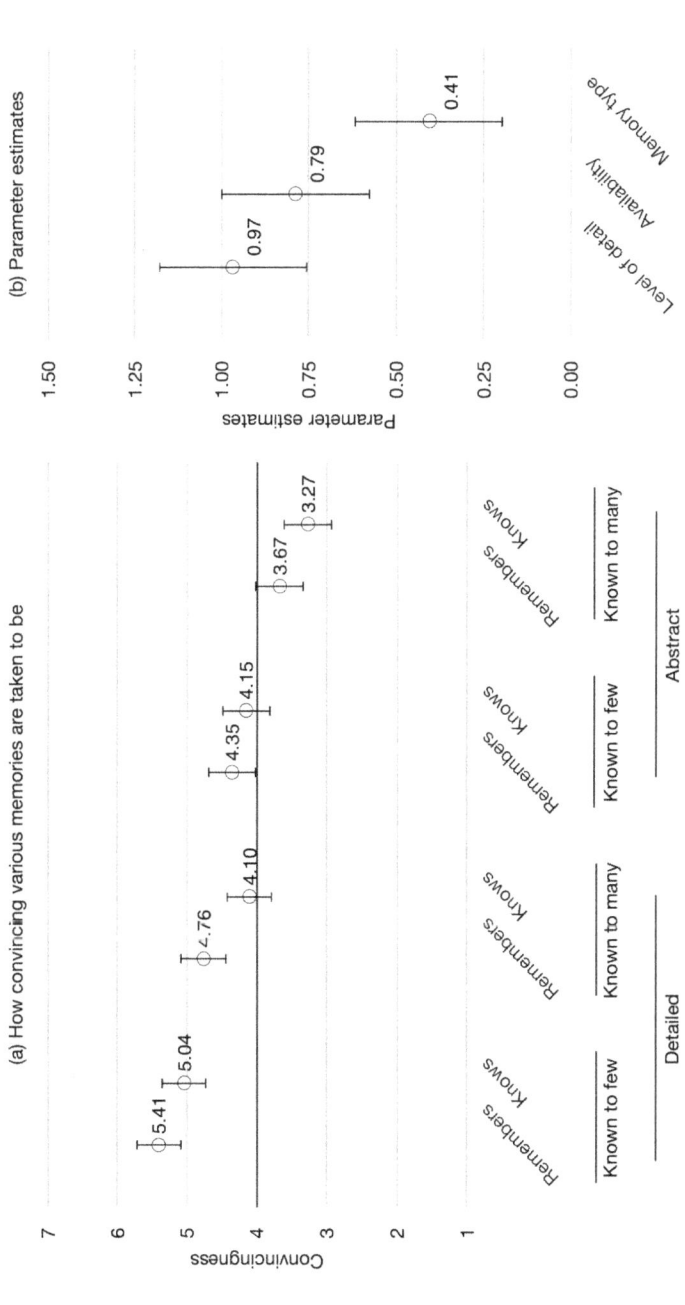

Figure 8.4 Estimated marginal means for how convincing various memories differing in level of detail, availability, and type of memory are taken to be (a) and parameter estimates of the three factors (b). Error bars indicate 95% CI.

him, this effect was considerably smaller than the effect of level of detail (detailed vs. abstract) or availability (known to few vs. known to many) of information contained in the memory claim.

III. General Discussion

The two studies presented in this chapter bear on the three descriptive questions discussed in the introduction. First, to what extent cases like Parfit's Celtic warrior case are judged to provide evidence supporting the belief in reincarnation depends on prior willingness to believe in reincarnation and what other potential explanations are salient (Study 1). On average, the case was not judged to constitute strong evidence in support of belief in reincarnation. There were, however, striking differences between groups holding different afterlife beliefs on a number of measurements: how plausible reincarnation was taken to be as an explanation of the case, how good was evidence for a belief in reincarnation taken to be, how likely participants thought it is that they would ascribe personal identity and remembering should they encounter such a case, and how often participants suggested an explanation in terms or reincarnation in a free text response. In all cases, those who believe in reincarnation scored high and those who believe that the person ceases permanently after death scored low. Furthermore, considering alternative explanations, some of which did not presuppose personal identity (telepathy, clairvoyance, artificial memory insertion by the technologically advanced extra-terrestrials), led participants to lower ascriptions of personal identity and remembering.

Second, written responses in Study 1 did not contain any clear hints that study participants interpret reincarnation in a way that does not assume personal identity. Furthermore, a measure of perceived identity was strongly correlated with measures of plausibility of explanation in terms of reincarnation, $r = .760$, and judgments of quality of evidence in support of the belief in reincarnation, $r = .759$, both $ps < .001$, suggesting that the concept of reincarnation employed by the participants implied preservation of personal identity. Furthermore, in factor analysis, explanation in terms of reincarnation loaded with other explanations that assume the presence of the Celtic warrior in the Japanese woman: immortality and possession.

In relation to the third question, the two studies collectively suggest that third-personal evidence of reincarnation is mostly constituted by otherwise hard-to-explain possession of knowledge rather than that knowledge being presented in a format of a memory claim that stresses that the event is personally remembered. This is most clearly demonstrated by direct comparisons between the level of detail, availability of information about the event, and memory type, as well as by relatively rare references to remembering in free text responses in Study 2. Free text responses in Study 1 also point to the fact that what was often taken to call for an explanation was the unlikely knowledge of facts: 26% of participants proposed explanations in terms of an educated guess, 12% speculated about other ways to obtain this kind of knowledge (testimony via family, access to authentic written sources, non-invasive archaeology), 13% entertained the possibility of sheer coincidence (made more palatable by pointing to the possibility that perhaps many people were making such claims and thereby someone was likely to guess just by luck, or portraying the claims made to be relatively vague).

In summary, the extent to which verifiable memory claims are taken to constitute evidence of personal identity in reincarnation depends on background beliefs. Furthermore, it seems that when potential past lives memories are considered, the element of verifiable memory claims that calls for an explanation—and that is sometimes explained in terms of reincarnation—is the possession of otherwise-hard-to-obtain knowledge about past events rather than whether the memory claim is presented as based on personally remembering the event.[5,6]

Notes

1. Excerpt from "Derek Parfit, Reasons and Persons" © 1984 Oxford Publishing Limited (Academic). Reproduced with permission of The Licensor through PLS clear.
2. Thus, when Claire White and her colleagues interpret eyewitness accounts of the selection procedures of the fourteenth Dalai Lama (which included the boy correctly choosing the items that belonged to the late thirteenth Dalai Lama and also handling those objects in a distinctive fashion) in terms of essentialism about personal identity (White, Sousa, and Berniunas 2014), they seem to underestimate the vast doctrinal resources available to the Tibetan bureaucrats.
3. Labels in brackets (in both studies) were not shown to the participants.
4. For example:

    Event known only to very few.
    Event is described with a lot of detail.
    Associate claims "I personally remember this event."

5. At least in third-personal scenarios based on observable evidence in a form of memory claims. The role of memory may be different in first-personal scenarios (White et al. 2016) or when presence of memories is stipulated in a vignette rather than inferred from memory claims (White 2015, 2016a, Woike et al. 2020).
6. I would like to thank members of the Centre for Philosophy of Memory at the Université Grenoble Alpes for comments on a previous version of this chapter and Phyllis Zych Budka for linguistic edits. This research has received funding from the European Research Council (ERC) under the European Union's Horizon 2020 research and innovation program (grant agreement 805498).

Bibliography

Ayer, A. J. (1956). *The Problem of Knowledge*. London: Macmillan.
Blok, S., G. Newman and L. J. Rips (2005). "Individuals and their Concepts." In W.-K. Ahn, R. L. Goldstone, B. C. Love, A. B. Markman and P. Wolff (eds.), *Categorization Inside and Outside the Lab*, 127–49. Washington: American Psychological Association.
Ducasse, C. J. (1961). *A Critical Examination of the Belief in a Life after Death*. Springfield: Charles C Thomas.

Hales, S. D. (2001). "Evidence and the Afterlife." *Philosophia*, 28 (1): 335–46.
Nichols, S. and M. Bruno (2010). "Intuitions about Personal Identity: An Empirical Study." *Philosophical Psychology*, 23 (3): 293–312.
Parfit, D. (1984). *Reasons and Persons*. Oxford: Oxford University Press.
Perrett, R. W. (1987). "Rebirth." *Religious Studies*, 23 (1): 41–57.
Siderits, M. (2015). *Personal Identity and Buddhist Philosophy: Empty Persons*, 2nd ed. Aldershot: Ashgate.
White, C. (2015). "Establishing Personal Identity in Reincarnation: Minds and Bodies Reconsidered." *Journal of Cognition and Culture*, 15 (3–4): 402–29.
White, C. (2016a). "Cross-cultural Similarities in Reasoning about Personal Continuity in Reincarnation: Evidence from South India." *Religion, Brain & Behavior*, 6 (2): 130–53.
White, C. (2016b). "The Cognitive Foundations of Reincarnation." *Method & Theory in the Study of Religion*, 28 (3): 264–86.
White C., R. Kelly and S. Nichols (2016). "Remembering Past Lives: Intuitions about Memory and Personal Identity in Reincarnation." In H. De Cruz and R. Nichols (eds.), *Advances in Religion, Cognitive Science, and Experimental Philosophy*, 169–95. London: Bloomsbury Academic.
White, C., P. Sousa and R. Berniunas (2014). "Psychological Essentialism in Selecting the 14th Dalai Lama: An Alternative Account." *Journal of Cognition and Culture*, 14 (1–2): 157–8.
Woike, J. K., P. Collard and B. Hood (2020). "Putting your Money Where Your Self Is: Connecting Dimensions of Closeness and Theories of Personal Identity." *PloS One*, 15 (2): e0228271.

9

The Importance of Morality for One's Self-Concept Predicts Perceptions of Personal Change after Remembering Wrongdoings

Matthew L. Stanley and Felipe De Brigard

Most people think of themselves as fundamentally morally good (De Freitas et al. 2018; Strohminger, Knobe, and Newman 2017; Tappin and McKay 2017) and express a desire to exemplify positive moral traits and virtues (Aquino and Reed 2002). Extant evidence has solidified the observation that morality features prominently in people's self-concept—roughly, the set of ideas that constitute our notions of who we are (Leary and Tangney 2011; Markus and Kunda 1986)—perhaps to a greater extent than any other features of our mental lives (Molouki and Bartels 2017; Strohminger et al. 2017; Strohminger and Nichols 2014, 2015). Prentice and colleagues (2019) have even offered evidence that we *need* to believe we possess positive moral traits and virtues, and that satisfying this moral need is closely linked to the realization of positive psychological outcomes (e.g., well-being, flourishing).

Yet, people commit moral transgressions with striking frequency in everyday life. Using ecological momentary assessment over a three-day period, Hofmann and colleagues (2014) found that participants reported 14% of the time that they had "committed, were the target of, witnessed, or learned about" a moral transgression within the past hour. Moreover, when asked to do so, people can readily recall having committed many different moral transgressions (Stanley and De Brigard 2019), including some which participants themselves judge as having been very morally wrong (Stanley et al. 2017; Stanley, Henne, and De Brigard 2019; Stanley et al. 2020a). Our more egregious past wrongdoings also tend to be more frequently ruminated upon (Huang et al. 2020; Stanley, Stone, and Marsh 2021), even though they should be more threatening to our morally good self-concept.

How can we reconcile the fact that positive moral traits feature prominently in people's self-concept with the overwhelming evidence that people frequently behave immorally? Recently, we have leveraged research on autobiographical memory to offer a possible way to reconcile this apparent discrepancy (Stanley and De Brigard 2019). Even though people commit and remember their moral transgressions quite frequently, they might still use those memories to create a morally good self-concept in the present. Personal past events can be woven into a life story in a way that ensures our worst failures, improprieties, and shortcomings can be attributed to a distant, dissimilar past self who has changed considerably for the better. Outside of the moral domain, Wilson and Ross (2000) showed that when instructed to evaluate themselves favorably, participants were more likely to describe inferior past selves than when instructed to evaluate themselves accurately. In a related study, Ross and Wilson (2002) found that participants reported having more positive views of themselves in the present when they were encouraged to feel distant from their former disappointments and close to their former successes (see also Demiray and Janssen 2015).

In the moral domain, Stanley and colleagues (2017) found that participants judged their own moral transgressions from the more distant past (e.g., ten years ago) to be morally worse than their more recent transgressions, which was not the case for moral transgressions committed by others. Similar results emerge when measuring *subjective* distance between past events and the present, as opposed to *objective* calendar time. When remembering certain events, people can feel detached from and dissimilar to some past selves, but close to and similar to other past selves (Wilson and Ross 2003). Although objective temporal distance (calendar time) and subjective distance are related, they do not always track one another. We can feel subjectively close to past selves who acted in events that occurred a very long time ago, and we can feel subjectively distant from past selves who acted in events that occurred very recently. Stanley and colleagues (2017) found that when participants were cued to remember events during periods of time when they were very dissimilar to their current selves, they judged their moral transgressions to be more morally wrong than similar kinds of transgressions they committed during periods of time when they believed they were very similar to their current selves. Complementary research has found that, regardless of when the events actually occurred in the past (i.e., calendar time), people perceive considerable dissimilarity in their selves over time after reflecting on their own past moral transgressions, but they perceive stability in others after reflecting on past events in which said others committed moral transgressions (Stanley et al. 2019).

The fact that these effects are consistently obtained for remembered transgressions committed by oneself, but not for transgressions committed by others, suggests that the way in which these personal past events are woven into a life story may serve a self-related function. People seem to advantageously utilize temporal and subjective distancing in a way that selectively links together different past events within a life story to buttress a belief in their own personal moral improvement over time. Doing so may help to dismiss or explain away their more serious past wrongdoings (e.g., "My worst transgressions were committed by a dissimilar self who has changed considerably for the better") and to portray the current self favorably. With that being said, the evidence supporting this self-related function has been indirect; there is currently a lack of direct evidence that these autobiographical memory effects help people to enhance and protect their otherwise morally good self-concept.

The primary purpose of this chapter is to provide more direct evidence that these memory-mediated mechanisms serve a self-related function. To this end, we leverage research indicating that, although most people report that positive moral traits are central to their self-concept, there are still individual differences in the degree to which such moral traits are central to their self-concept (Aquino and Reed 2002). The extent to which people report that moral traits are central to their self-concept predicts charitable behaviors (Reed et al. 2016), the experience of moral emotions (Aquino et al. 2011), responses to intergroup conflict (Reed and Aquino 2003), and contributions to public goods (Aquino et al. 2009). However, the importance of morality to our self-concept has not previously been linked to memory-mediated perceptions of personal change or psychological distancing after committing transgressions.

Across three studies, we investigate whether the degree to which morality is central to people's self-concept predicts how much they distance themselves from their past moral transgressions and facilitate a sense of personal change. Using different experimental methods and measures, we consistently find that individuals for whom moral traits are more central to their self-concept tend to foster a stronger sense of memory-mediated personal change. We report all measures, manipulations, and participant exclusions in all three studies.

I. Study 1

In Study 1, we cued participants to recall their own past moral transgressions from a time during which they thought of themselves as being very *different* from their current selves, as well as from a time during which they thought of themselves as being very *similar* to (or the same as) their current selves. Participants reported the severity of each of their moral transgressions. They also completed a well-validated scale to measure individual differences in the importance of morality to the self-concept (Aquino and Reed 2002). This paradigm was developed to test two hypotheses. First, we tested the hypothesis that people would judge their transgressions when they were very different from their current selves to be morally worse than their transgressions when they were very similar to their current selves (this is a conceptual replication of Stanley et al. 2017). Second, and more importantly, we tested the novel hypothesis that the extent to which people perceive positive moral change when reflecting on their past wrongdoings will be moderated by the importance of positive moral traits for their own self-concept. To address this second hypothesis, a *moral change* score was computed for each participant operationalized as the difference in the severity of moral wrongness judgments between wrongdoings recalled when they were very different from their current selves and wrongdoings recalled when they were very similar to their current selves. Higher values on this *moral change* score indicate a stronger tendency to perceive moral improvement in the self. So, we expected higher values on this moral change score to be positively related to the importance people place on morality in constructing their personal identities.

A. Materials and Methods

Participants: One-hundred thirty individuals completed this study via Amazon's MTurk for monetary compensation. In all three studies reported herein, participant recruitment was restricted to individuals in the United States who had completed at least 500 HITs and had a prior approval rating of at least 95%. Nine participants in Study 1 were excluded for failing the check question at the end or for providing clearly nonsensical responses to a memory cue (e.g., "good" was the entire response). As such, data were analyzed with the remaining 121 participants (M_{age} = 38 years, SD = 10, age range = [20, 67], 45 females, 75 males, 1 non-binary). We aimed to recruit a total of 130 participants to provide sufficient power (.85) to detect moderate-sized correlations (r = .30; two-tailed), after expected exclusions. All participants in all studies reported being fluent English speakers. Informed consent was obtained from each participant in all studies in accordance with protocol approved by the Duke University Campus Institutional Review Board.

Materials: Participants completed a ten-item individual difference questionnaire assessing the importance of morality to the self-concept—the Moral Identity scale (Aquino and Reed 2002; see Appendix). This scale is based on a conceptualization of moral identity as a schema organized around a set of moral trait associations (e.g., compassionate, kind, honest) and loads on two dimensions: Internalization and Symbolization. The five Internalization items index the degree to which moral traits are central to the self-concept; the five Symbolization items index the degree to which moral traits are reflected in the respondent's actions in the world. Sample items for the Internalization subscale include "Being someone who has these characteristics is an important part of who I am" and "It would make me feel good to be a person who has these characteristics." The Symbolization subscale includes items like "I am actively involved in activities that communicate to others that I have these characteristics" and "The types of things I do in my spare time (e.g., hobbies) clearly identify me as having these characteristics." Participants rated all ten items on a seven-point Likert-type scale (1 = *completely disagree*, 7 = *completely agree*). Both subscales were reliable (Internalization: M = 6.24, SD = .92, α = .85; Symbolization: M = 3.89, SD = 1.58, α = .92).

Procedure: This study was self-paced and consisted of a single session. Participants were asked to recall two different events from their personal pasts and to provide several ratings for each recalled event. They were instructed to provide memories of actions they believed to be morally wrong, and they were assured that their responses would be confidential (see Stanley et al. 2017 for an analogous cuing procedure). Specifically, participants were instructed to provide one memory from each of the following cues: (1) during a period of time in which you felt you were a very different person than the person you are now, please recall a specific memory of an event in which you did something that you believe to be morally wrong; (2) during a period of time in which you felt you were very similar to or the same as the person you are now, please recall a specific memory of an event in which you did something that you believe to be morally wrong. We refer to the former as the *different self* condition and to the latter as the *similar self* condition. The order of these two cues was randomized across participants.

For each memory, participants described the event in two to six sentences and typed in the month and year when the event occurred. As a manipulation check question, participants answered the following *personal change* question: To what extent have you changed as a person since this event occurred? (1 = *not at all*, 7 = *a lot*). Participants then reported how morally wrong their behavior was (1 = *slightly morally wrong*, 7 = *very morally wrong*).

Participants were randomly assigned to complete the Moral Identity scale either before or after recalling, describing, and making judgments about the two events. At the end, participants answered basic demographic questions and responded to the following attention-check question: Do you feel that you paid attention, avoided distractions, and took the survey seriously? They responded by selecting one of the following: (1) no, I was distracted; (2) no, I had trouble paying attention; (3) no, I did not take the study seriously; (4) no, something else affected my participation negatively; or (5) yes. Participants were ensured that their responses would not affect their payment or their eligibility for future studies. Only those participants who selected "5" were included in the analyses (see exclusions in the previous paragraphs). This same attention-check question has been used in recent published research (e.g., Stanley, Marsh, and Kay 2020b; Stanley et al. 2021). We have reported all measures, conditions, and data exclusions. Upon completion of the study, participants were monetarily compensated for their time.

Data analyses: Due to severe violations of normality, we conducted non-parametric Sign Tests for related samples and Spearman's rank-order correlations.

B. Results and Discussion

Manipulation check: To ensure that participants responded as expected to the *different self* and *similar self* memory cues, we first conducted a Sign Test with memory cue condition (*different self* vs. *similar self*) on participants' *personal change* judgments. Participants reported that they had changed more over time since the event occurred in the *different self* condition ($M = 6.40$, $SD = .84$, $Median = 7.00$) than in the *similar self* condition ($M = 3.10$, $SD = 1.85$, $Median = 2.00$; $p < .001$).

Next, we tested the hypothesis that participants tend to judge their transgressions to be more morally wrong when they believe themselves to be different than—as opposed to similar to—their current selves. A Sign Test revealed that memories of moral transgressions in the *different self* condition ($M = 5.92$, $SD = 1.23$, $Median = 6.00$) were judged to be more morally wrong than memories of transgressions in the *similar self* condition ($M = 4.79$, $SD = 1.63$, $Median = 5.00$; $p < .001$). Figure 9.1 graphically depicts these results.

Finally, we hypothesized that the extent to which people perceive positive moral change when reflecting on their past wrongdoings will be moderated by the importance of morality to their self-concept. To address this hypothesis, a *moral change* score was computed for each participant (the moral wrongness judgment in the *different self* condition *minus* the moral wrongness judgment in the *similar self* condition). Higher values on this *moral change* score indicate a stronger tendency to perceive moral improvement in the self. Using Spearman's rank-order correlations, the Internalization subscale of the Moral Identity scale was positively correlated with participants' moral change scores ($r(119) = .21$, $p = .021$), but there was no significant relationship between the Symbolization subscale and participants' moral change scores ($r(119) = .07$, $p = .47$). So, those individuals for whom positive moral traits are more central to their self-concept tend to perceive more positive moral change in themselves when reflecting on their past wrongdoings.

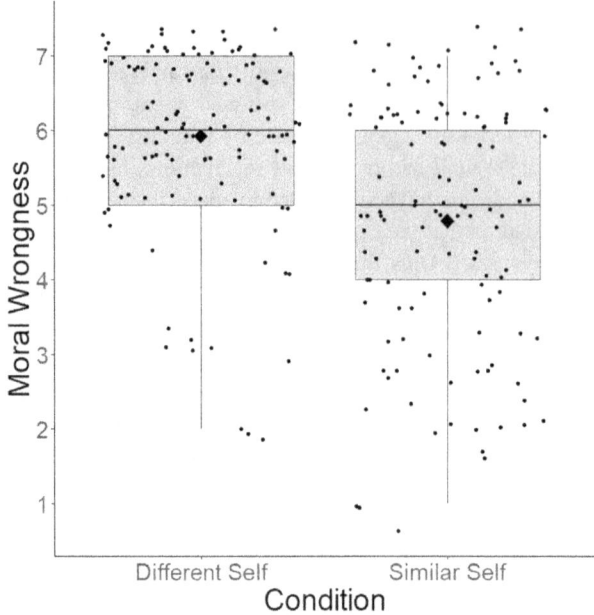

Figure 9.1 Boxplots for moral wrongness judgments split by condition (*different self* vs. *similar self*) are depicted for Study 1. Each participant's moral wrongness rating is represented by the small black dots, which were jittered for visualization purposes. The averages across participants of moral wrongness ratings are represented with the large black diamonds.

II. Study 2

Study 1 provides some support for our initial two hypotheses: (1) that people judge their remembered moral transgressions to be worse when they believe themselves to be different than—as opposed to similar to—their current selves; and (2) that people perceive more positive moral change when positive moral traits are more central to their self-concept. Study 2 extends Study 1 by including an additional condition: participants were asked to recall events in which they witnessed someone else commit a moral transgression in the *different self* and *similar self* conditions. We expected the effects from Study 1 to hold only for memories of past events in which the participant committed the moral transgression, and not for events in which the participant witnessed someone else commit a moral transgression. If these effects hold only for memories of past events in which the participant committed the moral transgression, then we can be more certain that these effects are serving a self-related function.

A. Materials and Methods

Participants: One-hundred thirty individuals completed this study via Amazon's MTurk for monetary compensation. Fifteen participants were excluded for failing the check question at the end (same as in Study 1) or for providing clearly nonsensical responses to a memory cue (e.g., "good" was the entire response). As such, data were analyzed with the remaining 115 participants (M_{age} = 37 years, SD = 10, age range = [20, 69], 46 females, 69 males, 0 non-binary). As in Study 1, we aimed to recruit a total of 130 participants to provide sufficient power (.85) to detect moderate-sized correlations (r = .30; two-tailed), after expected exclusions.

Materials: As in Study 1, participants completed the ten-item Moral Identity scale (Aquino and Reed 2002). Both subscales of the Moral Identity scale were reliable (Internalization: M = 6.24, SD = .92, α = .85; Symbolization: M = 3.89, SD = 1.58, α = .92).

Procedure: The procedure in Study 2 was the same as in Study 1, but with the addition of a new condition. In Study 1, the two memories that participants provided were from an *actor* perspective, meaning that participants only recalled their own past moral transgressions (i.e., the participants were the actors in the memories). In Study 2, participants were instructed to recall two additional memories from an *other* perspective (i.e., the participant witnessed some other person commit the moral transgression). Specifically, participants recalled two additional memories in accordance with the following two memory cues: (1) during a period of time in which you felt you were a very different person than the person you are now, recall a specific memory of an event in which you witnessed someone else do something you believe to be morally wrong; (2) during a period of time in which you felt you were very similar to or the same as the person you are now, recall a specific memory of an event in which you witnessed someone else do something you believe to be morally wrong.

The four memories provided by each participant in Study 2 yielded a 2 (different self vs. similar self) x 2 (actor perspective memory vs. other perspective memory) experimental design.

Statistical analyses: Due to severe violations of normality, we conducted non-parametric Sign Tests for related samples and Spearman's rank-order correlations.

B. Results and Discussion

Manipulation check: To ensure that participants responded as expected to the *different self* and *similar self* memory cues, we first conducted Sign Tests with memory cue condition (*different self* vs. *similar self*) on participants' *personal change* judgments. For actor perspective memories, participants reported that they had changed more over time since the event occurred in the *different self* condition (M = 6.10, SD = 1.12, Median = 6.00) than in the *similar self* condition (M = 2.60, SD = 1.71, Median = 2.00; p < .001). Similarly, for other perspective memories, participants reported that they had changed more over time since the event occurred in the *different self* condition (M = 5.97, SD = 1.18, Median = 6.00) than in the *similar self* condition (M = 2.38, SD = 1.77, Median = 2.00; p < .001).

We then tested the hypothesis, supported by Study 1, that participants tend to judge past transgressions of which they were the perpetrators (i.e., the actors) to be more morally wrong when they believe themselves to be different than—as opposed to similar to—their current selves. For actor perspective memories, a Sign Test revealed that memories of moral transgressions in the *different self* condition ($M = 5.67$, $SD = 1.35$, $Median = 6.00$) were judged to be more morally wrong than memories of transgressions in the *similar self* condition ($M = 4.63$, $SD = 1.64$, $Median = 5.00$; $p < .001$). In contrast, for other perspective memories, another Sign Tested revealed no significant difference in moral wrongness judgments between the different self ($M = 5.97$, $SD = 1.26$, $Median = 6.00$) and similar self ($M = 5.83$, $SD = 1.20$, $Median = 6.00$) conditions ($p = .08$). Figure 9.2 graphically depicts these results.

We then attempted to replicate the finding from Study 1 that the extent to which people perceive positive moral change in themselves when reflecting on their past wrongdoings will be moderated by the importance of morality to their self-concepts. As in Study 1, a *moral change* score was computed for each participant (the moral wrongness judgment in the *different self* condition *minus* the moral wrongness judgment in the *similar self* condition). Using Spearman's rank-order correlations for actor perspective memories, the Internalization subscale of the Moral Identity scale was positively correlated with participants' moral change scores ($r(113) = .25$, $p = .006$), but there was no significant relationship between the Symbolization subscale and participants' moral change scores ($r(113) = -.05$, $p = .58$). For other perspective memories, in contrast, moral change scores were not significantly related to the Internalization scores ($r(113) = .14$, $p = .13$) or the Symbolization scores ($r(113) = -.16$, $p = .10$). Thus, participants for whom positive moral traits are more central to their self-concept tended to perceive more positive moral change in themselves but less positive moral change in others, when reflecting on past wrongdoings.

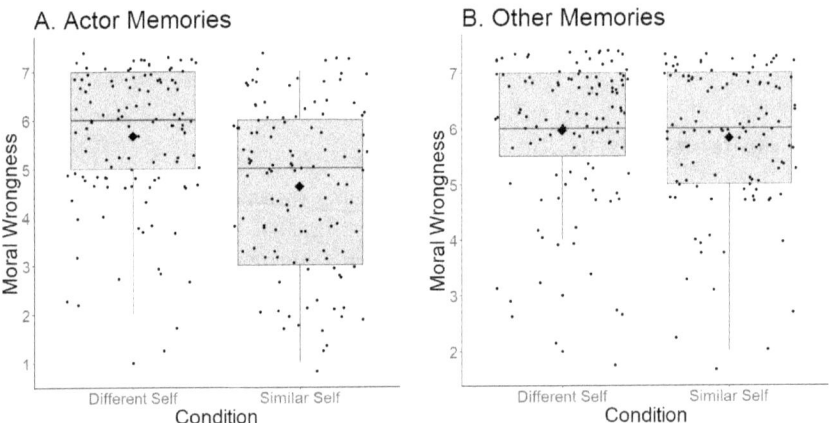

Figure 9.2 For actor perspective memories (A) and other perspective memories (B), boxplots are depicted for moral wrongness judgments split by self condition (*different self* vs. *similar self*) for Study 2. Each participant's moral wrongness rating is represented by the small black dots, which were jittered for visualization purposes. The averages across participants of moral wrongness ratings are represented with the large black diamonds.

III. Study 3

The purpose of Study 3 is twofold. First, Study 3 directly measures impressions of personal change after committing moral transgressions in actor and other memory perspective conditions. This allows us to test the hypothesis that people who hold positive moral traits to be more central to their self-concept will also perceive more change in their selves since committing moral transgressions (but not change in others after witnessing those others commit moral transgressions). Second, Study 3 directly measures impressions of subjective distance from remembered events (Ross and Wilson 2002). We can feel detached from and dissimilar to some former selves who committed certain actions, but close to and similar to other past selves who committed other actions. These feelings of subjective closeness and farness to former selves can help foster a favorable view of the self in the present (Wilson and Ross 2003). By measuring subjective distance from past events, we tested the hypothesis that people who hold moral traits to be more central to their self-concept will also feel more distant from past selves who committed moral transgressions—but no relationship between subjective distance and the importance of morality to the self-concept for events where participants witnessed someone else's wrongdoing.

A. Materials and Methods

Participants: Four-hundred one individuals completed this study via Amazon's MTurk for monetary compensation. Sixty-two participants were excluded for failing the check question at the end (same as in previous studies), for providing clearly nonsensical responses to a memory cue (e.g., "good" was the entire response), or for providing a memory outside the specified temporal range (five to ten years ago). As such, data were analyzed with the remaining 339 participants ($M_{age} = 40$ years, $SD = 12$, age range = [18, 76], 140 females, 199 males, 0 non-binary). We aimed to recruit roughly 200 participants in each cell of the experimental design to provide sufficient power (.85) to detect small-to-moderate-sized correlations ($r = .25$, two-tailed), after expected exclusions.

Materials: As in the previous studies, participants completed the ten-item Moral Identity scale (Aquino and Reed 2002). Both subscales of the Moral Identity scale were reliable (Internalization: $M = 6.11$, $SD = .99$, $\alpha = .83$; Symbolization: $M = 4.06$, $SD = 1.37$, $\alpha = .88$).

Procedure: This study was self-paced and consisted of a single session. Participants were randomly assigned to provide a memory from one of the following two cues (between-subjects design): (1) please recall the most morally wrong action you committed between five and ten years ago; (2) please recall the most morally wrong action you witnessed someone else commit between five and ten years ago. Adapting the terminology utilized in Study 2, we refer to the former as an *actor perspective memory*, and to the latter as an *other perspective memory*. Regardless of the kind of event participants were asked to recall, they described the event in two to six sentences and typed in the month and year when the event occurred. Participants then reported how much the person who committed the moral transgression has changed since the event occurred (1 = *not at all*, 7 = *a lot*) and how subjectively distant from the event they currently feel (1 = *feels very close*, 7 = *feels very distant*). This measure of subjective distance was adapted from Ross and Wilson (2002).

Participants were randomly assigned to complete the Moral Identity scale (described earlier) either before or after recalling, describing, and making judgments about event. At the end, participants answered the same demographics questions and attention-check question as in the previous studies. Upon completion, participants were monetarily compensated for their time.

Data analyses: Due to some variables exhibiting severe violations of normality, we conducted non-parametric Mann-Whitney U Tests for independent samples and Spearman's rank-order correlations.

B. Results and Discussion

We first tested the hypothesis that participants would tend to report that they have changed more since committing past moral transgressions than other people have changed since committing past moral transgressions. A Mann-Whitney U Test revealed that participants reported more personal change in their selves after committing a moral transgression ($M = 5.48$, $SD = 1.56$, $Median = 6.00$) than personal change in others after those others committed a moral transgression ($M = 3.12$, $SD = 1.74$, $Median = 3.00$; $p < .001$). We then tested the hypothesis that people tend to feel more psychologically distant from events in which they committed a moral transgression relative to events in which they witnessed someone else commit a moral transgression. A Mann-Whitney U Test revealed that participants did indeed report feeling more distant to their past selves when recalling their own past transgressions ($M = 5.08$, $SD = 1.53$, $Median = 5.00$) than when recalling transgressions they witnessed others commit ($M = 4.61$, $SD = 1.76$, $Median = 5.00$; $p = .016$). Figure 9.3 graphically depicts these results. Note that there were no differences in actual calendar time between actor and other perspective memory conditions ($p > .10$).

Next, we tested the hypothesis that the extent to which participants perceive change in the self over time after reflecting on their moral transgressions will be moderated by the importance of morality to their self-concept. Using Spearman's rank-order correlations for memories from the actor perspective, participants' perceived change in themselves after having committed a moral transgression was positively correlated with both the Internalization subscale ($r(166) = .43$, $p < .001$) and the Symbolization subscale ($r(166) = .33$, $p < .001$) of the Moral Identity scale. In contrast, for other perspective memories, participants' perceived change in others after they committed a moral transgression was *negatively* correlated with the Internalization subscale ($r(169) = -.19, p = .013$), and there was no significant correlation with the Symbolization subscale ($r(169) = .12, p = .12$).

Finally, we tested the hypothesis that the extent to which participants subjectively distance themselves from their past moral transgressions would be moderated by the

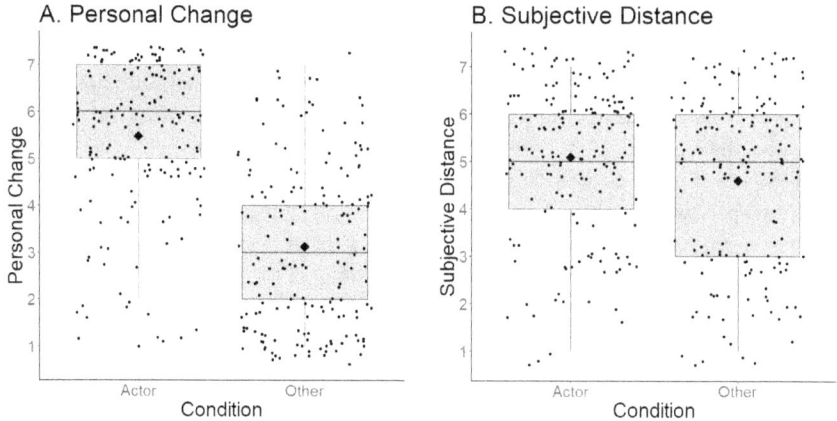

Figure 9.3 For personal change (A) and subjective distance (B) outcome variables, boxplots are depicted for ratings split by condition (actor perspective memories vs. other perspective memories) for Study 3. Each participant's individual rating is represented by the small black dots, which were jittered for visualization purposes. The averages across participants' ratings are represented with the large black diamonds.

importance of morality for their self-concept. Using Spearman's rank-order correlations for memories from the actor perspective, participants' tendency to subjectively distance themselves from their own past moral transgressions was not significantly correlated with the Internalization subscale ($r(166) = .05$, $p = .57$) or the Symbolization subscale ($r(166) = .09, p = .23$) of the Moral Identity scale. For memories from the other perspective, participants' perceived change in others after they committed a moral transgression was not significantly correlated with the Internalization subscale ($r(169) = -.06, p = .45$), but it was negatively correlated with the Symbolization subscale ($r(169) = -.17, p = .023$).

IV. General Discussion

In recent years, we have argued that our autobiographical memories may help to reconcile two seemingly conflicting tendencies: the fact that people take positive moral traits to be central to their self-concept and, while at the same time, they tend to behave immorally quite frequently (Stanley and De Brigard 2019). Specifically, we have argued that people distance themselves from past selves that committed wrongdoings in the service of protecting a morally good self-concept in the present. In this chapter, we sought to provide more direct evidence for these memory-mediated self-serving effects by testing whether the importance of morality for participants' self-concept predicts perceptions of personal change and psychological distancing for remembered moral transgressions committed by previous selves.

Our results indicate that participants tend to report having undergone significant personal change when reflecting on their own past wrongdoings, and that they tend to report feeling psychologically distant from their past selves who committed wrongdoings. But participants perceived less change in others after recalling events in which those others committed moral transgressions, and they did not report feeling as psychologically distant from the wrongdoings of others. Most importantly, we found that individuals for whom morality is more central to their self-concepts tend to believe they have undergone more positive change when confronted with their own past wrongdoings (however, there was no significant relationship between the self-importance of morality and psychological distancing from participants' own past wrongdoings). These results more directly support the theoretical position that memory can be employed to construct a morally good self-concept in the present—even if people frequently recall and ruminate upon their wrongdoings. Personal past wrongdoings can be woven into a life story where those events are indicative of turning points in the life story, and as indications of personal moral improvement. In this way, memory may play a critical role in creating a morally good self-concept.

The relationships between the importance of morality to the self-concept and perceptions of personal change over time were larger and more consistent across studies for the Internalization subscale of the Moral Identity scale than for the Symbolization subscale. This discrepancy suggests that perceptions of personal change more closely track personal beliefs about the value of possessing positive moral traits rather than how we actually act in the world and how we portray ourselves to the rest of the world. Future work could further explore when and why these subscales diverge in predicting people's moral beliefs and judgments.

Bibliography

Aquino, K., D. Freeman, A. Reed II, V. K. Lim and W. Felps (2009). "Testing a Social-Cognitive Model of Moral Behavior: The Interactive Influence of Situations and Moral Identity Centrality." *Journal of Personality and Social Psychology*, 97 (1): 123–41.

Aquino, K., B. McFerran and M. Laven (2011). "Moral Identity and the Experience of Moral Elevation in Response to Acts of Uncommon Goodness." *Journal of Personality and Social Psychology*, 100 (4): 703–18.

Aquino, K. and A. Reed II (2002). "The Self-Importance of Moral Identity." *Journal of Personality and Social Psychology*, 83 (6): 1423–40.

De Freitas, J., H. Sarkissian, G. E. Newman, I. Grossmann, F. De Brigard, A. Luco and J. Knobe (2018). "Consistent Belief in a Good True Self in Misanthropes and Three Interdependent Cultures." *Cognitive Science*, 42 (Supplement 1): 134–60.

Demiray, B. and S. M. Janssen (2015). "The Self-Enhancement Function of Autobiographical Memory." *Applied Cognitive Psychology*, 29 (1): 49–60.

Hofmann, W., D. C. Wisneski, M. J. Brandt and L. J. Skitka (2014). "Morality in Everyday Life." *Science*, 345 (6202): 1340–43.

Huang, S., M. L. Stanley and F. De Brigard (2020). "The Phenomenology of Remembering Our Moral Transgressions." *Memory and Cognition*, 48: 277–86.

Leary, M. R. and J. P. Tangney, eds. (2011). *Handbook of Self and Identity*. New York: Guilford Press.

Markus, H. and Z. Kunda (1986). "Stability and Malleability of the Self-Concept." *Journal of Personality and Social Psychology*, 51 (4): 858–66.

Molouki, S. and D. M. Bartels (2017). "Personal Change and the Continuity of the Self." *Cognitive Psychology*, 93: 1–17.

Prentice, M., E. Jayawickreme, A. Hawkins, A. Hartley, R. M. Furr and W. Fleeson (2019). "Morality as a Basic Psychological Need." *Social Psychological and Personality Science*, 10 (4): 449–60.

Reed II, A. and K. F. Aquino (2003). "Moral Identity and the Expanding Circle of Moral Regard Toward Out-Groups." *Journal of Personality and Social Psychology*, 84 (6): 1270–86.

Reed II, A., A. Kay, S. Finnel, K. F. Aquino and E. Levy (2016). "I Don't Want the Money, I Just Want Your Time: How Moral Identity Overcomes the Aversion to Giving Time to Prosocial Causes." *Journal of Personality and Social Psychology*, 110 (3): 435–57.

Ross, M. and A. E. Wilson (2002). "It Feels Like Yesterday: Self-Esteem, Valence of Personal Past Experiences, and Judgments of Subjective Distance." *Journal of Personality and Social Psychology*, 82: 792–803.

Stanley, M. L., A. Bedrov, R. Cabeza and F. De Brigard (2020a). "The Centrality of Remembered Moral and Immoral Actions in Constructing Personal Identity." *Memory*, 28 (2): 278–84.

Stanley, M. L., R. Cabeza, R. Smallman and F. De Brigard (June 2021). "Memory and Counterfactual Simulations for Past Wrongdoings Foster Moral Learning and Improvement." *Cognitive Science*, 45 (6). https://doi.org/10.1111/cogs.13007.

Stanley, M. L. and F. De Brigard (2019). "Moral Memories and the Belief in the Good Self." *Current Directions in Psychological Science*, 28 (4): 387–91.

Stanley, M. L., P. Henne and F. De Brigard (2019). "Remembering Moral and Immoral Actions in Constructing the Self." *Memory and Cognition*, 47 (3): 441–54.

Stanley, M. L., P. Henne, V. Iyengar, W. Sinnott-Armstrong and F. De Brigard (2017). "I'm not the Person I Used to Be: The Self and Autobiographical Memories of Immoral Actions." *Journal of Experimental Psychology: General*, 146 (6): 884–95.

Stanley, M. L., E. J. Marsh and A. C. Kay (2020b). "Structure-Seeking as a Psychological Antecedent of Beliefs about Morality." *Journal of Experimental Psychology: General*, 149: 1908–18.

Stanley, M. L., A. R. Stone and E. J. Marsh (2021). "Cheaters Claim They Knew the Answers All Along." *Psychonomic Bulletin & Review*, 28: 341–50.

Strohminger, N., J. Knobe and G. Newman (2017). "The True Self: A Psychological Concept Distinct from the Self." *Perspectives on Psychological Science*, 12 (4): 551–60.

Strohminger, N. and S. Nichols (2014). "The Essential Moral Self." *Cognition*, 1: 159–71.

Strohminger, N. and S. Nichols (2015). "Neurodegeneration and Identity." *Psychological Science*, 26 (9): 1469–79.

Tappin, B. M. and R. T. McKay (2017). "The Illusion of Moral Superiority." *Social Psychological and Personality Science*, 8 (6): 623–31.

Wilson, A. E. and M. Ross (2000). "The Frequency of Temporal-Self and Social Comparisons in People's Personal Appraisals." *Journal of Personality and Social Psychology*, 78: 928–42.

Wilson, A. E. and M. Ross (2003). "The Identity Function of Autobiographical Memory: Time is on Our Side." *Memory*, 11: 137–49.

Appendix: Moral Identity Scale (Aquino and Reed 2002)

Here is a list of some characteristics that might describe a person: caring, compassionate, fair, friendly, generous, helpful, hardworking, honest, kind. For a moment, visualize in your mind the kind of person who has these characteristics. The person with these characteristics could be you or it could be someone else. Imagine how that person would think, feel, and act. When you have a clear image of what this person would be like, please answer the questions below on scale from 1 (completely disagree) to 7 (completely agree).

Internalization Subscale:

1. It would make me feel good to be a person who has these characteristics.
2. Being someone who has these characteristics is an important part of who I am.
3. I would be ashamed to be a person who has these characteristics. (R)
4. Having these characteristics is not really important to me. (R)
5. I strongly desire to have these characteristics.

Symbolization Subscale:

1. The types of things I do in my spare time (e.g., hobbies) clearly identify me as having these characteristics.
2. The kinds of books and magazines that I read identify me as having these characteristics.
3. The fact that I have these characteristics is communicated to others by my membership in certain organizations.
4. I am actively involved in activities that communicate to others that I have these characteristics.
5. I often wear clothes that identify me as having these characteristics.

10

Uncomfortable Decisions

Paul Bloom and L. A. Paul

A behavioral economist gets a tempting job offer and agonizes over it. She meets with a friend and tells him that she is struggling to decide. It's a very tempting offer, she says, but she's happy in her current department. The offer is at a more prestigious university, but in a less attractive city. The pay is better, but the move would put her farther away from her aging parents. She goes on and on, describing her anguish, and then her friend puts up his hand and gently tells her to stop.

He says to her:

> Look, you study decision-making for a living. You teach about it, write papers about it. So, you know what to do. Write a list of the pros and cons of moving and another list of the pros and cons of staying. For each item, give it a weight corresponding to its importance. Then, just add it up: do the math, treating the pros as positive and the cons as negative.

She stares at him, getting madder and madder as he speaks, until she finally yells at him: "For God's sake, this is serious!"

* * *

We like this joke because it rings true. There is something that seems wrong about making a significant decision through this type of process. It might be useful to make a list of pros and cons, and even to weigh them, but few of us would act solely on the outcome of this mathematical calculation.

Other decision processes are similarly unpalatable. We do not like to make significant decisions based on social science research. We do not like to choose randomly, even in cases where flipping a coin is plainly the wisest choice (Keren and Tiegen 2010)—as when the values of the options are impossible to distinguish and decision-making is very costly. Many of us are reluctant to defer to another person, even if we believe that the other person is wiser. We also often do not want to appeal to an artificial intelligence (AI), even if we believe it to have decision-making powers superior to those of humans, a bias dubbed "algorithm aversion" (e.g., Dietvorst, Simmons, and Massey 2015; Castelo, Bos, and Lehmann 2019; though see Logg, Minson, and Moore 2019 for cases in which this does not apply).

What do these uncomfortable decision processes share? We can characterize them as *impersonal*. It's not you who is making the decision; it is someone or something else. This is to be contrasted with personal decision-making, where, well, you just decide, perhaps after mulling it over for a long time. To put it colloquially, for normal acceptable choices, you "own" your decision. Now, at some level, this distinction is an illusion—one's personal decisions are determined by causal processes and might themselves reduce to algorithms of the sort that the friend of the behavioral economist urged her to rely on. But, nonetheless, it doesn't feel this way; a satisfying decision-making process is more than an algorithmic process. It's something that *we* do, and in a certain way.[1]

But what, precisely, makes certain decision-making processes seem impersonal? What do we want from our decisions?

* * *

Before looking at options, we should note two subtleties about the phenomenon we're talking about.

First, our concern about impersonal decision-making processes applies to significant decisions, not so much to trivial ones. There are those who allow their partners, or sometimes even their waiters, to choose what dishes they will eat in a restaurant, and we do flip coins to resolve small dilemmas. Studies find that people are uncomfortable using a coin toss to decide which life to save but are fine with flipping a coin to decide authorship order or whether to attend the opera or the theater (Keren and Tiegen 2010). We suspect, though, that even here there is some discomfort with relying entirely on these processes. We often want to be able to *approve* the dinner recommendation, and it's a cliché that some people, finding that the coin's outcome wasn't what they wanted, might choose to flip again.

Still, we are especially interested in significant decisions here. Even people who are comfortable making trivial decisions impersonally will balk at making big ones this way. One of the authors of this chapter has argued that this distrust of such impersonal procedures is particularly salient in the case of "transformative experiences"—experiences, like choosing to become a parent or emigrating or going to war, where you must choose between new lives, or choose between having a new life or keeping your old one (Paul 2014). Notably, with these types of decisions, there's an inability to properly imagine what this new life is like.

Second, we have no qualms about using impersonal sources of information to *help* us make important decisions. We assume that every reader of this chapter regularly uses ratings—from Yelp, TripAdvisor, Amazon, and so on—when deciding where to eat, which hotel to stay at, what book to read, and so on. This is true for even the most significant of choices. Someone deciding whether to have a child is likely to be very interested in the data on whether children make you happy or give meaning to your life and very likely to want to talk to new parents and hear about their experiences. Someone who was wrestling with a decision about cancer treatment might well be very interested in data on outcomes and survival rates.

We are similarly happy to get information from more "internal" procedures such as list making and priority rankings. It would kill the joke if her friend suggested that she write down the pros and cons of each option and they talk them through together—Who would get upset at that? Indeed, Charles Darwin famously wrote a list of pros and cons in his journal when deciding whether to marry his cousin Emma Wedgwood—"a nice soft wife on a sofa with good fire, & books & music perhaps," but then again, "perhaps quarrelling"—but it's clear that he's just spitballing ideas to himself and the decision is all his own (see Quammen 2007). Other internal procedures include imagining that you made a decision and assessing how you feel about it or figuring out what one would recommend to a third party (Galef 2021 enumerates several processes of this sort). We are comfortable with all of these—so long as the final decision is left up to us.

* * *

What is the source of our reluctance?

One possibility is that we don't trust the reliability of certain impersonal decision-making processes. This concern is clearest enough when it comes to survey data. Perhaps this is because we believe we are special. This can be rational in certain cases. One of the authors dislikes cheese, and if he went to a restaurant with the best reviews, he might end up at one that specializes in cheese—most people do like cheese—and this would be terrible.

Taken to the extreme, though, this skepticism is unreasonable. Nobody should refuse a vaccine because, though it works for others, they believe (without any evidence) that their body is different. The same holds for preferences. One can imagine, along the lines of philosophical thought experiments, Perverse Man—a person whose tastes are the opposite of most everyone else's. A hotel that gets 9.8/10 on TripAdvisor—"best hotel in Cancun," "a perfect paradise"—would be misery for Perverse Man, while a hotel ranked 1.4—"disgusting," "horrible"—would be perfect for him. But there is no Perverse Man. While everyone is unique and nobody should choose just by the numbers (a hotel can be ranked highly because of its golf course, but what if you don't golf?), surely, in the absence of other information, everyone should prefer a highly ranked hotel to one that everyone else hates.

Our suspicion is that the source of the reluctance to rely on certain decision-making processes isn't actually concern about their utility. For one thing, as mentioned before, most people believe that ratings, anecdotes, and so on *are* useful. They're just not sufficient. The behavioral economist in the joke might believe, sincerely, that ranking the pros and cons of a decision is a useful way to proceed, but nonetheless not want to rely solely on such a process.

We suggest instead that this aversion has deeper roots, and we are interested in two of them here—one concerning authenticity, the other autonomy. (These terms are used in many ways, and we don't have settled views on how to capture all their ordinary or even technical connotations, so we will work with a rough distinction.)

A certain type (not the only type) of authentic decision-making, as we'll understand it, is decision-making in which an agent intentionally and knowledgably chooses an option in a way that is "true to themselves." This way of choosing requires a certain kind of understanding of one's options, which we'll expand upon in the following paragraphs. Such decision-making can be important in contexts where one is making a life-changing decision of great import, such as the choice to emigrate, start a family, or embark on a major career change. A paradigm case of making such an authentic decision concerning oneself requires this type of understanding, which is (arguably) gained through reflection, careful assessment, and imaginatively evolving the world forward under different possible actions in order to knowledgeably and volitionally choose the outcome that will lead to the most happiness or greatest life satisfaction for oneself (and relevant others).[2]

As one of us, a fan of authenticity, has put it:

> You use your memories from the past, your beliefs about the present, and your anticipations about possible subjective futures to formulate your current and evolving [preferences], as well as to develop temporally extended, forward-looking, subjective projections about what will happen. . . . You use this reflection on what you think these events will be like, that is, what you think your lived experience will be like, to authentically determine your preferences about your future. (Paul 2014: 106–7)

Autonomy, on the other hand, involves control. It involves making the decision yourself, and not off-loading the process to ratings, polls, an algorithm, an oracle, and so on, though, again, you might be receptive to information from these other sources.

There's a sense of which this prizing of autonomy might be perverse. Suppose a website is better at choosing books for you to read than you are—and you know it. The books it chooses make you happier, more engaged, you learn more, and so on than the books you choose for yourself. If your goal is to be happier, you should just let the website choose, even if it's not the choice that you want to make at the time. But autonomy considerations would push against this.

Note critically that autonomous choices can be made on any grounds at all. One can make an autonomous choice based on a gut feeling or even based a criterion you might acknowledge as foolish ("I want to go to this hotel because its name reminds me of the hotel I went to on my honeymoon."). There's certainly no requirement that one imaginatively reconstruct the outcome of a decision-making process. Many authentic processes are autonomous ones. But what we are interested in here is in exploring the discomfort involved with certain kinds of autonomous decisions that are not, in the way we are defining it here, authentic.

* * *

Now let's go back to our questions about comfortable and uncomfortable decisions. If we are choosing whether to embark upon a new life, we can do it comfortably by deliberating about our options, accurately assessing the value of each possibility through imagining what it would be like to be those possible new selves leading those new lives, and personally choosing the best one. This approach hits all the "like" buttons. It is both authentic and autonomous in the way we've been framing these features. It involves making the choice ourselves, in an informed way, where we undertake an appropriately informed process of evaluating our options and comparing them in order to make the best choice.

In the case of the job offer, if our behavioral economist were to authentically engage in making this decision, she'd imaginatively put herself in each possible job, and assess (or maybe create) the value of that option. Then she'd compare these values to form a preference, either preferring Job A over Job B (if A's value is higher than B's value) or vice versa. And then she would act on this preference. Autonomy plus authenticity—what's not to like?

But then there are decisions that are neither autonomous nor authentic. Indeed, if the relevant kind of authenticity requires an imaginative recreation, a simulation, of the life one would end up taking, then perhaps transformative experiences are simply not amenable to this kind of authentic decision-making process. We can't decide in a satisfying way to become a parent, say, because someone without children cannot fully imagine what it is to have children (Paul 2014). Perhaps the same is true for a decision like taking a new job.

Consider now a less welcome alternative. Perhaps we are not far away from the day when our behavioral economist would be able to hire a benevolent AI to do the calculation for her. She might engage the Google Deepmind Concierge to have a bespoke algorithm provide an analysis based on masses of data collected on her (and the rest of humanity) since the birth of the internet. The AI uses the algorithm to assess what jobs that others relevantly similar to her have liked most, scales these results (somehow) to make comparisons meaningful, and chooses the highest-scoring job. For a small added fee, it informs her prospective employers and politely declines the alternative position on her behalf. Our professor is highly likely (let's assume) to get a result that, afterwards, she will testify to as making her happier than other options would have. But her decision is neither authentic nor autonomous.

There are similar decision processes that also don't meet these two criteria. She might flip a coin. Or be paralyzed with indecision, so that the offer goes away. Or consider decisions that are made through involving certain forms of nudging: perhaps someone else sets up the world for her in ways that unobtrusively guide her to the choice that is her best option. Or, perhaps someone else simply makes the choice for her, acting in her best interests, someone like the AI, only made of flesh and blood. None of these alternatives are autonomous or authentic.

But now, as a distinct class of cases, consider choices that are autonomous but not authentic. Imagine, in search of doing something a little more satisfying, our professor rejects the services of the AI, opting instead to have Google package all the relevant numbers, including the assigned, scaled values, and deliver it to her in easy-to-read, bite-sized chunks. Given this information, she maps out the decision tree, does the math—and perhaps sleeps on it, indulges in silent prayer—and then decides on which job to take. This is likely to get the same result as using the benevolent AI. (Maybe it's still worth it to hire the AI to decline the offer she doesn't want.) But it's not authentic in the sense we are exploring, because it doesn't require simulating the different alternative lives and making the comparisons based on this knowledge.

* * *

The two authors of this chapter agree on the importance of autonomy. People are happier when they themselves are making the decision, rather than when it's offloaded to a coin toss, an AI, and so on.[3] The authors also agree that for non-trivial decisions, the assumed efficacy of the procedure matters. Our behavioral economist is unlikely to ask her four-year-old niece for advice or bring out an Ouija board.

We disagree about the authenticity requirement, however. One of us (Paul Bloom) thinks that people would be comfortable appealing to the AI-facilitated process described earlier, so long as the ultimate choice in their hands; the other (L. A. Paul) is skeptical. To make this sort of decision authentically, she skeptically argues, one has to get a real sense of what each new life will bring, and to do so, one has to be able to accurately imagine themselves, or perhaps a transformed version of themselves, in the new situation.

The problem, she thinks, is that it simply isn't acceptable to rely on the happiness utilities assigned by an expert AI to make this sort of choice. There just seems to be something wrong, at an intuitively deep level, with using numerical quantities to capture what matters. For her, this is why the joke works. Officially, experts in behavioral economics and other social sciences endorse rigorous, mathematically based treatments of decision-making and evidentially based policy formation. Officially, the right way for our economist to make the decision between job offers is to assign numerical values, calculate expected utilities, and choose in a way that maximizes expected value. But, as the joke illustrates, this feels wrong, at a gut level—it's not at all how we feel we should make the decision.

Is this just some sort of residual anti-scientific bias, some fear of being reduced to mere mathematics, a last gasp of religiosity that needs to be put to rest in the modern world? Perhaps we simply need to bring our gut feeling to heel and impose, as careful thinkers, a more rational approach. But our pro-authenticity author argues otherwise. She thinks, rather, that our gut intuition reflects our knowledge of a real fact: numerical quantities, while useful in many contexts, are inadequate for representing the value of the nature and character of the kinds of lives we are contemplating. (In fact, she'd argue, doing the work of imaginative evaluation can be itself seen as a rational process.)

The need for a deep, intuitive understanding of how each job choice would change one's life is why the imaginative evaluation is so important. The point isn't that you can't compare the values on this approach. You can: you can compare them, and have a defined preference, and understand which option it is that you'd prefer. The point is that there's a richness to the way we want to assign values to these life choices that isn't being captured by the numbers. There's something about the experience of imaginatively understanding these different lives and the different ways that you would respond to each job choice that allows you to make a more informed assessment about the pros and cons, and thus know how to assign and represent their values in a way that will let you make a fully informed, and thus authentic, choice. However it is that we want to represent and assign values to our life options, it isn't captured by the official approach.

And, she thinks, as the joke shows, we will not be fully satisfied with a process that lacks such authenticity. Knowing, say, that becoming a parent made 65% of people happier, or that declining a job most likely will maximize one's priorities (the pros will outweigh the cons) just isn't enough in this context.

To illustrate the kind of details that could be obscured by simply looking at the numbers, consider the following point about these kinds of transformative decisions.

Making a major job change does more than change what you are doing with your life. It changes who you are. This is most obvious when we think about choosing between very different careers. If you become a dentist, who you are and what you care about will be very different from who you are and what you care about if you become a pianist. In this sense, the choice between careers is a deeply personal transformative choice about whom you want to become, about what to give up and what to embrace, and about choosing the life you want to live. As we can put it, it's a choice between your future selves. Which self do you want to become? This is the problem that the person must solve.

This, L. A. Paul argues, suggests that in such cases, the decision-making process matters. The process is internal in a special way because your choice determines what you want. If you choose to become a dentist and it makes you happy, it's the process of becoming a dentist that makes you happy. You are glad, at that point, that you hadn't decided to become a pianist! On the other hand, if you choose to become a pianist, it's the process of becoming a pianist that makes you happy about being a pianist. You're glad, at that point, that you hadn't decided to become a dentist!

To put it differently, such a choice is partially endogenous. And this endogeneity creates a problem with our interpretation of the results of the choice. What if your dentist self would testify to a +4 happiness, saying that your wealthy, comfortable life is fantastic, while the pianist would testify to a +2 happiness, but claim that your life, devoted as it is to music, is so much more satisfying? Given that the future self you choose will replace the self that you are now, how are you to know which of them is the best, most natural extension of who you are right now? How are those selves comparable to who you are now, as you choose, and by extension, how are they to be compared with each other (Paul and Healy 2018; Paul 2020)?

The job choice faced by our behavioral economist is like this—the choice isn't quite as stark, but if making a major job change can endogenously affect you in the way that choosing a career can, then the structure reappears. If the behavioral economist chooses the more prestigious university, as she embeds herself into her new life, it will change her in ways that, in the end, will make her value her new life over her old one. If she stays put, she'll strengthen her current values and be glad she chose being close to her parents over a fancy intellectual climate.

With so much to lose (or gain) and so many unknowns to face, the stakes are high. Which life is the better one for her to choose? Which one of these lives is most authentically the extension of the life she is living right now, as she makes her choice? It's tempting to think the question could be resolved if she could just imagine herself into the lives of her different possible selves and compare them. Then, at least, she could decide which possible self better captures who she is and what she really wants from life.

Unfortunately, this is precisely what she can't do. And, in the case where you are supposed to appeal to an AI-facilitated process, you can't either. You can't, and don't, simulate these new lives and compare them yourself. Instead, you turn to an impersonal process of assessment and scaling performed by an AI. And it simply isn't clear whether the AI has the resources to assess the options and thus determine your preferences in the right way. If all that matters to the AI is maximizing happiness, other things that seem important could be left out. In particular, the choice that the AI makes for you could fail to be a legitimate extension of your current preferences. Rather, it could be a choice that involves a replacement of your current preferences. Say the AI tells you to choose the dentist option: after all, it brings greater happiness (+4 over +2). In this scenario, you could be choosing to replace your life with a new life that, while it is +4 happier, isn't really an extension of what you care about now. In other words, it is not a choice that truly captures who you are, at this moment of choosing. Rather, the replacement life brings with it a kind of psychological rearrangement, making you glad, as a result of the process, that the replacement has occurred. If you rely solely on the AI, there is no way of knowing whether your current preferences will be satisfied, as opposed to merely replaced.

Our authenticity-friendly author doesn't think that people would be worried about this particular problem. Rather, she thinks they would be worried that, in some more general sense, simply using AI-generated numerical values won't capture the experiential complexity and meaningfulness of each option. In this situation, discomfort stems from the fact that the numbers might not represent all the factors that matter to you, since these factors go beyond what they can capture. If you simply rely on the AI, you must choose without thinking it through for yourself. All you have are the outcome-numbers gathered by the AI. And this is uncomfortable.

* * *

The other author, less persuaded about the importance of authenticity, agrees with many of the discussed points. Paul Bloom very much agrees that people want more than happiness—we also want to live meaningful lives, to be moral, to have purpose, and other things as well. (Indeed, he has just published a book making exactly this argument: Bloom 2021.) Our motivational pluralism makes decision-making difficult, as these values often clash. And it suggests that we would be most interested in a decision-making process that draws upon multiple sources of information about how we will end up after the decision has been made. If the AI only took happiness into account, it would be inadequate.

Bloom agrees as well that the choices one makes influence how one evaluates the outcome. This is one of the more robust findings in social psychology, a classic example of the phenomenon of cognitive dissonance (see Cushman 2020 for review). Get people to choose between two things that are valued roughly equally, and, later, they will tend to like the chosen one more and the unchosen one less (e.g., Egan, Santos, and Bloom 2007). This effect occurs even when the choice is blind, where they don't know what they're choosing (Sharot, Velasquez, and Dolan 2010).

Finally, he agrees that people often don't like to think about important decisions in terms of numerical rankings. Among other things, it's rather unseemly. It would be a poor marriage proposal indeed if the suitor, on bended knee, proudly states to his beloved the precise estimated values of "married' versus "not married" ("Married wins!," he sings to her.). Better to say instead, "I couldn't imagine any other life than one with you. It was no choice at all." Indeed, there may be some intrapersonal benefit to thinking of important and difficult-to-reverse decisions (getting married, having children, religious conversions) as no-brainers, the only conceivable thing to do. It certainly reduces regret. Perhaps this is one function of cognitive dissonance.

Decision-making has to happen, though. To choose A over other options is to come to believe that A ranks above the rest, and this requires putting the options on a common scale. Yes, if you make the decisions through simulating alternative possibilities, you will have access to information that is rich and qualitative, and yes, assigning the values is a complex matter. Perhaps the values you assign are represented as numbers, or perhaps they are in some non-numerical representational format, but in the end, comparing values is what decision-making comes down to. If the suitor insists that his own decision-making process is exempt from this, then he is deluding himself.

More generally, both authors agree that none of these points—our motivational pluralism, our distaste for numerical comparison, and the fact that making a decision influences what we think about the outcome—entail that we want authenticity in our decision-making process. If you concede that non-authentic processes can tell you that some choice is likely to make you happier, then it suggests that this process can also tell you that this choice will make you more satisfied with your life in some more abstract sense. To take a real example, while there is a lot of debate over the interpretation of the data (e.g., Nelson, Kushlev, and Lyubomirsky 2014), there is some evidence that parents report having less pleasurable experiences than non-parents—but also report more meaningful lives (see Bloom 2021 for review and discussion). Pluralistic decision-making does not require authenticity.

Similarly, both agree that cognitive dissonance is a phenomenon that is general to decision-making, applying both to major life experiences and to totally mundane choices like deciding which of two identical cookies to pick up. Thus, the partially endogenous nature of decision-making does not in itself provide evidence for a desire for authentic decision-making processes, nor does the fact that people often don't like to think in terms of quantitative comparisons. This is again compatible with all sorts of processes that are not authentic.

In the end, the core disagreement between the authors might be about how people construe decisions, particularly high-stakes decisions. The author who is sympathetic to authenticity concerns sees such decisions in terms of changes of self, and perhaps the replacement of one self by another—and she believes that, at some level, when making high-stakes decisions, non-philosophers recognize that such choices bring major changes in the kind of person one is. And so authenticity becomes important; people want to know how the choice will change them. The author who is skeptical about the importance of authenticity rejects this view of common-sense decision-making. Someone deciding whether to be a parent, say, will want to make the choice that will lead to a life that has the most happiness, purpose, and meaning—and won't naturally construe it as involving a change in the sort of person they are. And so authenticity, as defined here, doesn't matter—if they trust the data and can choose autonomously, that's all they need.

While the authors disagree about the actual importance of authenticity and about whether people value it, we agree that at least the second question is an empirical one. What *do* people think of authentic and non-authentic decision-making processes? And so we will end with a clichéd proposition—but one that we believe really applies here: more research is needed.[4]

Notes

1. Indeed, the same psychological forces that make us want to "own" decisions we make in the world might also lead us to discomfort about theories of the mind that deny a singular agentic self. As part of a critique of massive modularity, Jerry Fodor (1998) expresses this desire for decision-making "ownership" with characteristic verve: "If, in short, there is a community of computers living in my head, there had also better be somebody who is in charge; and, by God, it had better be me."
2. "True to themselves" and "knowledgeably and volitionally" admit of many interpretations, but we will work with these intuitive glosses in hopes of making incremental progress.
3. This is a claim about how people like to make decisions when we have to; it is not meant to imply that we always enjoy making decisions. Often, we do not (e.g., Schwartz 2004).
4. For some research on this question, which came out as this chapter went to press, see "Deciding to be Authentic: Intuition is Favored over Deliberation When Authenticity Matters," by Kerem Oktar and Tania Lombrozo, forthcoming in Cognition.

Bibliography

Bloom, P. (2021). *The Sweet Spot: The Pleasures of Suffering and the Search for Meaning*. New York: Ecco.

Castelo, N., M. W. Bos and D. R. Lehmann (2019). "Task-Dependent Algorithm Aversion." *Journal of Marketing Research*, 56 (5): 809–25.

Cushman, F. (2020). "Rationalization is Rational." *Behavioral and Brain Sciences*, 43: 1–16.

Dietvorst, B. J., J. P. Simmons and C. Massey (2015). "Algorithm Aversion: People Erroneously Avoid Algorithms After Seeing Them Err." *Journal of Experimental Psychology: General*, 144 (1): 114.

Egan, L. C., L. R. Santos and P. Bloom (2007). "The Origins of Cognitive Dissonance: Evidence from Children and Monkeys." *Psychological Science*, 18 (11): 978–83.

Fodor, J. (1998). "The Trouble with Psychological Darwinism." *London Review of Books*, 20 (2): 11–13.

Galef, J. (2021). *The Scout Mindset: Why Some People See Things Clearly and Others Don't*. New York: Penguin.

Keren, G. and K. H. Teigen (2010). "Decisions by Coin Toss: Inappropriate but Fair." *Judgment and Decision Making*, 5 (2): 83.

Logg, J. M., J. A. Minson and D. A. Moore (2019). "Algorithm Appreciation: People Prefer Algorithmic to Human Judgment." *Organizational Behavior and Human Decision Processes*, 151: 90–103.

Nelson, S. K., K. Kushlev and S. Lyubomirsky (2014). "The Pains and Pleasures of Parenting: When, Why, and How is Parenthood Associated with More or Less Well-Being?" *Psychological Bulletin*, 140 (3): 846–95.

Oktar, K. and T. Lombrozo (forthcoming). "Deciding To Be Authentic: Intuition is Favored Over Deliberation When Authenticity Matters." Cognition.

Paul, L. A. (2014). *Transformative Experience*. Oxford: Oxford Univ. Press.

Paul, L. A. (2020). "Who Will I Become?" In J. Schwenkler and E. Lambert (eds.), *Becoming Someone New: Essays on Transformative Experience, Choice, and Change*, 16–36. Oxford: Oxford Univ. Press.

Paul, L. A. and K. Healy (2018). "Transformative Treatments." *Noûs*, 52: 320–35.

Quammen, D. (2007). *The Reluctant Mr. Darwin: An Intimate Portrait of Charles Darwin and the Making of his Theory of Evolution (Great Discoveries)*. New York: WW Norton & Company.

Schwartz, B. (2004). *The Paradox of Choice: Why More is Less*. New York: Ecco.

Sharot, T., C. M. Velasquez and R. J. Dolan (2010). "Do Decisions Shape Preference? Evidence from Blind Choice." *Psychological Science*, 21 (9): 1231–5.

11

Authenticity as a Pathway to Coherence, Purpose, and Significance

Rebecca J. Schlegel, Patricia N. Holte, Joe Maffly-Kipp,
Devin Guthrie, and Joshua A. Hicks

Authenticity has been defined in a myriad of ways across disciplines such as philosophy, sociology, and psychology. The meaning of authenticity also differs across domains such as people, art, products, and restaurants (Kovacs 2019). While there has been disagreement about what exactly authenticity is and how best to achieve it, theorists and laypeople alike tend to agree that authenticity is valuable across a wide variety of domains (Carroll 2015).

While it is beyond the scope of this chapter to review all the ways authenticity has been defined, we believe that it is important to adopt a working definition for the remainder of the chapter. To this end, we focus on two common themes that emerge across a variety of conceptualizations of authenticity in persons: knowing and expressing one's true self. These themes are represented in two of the most popular current models of trait authenticity in psychology (Kernis and Goldman 2006; Wood et al. 2008) as well as a more recently developed model of state authenticity (Sedikides et al. 2017). While these models differ in a variety of ways, they converge in suggesting that knowing and expressing one's true self are key components of the experience of authenticity. The importance of self-knowledge and self-expression is also well represented in people's lay theories about authenticity (Schlegel et al. 2013) as well as commonly used self-report measures of subjective authenticity (Kernis and Goldman 2006; Wood et al. 2008).

While there is some debate about whether people can accurately judge their levels of authenticity (e.g., Jongman-Sereno and Leary 2019), it is clear that subjective judgments of authenticity are important to a host of well-being indicators (e.g., Rivera et al. 2019a). In particular, subjective judgments of authenticity are important for the experience of meaning in life (MIL). Indeed, classical philosophical and humanistic theories surrounding what it means to "live the good life" hold both authenticity and MIL to be key components of eudaimonic well-being. In fact, several scholars hold that meaning in life can only be differentiated from more hedonic forms of well-being precisely by its association with authentic self-expression (Keyes and Haidt 2003; McGregor and Little 1998; Waterman 1984). The idea that authenticity and meaning are linked has a decades long history of supporting empirical work (e.g., Ménard and Brunet 2011; McGregor and Little 1998; Schlegel et al. 2009, 2011).

However, the research on authenticity and MIL to date has dealt with how authenticity relates to an abstract conceptualization of MIL. In these studies, assessments of MIL often involve face-valid items, leaving the word "meaning" up to interpretation and resulting in an idiosyncratic assessment of MIL. While this is certainly informative, recent research has converged on a multidimensional conceptualization of MIL, with coherence, purpose, and significance as three key facets of MIL (Martela and Steger 2016; George and Park 2017; Costin and Vignoles 2020). Empirical work suggests that ratings of each of these components explains approximately 60% to 70% (George and Park 2016; Costin and Vignoles 2019) of variation in global MIL judgments. Each of these components may relate differently to oft studied antecedents and outcomes of meaning, and, as such, there exists a call to revisit empirical and theoretical work on MIL with this multidimensional approach to understanding and measuring the construct. To date, work on authenticity and meaning has not examined this issue directly. However, there are theoretical and empirical cues that suggest how authenticity may lead to each of these three facets. Thus, the aim of the following sections is to lay out possible ways that authenticity may lead to meaning via coherence, purpose, and significance.

I. Coherence/Comprehension

Coherence is defined as "the feeling that one's experiences or life itself makes sense" (Martela and Steger 2016). One common way people make sense of their experiences is through autobiographical reasoning, the process of establishing causal or thematic links between your past, present, and projected future (Habermas and Bluck 2000; Habermas and de Silveira 2008). Establishing these links is a method of meaning-making that may be facilitated by feelings of and/or reflections on authenticity and the true self.

Although a great deal of theoretical and empirical work in a narrative context argues that telling your story helps you understand who you are (e.g., McAdams 2001), it is also probable that a sense of knowing who you are helps you tell your story. Authenticity can serve as a lens through which individuals interpret life events (Wilt, Thomas, and McAdams 2019), and metaphors of self discovery (Schlegel, Vess, and Arndt 2012; Waterman 1984) can create the structure of a compelling and coherent life narrative. This is reflected in the finding that individuals tend to believe they are becoming more authentic over the course of their lives and will continue to do so in the future (Seto and Schlegel 2018). Given that life stories are shaped, in part, by cultural expectations of what a healthy life narrative should look like (McLean, Pasupathi, and Pals 2007), this pattern suggests that there may be a cultural expectation that people "find" themselves as they move through their lives. When people perceive a trajectory of increasing authenticity, this may serve as a cue that one's life is moving in the right direction, which in turn should foster an overall sense of coherence. This idea is supported by findings that people also believe their life is becoming more meaningful over time (i.e., an authentic life is perceived as a meaningful life and vice versa; Seto and Schlegel 2018).

Another possibility is that when people feel connected to their true self, their true self-concept serves as a salient connecting thread between the past, present, and future. This aligns particularly well with the idea that people hold the belief that they should use their true self as a guide in decision-making (Schlegel et al. 2013). Our past work has revealed that most people agree that following the true self is likely to lead to personally satisfying decisions and that people use the true self to lend credence and value to the choices they make. We have found that such framing (even in retrospect) makes decisions feel more satisfying (Kim et al. 2021). Similarly, we suspect that people can distance themselves from past decisions that did not turn out well by framing those decisions as not being guided by their true selves (e.g., due to social pressure or to not knowing one's true self yet). In this way, the idea of the true self provides a lens through which to make sense of one's story. Feelings of self-knowledge are a likely prerequisite for such feelings of coherence. If we think of coherence as the ability to create a narrative about life that makes sense, then a perceived lack of knowledge of/connection to the true self would likely lead to a feeling of telling a story without knowing the main character.

Viewed at a lower level of abstraction, coherence can also be thought of as the process of finding patterns and connections (Martela and Steger 2016). Heintzelman, Trent, and King (2013) found that simple exposure to coherent stimuli (i.e., words or pictures that "go together") enhanced feelings of meaning in life (theoretically via coherence). It may follow, then, that a sense of consistency between internal conceptions of self and external behavior contributes to feelings of coherence as well. The same may be said for consistency between the self and the environment. Schmader and Sedikides (2018) propose that authenticity is an emotional response cued by person-environment-fit. The resulting cognitive, motivational, and social fluency (Schmader and Sedikides 2018) may also contribute to a sense of coherence in the moment as opposed to in the grander scheme of one's life story.

II. Purpose

Purpose is defined as the extent to which a person feels that their life is directed toward goals that reflect core values (e.g., George and Park 2017; McKnight and Kashdan 2009). A sense of purpose helps provide momentum and engagement, and without it an individual might feel aimless. Critically, in order to move toward life goals that are valued, one must have an idea of what their core values and beliefs are (McKnight and Kashdan 2009). This requires the development of a clear sense of identity (Emmons 2003; Hitlin 2003; Rogers 1963). Once an individual has clear values tied to their identity, they must be able to engage with their environment in a way that creates momentum toward value-based goals (George and Park 2016). This conceptualization has clear and concrete implications for a felt sense of personal authenticity, particularly the extent to which a person feels they know and are able to express who they truly are.

In other words, subjective authenticity seems central to the construction of a life that feels purposeful.

The broad idea that people must know and express themselves in order to create a purposeful existence is consistent with multiple areas of previous research. For example, Sheldon and Elliott (1999) demonstrated across multiple investigations that the pursuit of goals consistent with core values leads to higher levels of goal attainment and well-being over time (see also Sheldon and Houser-Marko 2001). Furthermore, Acceptance and Commitment Therapy (Hayes 2004), an intervention that overtly targets the construction of a value-oriented sense of self and a commitment to goal attainment, has been shown to lead to a variety of positive mental health outcomes (Brown et al. 2016), including meaning in life (Datta et al. 2016; Moghebel Esfahani and Haghayegh 2019). There is also reason to believe that this relationship might be bidirectional (i.e., that purposeful goal attainment can lead to authenticity). This idea is consistent with a self-regulation framework (Carver and Scheier 2000), which asserts (in part) that people set goals at a high level of abstraction/construal ("be goals") in order to strive toward desired states of being. A recent investigation found that framing academic goals at a higher level of construal (by focusing on the meaning/purpose of the task) led students to feel more self-concordant (Davis et al. 2016). These separate areas of research all generally support the notion that self-knowledge/expression (i.e., authenticity) can lead to a more purposeful existence, and vice versa.

A recent body of research has further investigated this relationship based on the idea that knowing and expressing one's *true* self (rather than broader conceptualizations of identity) holds particularly important implications for meaning and purpose. Schlegel and colleagues (2009, 2011) have demonstrated that people's belief in, and sense of connection to, true selves positively predicts MIL. No existing research has focused on the specific relationship between the true self and purpose, but related research on life decisions and goal pursuit can provide important conceptual context. For example, McGregor and Little (1998) found that setting goals consistent with who a person feels like they "truly" are led to a greater sense of MIL. Schlegel and colleagues (2013) extended this by demonstrating that important life decisions felt more satisfying when people felt a high degree of true self-knowledge, and suggested that people use their true self as a "guide" to navigate critical moments in life. Kim and colleagues (2021) found similar effects when decisions were simply framed as being made by following the true self, even if that framing happened after the decision had been made. These particular studies suggest that even illusions of authenticity can promote a feeling that one's decisions are satisfying and meaningful. Finally, a 2019 investigation found that a promotion-focused orientation toward goals was positively associated with perceptions of knowledge and expression of one's true self (Kim et al. 2019), again hinting at the possible bidirectional relationship between purpose and authenticity. To the extent that the pursuit of important life goals can be understood as a fundamental component of purpose (see George and Park 2016), these findings help to illustrate how true self-knowledge and expression are important for a sense of purpose in life.

Existing research is limited by the recency of the tripartite meaning model and more recent conceptualizations of authenticity, but compelling evidence suggests that subjective authenticity and a sense of purpose in life can bidirectionally impact each other, ultimately leading to greater overall well-being. Future research should further explicate this relationship using more recently adopted measures of tripartite MIL (e.g., George and Park 2016; Martela and Steger 2016). Important work can also be done examining exactly *how* people can identify values and goals that feel connected to their true self, with the intention of deriving more purposeful life pursuits. While authenticity and meaning are generally studied as trait-level variables, clinical approaches to mental health often involve the active construction of identity and self (e.g., Hayes 2004; Yalom 1980), which could perhaps inform research on authenticity and purpose. Given the potentially complex interplay between these constructs, there may be many points at which intervention is possible.

III. Significance

The third component of MIL in the tripartite models is a feeling of significance. Martela and Steger define significance as "a sense of life's inherent value and having a life worth living" (532). According to these authors, significance represents "a value-laden evaluation of one's life as a whole regarding how important, worthwhile, and inherently valuable it feels." Within the MIL literature, the term "mattering" is often used interchangeably with significance. George and Park (2016) argue that existential mattering represents "the degree to which individuals feel that their existence is of significance, importance, and value in the world" (212). Essentially, perceptions of mattering revolve around the belief that one's behaviors have had a lasting influence on the world. Research has shown that believing that one's life matters "in the grand scheme of the things" (George and Park 2017) as well as to other people specifically are each robust and unique predictors of MIL (Costin and Vignoles 2019).

How might authenticity contribute to a sense of mattering? One likely pathway is linked to the idea that people tend to perceive the true self as a morally good entity (Strohminger, Knobe, and Newman 2017). Research has shown that when people feel they have committed a moral transgression, they feel out of touch with their true self (Christy et al. 2016). Conversely, feeling authentic predicts behaviors associated with civic virtue (e.g., participating in democratic processes; Maffly-Kipp et al. under review). Moreover, people are more likely to make morally righteous decisions when instructed to be authentic (i.e., by following one's true self) while making the decisions compared to when they are instructed to follow other decision-making strategies (e.g., thinking rationally or using intuition; Kim et al. 2018; Zhang et al. 2019). These findings suggest that feelings of authenticity are often connected to the moral correctness of one's actions. In many instances, these behaviors are aimed at transcending the self and helping other people. As such, behaving authentically may often engender the perception of mattering due to the belief that one is doing good in the world. The feeling of authenticity may, therefore, serve as a barometer for whether one matters both to other people and to the world at large.

Another way authenticity might promote feelings of mattering is via satisfying personal relationships. For example, Baker et al. (2017) found that people with higher levels of trait authenticity reported more positive interpersonal interactions over a period of two weeks. Authenticity has also been linked to having more compassionate goals in interpersonal relationships (Tou et al. 2015) and higher relationship satisfaction (Brunell et al. 2010). Similarly, the perception that one's partner is authentic predicts relationship satisfaction (Wickham 2013) as do perceptions that one's partner knows your true self (Rivera et al. 2019b). Taken together, this work suggests that authenticity is an important part of positive interpersonal relationships. Having these kinds of positive relationships is likely a fundamental part of feeling like you matter to other people, and feeling like you matter to other people is a strong predictor of global MIL judgments (Guthrie, Holte, and Hicks unpublished).

As noted earlier, definitions of significance also include how much one values life itself. This latter component of significance has been labeled experiential appreciation (EA) and it serves as a unique pathway to MIL over and above mattering (Kim et al., under review). People tend to value and appreciate a wide variety of experiences, but those that are intrinsically valuable are often linked to higher levels of MIL (Audi 2005). The feeling of authenticity is likewise associated with intrinsically valuable experiences (Ryan and Ryan 2019), and some might consider authenticity itself to be intrinsically rewarding. In fact, it is likely that feelings of authenticity, and the subsequent experience of EA, might help explain how many known antecedents of MIL that represent intrinsically rewarding experiences, such as flow (Csikszentmihalyi 1990), positive affect (King et al. 2006), mindfulness (Pandya 2019), nostalgic reflection (Juhl and Routledge 2013), and basic need satisfaction (Ryan and Deci 2001) contribute to the experience of MIL.

IV. Unanswered Questions about Authenticity and Meaning in Life

A. The Nature of Authenticity

One idea touched upon but not directly addressed throughout this chapter is the distinction between subjective authenticity as we have described it and more "objective" conceptualizations of authenticity rooted in consistency. The latter conceptualization operationalizes authenticity as behaviors consistent with inner traits across contexts (Sherman, Nave, and Funder 2012). However, subjective feelings of authenticity do not always track this type of consistency. Thus, it is possible to feel authentic while behaving in a fashion that would be deemed "inauthentic" by more objective standards. One often cited example deals with the authentic expression of self-identified introverts. According to more objective conceptions of authenticity, introverts are being authentic (and thus should experience subjective authenticity) when behaving in an introverted fashion. Paradoxically, research has shown the opposite to be the case—introverts feel more authentic when behaving in an extroverted fashion (Fleeson and Wilt 2010). Some scholars (Baumeister 2019; Sherman et al. 2012) have interpreted this finding as evidence that subjective authenticity does not reflect an emotional experience of being true to one's self, but rather is nothing more than positive feelings associated with socially desirable behavior (i.e., extraversion is culturally valued above introversion and thus feels more "authentic," regardless of individual personality).

Of course, another thorny issue is whether there is such a thing as a true self. As we and others have argued in the past (Dennett 1991; Hood 2012; Rivera 2019a), there may be no true self to be true to. The true self may be a myth people hold on to (Baumeister 1991), in which case the question of whether there is any such thing as objective authenticity becomes somewhat moot. Future research on authenticity will likely need to continue to contend with the antecedents of subjective authenticity and what that might mean for the construct and its relationship with meaning.

Authenticity has also been conceptualized in different ways by philosophers, and the work on subjective authenticity in the psychological literature may not always map well onto philosophical conceptualizations. For example, Heidegger's conceptualization of authenticity requires people to reflect on MIL in spite of the inevitability of death (Heidegger 2013). Most psychological research on death reflection reveals that engaging in it tends to lead to negative psychological effects very much at odds with the positive psychological effects associated with what we label authenticity (Pyszczynski et al. 2006). Moreover, a recent study by Guthrie and colleagues (unpublished) found that the more often people think about MIL in their everyday lives, the lower their self-reported levels of MIL tend to be. Therefore, it seems unlikely that acting authentically in accordance with Heidegger's definition would promote feelings of authenticity or MIL as we currently measure them. Similarly, although Sartre's definition of bad faith may seem more congruent with our psychological definition of authenticity on the surface, Sartre's version of inauthenticity is intertwined with ideas of self-objectification and rejections of essential freedoms that little current psychological research touches on (Sartre 2010). If authenticity were operationalized in psychological research to be in line with such philosophical definitions, the relationships between authenticity and MIL could be drastically different.

B. The Role of Culture

It is important to note that almost all of the work cited in this chapter relies on WEIRD (Western, educated, industrialized, rich, and democratic) samples (Henrich, Heine, and Norenzayan 2010). Indeed, nearly all of this work on the links between authenticity and meaning has been conducted exclusively in the United States. However, our collaborators have conducted a number of studies that have found similar patterns in China, some of which we reviewed in this chapter (e.g., Zhang et al. 2016; Zhang, Chen, and Schlegel 2018; Zhang et al. 2019a, b). Additionally, preliminary data suggests that the true self as guide lay theory is widely endorsed in China, India, Singapore, and South Korea (Kim et al., under review). Nonetheless, it would be premature to say whether the link between authenticity and meaning generalizes to less WEIRD contexts than the United States. Indeed, the idea of the true self has an individualistic feel to it that may translate differently to less individualistic cultures, so this issue definitely deserves more attention.

C. The Illusion of Causality?

Thus far, we have described various processes where authenticity *leads* to the experience of meaning (or vice versa). It is also possible that these two experiences do not contribute to each other per se, but are instead separately elicited by similar causes or even part of the same phenomenon. After all, both subjective authenticity and MIL share similar antecedents. For example, both experiences are believed to be associated with the perception of interconnectivity and self-transcendence (Frankl 1963; Wong 2014). The more mental connections people feel, the more an experience feels meaningful (Baumeister 1991). Recent theoretical accounts of authenticity also suggest that the perception of person-environment fit is important because it leads to high levels of cognitive, motivational, or social fluency (Schmader and Sedikides 2017). That is, it is likely that each of these types of fluency are felt due to the perceived connection between one's personality and environment (see coherence sections for a similar idea). In a related vein, many scholars argue self-transcendence helps make life feel meaningful (Frankl 1963; Wong 2014). Although research on authenticity has been less explicit about the role of self-transcendence in the perception of authenticity, many behaviors and emotions connected to self-transcendence are similarly associated with feelings of authenticity (Hannah, Avolio, and Walumbwa 2011).

V. Conclusion

Both authenticity and MIL represent central components of the good life. In the past two decades, scholars in the psychological sciences and other disciplines have made great strides in understanding the causes and consequences of these two experiences (Hicks, Schlegel, and Newman 2019; King and Hicks 2021), yet many questions related to these experiences remain unanswered. This chapter focuses on one of these questions. Namely, how exactly does authenticity relate to MIL? While we know that these two experiences are highly correlated, we do not know the mechanism underlying this relationship. Our hope is that this chapter helps inspire scholars to better understand the connection between feeling authentic and experiencing meaning in life.

Bibliography

Audi, R. (2005). "Intrinsic Value and Meaningful Life." *Philosophical Papers*, 34 (3): 331–55.

Baker, Z. G., R. Y. W. Tou, J. L. Bryan and C. R. Knee (2017). "Authenticity and Well-Being: Exploring Positivity and Negativity in Interactions as a Mediator." *Personality and Individual Differences*, 113: 235–9.

Baumeister, R. F. (1991). *Meanings of Life*. New York: Guilford Press.

Baumeister, R. F. (2019). "Stalking the True Self Through the Jungles of Authenticity: Problems, Contradictions, Inconsistencies, Disturbing Findings—and a Possible Way Forward." *Review of General Psychology*, 23 (1): 143–54.

Brown, M., Glendenning, A. C., A. E. Hoon and A. John (2016). "Effectiveness of Web-Delivered Acceptance and Commitment Therapy in Relation to Mental Health and Well-Being: A Systematic Review and Meta-Analysis." *Journal of Medical Internet Research*, 18 (8): e6200.

Brunell, A. B., M. H. Kernis, B. M. Goldman, W. Heppner, P. Davis, E. V. Cascio and G. D. Webster (2010). "Dispositional Authenticity and Romantic Relationship Functioning." *Personality and Individual Differences*, 48 (8): 900–5.

Carroll, G. R. (2015). "Authenticity: Attribution, Value, and Meaning." *Emerging Trends in the Social and Behavioral Sciences: An Interdisciplinary, Searchable, and Linkable Resource*: 1–13.

Carver, C. S. and M. F. Scheier (2000). "Autonomy and Self-Regulation." *Psychological Inquiry*, 11 (4): 284–91.

Christy, A. G., E. Seto, R. J. Schlegel, M. Vess and J. A. Hicks (2016). "Straying from the Righteous Path and from Ourselves: The Interplay Between Perceptions of Morality and Self-Knowledge." *Personality and Social Psychology Bulletin*, 42 (11): 1538–50.

Costin, V. and V. L. Vignoles (2020). "Meaning is about Mattering: Evaluating Coherence, Purpose, and Existential Mattering as Precursors of Meaning in Life Judgments." *Journal of Personality and Social Psychology*, 118 (4): 864–84. https://doi.org/10.1037/pspp0000225.

Csikszentmihalyi, M. (1990). *Flow: The Psychology of Optimal Experience*. New York: Harper & Row.

Datta, A., C. Aditya, A. Chakraborty, P. Das and A. Mukhopadhyay (2016). "The Potential Utility of Acceptance and Commitment Therapy (Act) for Reducing Stress and Improving Wellbeing in Cancer Patients in Kolkata." *Journal of Cancer Education*, 31 (4): 721–9.

Davis, W. E., N. J. Kelley, J. Kim, D. Tang and J. A. Hicks (2016). "Motivating the Academic Mind: High-level Construal of Academic Goals Enhances Goal Meaningfulness, Motivation, and Self-Concordance." *Motivation and Emotion*, 40 (2): 193–202.

Dennett, D. C. (1991). "Real Patterns." *The Journal of Philosophy*, 88 (1): 27–51.

Emmons, R. A. (2003). *The Psychology of Ultimate Concerns: Motivation and Spirituality in Personality*. New York: Guilford Press.

Fleeson, W. and J. Wilt (2010). "The Relevance of Big Five Trait Content in Behavior to Subjective Authenticity: Do High Levels of Within-Person Behavioral Variability Undermine or Enable Authenticity Achievement?" *Journal of Personality*, 78 (4): 1353–82.

Frankl, V. E. (1963). *Man's Search for Meaning: An Introduction to Logotherapy*. Boston: Beacon Press.

George, L. S. and C. L. Park (2016). "Meaning in life as Comprehension, Purpose, and Mattering: Toward Integration and New Research Questions." *Review of General Psychology*, 20 (3): 205–20.

George, L. S. and C. L. Park (2017). "The Multidimensional Existential Meaning Scale: A Tripartite Approach to Measuring Meaning in Life." *The Journal of Positive Psychology*, 12 (6): 613–27. https://www.issep.org/workshops-webinars.

Guthrie, D., P. Holte and J. A. Hicks (unpublished). "Does Meaning Disappear When You Think About It? Paradoxical Relationships Between Reflections on and Feelings of Meaning in Life."

Habermas, T. and S. Bluck (2000). "Getting a Life: the Emergence of the Life Story in Adolescence." *Psychological Bulletin*, 126 (5): 748.

Habermas, T. and C. de Silveira (2008). "The Development of Global Coherence in Life Narratives Across Adolescence: Temporal, Causal, and Thematic Aspects." *Developmental Psychology*, 44 (3): 707.

Hannah, S. T., B. J. Avolio and F. O. Walumbwa (2011). "Relationships between Authentic Leadership, Moral Courage, and Ethical and Pro-Social Behaviors." *Business Ethics Quarterly*, 21 (4): 555–78.

Hayes, S. C. (2004). "Acceptance and Commitment Therapy, Relational Frame Theory, and the Third Wave of Behavioral and Cognitive Therapies." *Behavior Therapy*, 35 (4): 639–65.

Heidegger, M. (2013). *Being and Time*. Oxford: Stellar Books.

Heintzelman, S. J., J. Trent and L. A. King (2013). "Encounters with Objective Coherence and the Experience of Meaning in Life." *Psychological Science*, 24 (6): 991–8.

Henrich, J., S. J. Heine and A. Norenzayan (2010). "Most People are not WEIRD." *Nature*, 466 (7302): 29.

Hicks, J. A., R. J. Schlegel and G. E. Newman (2019). "Introduction to the Special Issue: Authenticity: Novel Insights into a Valued, yet Elusive, Concept." *Review of General Psychology*, 23 (1): 3–7.

Hitlin, S. (2003). "Values as the Core of Personal Identity: Drawing Links between Two Theories of Self." *Social Psychology Quarterly*, 66 (2): 118–37.

Hood, B. (2012). *The Self Illusion: How the Social Brain Creates Identity*. Oxford: Oxford University Press.

Jongman-Sereno, K. P. and M. R. Leary (2019). "The Enigma of Being Yourself: A Critical Examination of the Concept of Authenticity." *Review of General Psychology*, 23 (1): 133–42.

Juhl, J. and C. Routledge (2013). "Nostalgia Bolsters Perceptions of a Meaningful Self in a Meaningful World." In J. A. Hicks and C. Routledge (eds.), *The Experience of Meaning in Life: Classical Perspectives, Emerging Themes, and Controversies*, 213–26. Netherlands: Springer.

Kernis, M. H. and B. M. Goldman (2006). "A Multicomponent Conceptualization of Authenticity: Theory and Research." *Advances in Experimental Social Psychology*, 38: 283–357.

Keyes, C. L. M. and J. Haidt, eds. (2003). *Flourishing: Positive Psychology and the Life Well-Lived*. Washington, D.C.: American Psychological Association.

Kim, J., K. Chen, W. E. Davis, J. A. Hicks and R. J. Schlegel (2019). "Approaching the True Self: Promotion Focus Predicts the Experience of Authenticity." *Journal of Research in Personality*, 78: 165–76.

Kim, J., K. Chen, G. N. Rivera, E. K. Hong, S. Kamble, C. N. Scollon, K. M. Sheldon, H. Zhang, and R. J. Schlegel (2022). "True-self-as-guide Lay Theory Endorsement across Five Countries, Self and Identity." DOI:10.1080/15298868.2022.2028670.

Kim, J., A. G. Christy, G. N. Rivera, J. A. Hicks and R. J. Schlegel (2021). "Is the Illusion of Authenticity Beneficial? Merely Perceiving Decisions as Guided by the True Self Enhances Decision Satisfaction." *Social Psychological and Personality Science*, 12 (1): 80–90.

Kim, J., A. G. Christy, G. N. Rivera, R. J. Schlegel and J. A. Hicks (2018). "Following One's True Self and the Sacredness of Cultural Values." *Journal of Experimental Social Psychology*, 76: 100–3.

King, L. A. and J. A. Hicks (2021). "The Science of Meaning in Life." *Annual Review of Psychology*, 72: 561–84.

King, L. A., J. A. Hicks, J. L. Krull and A. K. Del Gaiso (2006). "Positive Affect and the Experience of Meaning in Life." *Journal of Personality and Social Psychology*, 90 (1): 179.

Kovács, B. (2019). "Authenticity is in the Eye of the Beholder: The Exploration of Audiences' Lay Associations to Authenticity Across Five Domains." *Review of General Psychology*, 23 (1): 32–59.

Maffly-Kipp, J., Holte, P., Stichter, M., Hicks, J. A., Schlegel, R., & Vess, M. (under review). Civic hope and the perceived authenticity of democratic participation.

Martela, F. and M. F. Steger (2016). "The Three Meanings of Meaning in Life: Distinguishing Coherence, Purpose, and Significance." *The Journal of Positive Psychology*, 11 (5): 531–45. https://doi.org/10.1080/17439760.2015.1137623.

McAdams, D. P. (2001). "The Psychology of Life Stories." *Review of General Psychology*, 5 (2): 100–22.

McLean, K. C., M. Pasupathi and J. L. Pals (2007). "Selves Creating Stories Creating Selves: A Process Model of Self-Development." *Personality and Social Psychology Review*, 11 (3): 262–78.

McGregor, I. and B. R. Little (1998). "Personal Projects, Happiness, and Meaning: On Doing Well and Being Yourself." *Journal of Personality and Social Psychology*, 74 (2): 494–512.

McKnight, P. E. and T. B. Kashdan (2009). "Purpose in Life as a System that Creates and Sustains Health and Well-Being: An Integrative, Testable Theory." *Review of General Psychology*, 13 (3): 242–51.

Ménard, J. and L. Brunet (2011). "Authenticity and Well-Being in the Workplace: A Mediation Model." *Journal of Managerial Psychology*, 26 (4): 331–46.

Moghbel Esfahani, S. and S. A. Haghayegh (2019). "The Effectiveness of Acceptance and Commitment Therapy on Resilience, Meaning in Life, and Family Function in Family Caregivers of Patients with Schizophrenia." *The Horizon of Medical Sciences*, 25 (4): 298–311.

Pandya, S. P. (2019). "Meditation for Meaning in Life and Happiness of Older Adults: A Multi-City Experiment of the Brahma Kumaris' Raja Yoga Practice." *Journal of Religion, Spirituality & Aging*, 31 (3): 282–304.

Pyszczynski, T., J. Greenberg, S. Solomon and M. Maxfield (2006). "On the Unique Psychological Import of the Human Awareness of Mortality: Theme and Variations." *Psychological Inquiry*, 17 (4): 328–56.

Rivera, G. N., A. G. Christy, J. Kim, M. Vess, J. A. Hicks and R. J. Schlegel (2019a). "Understanding the Relationship Between Perceived Authenticity and Well-Being." *Review of General Psychology*, 23 (1): 113–26.

Rivera, G. N., C. M. Smith and R. J. Schlegel (2019b). "A Window to the True Self: The Importance of I-sharing in Romantic Relationships." *Journal of Social and Personal Relationships*, 36 (6): 1640–50.

Rogers, C. R. (1963). "The Concept of the Fully Functioning Person." *Psychotherapy: Theory, Research & Practice*, 1 (1): 17.

Ryan, R. M. and E. L. Deci (2001). "On Happiness and Human Potentials: A Review of Research on Hedonic and Eudaimonic Well-Being." *Annual Review of Psychology*, 52 (1): 141–66.

Ryan, W. S. and R. M. Ryan (2019). "Toward a Social Psychology of Authenticity: Exploring Within-Person Variation in Autonomy, Congruence, and Genuineness Using Self-Determination Theory." *Review of General Psychology*, 23 (1): 99–112.

Sartre, J. (2010). *Being and Nothingness: An Essay of Phenomenological Ontology*. London: Routledge.

Schlegel, R. J., J. A. Hicks, J. Arndt and L. A. King (2009). "Thine Own Self: True Self-Concept Accessibility and Meaning in Life." *Journal of Personality and Social Psychology*, 96 (2): 473.

Schlegel, R. J., J. A. Hicks, W. E. Davis, K. A. Hirsch and C. M. Smith (2013). "The Dynamic Interplay Between Perceived True Self-Knowledge and Decision Satisfaction." *Journal of Personality and Social Psychology*, 104 (3): 542–58.

Schlegel, R. J., J. A. Hicks, L. A. King and J. Arndt (2011). "Feeling Like You Know Who You are: Perceived True Self-Knowledge and Meaning in Life." *Personality and Social Psychology Bulletin*, 37 (6): 745–56.

Schlegel, R. J., M. Vess and J. Arndt (2012). "To Discover or to Create: Metaphors and the True Self." *Journal of Personality*, 80 (4): 969–93.

Schmader, T. and C. Sedikides (2018). "State Authenticity as Fit to Environment: The Implications of Social Identity for Fit, Authenticity, and Self-Segregation." *Personality and Social Psychology Review*, 22 (3): 228–59.

Sedikides, C., L. Slabu, A. Lenton and S. Thomaes (2017). "State Authenticity." *Current Directions in Psychological Science*, 26 (6): 521–25.

Seto, E. and R. J. Schlegel (2018). "Becoming Your True Self: Perceptions of Authenticity Across the Lifespan." *Self and Identity*, 17 (3): 310–26.

Sheldon, K. M. and A. J. Elliot (1999). "Goal Striving, Need Satisfaction, and Longitudinal Well-Being: the Self-Concordance Model." *Journal of Personality and Social Psychology*, 76 (3): 482.

Sheldon, K. M. and L. Houser-Marko (2001). "Self-Concordance, Goal Attainment, and the Pursuit of Happiness: Can there be an Upward Spiral?" *Journal of Personality and Social Psychology*, 80 (1): 152.

Sherman, R. A., C. S. Nave and D. C. Funder (2012). "Properties of Persons and Situations Related to Overall and Distinctive Personality-Behavior Congruence." *Journal of Research in Personality*, 46 (1): 87–101.

Strohminger, N., J. Knobe and G. Newman (2017). "The True Self: A Psychological Concept Distinct from the Self." *Perspectives on Psychological Science*, 12 (4): 551–60.

Tou, R. Y. W., Z. G. Baker, B. W. Hadden and Y.-C. Lin (2015). "The Real Me: Authenticity, Interpersonal Goals, and Conflict Tactics." *Personality and Individual Differences*, 86: 189–94.

Waterman, A. S. (1984). "Identity Formation: Discovery or Creation?" *The Journal of Early Adolescence*, 4 (4): 329–41.

Wickham, R. E. (2013). "Perceived Authenticity in Romantic Partners." *Journal of Experimental Social Psychology*, 49 (5): 878–87.

Wilt, J. A., S. Thomas and D. P. McAdams (2019). "Authenticity and Inauthenticity in Narrative Identity." *Heliyon*, 5 (7): e02178.

Wong, P. T. P. (2014). "Viktor Frankl's Meaning-Seeking Model and Positive Psychology." In A. Batthyany and P. Russo-Netzer (eds.), *Meaning in Positive and Existential Psychology*, 149–84. New York: Springer.

Wood, A. M., P. A. Linley, J. Maltby, M. Baliousis and S. Joseph (2008). "The Authentic Personality: A Theoretical and Empirical Conceptualization and the Development of the Authenticity Scale." *Journal of Counseling Psychology*, 55 (3): 385–399.

Yalom, I. D. (1980). *Existential Psychotherapy*. New York: Basic Books.

Zhang, H., K. Chen, C. Chen and R. Schlegel (2019a). "Personal Aspirations, Person-Environment Fit, Meaning in Work, and Meaning in Life: A Moderated Mediation Model." *Journal of Happiness Studies*, 20 (5): 1481–97.

Zhang, H., K. Chen and R. Schlegel (2018). "How Do People Judge Meaning in Goal-Directed Behaviors: The Interplay Between Self-Concordance and Performance." *Personality and Social Psychology Bulletin*, 44 (11): 1582–600.

Zhang, H., K. Chen, R. Schlegel, J. Hicks and C. Chen (2019b). "The Authentic Moral Self: Dynamic Interplay between Perceived Authenticity and Moral Behaviors in the Workplace." *Collabra: Psychology*, 5 (1). https://online.ucpress.edu/collabra/article/5/1/48/113039/The-Authentic-Moral-Self-Dynamic-Interplay-between.

Zhang, H., Z. Sang, D. K. S. Chan, F. Teng, M. Liu, S. Yu and Y. Tian (2016). "Sources of Meaning in Life among Chinese University Students." *Journal of Happiness Studies*, 17 (4): 1473–92.

12

Experimental Philosophical Bioethics of Personal Identity

Brian D. Earp, Jonathan Lewis, Joshua A. Skorburg, Ivar R. Hannikainen, and Jim A. C. Everett[1]

I. Introduction

The question of what makes someone the same person through time and change has long been a preoccupation of philosophers. In recent years, the question of what makes ordinary or laypeople (i.e., individuals from a wide range of backgrounds, including non-philosophers) judge that someone is—or isn't—the same person has caught the interest of experimental psychologists. These latter, empirically oriented researchers have sought to understand the cognitive processes and eliciting factors that shape ordinary people's judgments about personal identity and the self. Still more recently, practitioners within an emerging discipline, experimental philosophical bioethics or "bioxphi"—the focus of this chapter—have adopted a similar aim and employed similar methodologies, but with two distinctive features: (a) a special concern for enhanced ecological validity in the examples and populations studied, and (b) an interest in contributing to substantive normative debates within the wider field of bioethics (Earp et al. 2020, Earp, Lewis et al. 2021; Klenk 2020; Lewis 2020a).

Our aim in this chapter is to sample illustrative work on personal identity in bioxphi, explore how it relates to studies in psychology covering similar terrain, and draw out the implications of this work for matters of bioethical concern. Of course, the boundaries between fields and disciplines are often blurry, and many of the same practitioners are conducting research across these different areas. We are less concerned with whether a given study or line of work counts as an instance of bioxphi than with characterizing bioxphi more generally and exploring some of the ways in which data-driven studies using the methods of cognitive science, moral psychology, and experimental philosophy (x-phi) can inform bioethical argumentation and decision-making.

With this aim in mind, we begin by briefly reviewing classic studies in psychology and x-phi that bear on questions concerning lay judgments about personal identity change versus persistence: that is, the extent to which someone is regarded as the *same person* despite undergoing significant psychological transformation. We will discuss some strengths and limitations of this work with a view to articulating what is new and exciting about bioxphi studies investigating similar judgments. Subsequently, we share some candidate strategies for how empirical findings (i.e., descriptive information about how and why people make certain judgments) might appropriately be used in the service of normative arguments: for example, arguments about how personal identity *should* be understood in certain contexts or toward certain ends. We also explore how such empirical information could profitably be employed in the context of practical bioethical decision-making: for example, in helping us to draw conclusions about what *should* be done in various medical situations involving judgments about personal identity change.

In pursuing these issues, we highlight recent work in bioxphi that addresses a rich variety of topics touching on personal identity. These topics include the perceived validity of advance directives following neurodegeneration (Earp, Latham, and Tobia 2020), the right of psychologically altered study participants to withdraw from research (Tobia 2016; Dranseika et al. unpublished), how drug addiction may cause one to be regarded by others as "a completely different person" (Earp et al. 2019), the effect of deep brain stimulation on perceptions of the self (Skorburg and Sinnott-Armstrong 2020), and the potential influence of moral enhancement interventions on intuitive impressions of a person's character (Fabiano 2021). We conclude with some general observations and suggestions for future research.

II. A Broad Overview of Conceptions of Personal Identity Change in Philosophy, X-Phi and Moral Psychology

What determines your personal identity through time and change? Are "you" at age five the same person as "you" in old age, at the end of life? If you suffer a serious brain injury that causes you to lose most of your memories—or which permanently alters key aspects of your character—are you still yourself, and if so, in what sense? Suppose that two people could swap bodies (Williams 1970); how could we decide or track who was who? A long tradition in philosophy has debated puzzles like these. A prominent view, typically associated with John Locke, involves a diachronic conception of the self as a reasoning and reflective entity that persists over time (Locke 1689/1694 [1985], 2.27.9). For Locke, as he has classically been interpreted, "consciousness" of past actions—via the faculty of memory—is at the heart of personal identity (Reid 1785 [1969]). Broadly, according to this view, Person A who did x at Time 1 can be identified as Person B at Time 2 if B has the same "consciousness" as A, where this implies having a memory of doing x.

Whether this is the correct, or most justifiable, view of personal identity is an open question. As some philosophers have argued, a theory of a given scientific phenomenon is usually considered to be adequate if, among other things, it can explain the relevant data: for example, if it can explain why the contents of a test tube turn green under certain conditions, but red under others (Thomson 1986: 257; Kagan 2001: 47). When one seeks to explain personal identity, however, it is not as obvious what the relevant data are that need to be explained. Certainly, many of us have a strong sense that we exist in the form of a person or self that extends through time; and it seems that we live in a world full of other selves that are similarly diachronic. Moreover, experiences of continuity or discontinuity in oneself or in the selves of others—in the context of close interpersonal relationships, for instance—often matter a great deal. When we "lose ourselves" in periods of mental illness; when a loved one starts to seem like a stranger after developing an addiction (Tobia 2017); when a parent or grandparent with dementia doesn't recognize us, we may feel disoriented, disenchanted, or disturbed. Perhaps *these* are the data that need to be explained: our everyday beliefs, perceptions, and experiences of ourselves and the selves of others through time and change.

Philosophers, including Locke, have developed theories along these lines. However, in doing so, they most often have simply consulted their own intuitions about particular cases—whether real or imagined—that seem to implicate, or raise questions about, the nature of personal identity (e.g., Williams's "body swap" scenario mentioned in Chapter 1). Commonly, they will ask what is entailed by a given theoretical claim if applied to such a scenario, and then check to see whether the implication seems intuitively right or reasonable to them. If it doesn't seem reasonable, then they may go back to adjust the theory. But whether this is an appropriate strategy for building a general account of personal identity is unclear.[2] As Machery notes, philosophers who rely on such an approach "are neither inquiring about the actual world, collecting observational data or running experiments, nor examining our best scientific theories to [decide] what determines personal identity" (Machery 2017: 189). Moreover, even if it is granted that philosophers' intuitions should play some role in theory development, it is doubtful whether these intuitions should be accorded substantially more weight than those of non-philosophers when it comes to providing answers to certain philosophical questions (Machery 2017: 149–84). At the very least, it seems pertinent to know whether the philosophers' intuitions or associated judgments about cases are idiosyncratic or widely shared among relevant stakeholders.

As Kagan (2001) notes, philosophers have for the most part simply assumed that others—at least, other philosophers—will share their intuitions and judgments about cases. Until relatively recently, this assumption had not been tested much empirically (Machery 2017). However, this started to change in the early 2000s when "experimental philosophers" (Knobe 2007; Knobe et al. 2012) started to move away from proverbial armchair theorizing, toward investigating how ordinary people think about questions such as what it means to be the same person over time. For example, Blok, Newman, and Rips (2005) asked study participants to imagine that a team of doctors removed the brain of a patient ("Jim") and destroyed his body. In one scenario, the doctors successfully transplanted Jim's brain into a new body, so that Jim's memories were fully preserved: physically, he had a completely different body, but he could still remember everything from before the surgery. In another version of the scenario, all the other details were kept the same except that Jim's memories were not preserved during the transplantation.

Philosophical debates in the Lockean tradition show that there are sophisticated arguments both for and against someone's being the same person in a cases like these. However, one argument concludes that the brain recipient is the same person as Jim when the latter's memories are preserved, despite the bodily changes. And that is what the researchers found: participants agreed that the brain recipient was the same person as Jim when his memories remained intact but disagreed when his memories did not survive the operation (Blok et al. 2005; for a replication of the results of Blok, Newman, and Rips's third-person investigation, see Nichols and Bruno 2010). It seems, then, that ordinary people—not only those with advanced philosophical training—intuitively regard autobiographical memories as being at least one important contributing factor to personal identity preservation.

Other factors matter as well. In a recent, influential line of work, it has been demonstrated that *moral attributes*, even more so than memories, are widely judged to be at the core of personal identity (Strohminger and Nichols 2014; Prinz and Nichols 2016). In these studies, researchers gave participants a list of traits and asked them to imagine to what degree a change to each trait would influence whether someone was still the same person. In what is now known as the *moral self effect*, changes to a person's moral qualities were consistently judged to be the most identity-disruptive factor. As Strohminger and Nichols concluded, "moral traits are considered more important to personal identity than any other part of the mind" (Strohminger and Nichols 2014: 168). Furthermore, the *direction* of moral change also matters: evidence suggests that improvements to moral character, compared to deteriorations, tend to be seen as less threatening to personal identity persistence (Tobia 2015).

So far, these studies have overwhelmingly involved "WEIRD" participants (Henrich, Heine, and Norenzayan 2010), so that the range of cultural and other demographic contexts across which similar results might obtain is not yet known (but see, e.g., Dranseika et al. unpublished).[3] Nevertheless, in the meantime, philosophers have begun grappling with the (meta)philosophical implications of experimentally derived findings regarding people's judgments of personal identity (e.g., O'Neill and Machery 2014; Fisher 2015; Knobe 2016; Machery 2017; Nado 2021). In line with this approach, but focusing specifically on philosophical bioethics, we will now explore some of the implications of such findings for the burgeoning discipline of bioxphi.

III. From X-Phi and Moral Psychology to Bioxphi

The studies surveyed earlier, and others like them, have done much to increase our understanding of how ordinary people think about personal identity change or persistence, albeit sometimes in relation to unusual cases. Typically, these studies rely on vignette-based designs that hold everything constant between experimental conditions apart from a specific feature—such as a given trait or personal attribute—that is expected to make a difference to participant judgments. Although questions have been raised as to whether this contrastive-vignette technique (CVT) should be used so exclusively (Mihailov, Hannikainen, and Earp 2021; Earp, Lewis et al. 2021), an advantage of the approach is it allows researchers to zero in on well-defined aspects of the self that might change as a result of some imagined intervention, so that fine-grained discriminations can be made between potential factors shaping participant judgments (Reiner 2019).

When applied to questions of personal identity, such CVT studies oftentimes have employed far-fetched, even science-fiction-like examples: brain transplants, body switches, magic pills, time machines, reincarnation, and the like. This likely has to do with a typical aim of such studies, which is to validate or refute the premises of arguments made from the armchair. As Machery (2017: 113–16) argues, such "armchair" philosophizing often relies on cases that are deliberately "unusual" in order to achieve certain theoretical goals. However, researchers are increasingly showing an interest in how cases might be adjusted to be more realistic (or to track features of the world that are more representative of everyday situations).

As alluded to previously, this includes researchers in bioxphi, an emerging discipline that uses the tools of x-phi, moral psychology, and cognitive science to investigate topics in bioethics with a heightened emphasis on ecological validity. In a bioethical context, judgments about whether, to what extent, or in what sense someone is the same person despite having undergone various changes often matter for real-life decisions about how someone should be treated: for example, in the context of high-stakes decisions about what healthcare a person should receive at the end of life. Understanding the factors that influence these personal identity-related judgments in more realistic, ethically charged situations may thus be both theoretically and practically relevant (but see Shoemaker 2010).

Some work in the more established tradition of moral psychology has already taken a turn toward greater realism. For example, Strohminger and Nichols (2015) studied judgments of identity persistence made by actual family members of patients with different neurodegenerative diseases. The authors sought to determine the extent to which patients would be seen as a different person as a function of three types of changes: changes to moral faculties (as in some cases of frontotemporal dementia), changes to memories (as in Alzheimer's disease), and changes to physical motor functions (as in amyotrophic lateral sclerosis). Mirroring results from earlier abstract thought experiments, Strohminger and Nichols found that family members of patients with frontotemporal dementia—the condition most strongly associated with moral change—saw the patient as more of a different person compared with family members of patients with other forms of neurodegeneration (in line with the moral self effect). Strohminger and Nichols also found that moral changes led to more severe deterioration in the relationships between patients and family members. Reflecting on these results, the authors derived normative recommendations:

> While loss of identity may be feared as an undesirable clinical outcome unto itself, the present research highlights that identity deterioration has significant downstream consequences for healthy relationships. . . . *Future therapies ought to be aimed at—and take into account—preserving moral function*, a previously unappreciated factor in the well-being of patients and their families. (Strohminger and Nichols 2015: 1477, emphasis added)

The bioethical analysis here is straightforward. First, it is noted that certain kinds of neurodegeneration seem to impair both personal and interpersonal well-being through their impact on moral functioning. Since one of the main normative commitments of healthcare is to mitigate threats to well-being that stem from disease or disability—a premise Strohminger and Nichols implicitly accept—then, assuming sufficient resources, among other relevant considerations (e.g., ranking of research and funding priorities based on likely success, efficacy, distributive justice, and so on), it follows that therapies *should* be developed to address this mediating factor.

The moral self effect on judgments of personal identity also applies to the case of addiction (Earp et al. 2019), another real-world issue that can have major implications for personal and interpersonal well-being. Over a series of experiments involving contrastive vignettes inspired by real-life stories—and designed to be as believable as possible—three of us explored whether participants would judge that someone who became addicted to drugs would thereby become, in some sense, a different person; and, if so, whether this judgment would be driven by perceived changes in the individual's moral qualities (Earp et al. 2019). In an initial experiment, United States participants judged a character who became addicted to drugs as being closer to "a completely different person" than "completely the same person," while subsequent experiments revealed that these judgments were indeed driven by a perceived worsening of the moral character of the drug user. In particular, the user was seen as having drifted away from their (presumably morally good) "true self" (Earp et al. 2019).

Could findings like these have normative implications? Although we could only speculate based on our initial results, we suggested that public health messages framed around (re)discovering one's true self might be especially desirable in the case of addiction (for related work, see Schlegel and Hicks 2011; Schlegel et al. 2009, 2011). Another possibility is that campaigns aimed at *dissociating* drug use or addiction from negative moral character judgments could be beneficial (Hart 2021), for example, by inclining the public to believe that individuals who are dealing with addiction are still the same (good) people after all. In either case, the underlying bioethical reasoning would be similar to that employed by Strohminger and Nichols (2015). In short, if drug addiction harms individuals and relationships, and if some of this harm comes from the perception that drug addiction undermines the identity of the user, then, *ceteris paribus*, measures to address that perception should be pursued.

In the following section, we will look at other ways in which empirical results—derived from bioxphi studies—can help inform normative conclusions about bioethical issues involving judgments about personal identity. First, we will describe some general strategies for reaching normative conclusions from premises that include empirical information about the mind. Second, we will discuss these strategies in relation to specific examples drawn from the recent bioxphi literature.

IV. From Empirical Studies to Normative Conclusions: Four Recent Strategies from the Bioxphi Literature

We have argued that bioxphi studies should be designed with at least two aims in mind. The first aim is scientific: it is to understand the cognitive processes and eliciting factors that shape morally relevant judgments in the real world, so that we might build theoretically justified and descriptively accurate models of the—realistically situated—moral mind (Mihailov et al. 2021). The second aim is normative: it is to harness these models and associated findings to help reach ethically warranted conclusions in bioethics (e.g., regarding public health policy or clinical decision-making) (Earp, Lewis et al. 2021).

In a recent paper (Earp, Lewis et al. 2021), some of us drew on examples from the burgeoning bioxphi literature to outline four main strategies for reaching normative conclusions from premises that include empirical content about the mind: *parsimony*, *debunking*, *triangulation*, and *pluralism*. Here is a brief description of each strategy, followed by an illustrative example of how it might be applied to an ethical question involving judgments about personal identity:

1. **Parsimony**. If relevant stakeholders consistently make a judgment p which encodes moral claim M, then M has prima facie normative weight (inspired, in part, by consultative approaches to empirical bioethics as detailed in Davies, Ives, and Dunn 2015).
2. **Debunking**. A strategy seeking to show that a judgment or moral claim is unreliable using the following argument structure (inspired by Mukerji 2019):

    (A) Judgment p is the output of a psychological process that possesses the empirical property of being substantially influenced by factor F. (Empirical premise)
    (B) If a judgment is the output of a psychological process that possesses the empirical property of being substantially influenced by factor F, then it is pro tanto unreliable. (Bridging normative premise)
    (C) Judgment p is pro tanto unreliable.

3. **Triangulation**. Divergence among the judgments of various groups of experts and/or between expert and lay judgments requires the following: adjusting, pruning, or supplementing the normative conclusions derived from either expert or lay judgments in order to accommodate: (1) the normative implications of the opposing views; and (2) normative considerations derived from, for example, ethical or legal principles, background theories, morally relevant facts, and/or the best arguments for a normative position in the relevant expert literature (inspired, in part, by the model of reflective equilibrium, and, in part, by the concept of triangulation in philosophy of science as detailed in Kuorikoski and Marchionni 2016).
4. **Pluralism**. In cases where expert and lay stakeholders hold conflicting, yet pro tanto reliable, judgments, or where multiple and independent communities reveal persistent disagreement between two or more conflicting yet pro tanto reliable judgments, these judgments could all have comparable normative weight; associated normative conclusions may justifiably be agent- or community-relative and/or preference-sensitive (inspired by the model of Shared Decision-Making in clinical contexts as discussed in, e.g., Elwyn, Tilburt, and Montori 2013; Lewis 2020b).

A. Illustration #1: Parsimony

In a recent study (Earp et al., in press), some of us asked participants to consider the case of a late-stage dementia patient who currently lacks autonomous decision-making capacity. We told participants that the patient had previously, autonomously signed an advance directive (AD) instructing the withholding of treatment just in case she fell ill under certain conditions. When those conditions are fulfilled, however, the patient seems to be living a happy life apart from the illness, which is described as easily curable. We asked research participants whether the AD should be followed, and how much they agreed that the dementia patient was "still her true self" despite the effects of the disease on her personal characteristics.

We found that, among the participants who judged that the patient was still her true self, almost all of them felt that the AD should be ignored or overridden: that is, they said that the patient should be treated under the very conditions identified in the AD as sufficient grounds to withhold treatment.

Some bioethicists argue that the preferences of an autonomous individual at Time 1—as recorded in an AD—should determine how a non-autonomous individual at Time 2 is treated, just so long as the individual at Time 1 is the same person as the individual at Time 2 (Buchanan 1988; Buchanan and Brock 1990; see also Dworkin 1993; for a critical discussion of the debate, see Furberg 2012). Given such a bioethical argument, when we consider the relationship between judgments regarding an AD and judgments of personal identity change, the empirical result we obtained might seem surprising. First, still being one's true self at Time 2 (compared to Time 1) includes the concept of being the same person, which suggests that participants do not perceive *simply* being the same person between the two time points to be sufficient for following an AD. Instead, these participants judged that a person can still be her true self despite lacking autonomy (i.e., one's autonomous self and one's true self can come apart), and that under such conditions, her Time 1 preferences as recorded in an AD should *not* necessarily determine how she is treated at Time 2. Indeed, the participants judged that the patient's AD should be ignored or overridden despite her having undergone substantial personal change through neurodegeneration—precisely the situation an AD is meant to cover.

Of course, much more work will be needed to clarify this finding,[4] and to determine how robust it is across different measures or operationalizations. It may turn out that the apparent tension between the judgments of ordinary research participants about this case, and those of at least some philosophers and bioethicists, is illusory, and that—if the case were described differently, for example—there would be perfect agreement about what should be done in terms of treatment. But let us assume for the sake of argument that the finding does hold up in future studies. According to the parsimony strategy for reaching normative conclusions from empirical findings about people's morally relevant judgments, we should, in this case, assign at least some normative weight to the view that dementia patients who still seem like their "true selves" should be treated under the stated conditions (even if this conflicts with the person's previously expressed preferences as recorded in an advance directive).

An immediate objection to this approach is that it may seem to reduce bioethical reasoning to a popularity contest. The mere fact that a majority of research participants—even assuming that their views are representative of some wider population of relevant stakeholders—reaches a given moral conclusion about an identity-related case does not entail that this is the correct, most reasonable, or (otherwise) most justifiable conclusion. Perhaps, after all, it is the bioethicists and philosophers who have it right, while the laypeople are morally mistaken. In some cases that may well be true (in which case an error theory may need to be given of why ordinary people are reaching the wrong conclusion). The claim implied by the parsimony strategy is not that we should rely directly on *argumenta ad populum* to reach normative conclusions in bioethics. Rather, the claim is that the experimentally robust, consistent judgments of ordinary people (or other relevant stakeholders) about a given case or set of cases is one factor that counts in favor of the moral statement or conclusion embedded in, or entailed by, those very judgments.

However, this factor alone will never be normatively decisive. For example, if people's judgments can be shown to be unreliable using a debunking strategy (see below), or if their moral concerns are plausibly outweighed by other, competing moral considerations (triangulation), then it could be reasonable to discount those judgments when deciding what to do. Simply put, the parsimony approach puts the burden of proof on those who would argue that *no* normative weight should be assigned to the consistent judgments of relevant stakeholders about a given moral issue (Earp, Lewis et al. 2021).

B. Illustration #2: Debunking

The parsimony strategy is parsimonious in that it provides the simplest possible model for deriving normative content from descriptive information about people's moral judgments. It holds that these judgments should, defeasibly, be given *some* normative weight. However, suppose a researcher is skeptical about the normative conclusion consistently reached by a group of stakeholders about some case. The researcher might want to engage in a debunking strategy as outlined earlier, potentially using experimental methods to test whether the moral judgments in question are the output of a normatively unreliable factor or process. For example, the researcher might want to see if the judgments are susceptible to framing effects that should have no moral relevance to the issue at hand (but see Demaree-Cotton 2016); or whether, perhaps, they are influenced by factors that are themselves morally objectionable, such as racial bias or sexist attitudes.

Consider the moral self effect by way of illustration. As discussed previously, this effect refers to the tendency of participants to judge that someone who undergoes a significant moral change—especially moral deterioration—becomes in some sense a different person. As Tobia (2016) argues, whether someone is seen as undergoing a moral improvement versus a moral deterioration will, therefore, often have different effects on judgments about their personal identity persistence; and these effects, in turn, may influence judgments about matters of bioethical concern. As an example, Tobia refers to an ongoing debate in bioethics concerning the moral acceptability of cognitive enhancement.

Suppose that, in a society shaped by sexist values, a group of participants consistently judged that a certain cognitive enhancement procedure (geared toward boosting one's intelligence and agency) was less ethically worrisome if pursued by men than if pursued by women; and suppose this judgment was rooted in the perception that the procedure would be more threatening to the personal identity of women. Suppose we grant that if a procedure is more threatening to the personal identity of members of one group compared to another, then this is an ethically valid reason to object more strongly to its use in the relevant group.

Given the moral self effect, we can imagine a possible explanation for this hypothetical sex-based discrepancy in judgments: the procedure might be thought to cause greater *moral deterioration* in women. This, in turn, could be due to a sexist societal conception of the "moral woman" as passive, submissive, or (otherwise) lacking in agency (Garcia 2021). Our skeptical researcher, then, might undertake an experimental study to see whether manipulation of this sexist attitude has the predicted downstream effect on participants' judgments (i.e., about the perceived impact of the procedure on personal identity), and, hence, on the relative acceptability of its use by women as opposed to men.

Of course, the very same stakeholders who might judge that it is worse for women than for men to engage in cognitive enhancement might disagree with the researcher's normative premise, namely, that it is sexist (and therefore wrong) to believe that women ought to be more "submissive" than men. This raises a simple but important point: the debunking strategy for drawing normative implications from empirical findings about people's judgments always involves one or more normative premises which may themselves be a matter of contestation. As a result, the form of the argument is necessarily conditional: *if* you agree with this normative premise (e.g., that moral judgments rooted in sexist attitudes ought to be discounted, and that the attitude in question really is sexist), and *if* the empirical data suggest that this particular moral judgment is rooted in said attitude, then you should discount the judgment accordingly (i.e., assign less normative weight to it).

The point about potential normative disagreements between various stakeholders, and/or disagreements in moral judgment regarding particular cases, leads to the triangulation strategy, described next.

C. Illustration #3: Triangulation

The triangulation strategy holds that divergence among the judgments of various individuals or groups of stakeholders requires the following: adjusting, pruning, or supplementing the normative conclusions derived from the competing positions in order to accommodate: (1) the normative implications of the opposing view(s); and (2) normative considerations derived from, for example, ethical or legal principles, background theories, morally relevant facts, and/or the best arguments for a normative position in the relevant expert literature (Earp, Lewis et al. 2021). To illustrate this strategy, we will refer to recent work conducted by Dranseika and colleagues (unpublished) on judgments about the right of study participants to withdraw from research after undergoing significant personal change.

The study builds on earlier findings from Tobia (2016), who asked participants to consider the case of a man who enrolls in a research study and then suffers a terrible accident, as a result of which he experiences (depending on the experimental condition) either moral improvement or moral deterioration. Tobia asked participants whether the morally changed man should be allowed to have the research study data, which had already been collected before the moral change, destroyed. Participants tended to judge that the morally deteriorated research subject should be denied the right to destroy his data, whereas the morally improved research subject retained the right.

In addition to probing the intuitions of ordinary citizens about Tobia's case, Dranseika and colleagues' cross-cultural replication study included a group of lawyers, whose judgment is especially consequential in real-world decisions involving legal rights. Potentially owing to a legal concept of personhood, lawyers from different countries revealed a distinct pattern of moral judgments: though they were still susceptible to the basic effect (i.e., asymmetry in judgments between conditions), lawyers tended to ascribe identity persistence overall, regardless of the subject's direction of moral change. Thus, at a broad level, Dranseika and colleagues find that (one of)[5] the lay intuition(s) regarding personal identity is morally laden in a wide range of cultures, whereas among lawyers, the concept of identity is not equally affected by the same moral considerations.

Put another way, laypeople demonstrated a paternalistic attitude toward the hypothetical research subject, willing to deny that an individual who underwent moral deterioration retained the right to withdraw from research. This attitude conflicted with the legally informed opinion of lawyers, who were more likely to protect the right to withdraw from research in the same situation. When adopting the triangulation strategy, we would begin by acknowledging the divergence in judgments between stakeholder groups (in this case, lawyers and ordinary citizens) and, at least tentatively, assume that neither judgment is straightforwardly amenable to debunking (i.e., both judgments are pro tanto reliable). The triangulation approach presents a possible pathway toward prescriptive insights in circumstances like this.[6]

In relation to the current example, it may be the case that the judgments of lay participants concerning a change in personal identity drive their judgments regarding the right to withdraw from research. If there is good reason to think that a legal conception of personal identity or associated rights should control in such a context, the public might need to be educated so as to clarify, or remedy confusions in, their conception as it bears on the legal right.

Alternatively, consideration of lay judgments might lead us to conclude that the legal concept of identity is not fit for purpose when applied to the question of research subjects' right to withdraw. In such a case, we might advocate stakeholder-motivated "conceptual engineering" in law, as has been done with respect to certain concepts in clinical medicine (see, e.g., McMillan 2018; Lewis 2020a).

D. Illustration #4: Pluralism

The pluralist solution to normative inference differs fundamentally from the previous three approaches. Let us suppose that existing empirical studies reveal substantial disagreement on questions of personal identity and/or associated moral implications, and, further, that follow-up evidence does not provide a reason to deem either judgment normatively unreliable (i.e., in a way that would help to establish a debunking argument). Furthermore, perhaps other normative considerations (justice, autonomy, etc.) also fail to support one view over the other. In circumstances like this, empirical evidence may lend itself to a different normative inference strategy: the pluralist approach. This approach holds that in certain cases of two or more conflicting, yet pro tanto reliable, judgments between stakeholders, multiple judgments may reasonably be assigned comparable normative weight.

Here is an example. An important bioethical issue involving judgments about personal identity persistence over time is the set of criteria that should be used to determine whether someone has died. Consider a recent study by Neiders and Dranseika (2020), in which they asked participants to express their preference for the stage in the process of dying at which their death should be declared by healthcare practitioners. To support conditions for the prima facie normative credibility of participants' judgments, three of the stages from which participants could choose mimicked three expert conceptions of death in the bioethics literature: higher-brain death, whole-brain death, and cardiopulmonary death.

In terms of expert judgment, there is more than one medically and ethically reasonable option, which suggests that decisions regarding death determination are, at least in part, preference or goal sensitive (Veatch and Ross 2016). In other words, which concept of death we should use may depend on our values or aims. Furthermore, the data gathered by Neiders and Dranseika (2020) reveal different preferences concerning death determination criteria among study participants. Taken together, the diversity of opinion among experts and laypeople alike may support a pluralistic approach to death determination, according to which individuals should be allowed to choose—among reasonable options—what criterion will be applied in the case of their own death.

V. Two More Examples

In the previous section, we reviewed four strategies for reaching normative conclusions in bioethics (in part) from experimental findings about stakeholders' moral judgments concerning identity-related cases. However, the examples we used cover just some of the topics being studied in this area. To give a sense of the wider set of issues of potential interest to bioxphi, we will explore two more interventions that have received considerable bioethical attention, and which have potential implications for personal identity: deep brain stimulation and moral enhancement.

A. Deep Brain Stimulation

In recent work, Skorburg and Sinnott-Armstrong (2020) explored a bioxphi approach to personal identity and deep brain stimulation (DBS). DBS involves a surgically implanted, battery-operated device which delivers targeted electrical stimulation to a specific brain region. The most common application of DBS is in the treatment of Parkinson's disease. At least 200,000 people worldwide live with neural implants for Parkinson's and related conditions.

Many patients have reported significant changes to their identity after DBS. For example, Schüpbach and colleagues (2006) found that in a population of twenty-nine patients undergoing DBS for Parkinson's, most reported improvements in motor symptoms, activities of daily living, and quality of life. However, two-thirds expressed feelings of estrangement and unfamiliarity with themselves, saying things like "I don't feel like myself anymore," and "I haven't found myself again after the operation" (2006: 1813). In another study, by contrast, patients who underwent DBS for Obsessive Compulsive Disorder or Treatment Resistant Depression reported feeling like themselves but without mental illness feeling "back to" themselves, or "back to sort of a baseline" (Klein et al. 2016: 144).

These kinds of case reports raise the question of whether, or in what sense, DBS changes a person's identity. We do not take a stand on this metaphysical question here (but see Gilbert, Viaña, and Ineichen, 2018, for some important criticisms of the claim that DBS threatens identity). Instead, we want to point out that perhaps the central issue in these ongoing debates is, as Witt and colleagues (2013: 501) suggest, "an explication of what we mean when judging that someone has become 'another person.'" Bioxphi could contribute to this project by manipulating key elements of a hypothetical DBS/change case and measuring the effect of these manipulations on judgments of personal identity across multiple operationalizations of the concept. This would allow for an assessment of which specific senses of personal identity (Dranseika 2017) are at play in debates about DBS-induced personal changes.

The real-life phenomenon of post-DBS personal changes provides a good example of the kind of ecologically valid case that bioxphi seeks to study. In turn, the bioxphi of personal identity could guide the construction of new forms of assessment of technologies like DBS. Given the moral self effect, for example, assessment of the moral attributes of patients before and after undergoing neurostimulation could shed light on what leads some patients or their families to say, "they're not the same person anymore."

B. Moral Enhancement

The bioxphi of personal identity is also relevant to ongoing debates about moral enhancement. One argument holds that human psychology is ill-equipped to deal with the breakneck speed of recent technological developments and the pressing existential risks that they engender (climate change, nuclear weapons, artificial intelligence, and so on). As a result, proponents argue that (biomedical) enhancement of moral traits may be required in order to adequately address these and other issues (Persson and Savulescu 2012). Setting aside the many nuances of these debates, it is worth highlighting that worries about identity change have figured prominently in the enhancement literature from the outset (e.g., Douglas 2008). More specifically, the worry is that enhancing some trait(s) might threaten the psychological continuity often thought to be constitutive of personal identity.

As we noted earlier, much recent work in x-phi has treated these kinds of questions as empirical ones. The evidence we described on the moral self effect sheds light on which traits are more likely to be viewed as constitutive of identity, how the direction of change in these traits might alter judgments of identity change, and how different contexts shape these judgments. A recent paper by Fabiano (2021) explicitly connects this research program with the moral enhancement literature. He argues that one way to preserve, or even strengthen, the kinds of psychological relations constitutive of personal identity is "to focus on enhancing virtue because virtue and personal identity are often deeply connected. The relationship between virtue and personal identity is evidenced by the fact that many concepts of virtue are intimately related to personal identity" (2021: 95). Fabiano claims that much of the evidence we discussed in this chapter supports this conclusion. Whether or not virtues are indeed an appropriate target of moral enhancement, we contend that bioxphi approaches to personal identity may meaningfully contribute to these long-standing debates in bioethics.

VI. Conclusion and Future Directions

In healthcare or biomedical research contexts, judgments about whether a patient or participant is the same person matter, and they have real-world implications that rarely arise in armchair contexts. Rights, liberty, consent, autonomy, specific care decisions, social support, and educational interventions are all potentially at stake. We do not claim that bioxphi can establish or even seeks to establish a final theory of personal identity, including how personal identity should be understood in various contexts or with respect to certain ends. Nor do we claim that bioxphi can provide definitive answers to how patients or research participants *should* be treated when changes to their personal identity are judged to have occurred.

Our vision for the bioxphi of personal identity is more modest. Through examples discussed both here and in the burgeoning literature, we can see that this emerging discipline, at least relative to traditional approaches to analytic philosophy and x-phi, is in a better position to support *ethical* decision-making in healthcare-related contexts. This is because bioxphi seeks to understand the factors that influence judgments regarding personal identity in real-world settings: factors that include addiction, the effects of neurosurgical procedures such as DBS, and the decline of cognitive function associated with certain disorders. And it seeks to understand these factors in such a way that the resulting empirical data can be used to support normative arguments.

In attempting to establish, for example, whether stakeholder judgments are pro tanto (un)reliable, bioxphi approaches to personal identity can bring empirical data into the service of reaching normative conclusions that are of significance to healthcare practice and policy. As we have seen, these conclusions can relate to, for example, the conditions under which advance directives should be respected or ignored, the specification and enactment of the right to withdraw from research, and the development of therapeutic interventions for people with substance abuse disorders.

The strategies that we have discussed for developing normative inferences from premises that include empirical content are not exhaustive; nor should this chapter be viewed as defending any single approach. Furthermore, while bioxphi studies have relied on the employment of the CVT, proponents of x-phi have argued that we should seek to employ the full range of experimental methods used in the psychosocial sciences, in combination with non-experimental approaches, such as interviews, qualitative studies, studies of linguistic corpus data, and anthropological work (O'Neill and Machery 2014; Alfano, Loeb, and Plakias 2018; Nado 2021). We think this lesson can be applied to bioxphi as well.

Another way in which research in this area could benefit is by expanding the boundaries of how personal identity is conceived. So far, much of the attention has been on psychological continuity, memories, the self-contained body, or the metaphysically distinct person. In broad terms, the focus has been on "brains and bodies" (Tobia 2016). However, it is increasingly recognized that the self and identity are not only diachronic but also relational (e.g., Mackenzie and Stoljar 2000; Christman 2004; Meyers 2005; Earp, McLoughlin et al. 2021). Therefore, rather than focusing so exclusively on a liberal conception of the self as a rational, reflective, and unitary entity, future bioxphi research on personal identity could consider more *relational* approaches to identity that take into account how the self is shaped or even constituted by social and interpersonal relations, structures, and processes (Andersen and Chen 2002).

Persons are socially embedded. When social norms and interpersonal ways of relating are internalized, "this contributes to the individual's identity, and thus the identity of the self-as-social is invested in a community and its cultural heritage" (Meyers 2005: 29-30). This suggests that judgments regarding a change in one's personal identity or that of a close friend or family member may be causally affected by interpersonal relations and the social environment. The psychologically continuous, reflective, and embodied self cannot be isolated from its social-relational situatedness (Lewis 2021).

Consequently, interpersonal relations and social structures can support or impair not only perceptions of personal identity continuity but also cognitive and moral capacities, character traits, and other qualities relevant to such perceptions (Tobia 2016; Lewis 2021; Veit et al. 2021). Doubts that an individual is the same person can arise "not only because of internal factors such as illness, depression, addiction, anxiety and fatigue, but also on the basis of external causal factors such as brainwashing, internalized oppression, stigmatization, disrespect or inappropriate normative expectations resulting from previous encounters with overly paternalistic, demeaning or pressurising institutional practices" (Lewis 2021: 20).

These effects on judgments regarding personal identity are contingent rather than necessary, meaning that whether a specific individual experiences these effects will, ultimately, depend on their psychological states and dispositions, which, in part, constitute their identity. As a concluding thought, we suggest that the bioxphi of personal identity should explore the effects of interpersonal relationships and social situations on judgments regarding personal identity change and the moral relevance of these social-relational factors.

Notes

1. We are immensely grateful to Joshua Knobe and Kevin Tobia for their invaluable comments and suggestions during the writing process, and we wish to thank Kevin for inviting us to contribute to this collected edition.
2. For a critique of the philosopher's "thought-experiment" approach to questions concerned with personal identity, see Wilkes (1988).
3. For a broader debate regarding whether intuitions vary across demographic groups in general, see Knobe (2019a; 2019b); Stich and Machery (2022).
4. See Earp et al. (in press) for details of a follow-up study.
5. See Knobe (2022) for a discussion of personal identity as a "dual character" concept, suggesting that, even among ordinary people, there may be different concepts of personal identity at play.
6. However, as with the debunking strategy, the path to a single normative conclusion about what to do in such an instance is not straightforward. When attitudes are, for example, diametrically opposed, triangulation may not be as simple as adjusting or supplementing two or more pro tanto reliable judgments in order to achieve some sort of compromise. Instead, one might need to employ a model of "wide" reflective equilibrium (for discussion, see Earp, Lewis et al. 2021). The aim here would be to achieve as much coherence as possible (given the data and information available at the time) between not only the conflicting judgments in question, but also, for example, background theories, legal or philosophical principles, morally relevant facts, etc. (Cath 2016).

Bibliography

Alfano, M., D. Loeb and A. Plakias (2018). "Experimental Moral Philosophy." In E. N. Zalta (ed.), *The Stanford Encyclopedia of Philosophy*. Available online: https://plato.stanford.edu/archives/win2018/entries/experimental-moral/ (accessed October 26, 2021).

Andersen, S. M. and S. Chen (2002). "The Relational Self: An Interpersonal Social-Cognitive Theory." *Psychological Review*, 109 (4): 619–645.

Blok, S., G. Newman and L. J. Rips (2005). "Individuals and their Concepts." In W. Ahn, R. L. Goldstone, B. C. Love, A. B. Markman and P. Wolff (eds.), *Categorization Inside and Outside the Laboratory: Essays in Honor of Douglas L. Medin*, 127–49. Washington: American Psychological Association.

Buchanan, A. (1988). "Advance Directives and the Personal Identity Problem." *Philosophy & Public Affairs*, 17 (4): 277–302.

Buchanan, A. and D. Brock (1990). *Deciding for Others. The Ethics of Surrogate Decision Making*. Cambridge: Cambridge University Press.

Cath, Y. (2016). "Reflective Equilibrium." In H. Cappelen, T. S. Gendler and J. Hawthorn (eds.), *The Oxford Handbook of Philosophical Methodology*, 213–30. Oxford: Oxford University Press.

Christman, J. (2004). "Relational Autonomy, Liberal Individualism and the Social Constitution of Selves." *Philosophical Studies*, 117 (1/2): 143–64.

Davies, R., J. Ives and M. Dunn (2015). "A Systematic Review of Empirical Bioethics Methodologies." *BMC Medical Ethics*, 16 (15): 1–13.

Demaree-Cotton, J. (2016). "Do Framing Effects Make Moral Intuitions Unreliable?" *Philosophical Psychology*, 29 (1): 1–22.

Douglas, T. (2008). "Moral Enhancement." *Journal of Applied Philosophy*, 25 (3): 228–45.
Dranseika, V. (2017). "On the Ambiguity of 'the Same Person.'" *AJOB Neuroscience*, 8 (3): 184–6.
Dranseika, V., I. R. Hannikainen, P. Bystranowski, B. D. Earp, K. P. Tobia, G. Almeida, K. Kneer, N. Struchiner, K. Dolinina, B. Janik, E. Lauraityte, A. Liefgreen, M. Prochnicki, A. Rosas, N. Strohmaier and T. Żuradzki (unpublished manuscript). "Personal Identity, Direction of Change, and the Right to Withdraw from Research."
Dworkin, R. (1993). *Life's Dominion. An Argument about Abortion and Euthanasia*. London: Harper Collins.
Earp, B. D., I. Hannikainen, S. Dale and S. Latham (in press). "Experimental Philosophical Bioethics, Advance Directives, and the True Self in Dementia." In A. De Block and K. Hens (eds.), *Experimental Philosophy of Medicine*. London: Bloomsbury.
Earp, B. D., J. A. Skorburg, J. A. Everett and J. Savulescu (2019). "Addiction, Identity, Morality." *AJOB Empirical Bioethics*, 10 (2): 136–53.
Earp, B. D., J. Demaree-Cotton, M. Dunn, V. Dranseika, J. A. C. Everett, A. Feltz, G. Geller, I. Hannikainen, L. A. Jansen, J. Knobe, J. Kolak, S. Latham, A. Lerner, J. May, M. Mercurio, E. Mihailov, D. Rodríguez-Arias, B. Rodríguez López, J. Savulescu, M. Sheehan, N. Strohminger, J. Sugarman, K. Tabb and K. P. Tobia (2020). "Experimental Philosophical Bioethics." *AJOB Empirical Bioethics*, 11 (1): 30–3.
Earp, B. D., S. R. Latham and K. P. Tobia (2020). "Personal Transformation and Advance Directives: An Experimental Bioethics Approach." *The American Journal of Bioethics*, 20 (8): 72–5.
Earp, B. D., J. Lewis, V. Dranseika and I. Hannikainen (2021). "Experimental Philosophical Bioethics and Normative Inference." *Theoretical Medicine and Bioethics*, 42 (3–4): 91–111.
Earp, B. D., K. L. McLoughlin, J. T. Monrad, M. S. Clark and M. J. Crockett (2021). "How Social Relationships Shape Moral Wrongness Judgments." *Nature Communications*, 12 (5776): 1–13.
Elwyn, G., J. Tilburt and V. Montori (2013). "The Ethical Imperative for Shared Decision-Making." *European Journal for Person Centered Healthcare*, 1: 129–31.
Fabiano, J. (2021). "Virtue Theory for Moral Enhancement." *AJOB Neuroscience*, 12 (2–3): 89–102.
Fisher, J. C. (2015). "Pragmatic Experimental Philosophy." *Philosophical Psychology*, 28 (3): 412–33.
Furberg, E. (2012). "Advance Directives and Personal Identity: What is the Problem?" *The Journal of Medicine and Philosophy*, 37 (1): 60–73.
Garcia, M. (2021). *We Are Not Born Submissive: How Patriarchy Shapes Women's Lives*. Princeton: Princeton University Press.
Gilbert, F., J. Viaña and C. Ineichen (2018). "Deflating the 'DBS Causes Personality Changes' Bubble." *Neuroethics*, 14 (1): 1–17.
Hart, C. L. (2021). *Drug Use for Grown-Ups: Chasing Liberty in the Land of Fear*. New York: Penguin.
Henrich, J., S. J. Heine and A. Norenzayan (2010). "Most People are not WEIRD." *Nature*, 466 (7302): 29.
Kagan, S. (2001). "Thinking about Cases." *Social Philosophy and Policy*, 18 (2): 44–63.
Klein, E., S. Goering, J. Gagne, C. V. Shea, R. Franklin, S. Zorowitz, ... A. S. Widge (2016). "Brain-Computer Interface-Based Control of Closed-Loop Brain Stimulation: Attitudes and Ethical Considerations." *Brain-Computer Interfaces*, 3 (3): 140–8.

Klenk, M. (2020). "Charting Moral Psychology's Significance for Bioethics: Routes to Bioethical Progress, its Limits, and Lessons from Moral Philosophy." *Diametros*, 17 (64): 36–55.

Knobe, J. (2007). "Experimental Philosophy." *Philosophy Compass*, 2 (1): 81–92.

Knobe, J. (2016). "Experimental Philosophy is Cognitive Science." In J. Sytsma and W. Buckwalter (eds.), *A Companion to Experimental Philosophy*, 37–52. Oxford: Wiley-Blackwell.

Knobe, J. (2019a). "Philosophical Intuitions are Surprisingly Robust Across Demographic Differences." *Epistemology & Philosophy of Science*, 56 (2): 29–36.

Knobe, J. (2019b). "Difference and Robustness in the Patterns of Philosophical Intuition across Demographic Groups." Unpublished manuscript. Available online: https://cpb-us-w2.wpmucdn.com/campuspress.yale.edu/dist/3/1454/files/2019/12/Difference-Robustness-2.pdf (accessed October 26, 2021).

Knobe, J. (2022). "Personal Identity and Dual Character Concepts." In K. P. Tobia (ed.), *Experimental Philosophy of Identity and the Self*. London: Bloomsbury.

Knobe, J., W. Buckwalter, S. Nichols, P. Robbins, H. Sarkissian and T. Sommers (2012). "Experimental Philosophy." *Annual Review of Psychology*, 63: 81–99.

Kuorikoski, J. and C. Marchionni (2016). "Evidential Diversity and the Triangulation of Phenomena." *Philosophy of Science*, 83 (2): 227–47.

Lewis, J. (2020a). "From X-phi to Bioxphi: Lessons in Conceptual Analysis 2.0." *AJOB Empirical Bioethics*, 11 (1): 34–6.

Lewis, J. (2020b). "Getting Obligations Right: Autonomy and Shared Decision Making." *Journal of Applied Philosophy*, 37 (1): 118–40.

Lewis, J. (2021). "Autonomy and the Limits of Cognitive Enhancement." *Bioethics*, 35 (1): 15–22.

Locke, J. (1689/1694). *An Essay Concerning Human Understanding*. P. H. Nidditch (ed.). Oxford: Oxford University Press, 1975.

Machery, E. (2017). *Philosophy Within its Proper Bounds*. Oxford: Oxford University Press.

Mackenzie, C. and N. Stoljar (2000). "Autonomy Refigured." In C. Mackenzie and N. Stoljar (eds.), *Relational autonomy: Feminist Perspectives on Autonomy, Agency and the Social Self*, 3–31. Oxford: Oxford University Press.

McMillan, J. (2018). *The Methods of Bioethics: An Essay in Meta-Bioethics*. Oxford: Oxford University Press.

Meyers, D. T. (2005). "Decentralizing Autonomy: Five Faces of Selfhood." In J. Christman and J. Anderson (eds.), *Autonomy and the Challenges to Liberalism: New Essays*, 27–55. Cambridge: Cambridge University Press.

Mihailov, E., I. R. Hannikainen and B. D. Earp (2021). "Advancing Methods in Empirical Bioethics: Bioxphi Meets Digital Technologies." *The American Journal of Bioethics*, 21 (6): 53–6.

Mukerji, N. (2019). *Experimental Philosophy: A Critical Study*. London: Rowman & Littlefield.

Nado, J. (2021). "Conceptual Engineering via Experimental Philosophy." *Inquiry*, 64 (1–2): 76–96.

Neiders, I. and V. Dranseika (2020). "Minds, Brains, and Hearts: an Empirical Study on Pluralism Concerning Death Determination." *Monash Bioethics Review*, 38 (1): 35–48.

Nichols, S. and M. Bruno (2010). "Intuitions about Personal Identity: An Empirical Study." *Philosophical Psychology*, 23 (3): 293–312.

O'Neill, E. and E. Machery (2014). "Experimental Philosophy: What is it Good For?" In E. Machery and E. O'Neill (eds.), *Current Controversies in Experimental Philosophy*, vii–xxix. London: Routledge.

Persson, I. and J. Savulescu (2012). *Unfit for the Future: The Need for Moral Enhancement*. Oxford: Oxford University Press.

Prinz, J. J. and S. Nichols (2016). "Diachronic Identity and the Moral Self." In J. Kiverstein (ed.), *The Routledge Handbook of Philosophy of the Social Mind*, 465–80. London: Routledge.

Reid, T. (1785/1969). *Essays on the Intellectual Powers of Man*. Cambridge, MA: MIT Press.

Reiner, P. B. (2019). "Experimental Neuroethics." In S. K. Nagel (ed.), *Shaping Children: Ethical and Social Questions That Arise When Enhancing the Young*, 75–83. Cham: Springer.

Schlegel, R. J. and J. A. Hicks (2011). "The True Self and Psychological Health: Emerging Evidence and Future Directions." *Social and Personality Psychology Compass*, 5 (12): 989–1003.

Schlegel, R. J., J. A. Hicks, J. Arndt and L. A. King (2009). "Thine Own Self: True Self-Concept Accessibility and Meaning in Life." *Journal of Personality and Social Psychology*, 96 (2): 473–90.

Schlegel, R. J., J. A. Hicks, L. A. King and J. Arndt (2011). "Feeling Like You Know Who You Are: Perceived True Self-Knowledge and Meaning in Life." *Personality & Social Psychology Bulletin*, 37 (6): 745–56.

Schüpbach, M., M. Gargiulo, M. L. Welter, L. Mallet, C. Béhar, J. L. Houeto, D. Maltête, V. Mesnage and Y. Agid (2006). "Neurosurgery in Parkinson disease: a Distressed Mind in a Repaired Body?" *Neurology*, 66 (12): 1811–16.

Shoemaker, D. (2010). "The Insignificance of Personal Identity for Bioethics." *Bioethics*, 24 (9): 481–9.

Skorburg, J. A. and W. Sinnott-Armstrong (2020). "Some Ethics of Deep Brain Stimulation." In D. Stein and I. Singh (eds.), *Global Mental Health and Neuroethics*, 117–32. London: Academic Press.

Stich, S. P. and E. Machery (2022). "Demographic Differences in Philosophical Intuition: A Reply to Joshua Knobe." *Review of Philosophy and Psychology* (online ahead of print), https://doi.org/10.1007/s13164-021-00609-7.

Strohminger, N. and S. Nichols (2014). "The Essential Moral Self." *Cognition*, 131 (1): 159–71.

Strohminger, N. and S. Nichols (2015). "Neurodegeneration and Identity." *Psychological Science*, 26 (9): 1469–79.

Thomson, J. J. (1986). *Rights, Restitution, and Risk*. Cambridge, MA: Harvard University Press.

Tobia, K. P. (2015). "Personal Identity and the Phineas Gage Effect." *Analysis*, 75 (3): 396–405.

Tobia, K. P. (2016). "Personal Identity, Direction of Change, and Neuroethics." *Neuroethics*, 9 (1): 37–43.

Tobia, K. P. (2017). "Change Becomes You." *Aeon*. Available online: https://aeon.co/essays/to-be-true-to-ones-self-means-changing-to-become-that-self (accessed October 26, 2021).

Veatch, R. M. and L. F. Ross (2016). *Defining Death: The Case for Choice*. Washington: Georgetown University Press.

Veit, W., B. D. Earp, H. Browning and J. Savulescu (2021). "Evaluating Trade-Offs Between Autonomy and Well-Being in Supported Decision Making." *American Journal of Bioethics*, 21 (11): 21–4.

Wilkes, K. V. (1988). *Real People: Personal Identity Without Thought Experiments*. Oxford: Oxford University Press.

Williams, B. (1970). "The Self and the Future." *The Philosophical Review*, 79 (2): 161–80.

Witt, K., J. Kuhn, L. Timmermann, M. Zurowski and C. Woopen (2013). "Deep Brain Stimulation and the Search for Identity." *Neuroethics*, 6 (3): 49–511.

13

Corporate Identity

Mihailis E. Diamantis

I. Introducing Collective Identity

Legal scholars rarely talk about personal identity, even though unstated and unexamined assumptions about identity are essential to legal practice (Mott 2018; Diamantis 2019c). Any effort to pair people with conduct for which they are responsible must draw on an implicit view of where one person ends and another begins, in both space and time. If a hand shot a gun, the law needs some criteria for saying whose hand it was. If the gun went off ten years ago, the law must determine whether that person is still around today.

Lawyers' silence about personal identity may not be altogether surprising. Human beings are corporeally continuous creatures with relatively predictable life cycles. The terrible accidents that fascinate neuroscientists—like Phineas Gage's exploded rod—and the fanciful thought experiments that vex philosophers—like split brains, fused personalities, and mind-controlling tumors—are rare even when they are physically possible. If such cases do occur, the law accommodates them using ad hoc exceptions to previously settled doctrine. There is little perceived need to wrangle with the nuances of human identity. Most practitioners implicitly assume that biological continuity is a serviceable proxy for any question the law may ask in regard to personal identity. To find out whose hand was on a gun, the law simply asks to whose body it was attached. To find out if that person is still around today, the law asks whether that body is still breathing.

Lawyers' reticence to discuss personal identity may be more surprising when it comes to *legal* persons. Legal people are usually collectives of human beings, like business corporations and unions. The law formally designates such collectives as distinct "people" for purposes of assessing rights and responsibilities. Accordingly, corporations can be sued by private parties for offenses like discrimination and prosecuted by authorities for crimes like insider trading.

Just as for natural people, the law needs some implicit theory of identity for holding corporations accountable. The same basic questions need answers: When a violation occurs, how can the law determine whether what caused it is part of a corporation (Diamantis 2021)? And how can the law say which corporation today, if any, is the same as the one that caused the harm in the past (Diamantis 2019d)?

It is difficult to begin articulating identity conditions for corporations. There is no obvious way to generate a pre-theoretical list of constituent parts. Clearly corporations can include natural people, but which ones?[1] Unlike natural people, legal people have no scientifically discernible perimeter. No visible cue distinguishes an Apple employee from a Microsoft employee, or either from someone who has no corporate affiliation at all. Even after discovering (or stipulating) which natural people make up corporations, there are few pre-theoretical guides for determining what rearrangements and substitutions of parts corporations can survive. Corporations have no heartbeat and no uniform function by which to measure their death. In life, corporations are much more dynamic than natural people. They have no predictable life cycle.[2] For them, the sorts of transformations that captivate philosophers of identity are matters of course. Corporations revise their fundamental operating principles, lose and gain any of their parts, or split and merge, all with the stroke of a pen.

The stakes for finding a satisfactory account of corporate identity are high. Lawmakers recognized corporate personhood in large part to address the massive harms corporations can cause. Corporations operate on a scale—temporal, geographic, and material—that no natural person can achieve. They can darken the sky, poison entire communities, disrupt financial markets, and drive millions of people from their homes. By identifying responsible corporations and imposing penalties, the law hopes to deter corporations from socially destructive behavior and provide some measure of justice to their victims.

And yet, the law has no explicit position on corporate identity. One reason is that historically, lawmakers prefer to repurpose existing law rather than develop it anew. As the corporate form grew in social and economic significance, lawmakers responded by transposing onto the corporate context an ancient Roman doctrinal framework (discussed later in this chapter) that applied originally to simple master-slave relationships. Another reason is lack of philosophical reflection. It takes some creative insight, some puzzling thought experiment, or some pointed question to provoke a sense of urgency over matters of identity that we otherwise take for granted. These prompts are familiar to philosophers of identity, but they have yet to meaningfully enter legal discourse. This chapter aims to change that.

Even if the law has no explicit view on corporate identity, it is implicitly committed to certain parameters. The legal rules for imposing corporate liability encode assumptions about which things out in the world count as parts of corporations and what transformations corporations can survive. This chapter unearths those assumptions to paint a rough picture of the law's view on corporate identity.

Corporate identity also matters to us in our ordinary lives. In our routine socio-ethical interactions with corporations, we must draw intuitive lines between corporations so we know which, if any, to blame, or praise, or otherwise relate to in a new way going forward. Experimental philosophers have made some initial inroads into understanding how these intuitions function, but much work remains. This chapter presents what is known or can be inferred from available studies. It uncovers differences between how the law and the folk conceive corporate identity, both synchronic (Section II) and diachronic (Section III). A concluding section (Section IV) discusses the real-world significance of the discrepancy.

II. Synchronic Collective Identity: Pairing Collectives with Constituents

Synchronic identity refers to a thing's identity at a given time. As for natural people, a view of synchronic identity for corporations should pick out the things in the world that are constituents of them (Diamantis 2019a). When something happens in the world, synchronic identity will help to say whether the corporation, or something else, caused it. As a starting point, it should be relatively uncontroversial that employees are parts of corporations. Beyond that, there are few clear intuitive signs about which employees matter, who counts as an employee, or whether corporations encompass anything other than employees. In corporate law, "part," "constituent," and "identity" are not defined concepts. Nor do they have sufficiently coherent ordinary meanings to make surveying people's intuitions about those terms directly a worthwhile exercise.

A more productive path may be to investigate synchronic corporate identity indirectly. One issue about which legal doctrine and folk intuitions are more robust is corporate accountability. The conditions under which corporations are deemed responsible may give some insight into what corporate identity is supposed to be. For example, if an individual bribes a politician and a corporation is held to account, that is prima facie evidence that the corporation is functionally identifiable with that individual. As explained later in the chapter, the connection between liability and identity is particularly strong in criminal law. Investigating the conditions under which we hold corporations responsible could uncover a preliminary picture of synchronic corporate identity.

A. The Law's View

The law assumes that corporations can only function through natural people. The law also subscribes to the "identity principle," which prohibits punishing one person for another's crimes. (Korematsu v. United States, 323 U.S. 214 (1944); Locke 1690/1975; Parfit 1971). Accordingly, when the law holds a corporation accountable for human activity, it identifies that activity as corporate activity.

Respondeat superior ("let the master answer") is the general legal doctrine for assessing corporate criminal responsibility. In conjunction with the identity principle, it says when a natural person acts or thinks as an extension of a corporation (Diamantis 2016). It applies whenever an individual:

1. Is an employee of a corporation,
2. Operates within the scope of her employment, and
3. Has some intent to benefit the corporation.

Whatever the employee does or thinks under these conditions, she does or thinks both on her own account and as the corporation. For example, if a truck driver hits a pedestrian while speeding to make a timely delivery, then her corporate employer also hit the pedestrian.

"Employee," "scope of employment," and "intent to benefit" are legal terms of art. Who counts as an employee is a complicated question and a point of current controversy. In the interest of brevity, I skip over the nuances of labor law and focus the discussion on clear-cut, traditional examples of employees: that is, those with a current employment contract, an ongoing corporate relationship, and a wage from the corporation. "Scope of employment" and "intent to benefit" are a bit easier to characterize. Courts have interpreted both in very permissive ways. Scope of employment can exceed the four corners of an employment contract (United States v. Hilton Hotels Corp., 467 F.2d 1000 (9th Cir. 1972)). An employee may count as operating within the scope of her employment even if she acts contrary to direct orders. The only behaviors that are reliably beyond the scope of employment are victimizing one's employer (perhaps by embezzling funds) and pursuing purely private matters away from the workplace (like mowing one's own lawn). "Intent to benefit" is similarly broad (United States v. Sun-Diamond Growers of California, 138 F.3d 961 (D.C. Cir. 1998)). Any sort of benefit qualifies, as do intentions that are ineffectual, subsidiary, or confused.

Although *respondeat superior* does not paint a complete picture of synchronic corporate identity under the law, it does imply some general commitments. For example, according to the law, each corporation is entirely constituted by any one of its employees, from the C-suite to the custodial staff. Each employee potentially embodies the entire corporation because each in isolation can incur liability for it. To illustrate the oddity of this view, suppose one employee in a corporation's human resources department makes hiring decisions using objective criteria, another gives undue preference to men, a third gives undue preference to women, and a fourth runs compliance to ensure all hiring practices are nondiscriminatory. At one and the same time, *respondeat superior* would say that the corporation hires in a nondiscriminatory way, engages in gender discrimination (both in favor of and against women), and tries to prevent discrimination. For any natural person, this self-undermining pattern of behavior might be symptomatic of a rare dissociative disorder; *respondeat superior* effectively prescribes it for corporate people.

When *respondeat superior* identifies corporations with individual employees, it also excludes everything else. For example, internal organizational systems are irrelevant to corporate liability, and hence to identity. The same is true of a corporation's physical structures, brand, consumer products, technological systems, and so on. The law understands these all to be incidental features of corporations or property interests held by them, not constituent parts.

Perhaps paradoxically, *respondeat superior* even excludes *groups* of employees as possible constituents of corporate identity. While a corporation can be liable for the misconduct of any single employee, it is not liable if a group of employees engages in conduct that, though individually innocent, collectively amounts to criminal harm (Diamantis 2019b). For example, in one well-known case, a ferry capsized, killing nearly 200 passengers. (R. v. Her Majesty's Coroner for E. Kent, (1987) 3 B.C.C. 636, 638 (Eng.)). Since the ferry crew operated the boat in a manner that looked in the aggregate to be grossly negligent, prosecutors charged their corporate employer with manslaughter. Applying *respondeat superior*, the court found that, though the collective conduct of the crew was grossly negligent, none of the individual employees' acted with gross negligence. Accordingly, the court dismissed the manslaughter charge. This result seems to imply that a corporation can be identical to any individual employee, but not to a group of its employees, nor even to the sum total of all its employees.

B. The Folk View[3]

There is not much data on folk intuitions of synchronic corporate identity.[4] Early related research investigated conditions under which people are inclined to group objects (Rock 1997) or to identify moving groups of objects as unified loci of agency (Bloom and Veres 1999). As to groups of humans, researchers have described four types of groups that people intuitively recognize: intimacy groups (like families), task groups (like orchestras), social categories (like Christians), and loose associations (like people at a bus stop) (Lickel et al. 2000). However, people do not think of all these types of groups in the same way. Intimacy and task groups are distinctive in that they exhibit what cognitive scientists call entitativity, a high level of perceived coherence and interdependence/interactivity among their membership (Campbell 1958). Entitative groups occupy a special role in our cognitive economy, similar to the role that individuals occupy (Welbourne 1999; Abelson et al. 1998; Huebner 2016; Johnson and Queller 2003). We come to see such collectives as unified agents with an identity distinct from, but overlapping with, the individuals who compose them (Yzerbyt, Judd, and Corneille 2004). Corporations, with their generally hierarchical structure and profit-based organizing principle, are archetypical entitative groups (Clark 1994). Unfortunately, there is very little research into folk understandings of entitative group constitution, let alone corporate constitution.

Once again, judgments of corporate responsibility could yield insight into a folk picture of corporate identity. On this point, there is some good data, and it gestures toward a vision of synchronic corporate identity that departs significantly from the law's. As entitive groups, corporations activate our ordinary intuitions about responsible action (Dasgupta, Banaji, and Abelson 1999). This makes reactive attitudes, like blame, toward corporations psychologically sustainable (Sherman and Percy 2010; Knobe and Prinz 2008; Denson et al. 2006). We seem to assess corporate responsibly in much the same basic way that we assess individual responsibility (O'Laughlin and Malle 2002). For both, our assessment often turns on the intention (or lack thereof) behind their conduct, and we infer the presence (or absence) of intention from observed behavior and contextual clues (Bloom and Veres 1999). We even use the same neural systems to evaluate both individual and corporate behavior (Contreras et al. 2013).

These basic observations map out some important differences between the legal and folk conceptions of corporate identity. Since people ordinarily think of corporations as unified entities, they seem to conceive of corporations as consisting of an aggregate of employees, rather than individual employees. Recall the human resources and ferry examples from the previous section. The law views each corporate employee as individually embodying their entire corporate employer, undertaking distinct courses of behavior on the corporation's behalf. Laypeople, however, appear to be more likely to see the corporations as unified agents, acting out single courses of behavior or having single trains of thought, albeit through their multiple employees (Jenkins et al. 2014). Each employee's behavior adds to that course of conduct and provides context in light of which we understand and evaluate the whole. As a consequence, on the folk view, the ferry company described in the previous section may seem to have committed manslaughter (because the employees collectively acted with gross negligence) and the company with the human resources department may seem to have hired applicants equitably (because they collectively hired as many men as women).

Adding detail to this skeletal folk view would require much more experimental investigation. We do not know, for example, how people decide whether an individual is part of a task group like a corporation. Available studies ask participants directly about collectives, for example, "Microsoft" or "a university," or, to the extent they ask about individuals, the studies explicitly introduce the individuals as members of the collective, for example, "an employee of Microsoft" or "a university administrator." Accordingly, they yield little insight into what it intuitively takes for an individual to be a member of a corporation.[5] Nor can we presently answer whether non-employees who are under corporate control (e.g., an independent contractor hired by the corporation) or employees who are not under corporate control (e.g., a rogue employee who disobeys orders) are intuitive constituents of corporations too.[6]

We might also wonder whether, on the folk view, corporations can have non-human constituent parts. Available data makes a tentative case for an affirmative answer. Experimental studies show that people are more likely to identify an entity with its causally effective features (Blok, Newman, and Rips 2005). Organizational psychologists know that corporate structures—like performance metrics and institutional culture—can be more important drivers of employee behavior (and hence corporate behavior) than individual employees themselves (Coleman 1990; Lederman 2000). And technologists know that corporations increasingly rely on algorithms to carry out functions previously assigned to human employees. So corporate structures and digital systems could plausibly play a role in the folk view of synchronic corporate identity (Diamantis 2020). Studies directly targeted to that question, for example, by asking whether and when corporations could be responsible for harms caused by algorithms, would be helpful.

III. Diachronic Collective Identity: Pairing Present with Past

Diachronic identity refers to identity over time, even as an entity changes. For collectives like corporations, the list of routine but potentially transformative changes is long. They may lose or gain any number of employees throughout the corporate hierarchy, abandon divisions dedicated to specific operations, pivot to totally new product lines, acquire (or be acquired by) other corporations, merge with them, spin off parts of themselves into new corporations, rebrand themselves, or rework their internal corporate structure. Sometimes, many of these changes can happen in a very short span, like when a hedge fund purchases a corporation with a view to restructuring and reselling it.

As with synchronic corporate identity, there are not many explicit clues in the law or from experimental philosophy about corporate identity over time. However, there is enough to begin describing rough-hewn legal and folk views.

A. The Law's View

Since the law does not explicitly define diachronic corporate identity, we must once more turn to corporate liability for indirect insight. Here again, criminal law's identity principle offers an inroad. In its diachronic version, the identity principle requires that the law only punish a present-day defendant who is identical to the person who committed the past crime at issue. If there is no such defendant, for example, because the suspect has since died or otherwise ceased to exist, criminal law offers no remedy.

There are a few bright-line legal rules for tracing corporate criminal liability through time. Some procedures "kill" a corporation and thereby extinguish any criminal liability. For example, the state under whose law a corporation is organized may revoke the corporation's charter for failure to abide by the state's requirements. Or a court may divest a corporation of all its assets, for example, as criminal punishment or in bankruptcy, thereby bringing it and all its liabilities to an end. There are also important internal corporate changes that the law is equally clear do not affect corporate criminal liability, such as swapping owners, turning over management, or implementing compliance reform. The legal reasons are slightly different for each. The doctrine of separateness, a cornerstone of corporate law, ensures that corporations have a legal status distinct from their owners. Similarly, under *respondeat superior*, liability for criminal conduct attaches twice, to the firm and to the employee independently. Lastly, the fact that corporate criminal liability persists even after implementing new internal programs—like upgraded compliance protocols—is so axiomatic that few have thought to question it (Diamantis 2019d).

For external changes that involve other corporations—like mergers and acquisitions—the law is less settled, but overall such changes seem to have little impact on corporate identity. When two corporations merge (what philosophers might think of as "fusion cases"), the composite inherits any prior criminal liabilities that either had (Model Business Corporation Act § 11.07; United States v. Polizzi, 500 F.2d 856 (9th Cir. 1974)). If a corporation splits off and separately incorporates some of its business operations (what philosophers might think of as "fission cases"), both resulting corporations are potentially liable for any prior criminal misconduct of the predecessor.[7]

Insofar as criminal liability implies identity,[8] these liability doctrines gesture toward a rather stubborn view of diachronic corporate identity. Short of death, nothing will terminate or compromise a corporation's identity. No matter what sort of internal changes a corporation undergoes, how large a corporation it merges with, or how large a part of itself it spins off, it fully remains the same corporation.

B. The Folk View

Existing data on the folk view of diachronic collective identity paint a picture that differs significantly from the law's (Hamilton, Levine, and Thurston 2008).[9] Three conclusions from studies about individual identity have motivated modern experimental research on collective identity. The first result is that people intuitively distinguish between "accidental" and "essential" traits, where only changes to the latter effectuate changes in identity (Strohminger and Nichols 2014). The second is that accidental traits tend to be surface level, while essential traits tend to be deeper and causally efficacious (Blok et al. 2005; Rips, Hespos, and Albarracín 2015). And the third is that the normative valence of a trait—whether it is perceived as being good or bad, rather than neutral—can make it seem more essential (Newman, Bloom, and Knobe 2014; Newman, De Freitas, and Knobe 2015).

It would be unsurprising if these results extended to folk judgments about corporate identity. As discussed earlier, entitive collectives occupy a role in our cognitive economy similar to the one occupied by individuals. People are inclined to view social groups as having underlying essences (Rothbart and Taylor 1992), and when the group is entitive, people tend to conceive of that essence in behavioral-dispositional terms (Hamilton and Sherman 1996). Recent studies confirm that people are more likely to judge that a collective's essential identity has changed if its normatively valenced traits have been altered (De Freitas et al. 2016).[10] In one test of this effect, experimenters presented participants with scenarios about a fictional school in Nazi Germany. The scenarios described the school undergoing various changes and then asked participants whether the school after the change was the same school or a different one. Participants were significantly more likely to say the school lost its identity when it changed a normatively valenced trait, like shifting its curricular focus from Nazi ideology to traditional academic subjects. Normatively neutral changes, like a turnover in administration, did not induce the same effect. Though available studies have focused on collectives like universities and rock bands, investigators believe their results could extend to other collectives, like corporations (De Freitas et al. 2016; Tobia 2015).[11]

If future work bears out that prediction, then the folk view of diachronic corporate identity is significantly more nuanced than the law's. Recall that according to the law, nothing short of dissolution will extinguish a corporation's identity. In some cases, this approach aligns well with the folk view. Superficial alterations—such as a change in corporate headquarters, logo, or name—are unlikely to have much impact on the causally efficacious, normatively valenced traits to which folk pin their conception of corporate identity. However, replacing executive leadership or implementing new compliance protocols could positively impact how the corporation conducts business. While legally irrelevant, such changes could generate a change of identity on the folk view.

Along similar lines, the folk perspective departs from the law's stark approach to mergers and spin-offs. Suppose, for example, that in the course of a merger between A and B, one of predecessor A's causally effective, normatively valenced traits—perhaps a robust compliance culture—manages to subsume the analogous trait of predecessor B. Ordinary people should be more likely to identify the composite with A. For spin-offs, the folk perception of the predecessor's identity is likely to follow whichever of the two successors inherits the predecessor's salient, causally effective, normatively valenced traits. That might be both successors, but it could be just one of them if the traits were tied to a particular division within the predecessor.

IV. Does the Discrepancy Between Law and Intuition Matter?

This chapter has articulated the basic outlines of legal and folk perspectives on both synchronic and diachronic corporate identity. As to synchronic identity, the law identifies corporations with individual employees, while folk intuition is more likely to look to employees in the aggregate. As to diachronic identity, the law sees corporate identity as a very durable construct that ends only with the dissolution of the corporation. Folk intuition is more nuanced. It seems to pin corporate identity to the persistence of causally effective, normatively valanced traits.

The legal and folk perspectives give different answers across routine corporate events. For corporations and those who manage them, these differences can be important. When corporations misbehave, they face liability both in the court of law and in the court of public opinion. Effective corporate management attends to both. When it comes to synchronic identity, the law is more manipulable than folk understanding. For example, one common strategy among corporate management is to distribute responsibilities across several employees so that none is likely to satisfy all the elements of a crime. While this minimizes the chance that the law will identify the corporation as the author of criminal harm, the strategy is unlikely to impact public perception when that harm occurs. For diachronic identity, things are reversed—the folk view is more manipulable. After a scandal, corporations often try reinventing themselves. As a legal matter, there is little they can do to extinguish liability. However, business partners and customers may be more open to persuasion by measures like hiring more ethics-minded management and implementing better compliance protocols.

The discrepancy between the legal and the folk visions of corporate identity is also significant for legal policy. One goal of corporate criminal law is to satisfy "society's desire to see [corporations] responsible for misconduct punished" (Henning 2010). To accomplish that expressive ambition, the law must understand how people identify and distinguish between responsible corporations. The law falls short when it fails to identify the intuitively right corporate offender.

Notes

1 I write "can" here because some corporations have no natural person constituents (Reyes 2021).
2 It should be noted, though, that some researchers maintain that social groups do follow predictable patterns of development (Worchel and Coutant 2004). I suspect the patterns they identify hold less reliably for business corporations.
3 The studies discussed later in the chapter were largely conducted on Western audiences. While Eastern audiences have different intuitions about groups, the data seem to show that they are even more inclined to exhibit the psychological tendencies I discuss (Phelan, Arico, and Nichols 2013; Huebner, Bruno, and Sarkissian 2010; Kashima et al. 2005; Menon et al. 1999).
4 Sociologists and social psychologists have talked about "collective identity" for decades in the context of social movements (Melucci 1989; Polletta and Jasper 2001).

For them, collective identity is a social and psychological phenomenon, bound up with individual identity, that emphasizes the first-personal perspective of people who have a distinctive shared orientation (Worchel and Coutant 2004). This understanding of collective identity is likely orthogonal to the third-personal conception that is the focus of this chapter (Hamilton et al. 2008).

5 Phelan et al. (2013) perhaps come closest. They demonstrate that we intuitively attribute member mental states to the group as a whole only if the mental state is "saliently associated with the role of being a member of the group" (2013: 717). The authors do not, however, test how people understand group roles or come to associate different mental states as appropriate to it.

6 Some research shows that group members themselves reject those among them who deviate too far from group norms (Marques, Yzerbyt, and Leyens 1988; Marques et al. 2001).

7 The legal reasoning here is a bit complex: the general rule for spin-offs is that a predecessor cannot assign liabilities to the newly formed corporation without the permission of any third parties to whom the liabilities are owed (Kotran, Katz, and Khan 2010). In the criminal context, the relevant third party is the government, which, so far as I know, has never agreed to such a transfer of criminal liability. As a consequence, both parent and the spin-off could be liable—at the prosecutor's option—for crimes committed before the separation.

8 Noonan (this volume) also describes the intuitive principle that only the doer of a deed merits punishment or reward for it.

9 Because this chapter focuses primarily on third-personal metaphysical judgments, it does not discuss work on members' perception about the continuity of their own group. Research on that topic finds two variables drive judgments of collective continuity: transgenerational transmission of core values/beliefs/traditions and narrative cohesion across different events in history (Sani et al. 2007).

10 Though all normative changes seem to be disruptive of identity, people are more likely to register a negative change as signaling a change in identity (Tobia 2015; De Freitas et al. 2018). For human identity, this could be because we assume that humans' core essence is overall positive (Molouki and Bartels 2017). It is an open question whether the result would hold for business corporations, which we regard with more moral suspicion (Rai and Diermeier 2015; Newheiser, Sawaoka and Dovidio 2012).

11 It bears noting that some recent research concludes that perceived continuity of purpose is what really drives persistence judgments for social objects (Rose, Schaffer, and Tobia 2020).

Bibliography

Abelson, R., N. Dasgupta, J. Park and M. Banaji (1998). "Perceptions of the Collective Other." *Personality and Social Psychology Review*, 2 (4): 243–50.

Blok, S., G. Newman and L. Rips (2005). "Individuals and their Concepts." In W. Ahn, R. Goldstone, B. Love, A. Markman and P. Wolff (eds.), *Categorization Inside and Outside the Laboratory: Essays in Honor of Douglas L. Medin*, 127–49. Washington: American Psychological Association.

Bloom, P. and C. Veres (1999). "The Perceived Intentionality of Groups." *Cognition*, 71 (1): B1–B9.

Campbell, D. (1958). "Common Fate, Similarity, and Other Indices of the Status of Aggregates of Persons as Social Entities."*Behavioral Science*, 3 (1): 14–25.

Clark, A. (1994). "Beliefs and Desires Incorporated." *The Journal of Philosophy*, 91 (8): 404–25.

Coleman, J. (1990). *Foundations of Social Theory*. Cambridge, MA: Harvard University Press.

Contreras, J., J. Schirmer, M. Banaji and J. Mitchell (2013). "Common Brain Regions with Distinct Patterns of Neural Responses During Mentalizing About Groups and Individuals." *Journal of Cognitive Neuroscience*, 25 (9): 1406–17.

Dasgupta, N., M. Banaji and R. Abelson (1999). "Group Entitivity and Group Perception: Associations Between Physical Features and Psychological Judgment." *Journal of Personality and Social Psychology*, 77 (5), 991–1003.

De Freitas, J., M. Cikara, I. Grossmann and R. Schlegel (2018). "Moral Goodness is the Essence of Personal Identity." *Trends in Cognitive Science*, 22 (9): 739–40.

De Freitas, J., K. Tobia, G. Newman and J. Knobe (2016). "Normative Judgments and Individual Essence." *Cognitive Science*, 41 (S3): 382–402.

Denson, T., B. Lickel, M. Curtis, D. Stenstrom and D. Ames (2006). "The Roles of Entitativity and Essentiality in Judgments of Collective Responsibility." *Group Processes & Intergroup Relations*, 9 (1), 43–61.

Diamantis, M. (2016). "Corporate Criminal Mind." *Notre Dame Law Review*, 91 (5): 2049–89.

Diamantis, M. (2019a). "Corporate Essence and Identity in Criminal Law." *Journal of Business Ethics*, 154 (4): 955–66.

Diamantis, M. (2019b). "Functional Corporate Knowledge." *William and Mary Law Review*, 61 (2): 319–95.

Diamantis, M. (2019c). "Limiting Identity in Criminal Law." *Boston College Law Review*, 60 (7): 2011–99.

Diamantis, M. (2019d). "Successor Identity." *Yale Journal on Regulation*, 36 (1): 1–44.

Diamantis, M. (2020). "The Extended Corporate Mind: When Corporations Use AI To Break the Law." *North Carolina Law Review*, 98 (4): 893–931.

Diamantis, M. (2021). "The Body Corporate." *Law and Contemporary Problems*, 83 (4): 133–58.

Hamilton, D., J. Levine and J. Thurston (2008). "Perceiving Continuity and Change in Groups." In F. Sani (ed.), *Self Continuity: Individual and Collective Perspectives*, 117–30. New York: Psychology Press.

Hamilton, D. and S. Sherman (1996). "Perceiving Persons and Groups." *Psychological Review*, 103 (2): 336–55.

Henning, P. (2010). "Should Perceptions of Corporate Punishment Matter?" *Journal of Law and Policy*, 19 (1): 83–93.

Huebner, B. (2016). "The Group Mind: In Commonsense Psychology." In J. Sytsma and W. Buckwalter (eds.), *A Companion to Experimental Philosophy*, 292–305. West Sussex: John Wiley & Sons.

Huebner, B., M. Bruno and H. Sarkissian (2010). "What Does the Nation of China Think about Phenomenal States?" *Review of Philosophy and Psychology*, 1 (2): 225–43.

Jenkins, A., D. Dodell-Feder, R. Saxe and J. Knobe (2014). "The Neural Bases of Directed and Spontaneous State Attributions to Group Agents." *PLoS ONE*, 9 (8): 1–11.

Johnson, A. and S. Queller (2003). "The Mental Representations of High and Low Entitivity Groups." *Social Cognition*, 21 (2): 101–19.

Kashima, Y., E. Kashima, C. Chiu, T. Farsides, M. Gelfand, Y. Hong, U. Kim, F. Strack, L. Werth, M. Yuki and V. Yzerbyt (2005). "Culture, Essentialism, and Agency: Are Individuals Universally Believed To Be More Real Entities Than Groups?" *European Journal of Social Psychology*, 35 (2): 147–69.

Kotran, S., M. Katz and S. Khan (2010). *Spin-Offs*. New York: Practical Law Publishing. Available online: https://www.sullcrom.com/siteFiles/Publications/September2010_SpinOffs.pdf (accessed October 18, 2021).

Knobe, J. and J. Prinz (2008). "Intuitions About Consciousness: Experimental Studies." *Phenomenology and the Cognitive Sciences*, 7 (1): 67–83.

Lederman, E. (2000). "Models for Imposing Corporate Criminal Liability: From Adaptation and Imitation Toward Aggregation and the Search for Self-Identity." *Buffalo Criminal Law Review*, 4 (1): 641–708.

Lickel, B., D. Hamilton, G. Wieczorkowska, A. Lewis, S. Sherman and A. Uhles (2000). "Varieties of Groups and the Perception of Group Entitativity." *Journal of Personality and Social Psychology*, 78 (2): 223–46.

Locke, J. (1690 reprint 1975). *An Essay Concerning Human Understanding*. Oxford: Oxford University Press.

Marques, J., D. Abrams, D. Paez and M. Hogg (2001). "Social Categorization, Social Identification, and Rejection of Deviant Group Members." In M. Hogg and R. Tindale (eds.), *Blackwell Handbook of Social Psychology: Group Processes*, 400–24. Oxford: Blackwell Publishing.

Marques, J., V. Yzerbyt and J. Leyens (1988). "The 'Black Sheep Effect': Extremity of Judgments Towards Ingroup Members as a Function of Group Identification." *European Journal of Social Psychology*, 18 (1): 1–16.

Melucci, A. (1989). *Nomads of the Present: Social Movements and Individual Needs in Contemporary Society*. Philadelphia: Temple University Press.

Menon, T., M. Morris, C. Chiu and Y. Hong (1999). "Culture and the Construal of Agency: Attribution to Individual Versus Group Dispositions." *Journal of Personality and Social Psychology*, 76 (5): 701–17.

Molouki, S. and D. Bartels (2017). "Personal Change and the Continuity of the Self." *Cognitive Psychology*, 93: 1–17.

Mott, C. (2018). "Statutes of Limitations and Personal Identity." In T. Lombrozo, J. Knobe and S. Nichols (eds.), *Oxford Studies in Experimental Philosophy*, 243–69. Oxford: Oxford University Press.

Newheiser, A., T. Sawaoka and J. Dovidio (2012). "Why Do We Punish Groups? High Entitativity Promotes Moral Suspicion." *Journal of Experimental Social Psychology*, 48 (4): 931–6.

Newman, G., P. Bloom and J. Knobe (2014). "Value Judgments and the True Self." *Personality and Social Psychology Bulletin*, 40 (2): 203–16.

Newman, G., J. De Freitas and J. Knobe (2015). "Beliefs about the True Self Explain Asymmetries Based on Moral Judgment." *Cognitive Science*, 39 (1): 96–125.

O'Laughlin, J. and B. Malle (2002). "How People Explain Actions Performed by Groups and Individuals." *Journal of Personality and Social Psychology*, 82 (1): 33–48.

Parfit, D. (1971). "Personal Identity." *The Philosophical Review*, 80 (1): 3–27.

Phelan, M., A. Arico and S. Nichols (2013). "Thinking Things and Feeling Things: On an Alleged Discontinuity in Folk Metaphysics of Mind." *Phenomenology and the Cognitive Sciences*, 12 (4): 703–25.

Polletta, F. and Jasper, J. (2001). "Collective Identity and Social Movements." *Annual Review of Sociology*, 27 (1): 283–305.

Rai, T. and D. Diermeier (2015). "Corporations are Cyborgs: Organizations Elicit Anger But Not Sympathy When They Can Think But Cannot Feel." *Organizational Behavior and Human Decision Processes*, 126 (C): 18–26.

Reyes, C. (2021). "Autonomous Business Reality." *Nevada Law Journal*, 21 (2): 437–90.

Rips, L., S. Hespos and D. Albarracín (2015). "Divisions of the Physical World: Concepts of Objects and Substance." *Psychological Bulletin*, 141 (4): 786–811.

Rock, I., ed. (1997). *Indirect Perception*. Cambridge, MA: MIT Press.

Rose, D., J. Schaffer and K. Tobia (2020). "Folk Teleology Drives Persistence Judgments." *Synthese*, 197 (12): 5491–519.

Rothbart, M. and M. Taylor (1992). "Category Labels and Social Reality: Do We View Social Categories as Natural Kinds?" In G. Semin and K. Fiedler (eds.), *Language, Interaction and Social Cognition*, 11–36. London: Sage Publications.

Sani, F., M. Bowe, M. Herrera, C. Manna, T. Cossa, X. Miao and Y. Zhou (2007). "Perceived Collective Continuity: Seeing Groups as Entities That Move Through Time." *European Journal of Social Psychology*, 37 (6): 1118–34.

Sherman, S. and E. Percy (2010). "Psychology of Collective Responsibility: Why and When Collective Entities are Likely to be Held Responsible for the Misdeeds of Individual Members." *Journal of Law and Policy*, 19 (1): 137–70.

Strohminger, N. and S. Nichols (2014). "The Essential Moral Self." *Cognition*, 131 (1):159–71.

Tobia, K. (2015). "Personal Identity and the Phineas Gage Effect." *Analysis*, 75 (3): 396–405.

Welbourne, J. (1999). "The Impact of Perceived Entitivity on Inconsistency Resolution for Groups and Individuals." *Journal of Experimental Social Psychology*, 35 (5): 481–508.

Worchel, S. and D. Coutant (2004). "It Takes Two To Tango: Relating Group Identity to Individual Identity within the Framework of Group Development." In M. Brewer and M. Hewstone (eds.), *Self and Social Identity*, 182–202. Oxford: Blackwell Publishing.

Yzerbyt, V., C. Judd and O. Corneille, eds. (2004). *The Psychology of Group Perception: Perceived Variability, Entitativity, and Essentialism*. New York: Psychology Press.

14

The Essence of an Immigrant Identity

Children's Pro-social Responses to Others Based on Perceived Ability and Desire to Change

James P. Dunlea, Redeate G. Wolle, and Larisa Heiphetz

The philosopher Heraclitus mused that one cannot step into the same river twice, ostensibly because people and the world they inhabit are constantly in flux. Interestingly, laypeople's views do not always coincide with Heraclitus's view: people often report that others' characteristics are stable over time (e.g., Dunlea and Heiphetz 2020, 2021; Heiphetz, Gelman, and Young 2017; Hussak and Cimpian 2019). Such views reflect *psychological essentialism*—the belief that people possess internal, immutable, biologically based "essences" that constitute their identity (Gelman 2003; Medin and Ortony 1989).

While essentialism research has offered important insight regarding the extent to which children and adults view human characteristics as immutable, this work has largely treated immutability as one concept. However, the perception that a characteristic is unchanging could include multiple components, including a perceived lack of *ability* to change and a perceived lack of *desire* to change. Here, we highlighted one domain—immigration—where both components are relevant and investigated the developmental origins of concepts regarding immutability in this domain. Specifically, we probed elementary schoolers' views regarding the extent to which immigrants could and, separately, wanted to change by adopting the norms of their new country.

Many adults living in the United States—primarily those identifying as part of the native majority group—believe that immigrants do not readily adopt United States norms (Paxton and Mughan 2006). One interpretation of this scholarship is that many adults view immigrants' identities as immutable. However, adults may conceptualize immutability in this domain as arising in different ways. First, adults may believe that immigrants' identities are immutable because they lack the *desire* to adopt the norms of their new country (Piontkowski, Rohmann, and Florack 2002). Exemplifying this view, reporter Tucker Carlson once stated that immigrants "don't seem all that *interested in* [emphasis added] integrating" (as cited in Lalami 2017). Second, adults may believe that immigrants' identities are immutable because they lack the *ability* to adopt the norms of their new country (Suarez-Orozco and Suarez-Orozco 2001). In 2016,

Donald Trump reflected this view when stating that "not everyone who seeks to join our country will be *able to* [emphasis added] successfully assimilate" (as cited in Lalami 2017). Together, this evidence suggests that adults apply an essentialist framework when reasoning about immigrants. We build on prior evidence by investigating the extent to which children apply an essentialist framework when reasoning about immigrants.

Past work leads to three possibilities. One possibility is that children view immigrants as possessing both the motivation and ability to adopt the norms of their new country. Native majority-group elementary schoolers typically express greater positivity toward immigrant peers who assimilate (i.e., adopt the norms of their new country) over those who do not (Verkuyten, Thijs, and Sierksma 2014). Children of this age are also especially likely to hold positive views of others (Boseovski 2010). Therefore, children may be motivated to view immigrants as being both able and willing to adopt local norms. A second possibility is that children view immigrants as lacking both the motivation and ability to adopt the norms of their new country. This possibility stems from prior work suggesting that elementary schoolers readily employ an essentialist framework when reasoning about a wide range of entities, including abilities (Dweck 2006) and mental states (e.g., desires, beliefs, Heiphetz et al. 2017). Because essentialism includes the view that characteristics are immutable (Gelman 2003), children may infer that distinct aspects of immigrants' identities (i.e., desires, abilities) cannot change. A third possibility is that children's judgments regarding ability and desire diverge. Elementary schoolers understand that people may possess the desire—but not the ability—to act in a certain way (Kushnir 2018). For example, in one line of work, elementary schoolers learned about a character who *wanted* to prevent a crumbling building from collapsing and reported that she lacked the *ability* to carry out her desire (Lane 2020). If children employ this reasoning in the context of immigration, they may infer that immigrants may possess the desire, but not the ability, to adopt new norms. We tested among these possibilities.

In addition to probing children's own notions of immigrants' ability and desire to change, we investigated the social ramifications of these views. As mentioned earlier, native majority-group children are especially likely to report negativity toward immigrant peers who do not adopt the norms of their new country (Verkuyten et al. 2014). We built on this scholarship by providing children information about *why* others might not adopt these norms (lacking desire, lacking ability). We probed the role of each factor separately to examine the relative weight children place on information about desires and abilities when responding to others.

This work also has translational implications. As previously mentioned, native majority-group children favor immigrant peers who employ assimilationist acculturation strategies over those who do not (Verkuyten et al. 2014). Given children's pro-assimilationist views, one way to curb anti-immigrant sentiment during childhood may include teaching children that some immigrants do indeed possess the ability and desire to assimilate. This form of intervention may be easily implementable because it leverages children's existing pro-assimilationist biases to potentially promote social good (i.e., decreasing intergroup negativity; for similar reasoning, see Roberts, Ho, and Gelman 2019). However, there is reason to challenge this approach altogether because it does not work toward ameliorating children's pro-assimilationist preferences. Indeed, pro-assimilationist views devalue immigrants' native cultures and allow "no room for a positive role for the ethnic or racial group" (Alba and Nee 2003: 5). Therefore, it is important to consider the translational implications of this work alongside a potential longer-term goal of reducing pro-assimilationist views.

I. Method

Participants: We recruited children between five and ten years old. Five-year-olds were the youngest children we tested because younger children do not reason coherently about national groups (DeJesus et al. 2018). Moreover, testing children in this age range allowed us to compare our results with research on age-related changes in essentialist reasoning. While reports of essentialist perspectives typically decrease throughout the elementary school years (e.g., Heiphetz et al. 2017; Hussak and Cimpian 2019), younger (five- to seven-year olds) and older (eight- to ten-year olds) children in this work responded similarly to items probing essentialism's immutability component (see Results), suggesting that views of immutability within the context of immigration may be stable throughout the elementary school years.

Our final sample included 112 children (36% female, 63% male, remainder unspecified) between the ages of five and ten years (M_{age} = 7.47 years, SD_{age} = 1.62 years; $N_{younger}$ = 56, N_{older} = 56).[1] Children's parents completed a demographic questionnaire where they identified their children as white or European American (47%), Black or African American (14%), Asian or Asian American (8%), multiracial (24%), and "other" (5%); the remaining parents did not identify their child's race. Parents reported their child's ethnicity using a separate question, and 13% identified their children as Hispanic or Latinx. We excluded data from one additional younger child because she did not understand the experimental items and one additional older child because he heard another person's responses before participating.

We recruited participants from a lab database and at a children's museum in a large city in the northeastern United States. Forty-one percent of participants completed this study in person. Due to Covid-19, the remainder participated online. As in other studies (e.g., Dunlea and Heiphetz 2021; Marshall, Mermin-Bunnell, and Bloom 2020), testing venue did not predict children's responses. Children who participated in person received a small prize; children who participated online received a $5 gift card.

Procedure: First, the experimenter told children that he or she would ask them questions and that there were no (in)correct answers. The experimenter then introduced children to a five-point Likert-type scale consisting of stick figures arrayed from smallest to largest on a sheet of paper (or, online, on a PowerPoint slide). The experimenter then instructed participants on how to use the scale (e.g., "If your answer is 'not at all,' you would point here," said while pointing to the smallest picture). The remaining labels were "a little bit," "a medium amount," "a lot," and "completely." The experimenter then asked children two items to gauge their understanding of the scale ("Can you show me where you would point if your answer was 'not at all'?"; "Can you show me where you would point if your answer was 'a medium amount'?"). For online participants, each stick figure had a number beneath it ranging from *1* for the smallest figure to 5 for the largest figure; children reported the number underneath the figure they wished to select. Children largely used the scale correctly: 99% of children pointed to the scale floor when indicating "not at all," and 89% of children pointed to the scale midpoint when indicating "a medium amount." Participants who answered incorrectly received corrective feedback, and all children provided the correct answer on their second attempt.

The remainder of the study progressed in three parts (Blocks I, II, and III). Block I examined the extent to which children employed an essentialist framework when reasoning about immigrants. During Block I, the experimenter showed participants outlines of two countries. The experimenter described one outline as a map of "America"[2] and the other as a country "that we do not know the name of."[3] The experimenter then showed children a picture of a stick figure on a PowerPoint display and told participants that the character moved from the unknown country to America. The experimenter then asked children a comprehension check item ("Can you remind me, where does Val live now? Does [he/she] live in America, or this other country?"); all the children responded correctly. The experimenter referred to the character using pronouns matching the child's reported gender.

Next, the experimenter read three sets of statements, one set at a time, highlighting different norms across the aforementioned countries. One set of statements highlighted differences in cuisine ("In America, people eat American food. In this other country, people do not eat American food"), a second set highlighted linguistic differences ("In America, people speak English. In this other country, people do not speak English"), and a third set highlighted differences in holidays ("In America, people celebrate Christmas. In this other country, people do not celebrate Christmas"). After listening to each set of statements, participants indicated their agreement regarding the extent to which the character was *capable* of adopting and, separately, *desired* to adopt the norm that was just described. For example, after listening to the set of statements about differences in cuisine, children responded to the following items: (1) "How much do you agree that Val *can* eat American food now?" and (2) "How much do you agree that Val *wants to* eat American food now?" Participants indicated their agreement using the Likert-type scale described earlier. We selected topics based on prior work showing that food (Liberman et al. 2016), language (Kinzler 2020), and traditions (Litwicki 2004) are robust indicators of socio-cultural group membership. The order in which items referencing each cultural element appeared was counterbalanced across participants.

Blocks II and III examined how different messages about immigrants' ability and desire to change might influence intergroup relations. Although prominent theorists (e.g., Allport 1954) have argued that both prejudice (negative intergroup attitudes) and discrimination (negative intergroup behavior) shape intergroup relations, much intergroup research has examined attitudes without testing corresponding behavior. We included attitudinal and behavioral measures to reflect both aspects of intergroup relations. This approach allowed us to contribute to ongoing conversations in psychology regarding links between attitudes and behaviors (Wallace et al. 2005).

In Block II, the experimenter told children that they would learn about additional people, all of whom moved to America. The experimenter subsequently showed children a picture of four characters on a PowerPoint display. The experimenter pointed to each character, one at a time, and described that character's ability and, separately, desire to adopt a given American norm (either eating American cuisine, speaking English, or celebrating Christmas). Descriptions aligned with one of four possible conditions in a 2 (Ability: can vs. cannot) x 2 (Desire: wants vs. does not want) within-participants design. For example, the interviewer told participants that "[Character A] *can* speak English but *does not want* to, [Character B] *cannot* speak English and *does not want* to, [Character C] *cannot* speak English but *wants* to, and [Character D] *can* speak English and *wants* to."[4] The purpose of providing these descriptions was to familiarize children with each of the characters.

Next, the experimenter re-introduced participants to each character, one at a time (e.g., "Here's [Character A] again. Remember, [Character A] can speak English but [he/she] does not want to"). Participants then answered three items probing their attitudes toward each character: (1) "How much do you like [Character A]?" (2) "How much do you want to be friends with [Character A]?" (3) "How much do you want to play with [Character A]?" We adapted these measures from scholarship examining children's intergroup attitudes (Heiphetz and Young 2019). Participants indicated their responses using the same Likert-type scale described in Block I and answered all items about one character before moving on to items about the next character. After recording children's responses to all items regarding a given American norm (e.g., speaking English), the experimenter completed an analogous procedure for items regarding the remaining norms (in this example, eating American food and celebrating Christmas). Descriptions of a character's ability and desire to adopt the norms of their new country were consistent across norm types. For example, if participants learned that [Character A] could speak English but did not want to, participants also learned that [Character A] could celebrate Christmas but did not want to. The order of experimental items (e.g., items probing participants' attitudes toward characters) and the order in which participants answered questions about a specific cultural element (e.g., speaking English) were counterbalanced across participants.

In Block III, the experimenter showed children a picture of the four characters from Block II and specified that participants would be playing a "sharing game" with each character. The experimenter then reminded participants about each character at a broad level (e.g., "Remember, [Character A] can do the things that people in America do but does not want to"). After re-introducing a character, the interviewer said, "Now, here are some stickers. You can decide how many stickers you want to give to [Character A]. You can give as many stickers as you want, but you cannot keep any for yourself." Participants received five stickers.

The experimenter then showed children how to distribute the stickers between two envelopes, one of which was illustrated with a picture of a stick figure resembling the character that the experimenter had just re-introduced and the other of which was illustrated with a picture of a trash can. The experimenter told participants that the character being discussed would receive any stickers placed in the former envelope and that any stickers placed in the latter envelope would be discarded. Children who completed the task in person physically placed stickers into the corresponding envelopes. Participants who completed this study online completed a modified version of this task including pictures of stickers. Online participants indicated the envelopes into which they wanted to place the stickers and observed (via video camera) the experimenter placing actual stickers in the corresponding envelopes. Participants finished making resource allocation decisions for a given character before moving on to the next trial. The order in which participants distributed stickers to each character was counterbalanced across participants.

II. Results

Immutability judgments: An exploratory series of tests examined children's perceptions of immigrants (Figure 14.1). First, we used a series of one-sample t-tests to compare participants' agreement that immigrants are able to—and, separately, want to—adopt the norms of their new country with 3 (the midpoint of the scale indicating, on average, moderate agreement). We did so among younger and, separately, older children. This approach yielded four comparisons; thus, p values needed to be .013 or lower to pass the Bonferroni-corrected significance threshold. Children in both age groups reported high agreement that immigrants *can* (younger: ($t(55) = 4.67, p < .001$, Cohen's $d = .62$, 95% CI_{diff}: [.39, .98]); older: ($t(55) = 5.81, p < .001$, Cohen's $d = .78$, 95% CI_{diff}: [.53, 1.09])) and *want* to (younger: ($t(55) = 8.10, p < .001$, Cohen's $d = 1.08$, 95% CI_{diff}: [.72, 1.20]); older: ($t(55)=6.21, p<.001$, Cohen's $d=.83$, 95% CI_{diff}: [.53, 1.03])) adopt the norms of their new country.

Next, we used independent-samples t-tests to compare the extent to which younger versus older children reported that immigrants *can* and, separately, *want to* adopt the norms of their new country. This approach yielded two comparisons; thus, p values needed to be .025 or lower to pass the Bonferroni-corrected significance threshold. These analyses did not reveal differences in participants' reports of immigrants' ability ($t(110) = -.62, p = .538$, Cohen's $|d| = .12$, 95% CI_{diff}: [−.53, .28]) or desire ($t(110) = 1.04$,

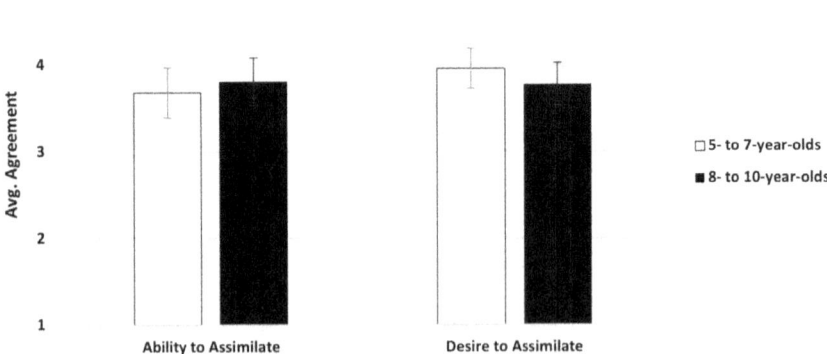

Figure 14.1 Average agreement that immigrants can (left) and want to (right) adopt American norms. Scores above the scale midpoint (3) indicate relatively high agreement, whereas scores below the scale midpoint indicate relatively low agreement. A score of 3 indicates moderate agreement. Error bars represent 95% confidence intervals.

p = .303, Cohen's $|d|$ = .20, 95% CI_{diff}: [−.16, .52]) to adopt their new country's norms. These findings suggest that both groups of children view immigrants as possessing the capacity and desire to change.

Attitudes: The three items measuring attitudes for each character had acceptable reliability ($\alpha_{can+wants}$ = .90, $\alpha_{can + does\ not\ want}$ = .92, $\alpha_{cannot + wants}$ = .92, $\alpha_{cannot + does\ not\ want}$ = .93). Thus, we created one composite attitude score for each character by averaging across the three items (how much participants liked, wanted to be friends with, and wanted to play with the character). In accordance with our pre-registration, we analyzed this composite using a 2 (Participant Age: five- to seven-year olds vs. eight- to ten-year olds) x 2 (Ability: can vs. cannot) x 2 (Desire: wants vs. does not want) mixed ANOVA with repeated measures on the last two factors (Figure 14.2). This analysis revealed a main effect of Ability ($F(1, 111)$ = 10.02, p = .002, η_p^2 = .08). Participants reported more positivity toward characters who were able (versus unable) to adopt their new country's norms. This analysis also revealed a main effect of Desire ($F(1, 111)$ = 83.45, $p < .001$, η_p^2 = .43). Participants reported more positivity toward characters who wanted (versus did not want) to adopt their new country's norms. No other main effects or interactions reached significance ($p \geq .057$).

Resource allocation: Next, consistent with our pre-registration, we analyzed participants' resource allocations using a 2 (Participant Age: five- to seven-year olds vs. eight- to ten-year olds) x 2 (Ability: can vs. cannot) x 2 (Desire: wants vs. does not want) mixed ANOVA with repeated measures on the last two factors (Figure 14.3). This analysis revealed a main effect of Ability ($F(1, 109)$ = 12.08, p = .001, η_p^2 = .10); participants shared more resources with characters who were able (versus unable) to adopt the norms of their new country. This analysis also revealed a main effect of Desire ($F(1, 109)$ = 73.63, $p < .001$, η_p^2 = .40); participants shared more resources with characters who wanted (versus did not want) to adopt the norms of their new country. Finally, this analysis revealed a main effect of Participant Age ($F(1, 109)$ = 4.77, p = .031, η_p^2 = .04); older children shared more resources than younger children. No interactions reached significance ($p \geq .121$).

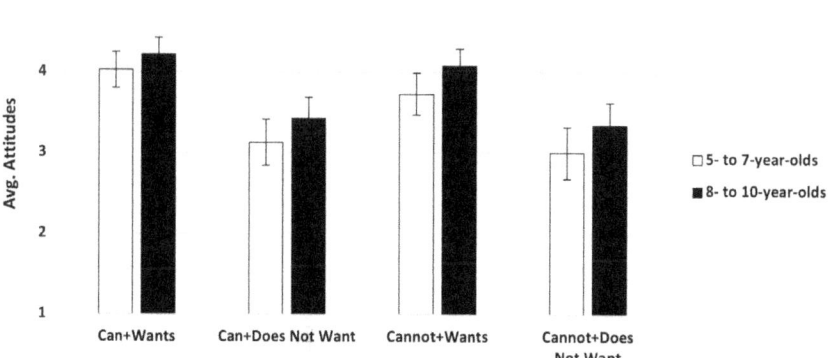

Figure 14.2 Average attitudes toward different characters. Higher values reflect more positive attitudes. Error bars represent 95% confidence intervals.

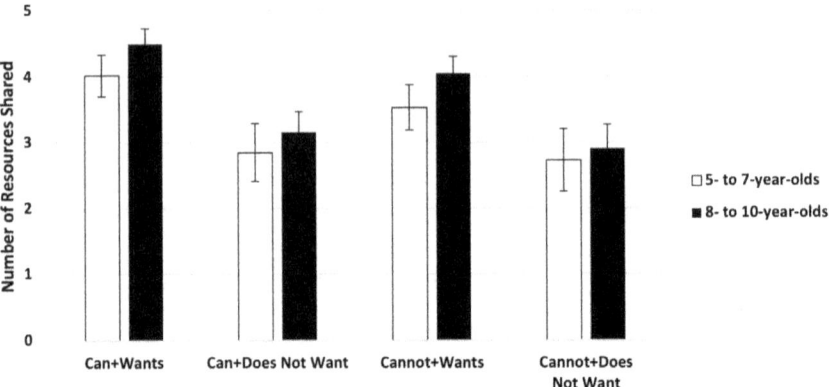

Figure 14.3 Average number of resources shared with different characters. Error bars represent 95% confidence intervals.

We also conducted exploratory analyses examining the extent to which children's attitudes toward a given character predicted the number of resources they shared with that character. We conducted this analysis for each of the four characters among younger and, separately, older children. This approach resulted in eight analyses; therefore, p values needed to be .006 or lower to reach the Bonferroni-corrected threshold. We observed a significant positive relation between younger children's attitudes and behaviors for three of the four characters ($rs \geq .44$, $ps \leq .001$). The relation between younger children's attitudes and behaviors toward characters who both could and wanted to adopt the norms of their new country passed the traditional .05 significance threshold ($r = .28$, $p = .037$); however, this relation dropped to non-significance after applying the Bonferroni correction. Additionally, we observed a significant positive relation between older children's attitudes and behaviors for all four characters ($rs \geq .43$, $ps \leq .001$). These findings suggest that, among elementary schoolers, more positive attitudes toward immigrants generally predict more pro-social behaviors toward immigrants.

III. General Discussion

Using immigration as an example domain, we examined the extent to which children's immutability concepts reflect beliefs about others lacking the *ability* and, separately, the *desire* to change. We also probed the consequences of such beliefs. In doing so, this work makes three contributions.

First, this work extends scholarship on essentialism by examining the development of immutability concepts. Immigration likely represents a domain in which adults' immutability concepts reflect notions of lacking the ability (Suarez-Orozco and Suarez-Orozco 2001) and desire (Piontkowski et al. 2002) to change. However, the origin of these "end state" immutability concepts is unclear. Past work led to three possibilities. First, because children exhibit positive attitudes toward immigrants who adopt the norms of their new country (Verkuyten et al. 2014) and are optimistic about others (Boseovski 2010), they could view immigrants as being able and willing to change. Second, because children view many characteristics as immutable (Gelman 2003), they could view immigrants as being unable and unwilling to change. Third, because children can distinguish ability from desire (Lane 2020), they could hold different views regarding immigrants' ability and desire to change. Our results supported the first possibility: children strongly agreed that immigrants could, and wanted to, adopt the norms of their new country. In conjunction with evidence suggesting that adults may not always share these views (Paxton and Mughan 2006; Piontkowski et al. 2002; Suarez-Orozco and Suarez-Orozco 2001), these results suggest that, at least in some domains, the view that others can and want to change wanes with age.

Second, this research also contributes to work on essentialism by probing the consequences of different messages about identity immutability. Participants felt more positively and behaved more pro-socially toward characters who were able and willing to change. Importantly, information about characters' *desires* played a greater role in shaping children's attitudes and behaviors than did information about characters' *abilities*: the effect size associated with differences in attitudes toward characters who wanted (versus did not want) to adopt the norms of their new country ($\eta_p^2 = .43$) was substantially larger than the effect size associated with differences in attitudes toward characters who could (versus could not) adopt such norms ($\eta_p^2 = .08$). A similar pattern of results emerged for participants' sharing behaviors: the effect size associated with differences in the number of resources shared with characters who wanted (versus did not want) to adopt the norms of their new country ($\eta_p^2 = .40$) was substantially larger than the effect size associated with differences in the number of resources shared with characters who could (versus could not) adopt such norms ($\eta_p^2 = .10$). Thus, perceptions regarding unwillingness to change may shape children's attitudes and behaviors toward immigrants more strongly than perceptions regarding a lack of ability to change. Such an interpretation dovetails with preliminary evidence suggesting that information about desires, versus abilities, may be more important in shaping children's social evaluations (Lin et al. 2019).

Finally, this work extends research investigating the link between attitudes and behaviors. Both attitudes and behaviors influence intergroup relations (Allport 1954); thus, this work included measures capturing both variables. Children's attitudes toward a given character generally predicted their behavior toward that character. Most correlation coefficients measuring the link between attitudes and behaviors in this work were "moderate" to "large" in size (above .30, Cohen 1988). This finding contrasts with prior research suggesting that correlation coefficients measuring the link between attitudes and behaviors are often relatively small (see Wallace et al. 2005, for a review of effect sizes reported in studies testing adults) and raises the possibility that the attitude-behavior link wanes over development.

In addition to these theoretical contributions, the present findings may have translational implications. Our results suggest that children favor immigrants who possess the ability and desire to assimilate over those who do not. Given these results, one way to attenuate anti-immigrant sentiment during childhood may include teaching children that some immigrants possess the ability and desire to assimilate. However, this approach may not be ideal because it does not work toward reducing children's pro-assimilationist preferences (Alba and Nee 2003). Thus, it is paramount to consider the practical implications of this work alongside the possible broader goal of reducing pro-assimilationist views.

While this work makes several contributions, additional questions remain ripe for inquiry. One fruitful future direction includes examining the extent to which children's judgments depend on *why* immigrants express (dis-)interest in changing certain aspects of their identities. For example, in future work, children can evaluate an immigrant who does not want to assimilate because she thinks doing so will be inauthentic or go against her "true" identity. Children and adults value authenticity (Silver, Newman, and Small 2021) and may report positivity toward immigrants who are disinterested in assimilating because doing so would go against their "true" identities. Future work can test this possibility.

Additionally, future research can measure the extent to which children essentialize immigrants' identities using a different paradigm. Some scholars have examined essentialist reasoning by probing the extent to which people view changes in certain characteristics as reflecting changes in personal identity (Heiphetz et al. 2018; Tobia 2016). This method uses the following logic: if participants view changing an individual's characteristic as changing who the person is overall, then participants view the characteristic in question as essential to identity. For example, in one study (Heiphetz et al. 2018), children and adults reported that changes to widely shared moral beliefs would elicit more change to identity than would changes to other mental states (e.g., preferences). The authors interpreted these findings as evidence that people view moral characteristics as especially essential to identity. Future studies can unite this work with this past scholarship by comparing children's views of identity change following different types of transformations, including changes in moral characteristics and national group membership (via immigration). Doing so can extend work on psychological essentialism by clarifying the extent to which children essentialize national group membership relative to another quality, such as moral characteristics.

IV. Conclusion

Using immigration as an example domain, we probed the extent to which children's immutability concepts reflect beliefs about others lacking the ability and, separately, the desire to change. Children expected that immigrants wanted to and were able to adopt the norms of their new country. Moreover, children's pro-social responses to immigrants more strongly depended on information about their desire, versus their ability, to change. This work highlights the need to study sub-components of a specific pillar of essentialist thought (i.e., separating the immutability component of essentialism into perceptions regarding people's perceived desire and, separately, perceived ability to change), partially because essentialism impacts social cognition and behavior differently across sub-components.

Notes

1 Our pre-registration (http://aspredicted.org/blind.php?x=b7b4th) specified a target sample size of eighty children per age group. This was an error. Initially, we planned to include a mediator in this study, and the mediation analysis would have required eighty children per group to detect our expected effect. We decided to forgo the mediation and revised the rest of our pre-registration accordingly. However, we failed to update the sample size. We ended data collection after recruiting a sample of sufficient size to conduct the actual analyses we pre-registered (e.g., ANOVA). We did not perform any statistical tests prior to completing data collection.
2 America consists of several countries spanning the North and South American continents. However, because people in the United States often use the term "America" as a synonym for the United States (Martinez-Carter 2013), we used the term "America" when interviewing children. The outline referring to "America" depicted an online of the United States.
3 Children use familiar country labels (e.g., "France," "Mexico") to make inferences about people living in a given country (Barrett, Wilson, and Lyons 2003). Because we did not want children's inferences about people immigrating from a specific country to influence their responses, we did not specify the character's country of origin.
4 Participants learned about characters named Kai, Lane, River, and Sage. Pairings of character names and descriptions (i.e., whether the character could and, separately, wanted to assimilate) were counterbalanced across participants.

Bibliography

Alba, R. and V. Nee (2003). *Remaking the American Mainstream: Assimilation and Contemporary Immigration*. Cambridge, MA: Harvard University Press.

Allport, G. W. (1954). *The Nature of Prejudice*. Reading: Addison-Wesley.

Barrett, M., H. Wilson and E. Lyons (2003). "The Development of National In-group Bias: English Children's Attributions of Characteristics to English, American and German People." *British Journal of Developmental Psychology*, 21: 193–220. doi: 10.1348/026151003765264048.

Boseovski, J. J. (2010). "Evidence for 'Rose-Colored Glasses': An Examination of the Positivity Bias in Young Children's Personality Judgments." *Child Development Perspectives*, 4: 212–18. doi: 10.1111/j.1750-8606.2010.00149.x.

Cohen, J. (1988). *Statistical Power Analysis for the Behavioral Sciences*, 2nd ed. Hillsdale: Erlbaum.

DeJesus, J. M., H. G. Hwang, J. B. Dautel and K. D. Kinzler (2018). "'American=English Speaker' before 'American=White': The Development of Children's Reasoning about Nationality." *Child Development*, 89: 1752–67. doi: 10.1111/cdev.12845.

Dunlea, J. P. and L. Heiphetz (2020). "Children's and Adults' Understanding of Punishment and the Criminal Justice System." *Journal of Experimental Social Psychology*, 87: 103913. doi: 10.1016/j.jesp.2019.103913.

Dunlea, J. P. and L. Heiphetz (2021). "Children's and Adults' Views of Punishment as a Path to Redemption." *Child Development*, 92: 398–415. doi: 10.1111/cdev.13475

Dweck, C. S. (2006). *Mindsets: The New Psychology of Success*. New York: Ballantine Books.

Gelman, S. A. (2003). *The Essential Child: Origins of Essentialism in Everyday Thought*. New York: Oxford University Press.

Heiphetz, L., S. A. Gelman and L. L. Young (2017). "The Perceived Stability and Biological Basis of Religious Beliefs, Factual Beliefs, and Opinions." *Journal of Experimental Child Psychology*, 156: 82–98. doi: 10.1016/j.jecp.2016.11.015.

Heiphetz, L., N. Strohminger, S. A. Gelman and L. L. Young (2018). "Who am I? The Role of Moral Beliefs in Children's and Adults' Understanding of Identity." *Journal of Experimental Social Psychology*, 78: 210–19. doi: 10.1016/j.jesp.2018.03.007.

Heiphetz, L. and L. L. Young (2019). "Children's and Adults' Affectionate Generosity Toward Members of Different Religious Groups." *American Behavioral Scientist*, 63: 1910–37. doi: 10.1177/0002764219850870.

Hussak, L. J. and A. Cimpian (2019). "'It Feels Like It's In Your Body': How Children in the United States Think about Nationality." *Journal of Experimental Psychology: General*, 148: 1153–68. doi: 10.1037/xge0000567.

Kinzler, K. D. (2020). *How You Say it: Why You Talk the Way You Do—and What it Says about You*. Boston: Houghton Mifflin Harcourt.

Kushnir, T. (2018). "The Developmental and Cultural Psychology of Free Will." *Philosophy Compass*, 13: e12529. doi: 10.1111/phc3.12529.

Lalami, L. (2017). "What Does it Take to 'Assimilate' in America?" *The New York Times*, August 1. Available online: https://www.nytimes.com/2017/08/01/magazine/what-does-it-take-to-assimilate-in-america.html (accessed December 10, 2020).

Lane, J. D. (2020). "Probabilistic Reasoning in Context: Socio-cultural Differences in Children's and Adults' Predictions about the Fulfillment of Prayers and Wishes." *Journal of Cognition and Development*, 21: 240–60. doi: 10.1080/15248372.2019.1709468.

Liberman, Z., A. L. Woodward, K. R. Sullivan and K. D. Kinzler (2016). "Early Emerging System for Reasoning about the Social Nature of Food." *Proceedings of the National Academy of Sciences*, 113: 9480–5. doi: 10.1073/pnas.1605456113.

Lin, Z., S.C. Levine, T. Berkowitz and A. Shaw (2019). "'Do You Reward Me for My Effort or My Achievement?': An Exploration of Developmental Intuitions on Deservingness in China." Poster presented at the Biennial Meeting of the Society for Research in Child Development, Baltimore, MD.

Litwicki, E. M. (2004). "'Our Hearts Burn with Ardent Love for Two Countries': Ethnicity and Assimilation." In E. Etzioni and J. Bloom (eds.), *We are What we Celebrate: Understanding Holidays and Rituals*, 213–46. New York: New York University Press.

Marshall, J., K. Mermin-Bunnell and P. Bloom (2020). "Developing Judgments about Peers' Obligation to Intervene." *Cognition*, 201: 104215. doi: 10.1016/j.cognition.2020.104215.

Martinez-Carter, K. (2013). "What Does 'American' Actually Mean?" *The Atlantic*, June 19. Available online: https://www.theatlantic.com/national/archive/2013/06/what-does-american-actually-mean/276999/ (accessed December 17, 2020).

Medin, D. L. and A. Ortony (1989). "Psychological Essentialism." In S. Vosniadou and A. Ortony (eds.), *Similarity and Analogical Reasoning*, 179–95. New York: Cambridge University Press.

Paxton, P. and A. Mughan (2006). "What's to Fear from Immigrants? Creating an Assimilationist Threat Scale." *Political Psychology*, 27: 549–68. doi: 10.1111/j.1467-9221.2006.00520.x.

Piontkowski, U., A. Rohmann and A. Florack (2002). "Concordance of Acculturation Attitudes and Perceived Threat." *Group Processes & Intergroup Relations*, 5: 221–32. doi: 10.1177/1368430202005003003.

Roberts, S. O., A. K. Ho and S. A. Gelman (2019). "The Role of Group Norms in Evaluating Uncommon and Negative Behaviors." *Journal of Experimental Psychology: General*, 148: 374–87. doi: 10.1037/xge0000534.

Suárez-Orozco, C. and M. M. Suárez-Orozco (2001). *Children of Immigration*. Cambridge, MA: Harvard University Press.

Silver, I., G. E. Newman and D. A. Small (2021). "Inauthenticity Aversion: Consumer Reactance Toward Tainted Actors, Actions, and Objects." *Consumer Psychology Review*, 4: 70–82. doi: 10.1002/arcp.1064

Tobia, K. P. (2016). "Personal Identity, Direction of Change, and Neuroethics." *Neuroethics*, 9: 37–43. doi: 10.1007/s12152-016-9248-9.

Verkuyten, M., J. Thijs and J. Sierksma (2014). "Majority Children's Evaluation of Acculturation Preferences of Immigrant and Emigrant Peers." *Child Development*, 85: 176–91. doi: 10.1111/cdev.12111.

Wallace, D. S., R. M. Paulson, C. G. Lord and C. F. Bond Jr (2005). "Which Behaviors do Attitudes Predict? Meta-analyzing the Effects of Social Pressure and Perceived Difficulty." *Review of General Psychology*, 9: 214–27. doi: 10.1037/1089-2680.9.3.214.

15

"Human" Is an Essentially Political Category

David Livingstone Smith

What is it to regard a being as a human being? You might think that the answer to this question is obvious. As an educated person, you probably think that to be human is to be a particular kind of primate—a member of the species Homo sapiens. Or you might think that to be human is equivalent to possessing a suite of psychological attributes that distinguish humans from all other sorts of beings. In the former case, to regard a being as human is to regard them as a member of a certain biological taxon, and in the latter case it is to identify them as possessing certain manifest properties. I believe all such accounts of humanness to be mistaken. I will begin by setting out why biological accounts of the human are problematic, and why efforts to cash out humanity by citing uniquely human properties cannot succeed. Having done this, I propose and explore an alternative approach, suggesting that categorizing others as human amounts to regarding them as belonging to one's own basic, essentialized natural kind. Finally, because my interest in this topic stems from my long-standing research into the phenomenon of dehumanization, I discuss how this way of making sense of what goes on when we categorize being as human beings may help us understand how dehumanization happens.

I. A Problem

Is "human" a biological category? If so, which biological category and why that one in particular rather than some other? Surely, you might think, science has proven that to be human is nothing more than being a member of the species Homo sapiens. If that's what you think, you are wrong. Anthropologists, biologists, and geneticists do not univocally assert that beings are human just in case they belong to the species Homo sapiens. For sure, they agree that all Homo sapiens are human, but they do not all agree that all humans are Homo sapiens. Often, they claim that being human is belonging to the genus Homo, which includes several extinct species in addition to Homo sapiens. This makes the category of the human even fuzzier, because the criteria for inclusion in the genus are far from clear. Paleoanthropologist Ian Tattersall writes:

> You might . . . be tempted to imagine that, in the century and a half since Charles Darwin pointed out that we are joined to the rest of nature by common ancestry,

science might have begun to make some progress toward a biological definition of the human genus. But if so, you would be doomed to disappointment. Scientists are still arguing vehemently over which ancient fossil human relatives should be included in the genus Homo. And they are doing so in the absence of any coherent idea of what the genus that includes our species Homo sapiens might reasonably be presumed to contain. (Tattersall 2016)

Some people have even suggested that chimpanzees and bonobos should be allocated a seat at this taxonomic table, in which case, on one interpretation of what it is to be human, chimps and bonobos turn out to be human.[1] Often, a distinction is made between Homo sapiens and what are called, rather vaguely, "early humans." A page titled "What Does It Mean to Be Human?" on the website of the Smithsonian National Museum of Natural History lists twenty-one "early human" species. Their list not only is confined to genus Homo but also includes members of genus Ardipithecus and genus Australopithecus.

These wide discrepancies are not explicitly discussed or scientifically scrutinized: the meaning of "human" is simply assumed and conveyed only implicitly and in passing, if at all. The following excerpt from an article titled "How Many Human Species Existed on Earth?" is typical of the way the issue is addressed in science journalism and the professional scientific literature.

> We *Homo sapiens* didn't used to be alone. Long ago, there was a lot more human diversity; *Homo sapiens* lived alongside an estimated eight now-extinct species of human about 300,000 years ago. As recently as 15,000 years ago, we were sharing caves with another human species known as the Denisovans. And fossilized remains indicate an even higher number of early human species once populated Earth before our species came along. "We have one human species right now, and historically, that's really weird," said Nick Longrich, an evolutionary biologist at the University of Bath in the United Kingdom. "Not that far back, we weren't that special, but now we're the only ones left." (Plackett 2021)

Why is there so much confusion about what biological category corresponds to being human? It's not because the fossil record is incomplete. The fossil record is scanty, but even if the scientists knew all that there is to know about the hominin lineage, this would not be enough to establish which primate taxa are human and which were not (and, correspondingly, what it is about us that accounts for our being human). The problem would remain because the question "What is a human being?" is a conceptual, philosophical question rather than an empirical one. It is a question about the interface between two taxonomic schemes, each of which is structured on the basis of distinct and incommensurable principles.

II. Natural and Invented Kinds

To be human is to be a certain kind of being—a member of humankind. There are many ways that the natural world can be divided up into kinds, depending on what organizing principle one brings to the table. Scientific taxonomies are built on the principle that the natural world consists of an array of relatively discrete natural kinds. They purport to map the objective categorical landscape of the world. The success of scientific taxonomy is evidenced by the inferential power that flows from correctly subsuming individuals under natural kinds. Correctly classifying a piece of matter as a chemical element—say, a sample of uranium—allows one to infer a great number of its chemical properties, and correctly classifying an animal as belonging to a certain biological species—say, as a North American porcupine—allows one to reliably draw very many conclusions about its anatomy, physiology, and behavior. These inferences would otherwise be impossible to make. Scientific taxonomies are supposed to be purely descriptive, despite often having normative implications. These evaluative features are not constitutive elements of the classificatory scheme. For example, deer ticks and anopheles mosquitos both carry dangerous diseases. They are animals that we should avoid being bitten by. But their dangerousness does not play any role in how they are scientifically taxonomized.

Not all taxonomies are scientific ones. There are also folk taxonomies that purport to carve nature at its joints. Sometimes, these folk categories are isomorphic, or near-isomorphic, to their scientific counterparts. For instance, when the biologist Ernst Mayr visited the Arfak mountains of New Guinea in 1928, he found that the indigenous people classified native birds into 136 species. These corresponded almost exactly to the 137 species identified by ornithologists (Mayr 1932).

To the extent that folk-taxonomic categories agree with scientific ones, their categories are interchangeable. But folk taxonomies don't always map onto scientific ones. The pale green substance known as "jade" can be either jadeite or nephrite, but these two substances are chemically distinct and united only in virtue of being superficially indistinguishable. Sometimes, scientific categories turn out to be folk categories in disguise. Linnaeus, the father of modern biological taxonomy, distinguished reptiles from birds, and included snakes, turtles, lizards, and crocodiles in the former category. But now we know that crocodiles are more closely related to birds than they are to lizards—upsetting the traditional assumption that is sedimented into vernacular speech and persists in scientific discourse. Linnaeus also divided the human family into five human "species" or races. Racial taxonomies were taken for granted by scientists until well into the twentieth century, but now we know that they are folk taxonomies with at most a very loose relationship to the biological facts about human variation.

Some folk taxonomies are based on superficial similarities (e.g., jade, reptiles), but others draw on different constitutive principles. Consider weeds. "Weed" is a folk category. The plants grouped together as weeds belong to many different biological taxa, and there are no intrinsic properties that unite them all. The category "weed" is essentially evaluative. "The best known and simplest definition," writes nature writer Richard Mabey, "is that 'a weed is a plant in the wrong place,' that is, a plant growing where you would prefer other plants to grow, or sometimes no plants at all" (Mabey 2010: 4). Weeds are "plants that sabotage human plans. They rob crops of nourishment, ruin the exquisite visions of garden designers, break our codes of appropriate behavior, make unpleasant and impenetrable hiding places for urban ne'er-do-wells" (Mabey 2010: 11).

Some plants are weeds, but their inclusion in the category, and the integrity of the category itself, is a product of human preferences and practices. A plant that is a weed in one society, or at one historical moment, need not be one in another, and a plant may be a weed when it grows in one location (say, a flower bed) but not in another (say, a pasture). Imagine that a team of intrepid botanists enter a time machine and decided to travel back one million years—long before the invention of horticulture—to determine whether a now-extinct plant, known only from the fossil record, was or was not a weed. This would be a foolish mission to embark upon, because although the botanists could learn a great deal about the plant species in question, there would be no possible evidence to decide whether or not these plants were weeds, because the category "weed" is meaningless in the absence of horticulture.

I believe that the category "human" is similar to the category "weed" insofar as its boundaries are fixed by our social practices and, flowing from this, because of its essentially normative character. This is not merely to say that people *disagree* about what beings belong in the category of the human. If that were the case then such disagreements could be settled by appealing to facts about the intrinsic properties of the beings in question. The question of whether any individual or group is human or not can't be settled in this way any more than a dispute about whether or not dandelions are weeds can be settled by appealing to facts about their intrinsic properties.

I've mentioned that when scientific writers refer to one or another primate taxon as "human," they invariably do so in a casual, offhand manner. Even though one may associate humanness with one primate taxon, while another associates it with another, there are no debates about what kind of beings count as human and no calls for empirical studies to resolve it. I think that this is explained by the fact that the question of what humans are is a conceptual rather than a scientific one. "Human" belongs to the vernacular. Like "weed," it's part of a folk taxonomy rather than a scientific one. Grappling with the question of what humans are requires one to address the interface between two taxonomic schemes, and a lot hangs on whether the categories of the vernacular scheme are reducible, even approximately, to those of the scientific one (like the avian taxonomies described by Mayr) or whether they are incommensurable with them (like the relation between weeds and botanical taxa).

Answering the question of what beings are human is beyond the scientists' remit because it cannot be solved empirically. Suppose that a team of paleoanthropologists were to enter a time machine and travel back a million years to study Homo erectus *in vivo*. They could make observations that would answer very many questions about this species, but their *observations* could not tell them whether Homo erectus was human. If human equals Homo sapiens, then the answer would be (trivially) "no," and if human equals genus Homo, then the answer would be (trivially) "yes." The real questions are which, if either, of these options is correct what makes it correct?

Vernacular uses are even more variable than scientific ones. Scientists at least agree that all Homo sapiens are human. But others have excluded members of our species from the category of the human by dehumanizing them. White supremacists have often characterized Black people as beasts, and Nazis characterized Jews as *Untermenschen* (subhumans). It's not just extremists that do such things. Members of some indigenous societies refer to themselves as "the human beings." The anthropologist Claude Levi-

Strauss observed that in many cases, "Humanity is confined to the borders of the tribe, the linguistic group, or even, in some instances, to the village, so that many so-called primitive peoples describe themselves as 'the men' (or sometimes—though hardly more discreetly—as 'the good,' 'the excellent,' 'the well- achieved'), thus implying that the other tribes, groups or villages have no part in the human virtues or even in human nature" (Levi-Strauss 1952: 12).

It is tempting to think that people who restrict humanness to a proper subset of our species are simply mistaken. They have a wrong-headed view of what it is to categorize people as human. Many psychologists and philosophers hold that the right way to understand the human is in relation to a set uniquely human properties ("rationality" is a perennial favorite) that are not restricted to any particular race or culture. Anne Phillips (2015) calls these "substantive" notions of humanness, and argues that substantive accounts are inevitably problematic because they exclude members of our species. If we insist (for example) on rationality as the criterion of the human, then we exclude infants and some of the mentally impaired. If we say that to be human is to be a free, autonomous agent, then drug addicts might slip through the conceptual cracks. One way that philosophers have tried to fix this so-called problem of marginal cases is to make the criteria so thin, abstract, and nebulous (in Phillips's language, so "contentless") that they allow that those who do not *manifest* the property may nevertheless *possess* it. Although newborn babies, or severely brain-damaged people, do not manifest rationality, they still, in some mysterious sense, "have it in them." This is epistemically awkward. If a putative property can't be observed, either directly or indirectly, then what basis can there be for asserting its existence? Saying that an individual possesses the property just in virtue of being human would be blatantly circular. And, as Phillips argues, abstracting away to this degree runs the risk of spreading the net too thin and allowing that other species only distantly related to us—for example, some cetaceans—get included in the human club.

Philosophers mostly ignore these problems. They treat "human" as a transparently biological category and turn their attention to the notion of "personhood" instead. John Locke defined a person as "a thinking, intelligent being that has reason and reflection and can consider itself as itself, the same thinking thing, in different times and places" (Locke 1975: 335) "To be a person in the full sense," writes Charles Taylor, "you have to be an agent, a being that can thus make plans for your life, one who also holds values in virtue of which different such plans seem better or worse, and who is capable of choosing between them" (Taylor 1985: 257). On such accounts, personhood can come apart from humanness. When you were an embryo you were a human embryo, but you were not a human person. Swampman is a person (given that he is an exact replica of Donald Davidson), but he is not a biologically human person because he does not belong to any taxon and has no ancestor in common with any member of our species.

The retreat from humanness to personhood is aimed at justifying the moral status that we assign to ourselves. It is difficult to see how the mere fact of belonging to a certain biological kind could endow one with this special status. So, personhood is invoked to do the moral and political heavy lifting that presumptively biological humanness can't do. But the concept of personhood isn't really helpful in this regard. For it to be ethically serviceable, every human being must be counted as a person. As Taylor says, "we believe that it would be utterly wrong and unfounded to draw the boundaries any narrower than around the whole human race," and "Should anyone propose to do so, we should immediately ask what distinguished those left in from those left out. And we should seize on this distinguishing characteristic in order to show that it has nothing to do with commanding respect" (Taylor 1992: 6–7). The problem is that substantive notions of personhood fare no better than substantive notions of humanness. Either personhood is a matter of displaying properties, in which case some members of our species lack it, or it is unobservable, in which case there are no empirical grounds for imputing it to some beings and not to others.

III. Maybe a Solution

I think that to properly understand what's going on when we consider others to be human is best explained by flipping substantivism on its head. Humanness is *constituted* not by intrinsic properties but instead by a certain sort of status. Anne Phillips's work on the politics of the human points in this direction. After discussing the problems that bedevil substantivism, she writes:

> The conclusion I derive from this is that we should jettison the human as a list of properties and stop thinking that we need this in order to justify human equality. Whatever candidates we choose as our descriptors, they lead us into questions about who fits and who does not, and may tempt us into treating these as matters of empirical investigation. . . . Recognizing others as equal is a political not cognitive matter. (Phillips 2015: 43–4)[2]

Seen from this perspective, humanity is claimed, or unclaimed, and granted or withheld, not observed or discovered. "People," she says, "assert, rather than prove, their claims to be regarded as human" (2015: 9). To assert one's humanity is to assert that one possesses a certain intrinsic value. Some philosophers call this "dignity." Michael Hauskeller highlights this dimension of attributions of humanness as follows:

> It shouldn't matter how we classify, what we call human and what not, but to many people it obviously does. Why is that so? Why do we care whether we are human or not, or someone else is? And why do we care what makes us human, that is, why do we care for the reason we call ourselves human? I think the answer to the first question (and thus, as we will see, also to the second) is that "human," to us, is usually more than just a descriptive predicate. It more often than not has a very strong prescriptive dimension. It is, just as the word "person" according to St Thomas Aquinas, a *nomen dignitatis*, that is a title of honour, or a dignity-conferring name. (Hauskeller 2009: 97–8)[3]

I agree with Phillips that asserting one's humanity in the face of its denial is laying claim to a political status, and I agree with Hauskeller that "human" is a dignity-conferring name. Hauskeller stops short of saying that facts about beings are irrelevant their human status. He says that human is *more than* just a descriptive predicate. I think that this is right. There at least *seem* to be intrinsic properties that are pertinent to granting humanity. A good account should explain this without collapsing into substantivism.

I think that there is a way to satisfactorily explain what goes into regarding entities as human—an anti-substantivist take that addresses the issues and reconciles the tensions that I have already remarked upon. As a point of departure, notice that in discussions of humanness it is always presumed that we are human. This is evident in the numerous article titles that pose variations on the question "What Makes Us Human?" "Well, of Course," you might say, "Only Humans Can Write Articles!" But look deeper. Consider the names that some ethnic groups use to designate themselves, mentioned in the passage from Levi-Strauss that I quoted earlier. Discussing this point, George Stewart remarks, "Tribal names are often not formal designations, but merely equivalents of the pronoun 'we'" (1975: 68). To be human, then, is to be one of *us*. It's to be part of the "we." We, the attributers of humanness, are always human, whereas they, the potential recipients, may or may not be. I propose that we treat this feature of humanizing discourse as the center of gravity for how the concept of the human really works. It suggests that "human" typically functions as an indexical term. Just as the word "here" names the place where that word is uttered, the word "now" names the time where that that it is uttered, and the word "human" names *the kind of being that the speaker is*. This interpretation of "human" draws together the various ways that this concept gets filled out. Saying that members of genus Homo were human boils down to saying that they were part of "us"—members of my (our) kind. Likewise, members of the societies alluded to by Levi-Strauss regard other members of their tribe as human (and outsiders as nonhuman) in virtue of restricting their kind to the tribe, and Neo-Nazis who deny humanness to Black people and reserve it for themselves do so because they conceive of "my kind" as the white kind.

"My kind" can designate many different things. This is both an advantage and a shortcoming. It's an advantage because it uncovers unity in diverse concepts of the human, but it's a shortcoming because any individual belongs to lots of nested kinds, most of which are not pertinent to ascriptions of humanity. Neo-Nazis are not only "white," they are also Homo sapiens, vertebrates, sons and daughters, residents of one or another nation, and so on. They might identify their kind with any or all of these. So, what's going on when they privilege their race as the criterion for being human?

To answer this question, we need to turn to the literature on psychological essentialism. "Psychological essentialism" (or "folk essentialism") refers to the very widespread cognitive disposition to carve the world of living things up into discrete natural kinds, the members of each of which are supposed to share a unique, unobservable property that psychologists call their "essence" (Medin and Ortony 1989). It is in virtue of possessing an essence that individuals are members of natural kinds. For example, from an essentialist perspective, what makes an individual animal a North American porcupine is not its appearance. Having four legs, being covered with quills, and so on are merely indicative and not constitutive of being a porcupine. What makes an animal a porcupine is something "inside" it that normally produces these phenotypic features. Although unobservable, essences are taken to be causally responsible for the manifest attributes that are typical of members of the kind. Normally, it is the unfolding of the porcupine essence that causes porcupines to grow quills, have four legs, and behave in their distinctive fashion. Needless to say, psychological essentialism is at odds with scientific conceptions of species. But it is a compelling intuitive theory of natural kinds with a powerful grip on the human psyche—one that is sometimes explicit and very often implicit, that can be overridden but apparently not extirpated.

Psychologists and cognitive anthropologists have found that we essentialize beings at a particular taxonomic level within the hierarchy of nested kinds. That is, the essentialistic mind tends to privilege one kind over all the others. Sarah-Jane Leslie explains how this works, using the term "quintessence" as a stand-in for "essence." She writes, "Quintessentialists . . . believe that there are a number of levels or degrees of similarity in quintessence, all of which are real and objective, in effect constituting a taxonomic hierarchy of kinds." She continues:

> At the lowest levels of this taxonomy, there are considerable similarities between the quintessences of members of some distinct kinds, while at the higher levels, there is considerable variation between the quintessences of members of the same kind. Importantly, there is a *privileged* level of this subjective taxonomy that occupies a "sweet spot" in this trade-off between within-kind variation in quintessence, and cross-kind quintessential distinctness. At this level, individual members of the same kind have only minimal differences in their quintessences, and these quintessences are quite dramatically different from the quintessences had by members of other kinds. (The Quintessentialists' cognitive psychologists call this taxonomic level "the basic level") The quintessentialists believe that this privileged taxonomic level is objectively determined, and so there is a privileged way of answering the question of whether a given individual is the *same kind of animal* (or *same kind of plant*) as another: namely whether they belong to the same basic-level kind. (Leslie 2013: 111–12)

These considerations suggest a rather different view of attributions of humanness than the one most prevalent in the psychological literature (see, e.g., Bain, Vaes, and Leyens 2013). According to Haslam's (2006) influential account, we attribute of humanness to others in virtue of attributing human *traits* to them (traits such as rationality and secondary emotions).[4] This approach suggests that we attribute humanness to others incrementally—that there are, psychologically speaking, degrees of humanness. In contrast, essences are supposed possessed absolutely. So, if regarding someone as human is attributing a human essence to them (in the specifically causal sense used in the literature on psychological essentialism) then the trait-based account of humanness is incorrect. One is either categorically human or not, with no gray area in between. Within this theoretical framework, talk of some people as semi-human should be understood as pertaining to the degree to which the human essence is *realized* rather than the degree to which it is possessed (see Smith 2021). Understanding the categorical character of humanness helps refine the indexical account of humanness. To conceive of someone as human is not just to regard them as a member of "my kind." It's to attribute to them the essence of the basic kind to which you take yourself to belong. What a person takes their basic kind to be is an upshot of complex psychological, social, cultural, and political factors. Explaining how it is formed and sustained is a task for the developmental psychologist rather than the philosopher, and need not concern us here.

IV. Humanness and Dehumanization

Attributions of humanity are political, in the broadest sense of the term. They demarcate "our kind" from "their kind," "us" and "them." They distinguish those whose lives matter from those whose lives do not, those who are exploitable from those who must be respected, those who deserve resources from those who can be denied them. These distinctions are salient in episodes of dehumanization. To dehumanize others is to deny that they are human. On the account of humanness given here, dehumanization is an act of disidentification at the most basic level. To deny the humanity of others—to exclude them from one's own kind—makes it permissible, or sometimes even obligatory, to treat them in ways that would otherwise be unacceptable. I have described the psychological and political mechanisms that drive dehumanization in considerable detail elsewhere (Smith 2011, 2020, 2021; for a range of other views, see Kronfeldner 2021; Bain et al. 2013). Here, I will focus on just one aspect of the logic of essentialism that is especially relevant to the essentially political function of the category of the human.

Recall that essences are supposed to be unobservable. They can only be inferred from the manifest properties of their bearers. Although these inferences are mostly thought to be reliable, they are fallible, because the essentialist framework allows that a thing's appearance may not correspond to its essence. Here is an illustration. In the year 1215 the Fourth Lateran Council of the Roman Catholic Church decided that the sacramental host is the body of Christ. Their point was not that the wafer symbolizes Christ. It was that the wafer is *literally* the body of Christ. The host's outward appearance was thought to come apart from the divine essence imparted to it through the miracle of transubstantiation, while remaining outwardly a wafer. This is why accusations that Jews stole and "tortured" them were accusations of the ultimate sin of assaulting Christ himself. This bizarre doctrine is only intelligible in light of our propensity to think that how a thing appears is not constitutive of what it is. Here is a less exotic example. Suppose mutant fox is born with floppy ears rather than perky ones. From the essentialist perspective although this animal might easily be mistaken for a puppy, it possesses the fox essence and is therefore a fox.

This manner of thinking is what makes dehumanization possible. Those who conceive of members of our species as really members of an alien kind do not hallucinate that these people are subhuman animals. They know that they have hands not paws, and that they speak rather than grunt. But dehumanizers think that their outwardly human appearance belies a subhuman essence. During the seventeenth and eighteenth centuries Europeans generally equated the human essence with the soul. Souls are unobservable. Their presence can only be inferred from their manifestations. Consequently, one could infer that others are human on the basis of their appearance. However, it was sometimes attractive to deny that others had human souls. In particular, it was sometimes attractive to deny that Africans had souls, because denying the humanity of enslaved people legitimated their exploitation and abuse. Although enslaved people looked and acted like human beings they weren't really human beings because they lacked a human essence—an essence that is easy to deny because it cannot be detected. The potential gap between the appearance and reality gave those who were motivated to abuse others for financial gain the metaphysical wiggle-room that they needed.

This is not speculation. It is evidenced by writings on slavery from the seventeenth, eighteenth, and nineteenth centuries. One clear example can be found in the writings of Morgan Godwyn. Godwyn was an English cleric who had been a student of John Locke. After leaving Oxford University in 1666 he sailed to the colonies, first to Virginia and later from there to Barbados. Godwyn was appalled that slaveholders self-servingly denied enslaved people admission into the church. He described and argued against the colonists' dehumanizing beliefs that functioned to legitimate their brutal oppression of Black people. Godwyn reported that white people told him that Black people do not possess souls, and that they therefore denied that Black people were human. He wrote that planters and their sympathizers held a "disingenuous position" that "the Negros, though in their Figure they carry some resemblances of Manhood, yet are indeed no men" (1680: 3), and that they advocated "Hellish Principles . . . that Negros are Creatures Destitute of Souls, to be ranked among Brute Beasts and treated accordingly" (1708: 3). These attitudes persisted in the American colonies for centuries to come. Historian Mia Bay recounts a former slave's recollection, collected in the 1930s, of being told by a white preacher that Black people "had no more soul than dogs" (2000: 124). Godwyn's testimony lays bare how essentialistic thinking facilitated the dehumanization of Black slaves. He made it clear that those who denied the humanity of the enslaved admitted that they *seemed* human ("carry some resemblances of Manhood"), but denied that they were really human. He explained that this was accomplished by denying that they possess a human essence ("destitute of Souls") and that this was thought to license their oppression ("ranked among the Brute beasts and treated accordingly"). Whatever theory of attributing humanness one chooses to adopt, it should—it must—have the resources to account for phenomena like this.

Notes

1 For a range of views, see, for example, Leakey and Lewin (1993), Falguères et al. (1999), Schmitt (2003), Potts (2003), Mikkelsen (2004), Foley and Lewin (2003), Pollard (2009).
2 Excerpt from "The Politics of the Human" © 2015 Anne Phillips, Cambridge University Press. Reproduced with permission of The Licensor through PLS clear.
3 Excerpt from "Michael Hauskeller, Making Sense of What We Are: A Mythological Approach to Human Nature" © 2009 Cambridge University Press. Reproduced with permission of The Licensor through PLS clear.
4 For an important methodological critique, see Over (2020).

Bibliography

Bain, P. G., J. Vaes and J. P. Leyens (2013). *Humanness and Dehumanization*. New York: Psychology Press.

Bay, M. (2000). *The White Image in the Black Mind: African-American Ideas about White People, 1830–1925*. New York: Oxford University Press.

Falguères, Christopher, Jean-Jacques Bahain, Yuji Yokoyama, Juan Luis Arsuaga, Jose Maria Bermudez de Castro, Eudald Carbonell, James R. Bischoff, and Jean-Michel Dolo (September 1999), "The Earliest Humans in Europe: The Age of TD6 Gran Dolina, Atapuerca, Spain," *Journal of Human Evolution*, 37 (3–4): 343–52.

Foley, R. A. and R. Lewin (2003). *Principles of Human Evolution*. London: Wiley-Blackwell.

Godwyn, M. (1680). *The Negro's & Indians Advocate, Suing for Their Admission into the Church, or, A Persuasive to the Instructing and Baptizing of the Negro's and Indians in Our Plantations*. London: J.D.

Godwyn, M. (1708). "A Brief Account of Religion, in the Plantations, with the Causes, of the Neglect and Decay Thereof in Those Parts." In F. Brokesby (ed.), *Some Proposals Towards Propagating of the Gospel in Our American Plantations*. London: G. Sawbridge.

Haslam, N. (2006). "Dehumanization: an Integrative Review." *Personality and Social Psychology*, 10 (3): 252–64.

Hauskeller, M. (2009). "Making Sense of What We Are: A Mythological Approach to Human Nature." *Philosophy*, 84 (372): 95–109.

Kronfeldner, M. E. (2021) *The Routledge Handbook of Dehumanization*. London: Routledge.

Leakey, Richard E. and Robert Lewin (1993). *Origins Reconsidered: In Search of What Makes Us Human*. New York: Doubleday.

Leslie, S.-J. (2013). "Essence and Natural Kinds: When Science Meets Preschooler Intuition." In T.S. Gendler and J. Hawthorne (eds.), *Oxford Studies in Epistemology*, Vol. 4, 108–65. New York: Oxford University Press.

Levi-Strauss, C. (1952). *Race and History*. New York: UNESCO.

Locke, J. (1975). *An Essay Concerning Human Understanding*. P. A. Nidditch (ed.). Oxford: Clarendon Press.

Mabey, R. (2010). *Weeds: In Defense of Nature's Most Unloved Plants*. New York: HarperCollins.

Mayr, E. (1932). "A Tenderfoot Explorer in New Guinea: Reminiscences of an Expedition For Birds in the Primeval Forests of the Arfak Mountains." *Natural History*, 32: 83–97.

Medin D. and A. Ortony (1989). "Psychological Essentialism." In S. Vosniadou and A. Ortony (eds.), *Similarity and Analogical Reasoning*, 179–95. Cambridge: Cambridge University Press.

Mikkelsen, T. (2004). "What Makes Us Human?" *Genome Biology* 5 (238), https://doi.org/10.1186/gb-2004-5-8-238.

Over, H. (2020). "Seven Challenges for the Dehumanization Hypothesis." *Perspectives on Psychological Science*, 16 (1): 3–13.

Phillips, A. (2015). *The Politics of the Human*. Cambridge: Cambridge University Press.

Plackett, B. (2021). "How Many Early Human Species Existed On Earth?" *LiveScience*. Available online: https://www.livescience.com/how-many-human-species.html (accessed on October 26, 2021).

Pollard, K. S. (2009). "What Makes Us Human?" *Scientific American* 300 (5): 44–9.

Potts, R. (2003). "Early Human Predation." In Patricia H. Kelley, Michael Kowalewski, Thor A. Hansen (eds.), *Predator-Prey Interactions in the Fossil Record*. New York: Springer.

Schmitt, D. (2003), "Insights into the Evolution of Human Bipedalism from Experimental Studies of Humans and Other Primates," *Journal of Experimental Biology*, 206: 1437–48.

Smith, D. L. (2011). *Less Than Human: Why We Demean, Enslave, and Exterminate Others*. New York: St. Martins Press.

Smith, D. L. (2020). *On Inhumanity: Dehumanization and How to Resist It*. New York: Oxford University Press.

Smith, D. L. (2021). *Making Monsters: The Uncanny Power of Dehumanization*. Cambridge, MA: Harvard University Press.

Smithsonian Natural Museum of Natural History. "What Does it Mean to be Human?." Available online: https://humanorigins.si.edu/evidence/human-fossils/species (accessed October 26, 2021).

Stewart, G. R. (1975) *Names on The Globe*. New York: Oxford University Press.

Tattersall, I. (2016). "The Genus Homo." *Inference: International Review of Science*, 2 (1). Available online: http://inference-review.com/article/the-genus-homo (accessed October 26, 2021).

Taylor, C. C. (1985). "The Person." In M. Carruthers, S. Collins and S. Lukes (eds.), *The Category of the Person: Anthropology, Philosophy, History*. Cambridge: Cambridge University Press.

Taylor, C. C. (1992). *Sources of the Self: The Making of the Modern Identity*. Cambridge, MA: Harvard University Press.

Index

Abele, A. E.   18–19, 22
Alba, R.   219, 226
Albahari, M.   115, 123 n.6, 124 n.18
Allport, G. W.   220, 225
animalism   3–4, 87, 91–4
anthropological view   3–5
Aquinas, T.   236
Aquino, K.   4, 7, 143–6, 149, 151, 156
authenticity   7, 159–66, 169–76, 226
autonomy   159–62, 190, 235
Ayer, A.   127

Bailey, A.   53
Bartels, D.   4, 5, 7, 17, 18, 39, 43, 58, 72–7, 79, 143, 212 n.10
Baumeister, R. F.   174–6
Bay, M.   240
Berniūnas, R.   5, 32, 141 n.2
bioethics   7, 183–98
Blok, S.   4, 40, 42, 44, 72–4, 77, 127, 185–6, 208, 210
Bloom, P.   4–6, 17, 32, 41, 43, 45, 49, 67, 71, 72, 75, 162, 164–5, 207, 210, 219
bodily criteria   2–4
Boseovski, J. J.   218, 225
Brambilla, M.   16, 18–19
Bruno, M.   1, 3, 4, 16, 41, 43–4, 127, 186, 211 n.3
Buddhism   16, 115–22, 128

causal centrality   77–81
Chen, S.   4, 6, 7, 73–4, 78–82, 175, 197
Christy, A. G.   4, 7, 173
Cikara, M.   17
Cimpian, A.   217, 219
Cohen, J.   222–3, 225
Costin, V.   170, 173
Coutant, D.   211 n.2, 212 n.4

Dalai, L.   117, 141 n.2
de Brigard, F.   7, 143, 153

decision-making   71–83, 157–66, 171–3, 184, 187, 194, 206, 219–24
de Freitas, J.   8, 17, 61, 67, 72, 75, 100, 143, 210, 212 n.10
Del Pinal, G.   50, 55
Demaree-Cotton, J.   191
Dennett, D.   39, 123 n.5, 124 n.14, 175
Descartes   41, 44–5, 111, 114, 120, 122
Diamantis, M.   8, 203, 205–9
direction of change   15–18, 32, 43, 49–50, 60–8, 107–8, 184
Dranseika, V.   5, 8, 32, 43, 60, 71, 184, 186, 192–5
dual character   6, 49–69, 107–8, 198 n.5
Dunlea, J.   7, 217, 219
Dweck, C. S.   50, 218
Dworkin, R.   190

Earp, B.   7, 8, 16, 43, 60, 62, 184, 186, 188–92, 197, 198 nn.4, 6
Ersner-Hershfield, H.   39, 76
essentialism   53, 141 n.2, 217–19, 224–6, 237–9
Everett, J.   4–5, 16, 32–33
expertise   8–9, 189, 194

Fabiano, J.   184, 196
Faraci, D.   100–4

Garfield, J.   16, 123 nn.6–7
Gelman, S. A.   77, 217–18, 225
Gendler, T. S.   123 n.5
Goodwin, G. P.   4, 16, 18, 44
Greene, P.   8, 122 n.3
Guo, C.   50, 55
Guthrie, D.   174, 175

Habermas, T.   170
Haidt, J.   169
Hamilton, D.   209–10, 212 n.4
Hannikainen, I.   50, 186

Haslam, N.   73, 77, 238
Hawthorne, J.   123 n.5
Heidegger, M.   175
Heine, S. J.   175, 186
Heiphetz, L.   4, 7, 16–17, 32, 59, 217–19, 221
Henne, P.   143
Henrich, J.   175, 186
Hicks, J.   174, 176, 188
Hood, B.   127, 175
Huebner, B.   207, 211 n.3
human   56, 91–5, 128, 203, 231–40
Hume   103
Hussak, L. J.   217, 219

identity of non-human entities   61–3, 203–11
intuitions   1–4, 32–3, 38–46, 49–69, 72, 87–96, 111–15, 121–2, 162, 184–6, 190–6, 205–8, 211

Josipovic, Z.   116, 123 n.9

Kagan, S.   184–5
Kahneman, D.   122 n.4
Kelly, L.   117–21, 124 nn.12–13, 124 nn.16–17
Kim, J.   4, 171–5
King, L. A.   171, 176
Knobe, J.   4, 6, 17, 50, 53–5, 67, 75, 100, 102, 106–8, 113, 143, 173, 185–6, 207, 210

Lane, J. D.   218, 225
Latham, S. R.   62, 184
Leary, M.   143, 169
Leslie, S.-J.   50, 238
Levi-Strauss, C.   235, 237
Lewis, D   86, 94, 96
Lewis, J.   183, 189, 193, 197
Leyens, J.   212 n.6, 238
Liao, S. Y.   50, 55
Little, B. R.   169–70, 172
Locke, J.   3, 4, 8, 15, 41–2, 57, 87–9, 91, 92, 95–6, 111, 184–5, 205, 235, 240

McGregor, I.   169–70, 172
Machery, E.   185–7, 197–8
McMahan, J.   111–14, 122

Malle, B.   207
Markus, H.   72, 81, 143
Marsh, E. J.   143, 147
Martela, F.   170–1, 173
meaning   7, 158–9, 164–5, 169–76
Medin, D. L.   217, 237
memory   32, 127–9, 140, 143–5, 153–4
Mihailov, E.   186, 189
Mingyur Rinpoche, Y.   116, 117
Molouki, S.   4–5, 17–18, 43, 72–5, 143, 212 n.10
moral self effect   4–6, 16–19, 24–33, 59, 79, 100–1, 186–96
Mott, C.   7, 58, 73, 203
Mughan, A.   217, 225

Nado, J.   186, 197
narrative   99–108, 170–1, 212 n.9
Nee, V.   219, 226
Newman, G.   4, 17, 44, 50, 53, 67, 72, 74–5, 100–2, 106, 113, 127, 143, 173, 176, 185–6, 208, 210, 226
Nichols, S.   1, 3–5, 7, 16, 18–20, 32, 41–4, 53, 58, 59, 72, 73, 77, 79, 123 n.7, 127, 143, 186–8, 210, 211 n.3
Noonan, H.   4, 88–90, 212
Norenzayan, A.   175, 186
numerical identity   5–6, 9–10, 32, 33, 37–46, 71–3, 82–3, 92, 162–6

Olson, E.   4, 33, 87, 92–3, 95, 96
O'Neill, E.   186, 197
Ortony, A.   217, 237

Parfit, D.   4–8, 39, 57, 60, 68, 72, 75–6, 83 n.1, 87–94, 112, 122, 127–30, 134, 140–1, 205
Paul, L.   6, 158, 160–3
Paxton, P.   217, 225
perdurantism   94–6
Phelan, M.   211 n.3, 212 n.5
Phillips, A.   235–7, 240 n.2
Piontkowski, U.   217, 224–5
Pizarro, D. A.   100
Plakias, A.   197
pluralism   5, 193–4
Ponlop Rinpoche, D.   117, 121
Prasada, S.   50

Prinz, J.   4, 7, 16, 18, 59, 186, 207
psychological   5–7, 71–7, 88, 111
　connectedness   116, 122
purpose   107, 164–5, 171–3

qualitative similarity   5–6, 32–3, 37–46, 52, 60–3, 71–3

Reed, II, A.   4, 7, 81, 143–6, 149, 151, 156
Reid, T.   16, 41, 184
Rips, L.   4, 39, 44, 72–4, 76, 127, 185–6, 208, 210
Rivera, G. N.   169, 174–5
Rosch, E.   73
Rose, D.   53, 107, 212 n.11
Ross, M.   144, 151–2
Rozin, P.   16, 44

Savulescu, J.   16, 195
Schaffer, J.   53, 90–1, 107, 212 n.11
Schechtman, M.   4, 69
Schlegel, R.   7, 169–72, 175–6, 188
Schmader, T.   171, 176
Schwenkler, J.   5–6, 69
Sedikides, C.   171, 176
self-continuity judgment   73–5
Shoemaker, D.   4, 8, 87–8, 90, 96, 100–4, 106, 108, 113, 187
Shtulman, A.   41
Sider, T.   5
Simmons, J. P.   4, 157
Sinnott-Armstrong, W.   184, 194–5
Skorburg, J.   16, 33, 184, 194–5
Sloman, S.   78
Smith, D. L.   8, 56, 238–9
Sousa, P.   100–1, 141 n.2
Stanley, M.   7, 143–7, 153

Starmans, C.   5, 32, 37, 39, 41, 43–5
Steger, M. F.   170–1, 173
Stich, S. P.   198 n.3
Strohminger, N.   4–5, 7, 16–20, 32, 42–4, 59, 67, 72–3, 77, 79, 106, 113, 122, 143, 173, 186–8, 210
Sullivan, M.   8, 122
Swinburne, R. G.   87–8, 90

Taylor, C.   235–6
teleology   53, 107
thought experiments   1, 6, 111–15, 127–9, 140, 184–6
Tierney, H.   5, 41, 58
Tobia, K.   4–10, 17–18, 43, 49–50, 53, 60–2, 64–5, 69, 101, 106–7, 108, 113, 184–6, 191, 193, 197, 198, 210, 212, 226
transformative experience   6, 158–64
true self   6, 17–19, 99–108, 188, 190
Turri, J.   4
Tversky, A.   122 n.4

Urminsky, O.   4, 6–7, 39, 58, 72–9, 81–2

Vess, M.   4, 170, 173

White, C.   127–9, 135, 141 nn.2, 5
Williams, B. A. O.   1–4, 42, 88–90, 92, 184–5
Wilson, A. E.   144, 151–2
Wojciszke, B.   18–19, 22, 44

Young, L.   16, 43, 59, 217, 221
Yzerbyt, V.   207, 212 n.6

Zhang, H.   173, 175

www.ingramcontent.com/pod-product-compliance
Lightning Source LLC
Chambersburg PA
CBHW062135300426
44115CB00012BA/1931